P9-CLO-374

THE NEW FOLGER LIBRARY SHAKESPEARE

Designed to make Shakespeare's great plays available to all readers, the New Folger Library edition of Shakespeare's plays provides accurate texts in modern spelling and punctuation, as well as scene-by-scene action summaries, full explanatory notes, many pictures clarifying Shakespeare's language, and notes recording all significant departures from the early printed versions. Each play is prefaced by a brief introduction, by a guide to reading Shakespeare's language, and by accounts of his life and theater. Each play is followed by an annotated list of further readings and by a "Modern Perspective" written by an expert on that particular play.

Barbara A. Mowat is Director of Academic Programs at the Folger Shakespeare Library, Executive Editor of *Shakespeare Quarterly,* Chair of the Folger Institute, and author of *The Dramaturgy of Shakespeare's Romances* and of essays on Shakespeare's plays and on the editing of the plays.

Paul Werstine is Professor of English at King's University College at The University of Western Ontario, Canada. He is general editor of the New Variorum Shakespeare and author of many papers and articles on the printing and editing of Shakespeare's plays.

AMISTAD ACADEMY
407 James Street
New Haven, CT 06513
How Do I Become A
Better Student and,
R

The Folger Shakespeare Library

The Folger Shakespeare Library in Washington, D.C., a privately funded research library dedicated to Shakespeare and the civilization of early modern Europe, was founded in 1932 by Henry Clay and Emily Jordan Folger. In addition to its role as the world's preeminent Shakespeare collection and its emergence as a leading center for Renaissance studies, the Folger Library offers a wide array of cultural and educational programs and services for the general public.

EDITORS

BARBARA A. MOWAT
Director of Academic Programs
Folger Shakespeare Library

PAUL WERSTINE
Professor of English
King's University College at The University of Western Ontario, Canada

FOLGER SHAKESPEARE LIBRARY

A Midsummer Night's Dream

By
WILLIAM SHAKESPEARE

EDITED BY BARBARA A. MOWAT
AND PAUL WERSTINE

SIMON & SCHUSTER PAPERBACKS
NEW YORK LONDON TORONTO SYDNEY

The sale of this book without its cover is unauthorized. If you purchased this book without a cover, you should be aware that it was reported to the publisher as "unsold and destroyed." Neither the author nor the publisher has received payment for the sale of this "stripped book."

Simon & Schuster Paperbacks
A Division of Simon & Schuster, Inc.
1230 Avenue of the Americas
New York, NY 10020

Copyright © 1993 by The Folger Shakespeare Library

All rights reserved, including the right to reproduce this book
or portions thereof in any form whatsoever. For information, address
Simon & Schuster Paperbacks Subsidiary Rights Department,
1230 Avenue of the Americas, New York, NY 10020.

Washington Square Press New Folger Edition March 1993
This Simon & Schuster paperback edition June 2009

SIMON & SCHUSTER PAPERBACKS and colophon are
registered trademarks of Simon & Schuster, Inc.

For information regarding special discounts for bulk purchases,
please contact Simon & Schuster Special Sales at
1-866-506-1949 or business@simonandschuster.com.

The Simon & Schuster Speakers Bureau can bring authors to your
live event. For more information or to book an event, contact the
Simon & Schuster Speakers Bureau at 1-866-248-3049 or visit our
website at www.simonspeakers.com.

Manufactured in the United States of America

25   24   23

ISBN 978-0-7434-7754-3

From the Director of the Library

For over four decades, the Folger Library General Reader's Shakespeare provided accurate and accessible texts of the plays and poems to students, teachers, and millions of other interested readers. Today, in an age often impatient with the past, the passion for Shakespeare continues to grow. No author speaks more powerfully to the human condition, in all its variety, than this actor/playwright from a minor sixteenth-century English village.

Over the years vast changes have occurred in the way Shakespeare's works are edited, performed, studied, and taught. The New Folger Library Shakespeare replaces the earlier versions, bringing to bear the best and most current thinking concerning both the texts and their interpretation. Here is an edition which makes the plays and poems fully understandable for modern readers using uncompromising scholarship. Professors Barbara Mowat and Paul Werstine are uniquely qualified to produce this New Folger Shakespeare for a new generation of readers. The Library is grateful for the learning, clarity, and imagination they have brought to this ambitious project.

Werner Gundersheimer,
Director of the Folger Shakespeare
Library from 1984 to 2002

Contents

Editors' Preface

In recent years, ways of dealing with Shakespeare's texts and with the interpretation of his plays have been undergoing significant change. This edition, while retaining many of the features that have always made the Folger Shakespeare so attractive to the general reader, at the same time reflects these current ways of thinking about Shakespeare. For example, modern readers, actors, and teachers have become interested in the differences between, on the one hand, the early forms in which Shakespeare's plays were first published and, on the other hand, the forms in which editors through the centuries have presented them. In response to this interest, we have based our edition on what we consider the best early printed version of a particular play (explaining our rationale in a section called "An Introduction to This Text") and have marked our changes in the text—unobtrusively, we hope, but in such a way that the curious reader can be aware that a change has been made and can consult the "Textual Notes" to discover what appeared in the early printed version.

Current ways of looking at the plays are reflected in our brief introductions, in many of the commentary notes, in the annotated lists of "Further Reading," and especially in each play's "Modern Perspective," an essay written by an outstanding scholar who brings to the reader his or her fresh assessment of the play in the light of today's interests and concerns.

As in the Folger Library General Reader's Shakespeare, which this edition replaces, we include explanatory notes designed to help make Shakespeare's language clearer to a modern reader, and we place the notes on the page facing the text that they explain. We also follow the earlier edition in including illustrations —of objects, of clothing, of mythological figures—from books and manuscripts in the Folger Library collection. We provide fresh accounts of the life of Shakespeare, of the publishing of his plays, and of the theaters in which his plays were performed, as well as an introduction to the text itself. We also include a section called "Reading Shakespeare's Language," in which we try to help readers learn to "break the code" of Elizabethan poetic language.

For each section of each volume, we are indebted to a host of generous experts and fellow scholars. The "Reading Shakespeare's Language" sections, for example, could not have been written had not Arthur King, of Brigham Young University, and Randal Robinson, author of *Unlocking Shakespeare's Language,* led the way in untangling Shakespearean language puzzles and shared their insights and methodologies generously with us. "Shakespeare's Life" profited by the careful reading given it by S. Schoenbaum, "Shakespeare's Theater" was read and strengthened by Andrew Gurr and John Astington, and "The Publication of Shakespeare's Plays" is indebted to the comments of Peter W. M. Blayney. We, as editors, take sole responsibility for any errors in our editions.

We are grateful to the authors of the "Modern Perspectives," to Leeds Barroll and David Bevington for their generous encouragement, to the Huntington and Newberry Libraries for fellowship support, to King's College for the grants it has provided to Paul Werstine, to the Social Sciences and Humanities Research Council of Canada, which provided him with a Research Time Stipend for 1990–91, and to the Folger Institute's Center for Shakespeare Studies for its fortuitous sponsorship of a workshop on "Shakespeare's Texts for Students and

Teachers" (funded by the National Endowment for the Humanities and led by Richard Knowles of the University of Wisconsin), a workshop from which we learned an enormous amount about what is wanted by college and high-school teachers of Shakespeare today.

Our biggest debt is to the Folger Shakespeare Library: to Werner Gundersheimer, Director of the Library, who has made possible our edition; to Jean Miller, the Library's Art Curator, who combed the Library holdings for illustrations, and to Julie Ainsworth, Head of the Photography Department, who carefully photographed them; to Peggy O'Brien, Director of Education, who gave us expert advice about the needs being expressed by Shakespeare teachers and students (and to Martha Christian and other "master teachers" who used our texts in manuscript in their classrooms); to the staff of the Academic Programs Division, especially Paul Menzer (who drafted "Further Reading" material), Mary Tonkinson, Lena Cowen Orlin, Molly Haws, and Jessica Hymowitz; and, finally, to the staff of the Library Reading Room, whose patience and support have been invaluable.

Barbara A. Mowat and Paul Werstine

Shakespeare's
A Midsummer Night's Dream

In *A Midsummer Night's Dream*, Shakespeare confronts us with mysterious images of romantic desire. There are Theseus and Hippolyta, about to be married; both are strange and wonderful figures from classical mythology. Theseus is a great warrior, a kinsman of Hercules; she is an Amazon, a warrior-woman, defeated in battle by Theseus. His longing for the wedding day opens the play, and the play closes with their exit to their marriage bed.

Within Theseus's world of Athens, two young men and two young women sort themselves out into marriageable couples, but only after one triangle, with Hermia at the apex and Helena excluded, is temporarily replaced by another, this time with Helena at the apex and Hermia excluded. At each point the fickle young men think they are behaving rationally and responsibly as infatuation (sometimes caused by a magic flower, sometimes not) leads them into fierce claims and counterclaims, and the audience is shown the power of desire to take over one's vision and one's actions. By presenting the young lovers as almost interchangeable, Shakespeare displays and probes the mystery of how lovers find differences—compelling, life-shaping differences —where there seem to be only likenesses.

In the woods outside of Athens, where the lovers suffer their strange love experiences, we find yet other images of desire, these involving the king and queen of Fairyland and an Athenian weaver transformed into an ass-headed monster. King Oberon and Queen Titania are engaged in a near-epic battle over custody of an orphan boy; the king uses magic to make the queen fall in love with the monster. The monster—a simple weaver named Bottom who came into the woods with his companions to rehearse a play for Theseus and Hippolyta's wedding—is himself the victim of magic. He has been turned into a monster by Oberon's helper, a hobgoblin or "puck" named Robin Goodfellow. The love-experience of Titania and Bottom is a playing out of the familiar "beauty and the beast" story, and, like the stories of the young lovers, it makes us wonder at the power of infatuation to transform the image of the beloved in the lover's eyes.

Finally, there is the tragic love story of "Pyramus and Thisbe," ineptly written and staged by Bottom and his workingmen companions. In this story romantic love leads to a double suicide—provoking only mirth in the onstage audience but reminding us once again of the extraordinary power of desire.

In *A Midsummer Night's Dream*, one of Shakespeare's most popular plays, Shakespeare stages the workings of love in ways that have fascinated generations of playgoers and readers. After you have read the play, we invite you to read "A Modern Perspective" on *A Midsummer Night's Dream* written by Professor Catherine Belsey of Cardiff University, printed at the back of this book.

Reading Shakespeare's Language

For many people today, reading Shakespeare's language can be a problem—but it is a problem that can be solved. Those who have studied Latin (or even French or German or Spanish) and those who are used to reading poetry will have little difficulty understanding the language of Shakespeare's poetic drama. Others, though, need to develop the skills of untangling unusual sentence structures and of recognizing and understanding poetic compressions, omissions, and wordplay. And even those skilled in reading unusual sentence structures may have occasional trouble with Shakespeare's words. Four hundred years of "static" intervene between his speaking and our hearing. Most of his immense vocabulary is still in use, but a few of his words are not, and, worse, some of his words now have meanings quite different from those they had in the sixteenth century. In the theater, most of these difficulties are solved for us by actors who study the language and articulate it for us so that the essential meaning is heard—or, when combined with stage action, is at least *felt*. When reading on one's own, one must do what each actor does: go over the lines (often with a dictionary close at hand) until the puzzles are solved and the lines yield up their poetry and the characters speak in words and phrases that are, suddenly, rewarding and wonderfully memorable.

Shakespeare's Words

As you begin to read the opening scenes of a play by Shakespeare, you may notice occasional unfamiliar words. Some are unfamiliar simply because we no longer use them. In the opening scenes of *A Midsummer Night's Dream*, for example, you will find the words *mewed* (i.e., caged), *an* (i.e., if), *beteem* (i.e., grant, give), *momentany* (i.e., momentary), and *collied* (i.e., coal black). Words of this kind are explained in notes to the text and will become familiar the more of Shakespeare's plays you read.

In *A Midsummer Night's Dream*, as in all of Shakespeare's writing, more problematic than discarded words are words that we still use but that we use with a different meaning. In the opening scene of *A Midsummer Night's Dream*, for example, the word *conceit* has the meaning of "a fancy trinket," the word *solemnity* is used where we would say "festive ceremony," *blood* where we would say "passions, feelings," *fantasy* where we would say "imagination," and *well possessed* where we would say "wealthy." Such words will be explained in the notes to the text, but they, too, will become familiar as you continue to read Shakespeare's language.

Some words are strange not because of the "static" introduced by changes in language over the past centuries but because these are words that Shakespeare is using to build a dramatic world that has its own space, time, history, and background mythology. *A Midsummer Night's Dream* is a particularly interesting example of this practice in that, in this play, Shakespeare creates three such worlds, each of which thinly veils other, very different worlds. In the play's first scene he builds a world that purports to be the city of Athens, home to the legendary characters Theseus and Hippolyta. That world exists in references to "Athenian youth," to "the law of Athens," and to "Athens' gates." But the language used in this Athens creates not a recognizable Greek city (in contrast to the opening scenes of, say, *Julius Caesar*, where the language creates a Rome of the classic past) but rather a placeless, almost timeless world of romantic love, of ritual, of mythology. This romance world is created through references to May Day "observances," to "Diana's altar," to "Venus' doves," to "winged Cupid," to "Cupid's strongest bow," and to "his best arrow with the golden head."

In the play's second scene, Shakespeare builds a world of supposedly Athenian workingmen (a world created primarily through the names of the men's occupations—joiner, bellows-mender, tinker) but here again language displaces this world and creates a world of theater, with its "scrolls," "scrips," "parts," "cues," and "bills of properties." References to mythological figures appear here, as they do in the world of Theseus's Athens, but now transformed through the language of the uneducated workers into comic references to "Phibbus' car" (i.e., the chariot of the sun god, Phoebus) and to "Ercles" (i.e., Hercules).

Finally, in the play's third scene, he creates the world of Fairyland, ruled over by Oberon, king of the fairies, and Titania, his queen. This world is made through references to "changelings," to "fairy ringlets" (i.e., circle dances), to "orbs" (i.e., the dancing ground of fairies), and to such magic flowers as "love-in-idleness." But more interesting are the other worlds created through the language of the fairies—first, the world of English country villagers affected by the doings of fairies, especially by that "lob of spirits," Robin Goodfellow, a world that is never shown onstage but that is created through references to the "villagery," the "quern," the "gossips' bowl," the old "aunt" with her "withered dewlap," the "quaint mazes in the wanton green," the "murrain flock," and "nine-men's-morris"; second, the world of Titania's past, with its mortal "vot'ress" who sat with her in the "spicèd Indian air" on "Neptune's yellow sands," watching "embarkèd traders on the flood"; and, third, the world of Oberon's past, with its "mermaid on a dolphin's back," its "bolt of Cupid," its "vestal thronèd by the West." This pattern of displacement, this creation of worlds that thinly veil quite different worlds, may well help to explain this play's magic, otherworldly quality.

Shakespeare's Sentences

In an English sentence, meaning is quite dependent on the place given each word. "The dog bit the boy" and "The boy bit the dog" mean very different things, even though the individual words are the same. Because English places such importance on the positions of words in sentences, on the way words are arranged, unusual arrangements can puzzle a reader. Shakespeare frequently shifts his sentences away from "normal" English arrangements—often to create the rhythm he seeks, sometimes to use a line's poetic rhythm to emphasize a particular word, sometimes to give a character his or her own speech patterns or to allow the character to speak in a special way. Again, when we attend a good performance of the play, the actors will have worked out the sentence structures and will articulate the sentences so that the meaning is clear. In reading for yourself, do as the actor does. That is, when you become puzzled by a character's speech, check to see if words are being presented in an unusual sequence.

Look first for the placement of subject and verb. Shakespeare often places the verb before the subject (e.g., instead of "He goes," we find "Goes he"). In *A Midsummer Night's Dream,* we find such a construction when Egeus says (1.1.23) "Full of vexation come I" (instead of "Full of vexation I come"); Lysander uses this same kind of construction when, at 1.1.163, he says "There, gentle Hermia, *may I* marry thee," as does Hermia at 1.1.209–10, when she says "Before the time I did Lysander see / *Seemed Athens* as a paradise to me." Helena's "But herein *mean I* to enrich my pain" (1.1.256) is another example of inverted subject and verb.

Such inversions rarely cause much confusion. More

problematic is Shakespeare's frequent placing of the object before the subject and verb (e.g., instead of "I hit him," we might find "Him I hit"). Egeus's "And what is mine my love shall render him" (1.1.98) is an example of such an inversion (the normal order would be "And my love shall render him what is mine"), as is Helena's "Things base and vile, holding no quantity, / Love can transpose to form and dignity" (1.1.238–39), where "things base and vile" is the object of the verb "transpose."

Inversions are not the only unusual sentence structures in Shakespeare's language. Often in his sentences words that would normally appear together are separated from each other. (Again, this is often done to create a particular rhythm or to stress a particular word.) Take, for example, Theseus's "But earthlier happy is the rose distilled / Than that which, withering on the virgin thorn, / Grows, lives, and dies in single blessedness" (1.1.78–80); here the phrase "withering on the virgin thorn" separates the pronoun ("which") from its verb ("grows"). Or take Lysander's lines that begin at 1.1.103: "My fortunes every way as fairly ranked / (If not with vantage) as Demetrius'," where the normal construction "as fairly ranked as Demetrius'" is interrupted by the insertion of the parenthetical "If not with vantage." In order to create for yourself sentences that seem more like the English of everyday speech, you may wish to rearrange the words, putting together the word clusters ("that which grows," "as fairly ranked as Demetrius'"). You will usually find that the sentence will gain in clarity but will lose its rhythm or shift its emphasis.

Locating and rearranging words that "belong together" is especially necessary in passages that separate basic sentence elements by long delaying or expanding interruptions. In some plays (*Hamlet,* for instance), long interrupted sentences are used to catch the audience up in the narrative or are used as a characterizing device. In *A Midsummer Night's Dream*, the interruptions are more often decorative lyrical passages. Hermia uses such an interrupted construction when she says to Lysander at 1.1.172–81:

> *I swear to thee* by Cupid's strongest bow,
> By his best arrow with the golden head,
> By the simplicity of Venus' doves,
> By that which knitteth souls and prospers loves,
> And by that fire which burned the Carthage queen
> When the false Trojan under sail was seen,
> By all the vows that ever men have broke
> (In number more than ever women spoke),
> In that same place thou hast appointed me,
> *Tomorrow* truly *will I meet with thee.*

Occasionally, rather than separating basic sentence elements, Shakespeare simply holds them back, delaying them until subordinate material has already been given. Lysander uses this kind of delaying structure when he says, at 1.1.134–36, "For aught that I could ever read, / Could ever hear by tale or history, / The course of true love never did run smooth" (where the basic sentence elements "The course of true love never did run smooth" are held back until two lines of explanatory material are introduced); Lysander's speech to Helena at 1.1.214–18 uses this same delayed construction:

> Tomorrow night when Phoebe doth behold
> Her silver visage in the wat'ry glass,
> Decking with liquid pearl the bladed grass
> (A time that lovers' flights doth still conceal),
> *Through Athens' gates have we devised to steal—*

delaying the basic sentence elements "we have devised

to steal through Athens' gates" and then doubly invert-
ing them.

Finally, in *A Midsummer Night's Dream*, as in other of
Shakespeare's plays, sentences are sometimes complicated not because of unusual structures or interruptions
but because Shakespeare omits words and parts of
words that English sentences normally require. (In
conversation, we, too, often omit words. We say "Heard
from him yet?" and our hearer supplies the missing
"Have you.") Frequent reading of Shakespeare—and of
other poets—trains us to supply such missing words. In
plays written ten years or so after *A Midsummer Night's
Dream*, Shakespeare uses omissions both of verbs and of
nouns to great dramatic effect. In *A Midsummer Night's
Dream* omissions are few and seem to result from the
poet's wish to create regular iambic pentameter lines.
At 1.1.76, for instance, Theseus says "Thrice-blessèd
they that master so their blood" instead of "Thrice-
blessèd *are* they." This omission creates a rhythmically
regular line. At 1.1.166 ("Steal forth thy father's house
tomorrow night"), the omission of the word *from* in the
phrase "forth from" again creates a regular rhythm.

Shakespearean Wordplay

Shakespeare plays with language so often and so vari-
ously that entire books are written on the topic. His
wordplay in *A Midsummer Night's Dream* is particularly
interesting in the way it varies his usual use of puns and
figurative language. A pun is a play on words that sound
the same but that have different meanings. In *A Midsummer Night's Dream*, puns are found only occasionally,
but, as with much of the language of this play, where
they are used, they are used complexly. When, for
example, Helena says (at 1.1.248–51),

> For, ere Demetrius looked on Hermia's eyne,
> He hailed down oaths that he was only mine;
> And when this hail some heat from Hermia felt,
> So he dissolved, and show'rs of oaths did melt—

the first use of the word *hail* means "to shower down, to pour," but, since it sounds exactly like the verb *hale*, it also carries the sense of "pull down," as if the oaths were being tugged down from the sky. The second use of the word *hail*, in the following line, is as a noun, and Demetrius's oaths are given the characteristics of hail: they feel heat, dissolve, and melt. This shift from *hail/hale* as a verb to *hail* as a noun is an interestingly complex pun.

More often, in *A Midsummer Night's Dream*, we find instead a variation on Shakespeare's usual puns. In a complex variant on the pun, he has characters *confuse* words with other words that sound (more or less) the same but have very different meanings. (Such verbal confusions are now called "malapropisms.") Bottom is particularly inclined to this kind of speech. When he says, for example, "But I will *aggravate* my voice so that I will roar you as gently as any sucking dove" (1.2.78–80) he seems to be confusing *aggravate* with *moderate* or *mitigate* (soften, tone down). (In a different kind of confusion, his reference to the "sucking dove" mixes up the sucking [i.e., unweaned] lamb and the sitting [i.e., hatching] dove.) When he says "there we may rehearse most obscenely and courageously" (1.2.103–4), he is confusing *obscenely* with some other word (probably *seemly*) and confusing *courageously* either with a word that sounds a bit like it (perhaps *correctly*) or perhaps with the word *bravely*, which had the meaning both of "courageously" and of "splendidly, in a fine fashion."

Not only are puns and related wordplay used unusually and complexly in *A Midsummer Night's Dream*, but figurative language is also shifted away from Shakespeare's usual patterns. Instead of finding straightforward metaphors (i.e., plays on words in which one object or idea is expressed as if it were something else, something with which it shares common features), one is more likely to find extended similes, buried similes, and elaborate personifications. In a simile, one thing is said to be *like* or *as* another, as when Theseus charges that the moon "lingers my desires / Like to a stepdame or a dowager / Long withering out a young man's revenue" (1.1.4–6). Here the moon is compared to a stepmother or a widow with rights in her husband's property, and Theseus's desires are compared to the young man who has to wait to claim his inheritance. Many of the similes in this play begin as simple similes and then extend themselves into elaborate comparisons that take on some of the qualities of what we sometimes call "epic similes." In Lysander's words to Hermia at 1.1.136–51, for example, he first compares the briefness of love to a series of things thought of as transient: sounds, shadows, dreams. Then, with the comparison of love to "lightning in the collied [coal-black] night," the simile takes on a life of its own, as the lightning "unfolds both heaven and earth" and then is devoured by the darkness:

> The course of true love never did run smooth. . . .
> [Since,] if there were a sympathy in choice,
> War, death, or sickness did lay siege to it,
> Making it momentany as a sound,
> Swift as a shadow, short as any dream,
> Brief as the lightning in the collied night,
> That, in a spleen, unfolds both heaven and earth,
> And, ere a man hath power to say "Behold!"
> The jaws of darkness do devour it up.
> So quick bright things come to confusion.

(Note the powerful puns in the final line of this speech, where "So quick bright things" means, simultaneously, "So quickly do bright things" and "Thus quick [living, intense] bright things," and where *confusion* means both "destruction, ruin" and "disorder.")

One finds a much simpler example of an extended simile in Helena's charge to Hermia (1.1.186–88):

Your eyes are lodestars and your tongue's sweet air
More tunable than lark to shepherd's ear
When wheat is green, when hawthorn buds appear—

where the third line elaborates the figure of the lark, to which Hermia's tongue has been compared.

Another kind of extended simile in this play is reminiscent of emblem books, where an idea is shown in the form of a picture under which is printed a name for the picture and an elaborate explanation. One finds the verbal equivalent of such an emblem in Helena's speech about Love (1.1.240–47). (Here the "picture" we are supposedly looking at is that of the boy Cupid, wearing a blindfold and bearing wings; Helena's words provide the standard "explanation" of the picture and its title, "Love"):

Love looks not with the eyes but with the mind;
And therefore is winged Cupid painted blind.
Nor hath Love's mind of any judgment taste.
Wings, and no eyes, figure unheedy haste.
And therefore is Love said to be a child
Because in choice he is so oft beguiled.
As waggish boys in game themselves forswear,
So the boy Love is perjured everywhere.

The entire speech could be transcribed as an extended

simile: "Love is like a boy who is winged and blind, because love is blind, without judgment, hasty, etc."

Often in *A Midsummer Night's Dream*, the simile, rather than being extended, is "buried" within the language. (Some readers might prefer to see these buried similes as metaphors.) For example, when Theseus says to Hermia (1.1.76–80):

> Thrice-blessèd they that master so their blood
> To undergo such maiden pilgrimage,
> But earthlier happy is the rose distilled
> Than that which, withering on the virgin thorn,
> Grows, lives, and dies in single blessedness—

under the surface of the language is a comparison of the unmarried woman to an unplucked rose and of the married woman to the rose that is plucked and its fragrance distilled into perfume. When Lysander says to Hermia (1.1.130–31): "How now, my love? Why is your cheek so pale? / How chance the roses there do fade so fast?" the buried simile likens red cheeks to roses. Hermia continues that simile when she responds (1.1.132–33): "Belike [probably] for want [lack] of rain, which I could well / Beteem [give] them from the tempest of my eyes," expanding the buried simile to include a comparison of weeping eyes to pouring rain. Hermia's "Keep word, Lysander. We must starve our sight / From lovers' food till morrow deep midnight" (1.1.227–28) includes a buried simile: the sight of the beloved is like food to the lover.

Finally, figurative language in *A Midsummer Night's Dream* often includes personification (i.e., abstract qualities are given human characteristics). To take a single example: when Theseus says to his master of the revels (1.1.14–16): "Awake the pert and nimble spirit of mirth.

/ Turn melancholy forth to funerals; / The pale companion is not for our pomp," he personifies both mirth and melancholy, expanding the personification of melancholy by describing it as pale and using the condescending term *companion* (which here means "fellow").

Implied Stage Action

Finally, in reading Shakespeare's plays we should always remember that what we are reading is a performance script. The dialogue is written to be spoken by actors who, at the same time, are moving, gesturing, picking up objects, weeping, shaking their fists. Some stage action is described in what are called "stage directions"; some is suggested within the dialogue itself. Learn to be alert to such signals as you stage the play in your imagination. When, in *A Midsummer Night's Dream* at 2.1.60, Robin Goodfellow says to the Fairy "room [i.e., stand aside], fairy. Here comes Oberon," and the Fairy responds "And here my mistress. Would that he were gone!" it is almost certain that Robin and the Fairy would move aside for the entrance of the king and queen of Fairyland. Similarly, a few lines later, when Titania orders her fairies to "skip hence," it is almost certain that they would obey her orders. Her later orders to them at line 149, "Fairies, away," show that, when they earlier "skip hence," they do not leave the stage. At many places in *A Midsummer Night's Dream*, signals to the reader are not quite so clear. When Demetrius says to Helena at line 242 "Let me go," it is clear that she has earlier taken hold of him, but it is not at all certain when she did so. Nor is it certain when she turns him loose (or, perhaps, when he pulls away from her) nor even when he exits. (In our text, we have shown him leaving the stage two lines before Helena's exit, but we could have placed his exit several lines earlier, or have left him onstage until Helena's exit.) In these uncertain situations, the director and the actors and you, as reader, must decide what makes for the most interesting, most likely, action.

Many scenes in this play give scope for imaginative "staging": Just how do Oberon and Robin "anoint" the eyes of their sleeping victims? How does Robin stage the mock combat between Lysander and Demetrius? What stage action accompanies the speeches of Titania to (and about) the transformed Bottom: "Out of this wood do not desire to go" (3.1.154); "Tie up my lover's tongue. Bring him silently" (3.1.208); "So doth the woodbine the sweet honeysuckle / Gently entwist; the female ivy so / Enrings the barky fingers of the elm" (4.1.43–45)?

Learning to read the language of stage action repays one many times over when one reaches scenes such as the final scene of *A Midsummer Night's Dream,* where much of the pleasure of the scene turns on our ability to visualize the performance of "Pyramus and Thisbe" before a scoffing court (as Wall provides a "chink" through which the lovers whisper, as "Moon" defends his bush and his lantern, as Thisbe imbrues her breast with a "trusty sword").

It is immensely rewarding to work carefully with Shakespeare's language so that the words, the sentences, the wordplay, and the implied stage action all become clear—as readers for the past four centuries have discovered. It may be more pleasurable to attend a good performance of a play—though not everyone has thought so. But the joy of being able to stage one of Shakespeare's plays in one's imagination, to return to passages that continue to yield further meanings (or further questions) the more one reads them—these are pleasures that, for many, rival (or at least augment) those of the performed text, and certainly make it worth considerable effort to "break the code" of Elizabethan poetic drama and let free the remarkable language that makes up a Shakespeare text.

Shakespeare's Life

Surviving documents that give us glimpses into the life of William Shakespeare show us a playwright, poet, and actor who grew up in the market town of Stratford-upon-Avon, spent his professional life in London, and returned to Stratford a wealthy landowner. He was born in April 1564, died in April 1616, and is buried inside the chancel of Holy Trinity Church in Stratford.

We wish we could know more about the life of the world's greatest dramatist. His plays and poems are testaments to his wide reading—especially to his knowledge of Virgil, Ovid, Plutarch, Holinshed's *Chronicles*, and the Bible—and to his mastery of the English language, but we can only speculate about his education. We know that the King's New School in Stratford-upon-Avon was considered excellent. The school was one of the English "grammar schools" established to educate young men, primarily in Latin grammar and literature. As in other schools of the time, students began their studies at the age of four or five in the attached "petty school," and there learned to read and write in English, studying primarily the catechism from the Book of Common Prayer. After two years in the petty school, students entered the lower form (grade) of the grammar school, where they began the serious study of Latin grammar and Latin texts that would occupy most of the remainder of their school days. (Several Latin texts that Shakespeare used repeatedly in writing his plays and poems were texts that schoolboys memorized and recited.) Latin comedies were introduced early in the lower form; in the upper form, which the boys entered at age ten or eleven, students wrote their own Latin orations and declamations, studied Latin historians and rhetoricians, and began the study of Greek using the Greek New Testament.

Since the records of the Stratford "grammar school" do not survive, we cannot prove that William Shakespeare attended the school; however, every indication (his father's position as an alderman and bailiff of Stratford, the playwright's own knowledge of the Latin classics, scenes in the plays that recall grammar-school experiences—for example, *The Merry Wives of Windsor*, 4.1) suggests that he did. We also lack generally accepted documentation about Shakespeare's life after his schooling ended and his professional life in London began. His marriage in 1582 (at age eighteen) to Anne Hathaway and the subsequent births of his daughter Susanna (1583) and the twins Judith and Hamnet (1585) are recorded, but how he supported himself and where he lived are not known. Nor do we know when and why he left Stratford for the London theatrical world, nor how he rose to be the important figure in that world that he had become by the early 1590s.

We do know that by 1592 he had achieved some prominence in London as both an actor and a playwright. In that year was published a book by the playwright Robert Greene attacking an actor who had the audacity to write blank-verse drama and who was "in his own conceit [i.e., opinion] the only Shake-scene in a country." Since Greene's attack includes a parody of a line from one of Shakespeare's early plays, there is little doubt that it is Shakespeare to whom he refers, a "Shake-scene" who had aroused Greene's fury by successfully competing with university-educated dramatists like Greene himself. It was in 1593 that Shakespeare became a published poet. In that year he published his long narrative poem *Venus and Adonis;* in 1594, he followed it with *The Rape of Lucrece.* Both poems were dedicated to the young earl of Southampton (Henry Wriothesley), who may have become Shakespeare's patron.

It seems no coincidence that Shakespeare wrote these narrative poems at a time when the theaters were closed because of the plague, a contagious epidemic disease that devastated the population of London. When the theaters reopened in 1594, Shakespeare apparently resumed his double career of actor and playwright and began his long (and seemingly profitable) service as an acting-company shareholder. Records for December of 1594 show him to be a leading member of the Lord Chamberlain's Men. It was this company of actors, later named the King's Men, for whom he would be a principal actor, dramatist, and shareholder for the rest of his career.

So far as we can tell, that career spanned about twenty years. In the 1590s, he wrote his plays on English history as well as several comedies and at least two tragedies (*Titus Andronicus* and *Romeo and Juliet*). These histories, comedies, and tragedies are the plays credited to him in 1598 in a work, *Palladis Tamia,* that in one chapter compares English writers with "Greek, Latin, and Italian Poets." There the author, Francis Meres, claims that Shakespeare is comparable to the Latin dramatists Seneca for tragedy and Plautus for comedy, and calls him "the most excellent in both kinds for the stage." He also names him "mellifluous and honey-tongued Shakespeare": "I say," writes Meres, "that the Muses would speak with Shakespeare's fine filed phrase, if they would speak English." Since Meres also mentions Shakespeare's "sugared sonnets among his private friends," it is assumed that many of Shakespeare's sonnets (not published until 1609) were also written in the 1590s.

In 1599, Shakespeare's company built a theater for themselves across the river from London, naming it the Globe. The plays that are considered by many to be Shakespeare's major tragedies (*Hamlet, Othello, King Lear,* and *Macbeth*) were written while the company was resident in this theater, as were such comedies as *Twelfth Night* and *Measure for Measure.* Many of Shakespeare's plays were performed at court (both for Queen Elizabeth I and, after her death in 1603, for King James I), some were presented at the Inns of Court (the residences of London's legal societies), and some were doubtless performed in other towns, at the universities, and at great houses when the King's Men went on tour; otherwise, his plays from 1599 to 1608 were, so far as we know, performed only at the Globe. Between 1608 and 1612, Shakespeare wrote several plays—among them *The Winter's Tale* and *The Tempest*—presumably for the company's new indoor Blackfriars theater, though the plays seem to have been performed also at the Globe and at court. Surviving documents describe a performance of *The Winter's Tale* in 1611 at the Globe, for example, and performances of *The Tempest* in 1611 and 1613 at the royal palace of Whitehall.

Shakespeare wrote very little after 1612, the year in which he probably wrote *King Henry VIII.* (It was at a performance of *Henry VIII* in 1613 that the Globe caught fire and burned to the ground.) Sometime between 1610 and 1613 he seems to have returned to live in Stratford-upon-Avon, where he owned a large house and considerable property, and where his wife and his two daughters and their husbands lived. (His son, Hamnet, had died in 1596.) During his professional years in London, Shakespeare had presumably derived income from the acting company's profits as well as from his own career as an actor, from the sale of his play manuscripts to the acting company, and, after 1599, from his shares as an owner of the Globe. It was presumably that income, carefully invested in land and other property, that made him the wealthy man that surviving documents show him to have become. It is also assumed that William Shakespeare's growing wealth and reputation played some part in inclining the crown, in 1596, to grant John Shakespeare, William's father, the coat of arms that he had so long sought. William Shakespeare died in Stratford on April 23, 1616 (according to the epitaph carved under his bust in Holy Trinity Church) and was buried on April 25. Seven years after his death, his collected plays were published as *Mr. William Shakespeares Comedies, Histories, & Tragedies* (the work now known as the First Folio).

The years in which Shakespeare wrote were among the most exciting in English history. Intellectually, the discovery, translation, and printing of Greek and Roman classics were making available a set of works and worldviews that interacted complexly with Christian texts and beliefs. The result was a questioning, a vital intellectual ferment, that provided energy for the period's amazing dramatic and literary output and that fed directly into Shakespeare's plays. The Ghost in *Hamlet,* for example, is wonderfully complicated in part because he is a figure from Roman tragedy—the spirit of the dead returning to seek revenge—who at the same time inhabits a Christian hell (or purgatory); Hamlet's description of humankind reflects at one moment the Neoplatonic wonderment at mankind ("What a piece of work is a man!") and, at the next, the Christian disparagement of human sinners ("And yet, to me, what is this quintessence of dust?").

As intellectual horizons expanded, so also did geographical and cosmological horizons. New worlds—

both North and South America—were explored, and in them were found human beings who lived and worshiped in ways radically different from those of Renaissance Europeans and Englishmen. The universe during these years also seemed to shift and expand. Copernicus had earlier theorized that the earth was not the center of the cosmos but revolved as a planet around the sun. Galileo's telescope, created in 1609, allowed scientists to see that Copernicus had been correct: the universe was not organized with the earth at the center, nor was it so nicely circumscribed as people had, until that time, thought. In terms of expanding horizons, the impact of these discoveries on people's beliefs—religious, scientific, and philosophical—cannot be overstated.

London, too, rapidly expanded and changed during the years (from the early 1590s to around 1610) that Shakespeare lived there. London—the center of England's government, its economy, its royal court, its overseas trade—was, during these years, becoming an exciting metropolis, drawing to it thousands of new citizens every year. Troubled by overcrowding, by poverty, by recurring epidemics of the plague, London was also a mecca for the wealthy and the aristocratic, and for those who sought advancement at court, or power in government or finance or trade. One hears in Shakespeare's plays the voices of London—the struggles for power, the fear of venereal disease, the language of buying and selling. One hears as well the voices of Stratford-upon-Avon—references to the nearby Forest of Arden, to sheep herding, to small-town gossip, to village fairs and markets. Part of the richness of Shakespeare's work is the influence felt there of the various worlds in which he lived: the world of metropolitan London, the world of small-town and rural England, the world of the theater, and the worlds of craftsmen and shepherds.

That Shakespeare inhabited such worlds we know from surviving London and Stratford documents, as well as from the evidence of the plays and poems themselves. From such records we can sketch the dramatist's life. We know from his works that he was a voracious reader. We know from legal and business documents that he was a multifaceted theater man who became a wealthy landowner. We know a bit about his family life and a fair amount about his legal and financial dealings. Most scholars today depend upon such evidence as they draw their picture of the world's greatest playwright. Such, however, has not always been the case. Until the late eighteenth century, the William Shakespeare who lived in most biographies was the creation of legend and tradition. This was the Shakespeare who was supposedly caught poaching deer at Charlecote, the estate of Sir Thomas Lucy close by Stratford; this was the Shakespeare who fled from Sir Thomas's vengeance and made his way in London by taking care of horses outside a playhouse; this was the Shakespeare who reportedly could barely read, but whose natural gifts were extraordinary, whose father was a butcher who allowed his gifted son sometimes to help in the butcher shop, where William supposedly killed calves "in a high style," making a speech for the occasion. It was this legendary William Shakespeare whose Falstaff (in *1* and *2 Henry IV*) so pleased Queen Elizabeth that she demanded a play about Falstaff in love, and demanded that it be written in fourteen days (hence the existence of *The Merry Wives of Windsor*). It was this legendary Shakespeare who reached the top of his acting career in the roles of the Ghost in *Hamlet* and old Adam in *As You Like It*—and who died of a fever contracted by drinking too hard at "a merry meeting" with the poets Michael Drayton and Ben Jonson. This legendary Shakespeare is a rambunctious, undisciplined man, as attractively "wild" as his plays were seen by earlier generations to be. Unfortunately, there is no trace of evidence to support these wonderful stories.

Perhaps in response to the disreputable Shakespeare of legend—or perhaps in response to the fragmentary and, for some, all-too-ordinary Shakespeare documented by surviving records—some people since the mid-nineteenth century have argued that William Shakespeare could not have written the plays that bear his name. These persons have put forward some dozen names as more likely authors, among them Queen Elizabeth, Sir Francis Bacon, Edward de Vere (earl of Oxford), and Christopher Marlowe. Such attempts to find what for these people is a more believable author of the plays is a tribute to the regard in which the plays are held. Unfortunately for their claims, the documents that exist that provide evidence for the facts of Shakespeare's life tie him inextricably to the body of plays and poems that bear his name. Unlikely as it seems to those who want the works to have been written by an aristocrat, a university graduate, or an "important" person, the plays and poems seem clearly to have been produced by a man from Stratford-upon-Avon with a very good "grammar-school" education and a life of experience in London and in the world of the London theater. How this particular man produced the works that dominate the cultures of much of the world almost four hundred years after his death is one of life's mysteries—and one that will continue to tease our imaginations as we continue to delight in his plays and poems.

Shakespeare's Theater

The actors of Shakespeare's time are known to have performed plays in a great variety of locations. They played at court (that is, in the great halls of such royal residences as Whitehall, Hampton Court, and Greenwich); they played in halls at the universities of Oxford and Cambridge, and at the Inns of Court (the residences in London of the legal societies); and they also played in the private houses of great lords and civic officials. Sometimes acting companies went on tour from London into the provinces, often (but not only) when outbreaks of bubonic plague in the capital forced the closing of theaters to reduce the possibility of contagion in crowded audiences. In the provinces the actors usually staged their plays in churches (until around 1600) or in guildhalls. While surviving records show only a handful of occasions when actors played at inns while on tour, London inns were important playing places up until the 1590s.

The building of theaters in London had begun only shortly before Shakespeare wrote his first plays in the 1590s. These theaters were of two kinds: outdoor or public playhouses that could accommodate large numbers of playgoers, and indoor or private theaters for much smaller audiences. What is usually regarded as the first London outdoor public playhouse was called simply the Theatre. James Burbage—the father of Richard Burbage, who was perhaps the most famous actor in Shakespeare's company—built it in 1576 in an area north of the city of London called Shoreditch. Among the more famous of the other public playhouses that capitalized on the new fashion were the Curtain and the Fortune (both also built north of the city), the Rose, the Swan, the Globe, and the Hope (all located on the Bankside, a region just across the Thames south of the city of London). All these playhouses had to be built outside the jurisdiction of the city of London because many civic officials were hostile to the performance of drama and repeatedly petitioned the royal council to abolish it.

The theaters erected on the Bankside (a region under the authority of the Church of England, whose head was the monarch) shared the neighborhood with houses of prostitution and with the Paris Garden, where the blood sports of bearbaiting and bullbaiting were carried on. There may have been no clear distinction between playhouses and buildings for such sports, for we know that the Hope was used for both plays and baiting and that Philip Henslowe, owner of the Rose and, later, partner in the ownership of the Fortune, was also a partner in a monopoly on baiting. All these forms of entertainment were easily accessible to Londoners by boat across the Thames or over London Bridge.

Evidently Shakespeare's company prospered on the Bankside. They moved there in 1599. Threatened by difficulties in renewing the lease on the land where their first theater (the Theatre) had been built, Shakespeare's company took advantage of the Christmas holiday in 1598 to dismantle the Theatre and transport its timbers across the Thames to the Bankside, where, in 1599, these timbers were used in the building of the Globe. The weather in late December 1598 is recorded as having been especially harsh. It was so cold that the Thames was "nigh [nearly] frozen," and there was heavy snow. Perhaps the weather aided Shakespeare's company in eluding their landlord, the snow hiding their activity and the freezing of the Thames allowing them to slide the timbers across to the Bankside without paying tolls for repeated trips over London Bridge. Attractive as this narrative is, it remains just as likely that the heavy snow hampered transport of the timbers in wagons through the London streets to the river. It also must be remembered that the Thames was, according to report, only "nigh frozen" and therefore as impassable as it ever was. Whatever the precise circumstances of this fascinating event in English theater history, Shakespeare's company was able to begin playing at their new Globe theater on the Bankside in 1599. After the first Globe burned down in 1613 during the staging of Shakespeare's *Henry VIII* (its thatch roof was set alight by cannon fire called for by the performance), Shakespeare's company immediately rebuilt on the same location. The second Globe seems to have been a grander structure than its predecessor. It remained in use until the beginning of the English Civil War in 1642, when Parliament officially closed the theaters. Soon thereafter it was pulled down.

The public theaters of Shakespeare's time were very different buildings from our theaters today. First of all, they were open-air playhouses. As recent excavations of the Rose and the Globe confirm, some were polygonal or roughly circular in shape; the Fortune, however, was square. The most recent estimates of their size put the diameter of these buildings at 72 feet (the Rose) to 100 feet (the Globe), but we know that they held vast audiences of two or three thousand, who must have been squeezed together quite tightly. Some of these spectators paid extra to sit or stand in the two or three levels of roofed galleries that extended, on the upper levels, all the way around the theater and surrounded an open space. In this space were the stage and, perhaps, the tiring house (what we would call dressing rooms), as well as the so-called yard. In the yard stood the spectators who chose to pay less, the ones whom Hamlet contemptuously called "groundlings." For a roof they had only the sky, and so they were exposed to all kinds of weather. They stood on a floor that was sometimes made of mortar and sometimes of ash mixed with the shells of hazelnuts. The latter provided a porous and therefore dry footing for the crowd, and the shells may have been more comfortable to stand on because they were not as hard as mortar. Availability of shells may not have been a problem if hazelnuts were a favorite food for Shakespeare's audiences to munch on as they watched his plays. Archaeologists who are today unearthing the remains of theaters from this period have discovered quantities of these nutshells on theater sites.

Unlike the yard, the stage itself was covered by a roof. Its ceiling, called "the heavens," is thought to have been elaborately painted to depict the sun, moon, stars, and planets. Just how big the stage was remains hard to determine. We have a single sketch of part of the interior of the Swan. A Dutchman named Johannes de Witt visited this theater around 1596 and sent a sketch of it back to his friend, Arend van Buchel. Because van Buchel found de Witt's letter and sketch of interest, he copied both into a book. It is van Buchel's copy, adapted, it seems, to the shape and size of the page in his book, that survives. In this sketch, the stage appears to be a large rectangular platform that thrusts far out into the yard, perhaps even as far as the center of the circle formed by the surrounding galleries. This drawing, combined with the specifications for the size of the stage in the building contract for the Fortune, has led scholars to conjecture that the stage on which Shakespeare's plays were performed must have measured approximately 43 feet in width and 27 feet in depth, a vast acting area. But the digging up of a large part of the Rose by archaeologists has provided evidence of a quite different stage design. The Rose stage was a platform tapered at the corners and much shallower than what seems to be

depicted in the van Buchel sketch. Indeed, its measure-
ments seem to be about 37.5 feet across at its widest
point and only 15.5 feet deep. Because the surviving
indications of stage size and design differ from each
other so much, it is possible that the stages in other
theaters, like the Theatre, the Curtain, and the Globe
(the outdoor playhouses where we know that Shakespeare's plays were performed), were different from
those at both the Swan and the Rose.

After about 1608 Shakespeare's plays were staged not
only at the Globe but also at an indoor or private
playhouse in Blackfriars. This theater had been constructed in 1596 by James Burbage in an upper hall of a
former Dominican priory or monastic house. Although
Henry VIII had dissolved all English monasteries in the
1530s (shortly after he had founded the Church of
England), the area remained under church, rather than
hostile civic, control. The hall that Burbage had purchased and renovated was a large one in which Parliament had once met. In the private theater that he
constructed, the stage, lit by candles, was built across
the narrow end of the hall, with boxes flanking it. The
rest of the hall offered seating room only. Because there
was no provision for standing room, the largest audience it could hold was less than a thousand, or about a
quarter of what the Globe could accommodate. Admis-
sion to Blackfriars was correspondingly more expensive. Instead of a penny to stand in the yard at the Globe,
it cost a minimum of sixpence to get into Blackfriars.
The best seats at the Globe (in the Lords' Room in the
gallery above and behind the stage) cost sixpence; but
the boxes flanking the stage at Blackfriars were half a
crown, or five times sixpence. Some spectators who
were particularly interested in displaying themselves
paid even more to sit on stools on the Blackfriars stage.

Whether in the outdoor or indoor playhouses, the

stages of Shakespeare's time were different from ours. They were not separated from the audience by the dropping of a curtain between acts and scenes. Therefore the playwrights of the time had to find other ways of signaling to the audience that one scene (to be imagined as occurring in one location at a given time) had ended and the next (to be imagined at perhaps a different location at a later time) had begun. The customary way used by Shakespeare and many of his contemporaries was to have everyone onstage exit at the end of one scene and have one or more different characters enter to begin the next. In a few cases, where characters remain onstage from one scene to another, the dialogue or stage action makes the change of location clear, and the characters are generally to be imagined as having moved from one place to another. For example, in *Romeo and Juliet*, Romeo and his friends remain onstage in Act 1 from scene 4 to scene 5, but they are represented as having moved between scenes from the street that leads to Capulet's house into Capulet's house itself. The new location is signaled in part by the appearance onstage of Capulet's servingmen carrying napkins, something they would not take into the streets. Playwrights had to be quite resourceful in the use of hand properties, like the napkin, or in the use of dialogue to specify where the action was taking place in their plays because, in contrast to most of today's theaters, the playhouses of Shakespeare's time did not use movable scenery to dress the stage and make the setting precise. As another consequence of this difference, however, the playwrights of Shakespeare's time did not have to specify exactly where the action of their plays was set when they did not choose to do so, and much of the action of their plays is tied to no specific place.

Usually Shakespeare's stage is referred to as a "bare stage," to distinguish it from the stages of the last two or three centuries with their elaborate sets. But the stage in Shakespeare's time was not completely bare. Philip Henslowe, owner of the Rose, lists in his inventory of stage properties a rock, three tombs, and two mossy banks. Stage directions in plays of the time also call for such things as thrones (or "states"), banquets (presumably tables with plaster replicas of food on them), and beds and tombs to be pushed onto the stage. Thus the stage often held more than the actors.

The actors did not limit their performing to the stage alone. Occasionally they went beneath the stage, as the Ghost appears to do in the first act of *Hamlet.* From there they could emerge onto the stage through a trapdoor. They could retire behind the hangings across the back of the stage (or the front of the tiring house), as, for example, the actor playing Polonius does when he hides behind the arras. Sometimes the hangings could be drawn back during a performance to "discover" one or more actors behind them. When performance required that an actor appear "above," as when Juliet is imagined to stand at the window of her chamber in the famous and misnamed "balcony scene," then the actor probably climbed the stairs to the gallery over the back of the stage and temporarily shared it with some of the spectators. The stage was also provided with ropes and winches so that actors could descend from, and reascend to, the "heavens."

Perhaps the greatest difference between dramatic performances in Shakespeare's time and ours was that in Shakespeare's England the roles of women were played by boys. (Some of these boys grew up to take male roles in their maturity.) There were no women in the acting companies, only in the audience. It had not always been so in the history of the English stage. There are records of women on English stages in the thirteenth and fourteenth centuries, two hundred years before

Shakespeare's plays were performed. After the accession of James I in 1603, the queen of England and her ladies took part in entertainments at court called masques, and with the reopening of the theaters in 1660 at the restoration of Charles II, women again took their place on the public stage.

The chief competitors for the companies of adult actors such as the one to which Shakespeare belonged and for which he wrote were companies of exclusively boy actors. The competition was most intense in the early 1600s. There were then two principal children's companies: the Children of Paul's (the choirboys from St. Paul's Cathedral, whose private playhouse was near the cathedral); and the Children of the Chapel Royal (the choirboys from the monarch's private chapel, who performed at the Blackfriars theater built by Burbage in 1596, which Shakespeare's company had been stopped from using by local residents who objected to crowds). In *Hamlet* Shakespeare writes of "an aerie [nest] of children, little eyases [hawks], that cry out on the top of question and are most tyrannically clapped for 't. These are now the fashion and . . . berattle the common stages [attack the public theaters]." In the long run, the adult actors prevailed. The Children of Paul's dissolved around 1606. By about 1608 the Children of the Chapel Royal had been forced to stop playing at the Blackfriars theater, which was then taken over by the King's Men, Shakespeare's own troupe.

Acting companies and theaters of Shakespeare's time were organized in different ways. For example, Philip Henslowe owned the Rose and leased it to companies of actors, who paid him from their takings. Henslowe would act as manager of these companies, initially paying playwrights for their plays and buying properties, recovering his outlay from the actors. Shakespeare's company, however, managed itself, with the principal actors, Shakespeare among them, having the status of "sharers" and the right to a share in the takings, as well as the responsibility for a part of the expenses. Five of the sharers themselves, Shakespeare among them, owned the Globe. As actor, as sharer in an acting company and in ownership of theaters, and as playwright, Shakespeare was about as involved in the theatrical industry as one could imagine. Although Shakespeare and his fellows prospered, their status under the law was conditional upon the protection of powerful patrons. "Common players"—those who did not have patrons or masters—were classed in the language of the law with "vagabonds and sturdy beggars." So the actors had to secure for themselves the official rank of servants of patrons. Among the patrons under whose protection Shakespeare's company worked were the lord chamberlain and, after the accession of King James in 1603, the king himself.

We are now perhaps on the verge of learning a great deal more about the theaters in which Shakespeare and his contemporaries performed—or at least of opening up new questions about them. Already about 70 percent of the Rose has been excavated, as has about 10 percent of the second Globe, the one built in 1614. It is to be hoped that soon more will be available for study. These are exciting times for students of Shakespeare's stage.

The Publication of Shakespeare's Plays

Eighteen of Shakespeare's plays found their way into print during the playwright's lifetime, but there is nothing to suggest that he took any interest in their publication. These eighteen appeared separately in editions called quartos. Their pages were not much larger than the one you are now reading, and these little books were sold unbound for a few pence. The earliest of the quartos that still survive were printed in 1594, the year that both *Titus Andronicus* and a version of the play now called *2 King Henry VI* became available. While almost every one of these early quartos displays on its title page the name of the acting company that performed the play, only about half provide the name of the playwright, Shakespeare. The first quarto edition to bear the name Shakespeare on its title page is *Love's Labor's Lost* of 1598. A few of these quartos were popular with the book-buying public of Shakespeare's lifetime; for example, quarto *Richard II* went through five editions between 1597 and 1615. But most of the quartos were far from best-sellers; *Love's Labor's Lost* (1598), for instance, was not reprinted in quarto until 1631. After Shakespeare's death, two more of his plays appeared in quarto format: *Othello* in 1622 and *The Two Noble Kinsmen*, coauthored with John Fletcher, in 1634.

In 1623, seven years after Shakespeare's death, *Mr. William Shakespeares Comedies, Histories, & Tragedies* was published. This printing offered readers in a single book thirty-six of the thirty-eight plays now thought to have been written by Shakespeare, including eighteen that had never been printed before. And it offered them in a style that was then reserved for serious literature and scholarship. The plays were arranged in double columns on pages nearly a foot high. This large page size is called "folio," as opposed to the smaller "quarto," and the 1623 volume is usually called the Shakespeare First Folio. It is reputed to have sold for the lordly price of a pound. (One copy at the Folger Library is marked fifteen shillings—that is, three-quarters of a pound.)

In a preface to the First Folio entitled "To the great Variety of Readers," two of Shakespeare's former fellow actors in the King's Men, John Heminge and Henry

Condell, wrote that they themselves had collected their dead companion's plays. They suggested that they had seen his own papers: "we have scarce received from him a blot in his papers." The title page of the Folio declared that the plays within it had been printed "according to the True Original Copies." Comparing the Folio to the quartos, Heminge and Condell disparaged the quartos, advising their readers that "before you were abused with divers stolen and surreptitious copies, maimed, and deformed by the frauds and stealths of injurious impostors." Many Shakespeareans of the eighteenth and nineteenth centuries believed Heminge and Condell and regarded the Folio plays as superior to anything in the quartos.

Once we begin to examine the Folio plays in detail, it becomes less easy to take at face value the word of Heminge and Condell about the superiority of the Folio texts. For example, of the first nine plays in the Folio (one quarter of the entire collection), four were essentially reprinted from earlier quarto printings that Heminge and Condell had disparaged; and four have now been identified as printed from copies written in the hand of a professional scribe of the 1620s named Ralph Crane; the ninth, *The Comedy of Errors*, was apparently also printed from a manuscript, but one whose origin cannot be readily identified. Evidently then, eight of the first nine plays in the First Folio were not printed, in spite of what the Folio title page announces, "according to the True Original Copies," or Shakespeare's own papers, and the source of the ninth is unknown. Since today's editors have been forced to treat Heminge and Condell's pronouncements with skepticism, they must choose whether to base their own editions upon quartos or the Folio on grounds other than Heminge and Condell's story of where the quarto and Folio versions originated.

Editors have often fashioned their own narratives to explain what lies behind the quartos and Folio. They have said that Heminge and Condell meant to criticize only a few of the early quartos, the ones that offer much shorter and sometimes quite different, often garbled, versions of plays. Among the examples of these are the 1600 quarto of *Henry V* (the Folio offers a much fuller version) or the 1603 *Hamlet* quarto (in 1604 a different, much longer form of the play got into print as a quarto). Early in this century editors speculated that these questionable texts were produced when someone in the audience took notes from the plays' dialogue during performances and then employed "hack poets" to fill out the notes. The poor results were then sold to a publisher and presented in print as Shakespeare's plays. More recently this story has given way to another in which the shorter versions are said to be recreations from memory of Shakespeare's plays by actors who wanted to stage them in the provinces but lacked manuscript copies. Most of the quartos offer much better texts than these so-called bad quartos. Indeed, in most of the quartos we find texts that are at least equal to or better than what is printed in the Folio. Many of this century's Shakespeare enthusiasts have persuaded themselves that most of the quartos were set into type directly from Shakespeare's own papers, although there is nothing on which to base this conclusion except the desire for it to be true. Thus speculation continues about how the Shakespeare plays got to be printed. All that we have are the printed texts.

The book collector who was most successful in bringing together copies of the quartos and the First Folio was Henry Clay Folger, founder of the Folger Shakespeare Library in Washington, D.C. While it is estimated that there survive around the world only about 230 copies of the First Folio, Mr. Folger was able to acquire more than seventy-five copies, as well as a large number of fragments, for the library that bears his name. He also amassed a substantial number of quartos. For example, only fourteen copies of the First Quarto of *Love's Labor's Lost* are known to exist, and three are at the Folger Shakespeare Library. As a consequence of Mr. Folger's labors, twentieth-century scholars visiting the Folger Library have been able to learn a great deal about sixteenth- and seventeenth-century printing and, particularly, about the printing of Shakespeare's plays. And Mr. Folger did not stop at the First Folio, but collected many copies of later editions of Shakespeare, beginning with the Second Folio (1632), the Third (1663–64), and the Fourth (1685). Each of these later folios was based on its immediate predecessor and was edited anonymously. The first editor of Shakespeare whose name we know was Nicholas Rowe, whose first edition came out in 1709. Mr. Folger collected this edition and many, many more by Rowe's successors.

An Introduction to This Text

A Midsummer Night's Dream was first printed in 1600 as a quarto. Then in 1619 someone slightly edited a copy of the 1600 quarto, adding a few stage directions and, perhaps, supplying some obvious verbal corrections, to make it the basis of a second quarto edition of the play. A copy of this 1619 quarto was, in turn, annotated and used as printer's copy for the First Folio text published in 1623. Again both stage directions and a few words of dialogue were affected. Chief among the changes introduced into the Folio text was the substitution of Egeus for Philostrate in Act 5, scene 1. Some scholars think that whoever annotated the 1619 text before it was reprinted in the Folio must have referred to a manuscript of the play that had actually been used in the theater, but this conjecture rests on the most slender evidence.

The present edition is based directly on the earliest quarto of 1600.* For the convenience of the reader, we have modernized the punctuation and the spelling of the quarto. Sometimes we go so far as to modernize certain old forms of words; for example, when *a* means "he," we change it to *he;* we change *mo* to *more* and *ye* to *you.* But it has not been our editorial practice in any of the plays to modernize some words that sound distinctly different from modern forms. For example, when the early printed texts read *sith* or *apricocks* or *porpentine,* we have not modernized to *since, apricots, porcupine.* When the forms *an, and,* or *and if* appear instead of the modern form *if,* we have reduced *and* to *an* but have not changed any of these forms to their modern equivalent, *if.* We also modernize and, where necessary, correct passages in foreign languages, unless an error in the early printed text can be reasonably explained as a joke.

Whenever we change the wording of the First Quarto or add anything to its stage directions, we mark the change by enclosing it in superior half-brackets ($\lceil \; \rceil$). We want our readers to be immediately aware when we have intervened. (Only when we correct an obvious typographical error in the First Quarto does the change not get marked.) Whenever we change the First Quarto's wording or change its punctuation so that meaning changes, we list the change in the textual notes at the

---

*We have also consulted the computerized text of the First Quarto provided by the Text Archive of the Oxford University Computing Centre, to which we are grateful.

back of the book, even if all we have done is fix an obvious error.

We, like a great many editors before us, regularize a number of the proper names. For example, more often than not, the character Robin Goodfellow enters and speaks (according to the stage directions and speech prefixes) under this, his proper name. Sometimes, however, he appears under the name "Puck." He is, as he himself tells us, a puck or a hobgoblin. Most editors since Nicholas Rowe in 1709 have used the name "Puck" for Robin throughout their editions, but we choose, instead, to employ the proper name "Robin Goodfellow" throughout this edition. Sometimes Nick Bottom, the weaver, is referred to as "Clown" in stage directions and speech prefixes; again we use his proper name throughout. Finally, the workers who rehearse and stage a play for Theseus and Hippolyta are often designated in the speech prefixes by the names of their roles rather than by their proper names; e.g., Bottom speaks as "Pyramus," his role. In our speech prefixes we supply both the name of the character and the name of his role. We expand the often severely abbreviated forms of names used as speech headings in early printed texts into the full names of the characters. Variations in the speech headings of the early printed texts are recorded in the textual notes.

This edition differs from many earlier ones in its efforts to aid the reader in imagining the play as a performance rather than as a series of fictional events. Thus stage directions are written with reference to the stage. For example, in Act 3, scene 1, when the workers are rehearsing their play, they want to know if the moon will shine the night that they hope to perform it. In the fiction of the play, they consult an almanac to find out, and some editors print a stage direction of the form *"Quince consults an almanac."* However, in staging the play, no actor need use an almanac itself; any book of reasonable size will do as a hand prop. And so, writing stage directions from the perspective of the stage, we print *"Quince takes out a book."* Whenever it is reasonably certain, in our view, that a speech is accompanied by a particular action, we provide a stage direction describing the action. (Occasional exceptions to this rule occur when the action is so obvious that to add a stage direction would insult the reader.) Stage directions for the entrance of characters in mid-scene are, with rare exceptions, placed so that they immediately precede the characters' participation in the scene, even though these entrances may appear somewhat earlier in the early printed texts. Whenever we move a stage direction, we record this change in the textual notes. Latin stage directions (e.g., *Exeunt*) are translated into English (e.g., *They exit*).

In the present edition, as well, we mark with a dash any change of address within a speech, unless a stage direction intervenes. When the *-ed* ending of a word is to be pronounced, we mark it with an accent.

Like editors for the past two centuries, we print metrically linked lines in the following way:

> HERMIA
> So is Lysander.
> THESEUS   In himself he is.

However, when there are a number of short verse-lines that can be linked in more than one way, we do not, with rare exceptions, indent any of them.

The Explanatory Notes

The notes that appear on the pages facing the text are designed to provide readers with the help that they may need to enjoy the play. Whenever the meaning of a word in the text is not readily accessible in a good contemporary dictionary, we offer the meaning in a note. Sometimes we provide a note even when the relevant meaning is to be found in the dictionary but when the word has acquired since Shakespeare's time other potentially confusing meanings. In our notes, we try to offer modern synonyms for Shakespeare's words. We also try to indicate to the reader the connection between the word in the play and the modern synonym. For example, Shakespeare sometimes uses the word *head* to mean "source," but, for modern readers, there may be no connection evident between these two words. We provide the connection by explaining Shakespeare's usage as follows: "**head:** fountainhead, source." On some occasions, a whole phrase or clause needs explanation. Then we rephrase in our own words the difficult passage, and add at the end synonyms for individual words in the passage. When scholars have been unable to determine the meaning of a word or phrase, we acknowledge the uncertainty.

A
MIDSUMMER
NIGHT'S DREAM

Characters in the Play

HERMIA
LYSANDER
HELENA
DEMETRIUS } *four lovers*

THESEUS, duke of Athens
HIPPOLYTA, queen of the Amazons
EGEUS, father to Hermia
PHILOSTRATE, master of the revels to Theseus

NICK BOTTOM, weaver
PETER QUINCE, carpenter
FRANCIS FLUTE, bellows-mender
TOM SNOUT, tinker
SNUG, joiner
ROBIN STARVELING, tailor

OBERON, king of the Fairies
TITANIA, queen of the Fairies
ROBIN GOODFELLOW, a "puck," or hobgoblin, in Oberon's service
A FAIRY, in the service of Titania
PEASEBLOSSOM
COBWEB
MOTE
MUSTARDSEED } *fairies attending upon Titania*

Lords and Attendants on Theseus and Hippolyta
Other Fairies in the trains of Titania and Oberon

A MIDSUMMER NIGHT'S DREAM

ACT 1

1.1 Theseus, duke of Athens, is planning the festivities for his upcoming wedding to the newly captured Amazon, Hippolyta. Egeus arrives with his daughter Hermia and her two suitors, Lysander (the man she wants to marry) and Demetrius (the man her father wants her to marry). Egeus demands that Theseus enforce Athenian law upon Hermia and execute her if she refuses to marry Demetrius. Theseus threatens Hermia with either lifelong chastity or death if she continues to disobey her father. Lysander and Hermia make plans to flee Athens. They reveal their plan to Helena, Hermia's friend, who is in love with Demetrius. To win Demetrius's favor, Helena decides to tell him about Lysander and Hermia's planned elopement.

---

1. **our nuptial hour:** the time for our wedding
4. **lingers:** delays, prolongs
5–6. **Like . . . revenue:** i.e., in the same way that a stepmother or a widow with rights in her dead husband's property (1) makes a young heir wait to inherit it, or (2) wastes it, or (3) has a claim on the young man's income until she dies
7. **steep themselves:** i.e., be absorbed (literally, soak themselves)
11. **solemnities:** festive ceremonies
14. **pert:** lively
16. **pale companion:** i.e., melancholy (**Companion** is a term of contempt, meaning "fellow.")
17–18. **I wooed . . . injuries:** In stories about Theseus, he overcomes Hippolyta in battle with the Amazons and then marries her.
20. **triumph:** public festivity

6

⌜ACT 1⌝

⌜Scene 1⌝

Enter Theseus, Hippolyta, ⌜and Philostrate,⌝ with others.

THESEUS
Now, fair Hippolyta, our nuptial hour
Draws on apace. Four happy days bring in
Another moon. But, O, methinks how slow
This old moon ⌜wanes!⌝ She lingers my desires
Like to a stepdame or a dowager   5
Long withering out a young man's revenue.

HIPPOLYTA
Four days will quickly steep themselves in night;
Four nights will quickly dream away the time;
And then the moon, like to a silver bow
⌜New⌝-bent in heaven, shall behold the night   10
Of our solemnities.

THESEUS   Go, Philostrate,
Stir up the Athenian youth to merriments.
Awake the pert and nimble spirit of mirth.
Turn melancholy forth to funerals;   15
The pale companion is not for our pomp.
                            ⌜*Philostrate exits.*⌝

Hippolyta, I wooed thee with my sword
And won thy love doing thee injuries,
But I will wed thee in another key,
With pomp, with triumph, and with reveling.   20

7

32. **feigning voice:** a voice singing softly; **feigning love:** pretended love

33. **the impression of her fantasy:** i.e., her imagination, on which you have impressed your image

34. **gauds:** (1) playthings; (2) showy things; **conceits:** fancy trinkets

35. **Knacks:** knickknacks

36. **prevailment:** influence

40. **Be it so:** i.e., if

44. **this gentleman:** Demetrius

46. **Immediately:** directly, i.e., with nothing intervening between sentence and actual punishment

47. **Be advised:** i.e., think carefully

*Enter Egeus and his daughter Hermia, and Lysander
and Demetrius.*

EGEUS
  Happy be Theseus, our renownèd duke!
THESEUS
  Thanks, good Egeus. What's the news with thee?
EGEUS
  Full of vexation come I, with complaint
  Against my child, my daughter Hermia.—
  Stand forth, Demetrius.—My noble lord,   25
  This man hath my consent to marry her.—
  Stand forth, Lysander.—And, my gracious duke,
  This man hath bewitched the bosom of my child.—
  Thou, thou, Lysander, thou hast given her rhymes
  And interchanged love tokens with my child.   30
  Thou hast by moonlight at her window sung
  With feigning voice verses of feigning love
  And stol'n the impression of her fantasy
  With bracelets of thy hair, rings, gauds, conceits,
  Knacks, trifles, nosegays, sweetmeats—messengers   35
  Of strong prevailment in unhardened youth.
  With cunning hast thou filched my daughter's heart,
  Turned her obedience (which is due to me)
  To stubborn harshness.—And, my gracious duke,
  Be it so she will not here before your Grace   40
  Consent to marry with Demetrius,
  I beg the ancient privilege of Athens:
  As she is mine, I may dispose of her,
  Which shall be either to this gentleman
  Or to her death, according to our law   45
  Immediately provided in that case.
THESEUS
  What say you, Hermia? Be advised, fair maid.
  To you, your father should be as a god,
  One that composed your beauties, yea, and one

52. **leave:** i.e., leave undisturbed; or, perhaps, abandon

56. **in this kind:** in this case; **wanting . . . voice:** lacking your father's support

62. **concern my modesty:** affect my reputation for proper maidenly behavior

67. **die the death:** be put to death

69. **question:** examine carefully

70. **Know of:** learn from; **blood:** passions, feelings

72. **livery of a nun:** a nun's distinctive clothing The term *nun* was used by writers in Shakespeare's day to refer not only to Christian nuns but also to pagan virgins dedicated to a life of chaste service to Diana or Vesta. (See page 12.)

73. **For aye:** forever; **mewed:** caged (A mew was a cage for hawks.)

75. **Chanting . . . moon:** Diana was both the moon goddess and the goddess of chastity.

76–77. **Thrice-blessèd . . . pilgrimage:** i.e., those who master their passions and live as chaste maidens separated from the world are **thrice-blessèd**

78–80. **But earthlier . . . blessedness:** i.e., those who marry have more happiness on this earth than those who live and die in **single blessedness**. (The image is of the married woman as a **rose distilled** [plucked and its fragrance distilled into perfume] as opposed to the rose that remains unplucked.)

To whom you are but as a form in wax 50
By him imprinted, and within his power
To leave the figure or disfigure it.
Demetrius is a worthy gentleman.

HERMIA
So is Lysander.

THESEUS   In himself he is, 55
But in this kind, wanting your father's voice,
The other must be held the worthier.

HERMIA
I would my father looked but with my eyes.

THESEUS
Rather your eyes must with his judgment look.

HERMIA
I do entreat your Grace to pardon me. 60
I know not by what power I am made bold,
Nor how it may concern my modesty
In such a presence here to plead my thoughts;
But I beseech your Grace that I may know
The worst that may befall me in this case 65
If I refuse to wed Demetrius.

THESEUS
Either to die the death, or to abjure
Forever the society of men.
Therefore, fair Hermia, question your desires,
Know of your youth, examine well your blood, 70
Whether (if you yield not to your father's choice)
You can endure the livery of a nun,
For aye to be in shady cloister mewed,
To live a barren sister all your life,
Chanting faint hymns to the cold fruitless moon. 75
Thrice-blessèd they that master so their blood
To undergo such maiden pilgrimage,
But earthlier happy is the rose distilled
Than that which, withering on the virgin thorn,
Grows, lives, and dies in single blessedness. 80

82. **my virgin patent:** my entitlement to my virginity; my freedom to live as a virgin.

83. **Unto his lordship:** i.e., to the mastery of a man

90. **he would:** i.e., your father wishes

91. **protest:** vow

92. **austerity:** i.e., a life of self-denial

94. **crazèd title:** flawed claim

96. **Do you:** i.e., you

100. **estate unto:** give to

101. **derived:** born, descended

102. **well possessed:** i.e., wealthy

103. **fairly:** attractively

104. **with vantage:** i.e., even more (than his)

108. **avouch . . . head:** declare it to his face

109. **Made love to:** courted

"The livery of a nun." (1.1.72)
From Johann Basilius Herold, *Heydenwelt* . . . (1554).

12

HERMIA
    So will I grow, so live, so die, my lord,
    Ere I will yield my virgin patent up
    Unto his lordship whose unwishèd yoke
    My soul consents not to give sovereignty.
THESEUS
    Take time to pause, and by the next new moon   85
    (The sealing day betwixt my love and me
    For everlasting bond of fellowship),
    Upon that day either prepare to die
    For disobedience to your father's will,
    Or else to wed Demetrius, as he would,   90
    Or on Diana's altar to protest
    For aye austerity and single life.
DEMETRIUS
    Relent, sweet Hermia, and, Lysander, yield
    Thy crazèd title to my certain right.
LYSANDER
    You have her father's love, Demetrius.   95
    Let me have Hermia's. Do you marry him.
EGEUS
    Scornful Lysander, true, he hath my love;
    And what is mine my love shall render him.
    And she is mine, and all my right of her
    I do estate unto Demetrius.   100
LYSANDER, ⌜*to Theseus*⌝
    I am, my lord, as well derived as he,
    As well possessed. My love is more than his;
    My fortunes every way as fairly ranked
    (If not with vantage) as Demetrius';
    And (which is more than all these boasts can be)   105
    I am beloved of beauteous Hermia.
    Why should not I then prosecute my right?
    Demetrius, I'll avouch it to his head,
    Made love to Nedar's daughter, Helena,
    And won her soul; and she, sweet lady, dotes,   110

112. **spotted:** i.e., morally stained, wicked

115. **self-affairs:** personal business

118. **schooling:** reproof, admonition

119. **arm:** prepare

122. **by no means we may extenuate:** i.e., I (speaking in my formal capacity) can in no way lessen or change

124. **What cheer . . . ?:** i.e., how are you? (literally, what is your mood or disposition?)

127. **Against:** in preparation for

128. **nearly that concerns yourselves:** i.e., that concerns you closely

131. **How chance . . . ?:** i.e., how does it happen that . . . ?

132. **Belike:** probably; **want:** lack

133. **Beteem:** grant, give

134. **For aught:** according to anything

137. **different in blood:** unequal in hereditary rank

138. **cross:** bar, barrier, obstruction

139. **misgraffèd . . . years:** mismatched in age

    Devoutly dotes, dotes in idolatry,
    Upon this spotted and inconstant man.
THESEUS
    I must confess that I have heard so much,
    And with Demetrius thought to have spoke thereof;
    But, being overfull of self-affairs,   115
    My mind did lose it.—But, Demetrius, come,
    And come, Egeus; you shall go with me.
    I have some private schooling for you both.—
    For you, fair Hermia, look you arm yourself
    To fit your fancies to your father's will,   120
    Or else the law of Athens yields you up
    (Which by no means we may extenuate)
    To death or to a vow of single life.—
    Come, my Hippolyta. What cheer, my love?—
    Demetrius and Egeus, go along.   125
    I must employ you in some business
    Against our nuptial, and confer with you
    Of something nearly that concerns yourselves.
EGEUS
    With duty and desire we follow you.
            ⌜*All but Hermia and Lysander*⌝ *exit.*
LYSANDER
    How now, my love? Why is your cheek so pale?   130
    How chance the roses there do fade so fast?
HERMIA
    Belike for want of rain, which I could well
    Beteem them from the tempest of my eyes.
LYSANDER
    Ay me! For aught that I could ever read,
    Could ever hear by tale or history,   135
    The course of true love never did run smooth.
    But either it was different in blood—
HERMIA
    O cross! Too high to be enthralled to ⌜low.⌝
LYSANDER
    Or else misgraffèd in respect of years—

141. **stood upon:** depended on

143. **if . . . choice:** i.e., if the lovers were suitably matched

145. **momentany:** lasting but a moment; instantaneous

147. **collied:** coal-black

148. **That:** the lightning; **in a spleen:** i.e., suddenly, in an impulsive action (The spleen was regarded as the seat of angry impulsiveness.); **unfolds:** reveals

149. **ere:** before

151. **quick:** (1) living, intense; (2) quickly; **confusion:** ruin, defeat

152. **ever crossed:** always frustrated or thwarted

157. **fancy's:** love's

158. **A good persuasion:** i.e., a good attitude for us to take

160. **revenue:** accented here on the second syllable

162. **respects me as:** i.e., regards me as much as if I were

166. **forth:** i.e., forth from

167. **without:** outside of

169. **To do . . . May:** i.e., to celebrate May Day (perhaps by collecting branches and flowers)

HERMIA
  O spite! Too old to be engaged to young.   140
LYSANDER
  Or else it stood upon the choice of friends—
HERMIA
  O hell, to choose love by another's eyes!
LYSANDER
  Or, if there were a sympathy in choice,
  War, death, or sickness did lay siege to it,
  Making it momentany as a sound,   145
  Swift as a shadow, short as any dream,
  Brief as the lightning in the collied night,
  That, in a spleen, unfolds both heaven and earth,
  And, ere a man hath power to say "Behold!"
  The jaws of darkness do devour it up.   150
  So quick bright things come to confusion.
HERMIA
  If then true lovers have been ever crossed,
  It stands as an edict in destiny.
  Then let us teach our trial patience
  Because it is a customary cross,   155
  As due to love as thoughts and dreams and sighs,
  Wishes and tears, poor fancy's followers.
LYSANDER
  A good persuasion. Therefore, hear me, Hermia:
  I have a widow aunt, a dowager
  Of great revenue, and she hath no child.   160
  From Athens is her house remote seven leagues,
  And she respects me as her only son.
  There, gentle Hermia, may I marry thee;
  And to that place the sharp Athenian law
  Cannot pursue us. If thou lovest me, then   165
  Steal forth thy father's house tomorrow night,
  And in the wood a league without the town
  (Where I did meet thee once with Helena
  To do observance to a morn of May),
  There will I stay for thee.   170

173. **arrow with the golden head:** Cupid, the mythological god of love, was said to use arrows with golden heads to cause love, and arrows with leaden heads to repel love.

174. **simplicity:** innocence; **Venus' doves:** Doves were sacred to Venus (goddess of love and mother of Cupid) and were sometimes pictured as drawing her chariot. (See page 46.)

176–77. **that fire . . . was seen:** Dido, queen of Carthage, both burned with love for Aeneas and burned herself on a pyre after Aeneas, **the false Trojan**, abandoned her by sailing off to found Rome.

183. **Godspeed:** a conventional greeting

185. **your fair:** your fairness, beauty; **happy:** fortunate

186. **lodestars:** stars (like the polestar) that sailors used to guide them

187. **tunable:** melodious

189. **catching:** contagious; **favor:** looks

190. **catch:** get as if by infection

194–95. **Demetrius . . . translated:** i.e., I'd give all the world, except for Demetrius, in order to be transformed into you **bated:** excepted, omitted **translated:** transformed

HERMIA   My good Lysander,
　I swear to thee by Cupid's strongest bow,
　By his best arrow with the golden head,
　By the simplicity of Venus' doves,
　By that which knitteth souls and prospers loves,   175
　And by that fire which burned the Carthage queen
　When the false Trojan under sail was seen,
　By all the vows that ever men have broke
　(In number more than ever women spoke),
　In that same place thou hast appointed me,   180
　Tomorrow truly will I meet with thee.
LYSANDER
　Keep promise, love. Look, here comes Helena.

　　　　　　　　Enter Helena.

HERMIA
　Godspeed, fair Helena. Whither away?
HELENA
　Call you me "fair"? That "fair" again unsay.
　Demetrius loves your fair. O happy fair!   185
　Your eyes are lodestars and your tongue's sweet air
　More tunable than lark to shepherd's ear
　When wheat is green, when hawthorn buds appear.
　Sickness is catching. O, were favor so!
　⌜Yours would⌝ I catch, fair Hermia, ere I go.   190
　My ear should catch your voice, my eye your eye;
　My tongue should catch your tongue's sweet
　　melody.
　Were the world mine, Demetrius being bated,
　The rest ⌜I'd⌝ give to be to you translated.   195
　O, teach me how you look and with what art
　You sway the motion of Demetrius' heart!
HERMIA
　I frown upon him, yet he loves me still.
HELENA
　O, that your frowns would teach my smiles such
　　skill!   200

206. **Would:** i.e., I wish

211. **what graces . . . dwell:** i.e., how much attractiveness lies in Lysander

214. **Phoebe:** i.e., the moon (Phoebe is another name for Diana, goddess of the moon.)

215. **wat'ry glass:** i.e., pond or lake, which acts as a **glass** or mirror

217. **still:** always

220. **faint:** pale; **wont:** accustomed

224. **stranger companies:** i.e., the company of strangers

Phoebe. (1.1.214)
From Johann Engel, *Astrolabium* (1488).

HERMIA
  I give him curses, yet he gives me love.
HELENA
  O, that my prayers could such affection move!
HERMIA
  The more I hate, the more he follows me.
HELENA
  The more I love, the more he hateth me.
HERMIA
  His folly, Helena, is no fault of mine.   205
HELENA
  None but your beauty. Would that fault were mine!
HERMIA
  Take comfort: he no more shall see my face.
  Lysander and myself will fly this place.
  Before the time I did Lysander see
  Seemed Athens as a paradise to me.   210
  O, then, what graces in my love do dwell
  That he hath turned a heaven unto a hell!
LYSANDER
  Helen, to you our minds we will unfold.
  Tomorrow night when Phoebe doth behold
  Her silver visage in the wat'ry glass,   215
  Decking with liquid pearl the bladed grass
  (A time that lovers' flights doth still conceal),
  Through Athens' gates have we devised to steal.
HERMIA
  And in the wood where often you and I
  Upon faint primrose beds were wont to lie,   220
  Emptying our bosoms of their counsel ⌐sweet,⌐
  There my Lysander and myself shall meet,
  And thence from Athens turn away our eyes
  To seek new friends and ⌐stranger companies.⌐
  Farewell, sweet playfellow. Pray thou for us,   225
  And good luck grant thee thy Demetrius.—

228. **lovers' food:** i.e., the sight of each other

232. **o'er other some:** i.e., in comparison to certain others

238. **holding no quantity:** i.e., out of all proportion

240–47. **Love . . . everywhere:** Helena uses the ways in which Cupid is often pictured (as a blind boy with wings) to describe the qualities of love—its blindness, lack of judgment, folly, and inconstancy. (See page 114.)

242. **of any judgment taste:** i.e., any taste of judgment

243. **figure:** represent; **unheedy:** heedless, reckless

245. **beguiled:** cheated

246. **game:** sport; **forswear:** swear falsely, perjure

247. **is perjured:** i.e., perjures himself

248. **eyne:** eyes

249. **hailed down:** showered, poured down like hail

254. **intelligence:** news

255. **If . . . expense:** Helena may be saying that she is purchasing Demetrius's thanks at great cost; or, she may mean that her efforts will be dear to her if they bring her Demetrius's thanks. **dear:** (1) high priced; (2) loved, precious

Keep word, Lysander. We must starve our sight
From lovers' food till morrow deep midnight.

LYSANDER
I will, my Hermia.   *Hermia exits.*
              Helena, adieu.   230
As you on him, Demetrius dote on you!
                              Lysander exits.

HELENA
How happy some o'er other some can be!
Through Athens I am thought as fair as she.
But what of that? Demetrius thinks not so.
He will not know what all but he do know.   235
And, as he errs, doting on Hermia's eyes,
So I, admiring of his qualities.
Things base and vile, holding no quantity,
Love can transpose to form and dignity.
Love looks not with the eyes but with the mind;   240
And therefore is winged Cupid painted blind.
Nor hath Love's mind of any judgment taste.
Wings, and no eyes, figure unheedy haste.
And therefore is Love said to be a child
Because in choice he is so oft beguiled.   245
As waggish boys in game themselves forswear,
So the boy Love is perjured everywhere.
For, ere Demetrius looked on Hermia's eyne,
He hailed down oaths that he was only mine;
And when this hail some heat from Hermia felt,   250
So he dissolved, and show'rs of oaths did melt.
I will go tell him of fair Hermia's flight.
Then to the wood will he tomorrow night
Pursue her. And, for this intelligence
If I have thanks, it is a dear expense.   255
But herein mean I to enrich my pain,
To have his sight thither and back again.
                              She exits.

1.2 Six Athenian tradesmen decide to put on a play, called "Pyramus and Thisbe," for Theseus and Hippolyta's wedding. Pyramus will be played by Bottom the weaver and Thisbe by Francis Flute the bellows-mender. The men are given their parts to study, and they agree to meet for a rehearsal in the woods outside Athens.

---

0 SD. **joiner:** carpenter, cabinetmaker

2. **You were best:** i.e., you had better; **generally:** Bottom's mistake for "individually"

3. **scrip:** a piece of paper with writing on it

4. **which:** i.e., who

6. **interlude:** an entertainment that comes between other events (here, a play to fill the time between the wedding and bedtime)

10. **grow to a point:** As in many of Bottom's lines, one gets a sense of what he means even though he uses language oddly. Here, he seems to mean "come to a conclusion."

11. **Marry:** i.e., indeed (originally an oath on the name of the Virgin Mary)

12–13. **Pyramus and Thisbe:** The story of Pyramus and Thisbe—a story very much like that of Romeo and Juliet—is told in Ovid's *Metamorphoses*, book IV.

23. **ask:** require

25. **condole:** grieve, lament (Bottom probably means that he will act the part of the grieving lover.)

26. **humor:** inclination, preference

27. **Ercles:** Hercules (This may be an allusion to a lost play about the Greek hero; or, the role of Her-

(continued)

⌜Scene 2⌝
Enter Quince the carpenter, and Snug the joiner, and
Bottom the weaver, and Flute the bellows-mender, and
Snout the tinker, and Starveling the tailor.

QUINCE   Is all our company here?

BOTTOM   You were best to call them generally, man by
man, according to the scrip.

QUINCE   Here is the scroll of every man's name which
is thought fit, through all Athens, to play in our   5
interlude before the Duke and the Duchess on his
wedding day at night.

BOTTOM   First, good Peter Quince, say what the play
treats on, then read the names of the actors, and so
grow to a point.   10

QUINCE   Marry, our play is "The most lamentable
comedy and most cruel death of Pyramus and
Thisbe."

BOTTOM   A very good piece of work, I assure you, and a
merry. Now, good Peter Quince, call forth your   15
actors by the scroll. Masters, spread yourselves.

QUINCE   Answer as I call you. Nick Bottom, the weaver.

BOTTOM   Ready. Name what part I am for, and proceed.

QUINCE   You, Nick Bottom, are set down for Pyramus.   20

BOTTOM   What is Pyramus—a lover or a tyrant?

QUINCE   A lover that kills himself most gallant for love.

BOTTOM   That will ask some tears in the true performing of it. If I do it, let the audience look to their
eyes. I will move storms; I will condole in some   25
measure. To the rest.—Yet my chief humor is for a
tyrant. I could play Ercles rarely, or a part to tear a
cat in, to make all split:

> *The raging rocks*
> *And shivering shocks*   30
> *Shall break the locks*

cules may have been famous as an extravagant, ranting part.)

27–28. tear a cat: i.e., rant and rave

33. Phibbus' car: the chariot of the sun god, Phoebus Apollo

38. Ercles' vein: the style of Hercules (See note on line 27, above.)

42. take . . . on you: i.e., play the part of

43. wand'ring knight: knight-errant (i.e., a hero's role in medieval romance)

47. That's all one: i.e., no matter; **mask:** perhaps alluding to the masks that women frequently wore when out of doors to protect their skin from the sun

48. small: shrill, high-pitched

49. An: i.e., if

50. monstrous little: extremely small

"Phibbus' car." (1.2.33)
From Hyginus, *Fabularum liber* (1549).

> *Of prison gates.*
> *And Phibbus' car*
> *Shall shine from far*
> *And make and mar*   35
> *The foolish Fates.*

This was lofty. Now name the rest of the players.
This is Ercles' vein, a tyrant's vein. A lover is more
condoling.

QUINCE   Francis Flute, the bellows-mender.   40

FLUTE   Here, Peter Quince.

QUINCE   Flute, you must take Thisbe on you.

FLUTE   What is Thisbe—a wand'ring knight?

QUINCE   It is the lady that Pyramus must love.

FLUTE   Nay, faith, let not me play a woman. I have a   45
   beard coming.

QUINCE   That's all one. You shall play it in a mask, and
   you may speak as small as you will.

BOTTOM   An I may hide my face, let me play Thisbe too.
   I'll speak in a monstrous little voice: "Thisne,   50
   Thisne!"—"Ah Pyramus, my lover dear! Thy Thisbe
   dear and lady dear!"

QUINCE   No, no, you must play Pyramus—and, Flute,
   you Thisbe.

BOTTOM   Well, proceed.   55

QUINCE   Robin Starveling, the tailor.

STARVELING   Here, Peter Quince.

QUINCE   Robin Starveling, you must play Thisbe's
   mother.—Tom Snout, the tinker.

SNOUT   Here, Peter Quince.   60

QUINCE   You, Pyramus' father.—Myself, Thisbe's
   father.—Snug the joiner, you the lion's part.—
   And I hope here is a play fitted.

SNUG   Have you the lion's part written? Pray you, if it
   be, give it me, for I am slow of study.   65

QUINCE   You may do it extempore, for it is nothing but
   roaring.

74. **were:** i.e., would be

78. **discretion:** judgment (Bottom seems to mean that they would have no choice but to hang them.); **aggravate:** Bottom's mistake for "moderate" or "mitigate" (i.e., soften, tone down)

79. **roar you:** i.e., roar for you;

79–80. **sucking dove:** Bottom's confusion of "sucking [i.e., unweaned] lamb" and "sitting [i.e., hatching] dove"

80. **an 'twere:** as if it were

82. **a proper:** i.e., as handsome a

84. **must needs:** i.e., must

88. **will:** i.e., wish

89. **discharge:** perform; **your:** i.e., a (a colloquialism)

90. **orange-tawny:** tan

90–91. **purple-in-grain:** crimson fast-dyed

91. **French-crown:** gold (the color of the French coin called a "crown" in English)

92. **perfit:** perfect (Since "perfect" became the preferred spelling around 1590, it is possible that the old form was deliberately chosen for Bottom—as again at line 105.)

93–94. **French . . . all:** an allusion to the baldness caused by syphilis (the "French disease")

96. **con:** learn

98. **without:** outside of

100. **devices:** plans; or, the plot of our play (The word *device* was sometimes used to denote a play or masque—as it is in Act 5 of this play.)

101. **bill of properties:** list of stage props

BOTTOM   Let me play the lion too. I will roar that I will do any man's heart good to hear me. I will roar that I will make the Duke say "Let him roar again. Let   70 him roar again!"

QUINCE   An you should do it too terribly, you would fright the Duchess and the ladies that they would shriek, and that were enough to hang us all.

ALL   That would hang us, every mother's son.   75

BOTTOM   I grant you, friends, if you should fright the ladies out of their wits, they would have no more discretion but to hang us. But I will aggravate my voice so that I will roar you as gently as any sucking dove. I will roar you an 'twere any nightingale.   80

QUINCE   You can play no part but Pyramus, for Pyramus is a sweet-faced man, a proper man as one shall see in a summer's day, a most lovely gentlemanlike man. Therefore you must needs play Pyramus.   85

BOTTOM   Well, I will undertake it. What beard were I best to play it in?

QUINCE   Why, what you will.

BOTTOM   I will discharge it in either your straw-color beard, your orange-tawny beard, your purple-   90 in-grain beard, or your French-crown-color beard, your perfit yellow.

QUINCE   Some of your French crowns have no hair at all, and then you will play barefaced. But, masters, here are your parts, ⌜*giving out the parts,*⌝ and I am   95 to entreat you, request you, and desire you, to con them by tomorrow night and meet me in the palace wood, a mile without the town, by moonlight. There will we rehearse, for if we meet in the city, we shall be dogged with company and our devices known. In   100 the meantime I will draw a bill of properties such as our play wants. I pray you fail me not.

BOTTOM   We will meet, and there we may rehearse

104. **obscenely:** Bottom perhaps means "seemly."

105. **perfit:** i.e., word-perfect

107. **Hold, or cut bowstrings:** This sounds like a proverb, or like an archery term, but seems to be Bottom's invention. (Perhaps it means "Keep your word or be disgraced.")

most obscenely and courageously. Take pains. Be
perfit. Adieu.   105
QUINCE   At the Duke's Oak we meet.
BOTTOM   Enough. Hold, or cut bowstrings.

They exit.

A
MIDSUMMER
NIGHT'S DREAM

ACT 2

2.1 Oberon and Titania, king and queen of the fairies, quarrel over possession of a young Indian boy. Oberon orders Robin Goodfellow, a hobgoblin or "puck," to obtain a special flower that makes people fall in love with the next creature they see. Oberon wants to make Titania fall in love with a beast and use her infatuation to get the Indian boy from her. Demetrius enters pursued by Helena, whom he tries to drive off. When Robin returns, Oberon, who sympathizes with Helena's love, orders him to find the Athenian man (i.e., Demetrius) and apply some of the flower's magic nectar to his eyes.

---

0 SD. **Robin Goodfellow:** a "puck," or mischievous spirit, whose activities are described in lines 33–59 (Since Nicholas Rowe's 1709 edition of the play, the character has been known as "Puck.") Robin appears in stories, plays, and books on witchcraft, sometimes as simply mischievous, sometimes as an evil goblin. (See page 58.)

3. **Thorough:** i.e., through

4. **pale:** fenced-in area

7. **moon's sphere:** In Ptolemaic astronomy, the moon (like the planets, the stars, and the sun) was carried around the earth in a crystalline sphere.

9. **orbs:** circles (A circle of darker, more luxuriant, grass in a meadow was called a "fairy ring" and was thought to be the dancing ground of fairies.)

10. **pensioners:** Because of their height and their brightly colored flowers (gold with ruby-red spots), **cowslips** are compared to the gaudily dressed bodyguards (**pensioners**) that served Queen Elizabeth.

16. **lob:** oaf, lout

(continued)

⌜ACT 2⌝

⌜Scene 1⌝

Enter a Fairy at one door and Robin Goodfellow at another.

ROBIN
How now, spirit? Whither wander you?
FAIRY
      Over hill, over dale,
        Thorough bush, thorough brier,
      Over park, over pale,
        Thorough flood, thorough fire;   5
      I do wander everywhere,
      Swifter than the moon's sphere.
      And I serve the Fairy Queen,
      To dew her orbs upon the green.
      The cowslips tall her pensioners be;   10
      In their gold coats spots you see;
      Those be rubies, fairy favors;
      In those freckles live their savors.
I must go seek some dewdrops here
And hang a pearl in every cowslip's ear.   15
Farewell, thou lob of spirits. I'll be gone.
Our queen and all her elves come here anon.
ROBIN
The King doth keep his revels here tonight.
Take heed the Queen come not within his sight,

17. **anon:** soon

18. **revels:** At the court of Queen Elizabeth, **revels** were presented at special seasons, and included plays, masques, and sports. Here, the king of fairyland's **revels** might also include dancing.

20. **passing:** i.e., surpassingly, extremely; **fell and wrath:** i.e., fiercely angry

25. **trace:** travel through

26. **perforce:** forcibly

29. **they:** i.e., the king and queen of fairies

30. **fountain:** spring

31. **square:** quarrel; **that:** i.e., so that

34. **shrewd:** mischievous, malicious; **sprite:** spirit

35. **Robin Goodfellow:** See the note on 2.1.0 SD.

36. **villagery:** villages

37. **Skim milk:** i.e., steal the cream from the milk; **labor in the quern:** i.e., work at the quern (a small mill for grinding corn), to frustrate the grinding

38. **bootless . . . churn:** i.e., make her churning produce no butter **bootless:** uselessly, fruitlessly **huswife:** pronounced "hussif"

39. **barm:** yeasty "head" on beer.

47. **beguile:** deceive, trick

49. **gossip's bowl:** the cup from which the gossiping or tattling woman is drinking

50. **crab:** crab apple (Roasted crabapples and spices were added to hot ale to make a winter drink.)

52. **dewlap:** the fold of skin hanging from the neck of certain animals (here applied to the neck of the old woman)

53. **aunt:** perhaps, old woman or gossip; **telling . . . tale:** "Winter's tales" and "old wives' tales," told to while away long evenings, could be merry or sad.

For Oberon is passing fell and wrath   20
Because that she, as her attendant, hath
A lovely boy stolen from an Indian king;
She never had so sweet a changeling.
And jealous Oberon would have the child
Knight of his train, to trace the forests wild.   25
But she perforce withholds the lovèd boy,
Crowns him with flowers, and makes him all her
   joy.
And now they never meet in grove or green,
By fountain clear, or spangled starlight sheen,   30
But they do square, that all their elves for fear
Creep into acorn cups and hide them there.

FAIRY
Either I mistake your shape and making quite,
Or else you are that shrewd and knavish sprite
Called Robin Goodfellow. Are not you he   35
That frights the maidens of the villagery,
Skim milk, and sometimes labor in the quern
And bootless make the breathless huswife churn,
And sometime make the drink to bear no barm,
Mislead night wanderers, laughing at their harm?   40
Those that "Hobgoblin" call you, and "sweet Puck,"
You do their work, and they shall have good luck.
Are not you he?

ROBIN   Thou speakest aright.
I am that merry wanderer of the night.   45
I jest to Oberon and make him smile
When I a fat and bean-fed horse beguile,
Neighing in likeness of a filly foal.
And sometime lurk I in a gossip's bowl
In very likeness of a roasted crab,   50
And, when she drinks, against her lips I bob
And on her withered dewlap pour the ale.
The wisest aunt, telling the saddest tale,
Sometime for three-foot stool mistaketh me;

56. **"Tailor":** Since "tail" could mean "buttocks," it has been suggested that the old woman's cry might be translated as "O my bum!" (It remains uncertain just what the expression means.)

57. **choir:** company

57–58. **loffe . . . waxen . . . neeze:** These archaic forms of "laugh," "wax" (i.e., increase), and "sneeze" seem to reproduce the country setting Robin is describing.

60. **room:** i.e., make room, stand aside

64. **forsworn:** renounced, formally rejected

65. **rash wanton:** foolish rebel; **lord:** husband (and therefore having the right to control his wife)

66. **lady:** wife (and therefore having the right to expect her husband to be faithful)

68. **in . . . Corin:** disguised as a lovesick shepherd

69. **of corn:** i.e., made from wheat straws

70. **Phillida:** traditional shepherdess of love poetry

71. **steep:** slope, cliff

72. **forsooth:** in truth, certainly; **Amazon:** In stories about Theseus, Hippolyta was one of the Amazon warriors (a tribe of women fighters) who attacked Athens. After four months of fighting, peace was reached through Hippolyta's efforts.

73. **buskined:** wearing buskins, or boots

74. **must be:** i.e., is to be

75. **their bed:** i.e., their marriage and offspring

77. **Glance at:** allude to; **credit:** reputation

81–83. **Perigouna . . . Aegles . . . Ariadne . . . Antiopa:** In stories about Theseus, these are lovers whom Theseus deserted. Oberon lays the blame for these desertions on Titania. **break . . . faith:** i.e., go back on his word, break his promise

Then slip I from her bum, down topples she,   55
And "Tailor!" cries, and falls into a cough,
And then the whole choir hold their hips and loffe
And waxen in their mirth and neeze and swear
A merrier hour was never wasted there.
But room, fairy. Here comes Oberon.   60

FAIRY
And here my mistress. Would that he were gone!

Enter ⌐Oberon⌐ the King of Fairies at one door, with his
train, and ⌐Titania⌐ the Queen at another, with hers.

OBERON
Ill met by moonlight, proud Titania.

TITANIA
What, jealous Oberon? ⌐Fairies,⌐ skip hence.
I have forsworn his bed and company.

OBERON
Tarry, rash wanton. Am not I thy lord?   65

TITANIA
Then I must be thy lady. But I know
When thou hast stolen away from Fairyland
And in the shape of Corin sat all day
Playing on pipes of corn and versing love
To amorous Phillida. Why art thou here,   70
Come from the farthest steep of India,
But that, forsooth, the bouncing Amazon,
Your buskined mistress and your warrior love,
To Theseus must be wedded, and you come
To give their bed joy and prosperity?   75

OBERON
How canst thou thus for shame, Titania,
Glance at my credit with Hippolyta,
Knowing I know thy love to Theseus?
Didst not thou lead him through the glimmering
   night   80
From ⌐Perigouna,⌐ whom he ravishèd,

84. **forgeries:** fictions, fictitious inventions

85. **middle summer's spring:** i.e., the beginning of midsummer

86. **mead:** meadow

87. **pavèd:** pebbled

88. **margent:** margin

89. **ringlets:** circle dances

91. **piping:** i.e., whistling, making music

94. **pelting:** paltry, insignificant

95. **continents:** i.e., banks (which contain them)

97–98. **green corn . . . beard:** As grain (called, in England, corn) ripens, its head develops bristle-like extensions; it is then called "bearded."

99. **fold:** i.e., sheepfold, or pen

100. **murrain flock:** i.e., sheep dead from murrain, an infectious disease

101. **nine-men's-morris:** an outdoor space carved, or cut in turf, for a game of the same name

102. **quaint:** elaborate; **mazes:** intricate interconnecting paths that lead confusingly to (and away from) a center; **wanton green:** luxuriant grass

103. **tread:** perhaps, human footsteps which, when tracing the maze, would keep its path clear; **undistinguishable:** not perceptible

104. **want:** lack

106. **Therefore:** i.e., (as in line 91) because of Oberon's disturbance of the fairy dances

108. **That:** i.e., so that; **rheumatic:** i.e., like colds or flu, with discharges of rheum or mucus (accent on first syllable)

109. **thorough:** i.e., through, as a consequence of; **distemperature:** (1) bad temper; (2) bad weather

112. **Hiems':** i.e., winter's

(continued)

And make him with fair ⌜Aegles⌝ break his faith,
With Ariadne and Antiopa?

TITANIA
These are the forgeries of jealousy;
And never, since the middle summer's spring, 85
Met we on hill, in dale, forest, or mead,
By pavèd fountain or by rushy brook,
Or in the beachèd margent of the sea,
To dance our ringlets to the whistling wind,
But with thy brawls thou hast disturbed our sport. 90
Therefore the winds, piping to us in vain,
As in revenge have sucked up from the sea
Contagious fogs, which, falling in the land,
Hath every pelting river made so proud
That they have overborne their continents. 95
The ox hath therefore stretched his yoke in vain,
The plowman lost his sweat, and the green corn
Hath rotted ere his youth attained a beard.
The fold stands empty in the drownèd field,
And crows are fatted with the murrain flock. 100
The nine-men's-morris is filled up with mud,
And the quaint mazes in the wanton green,
For lack of tread, are undistinguishable.
The human mortals want their winter here.
No night is now with hymn or carol blessed. 105
Therefore the moon, the governess of floods,
Pale in her anger, washes all the air,
That rheumatic diseases do abound.
And thorough this distemperature we see
The seasons alter: hoary-headed frosts 110
Fall in the fresh lap of the crimson rose,
And on old Hiems' ⌜thin⌝ and icy crown
An odorous chaplet of sweet summer buds
Is, as in mockery, set. The spring, the summer,
The childing autumn, angry winter, change 115
Their wonted liveries, and the mazèd world

113. **odorous:** fragrant

115. **childing:** fruitful (producing "children"); **change:** exchange

116. **wonted liveries:** usual outfits

116–17. **the mazèd world . . . which:** i.e., the bewildered world can no longer distinguish one season from another according to the produce (**increase**) normally brought forth in each **mazèd:** bewildered

118–19. **this same . . . debate:** these evils are the descendants of our quarrel **debate:** quarrel

120. **original:** origin

122. **cross:** oppose, resist

124. **henchman:** page, squire

127. **vot'ress . . . order:** woman vowed to serve me

129. **Full:** i.e., very

130. **Neptune:** the god of the sea (See page 110.)

131. **Marking:** noticing, watching; **embarkèd . . . flood:** i.e., merchant ships sailing on the ocean

133. **wanton:** (1) lewd; (2) playful

145. **round:** circle dance

147. **spare your haunts:** avoid the places you frequent

By their increase now knows not which is which.
And this same progeny of evils comes
From our debate, from our dissension;
We are their parents and original.   120

OBERON
Do you amend it, then. It lies in you.
Why should Titania cross her Oberon?
I do but beg a little changeling boy
To be my henchman.

TITANIA   Set your heart at rest: 125
The Fairyland buys not the child of me.
His mother was a vot'ress of my order,
And in the spicèd Indian air by night
Full often hath she gossiped by my side
And sat with me on Neptune's yellow sands,   130
Marking th' embarkèd traders on the flood,
When we have laughed to see the sails conceive
And grow big-bellied with the wanton wind;
Which she, with pretty and with swimming gait,
Following (her womb then rich with my young   135
   squire),
Would imitate and sail upon the land
To fetch me trifles and return again,
As from a voyage, rich with merchandise.
But she, being mortal, of that boy did die,   140
And for her sake do I rear up her boy,
And for her sake I will not part with him.

OBERON
How long within this wood intend you stay?

TITANIA
Perchance till after Theseus' wedding day.
If you will patiently dance in our round   145
And see our moonlight revels, go with us.
If not, shun me, and I will spare your haunts.

OBERON
Give me that boy and I will go with thee.

150. **chide:** fight, brawl; **downright:** i.e., outright
151. **from:** i.e., go from
152. **injury:** wrong, insult
154. **Since:** i.e., when
158. **stars . . . spheres:** See note on 2.1.7, above
164. **vestal:** i.e., virgin (This passage is often explained as referring to Queen Elizabeth I.)
165. **smartly:** briskly
166. **As:** i.e., as if
167. **might:** i.e., could
168. **wat'ry moon:** Because the moon controls the tides, it is often associated with water.
169. **imperial:** commanding, majestic; perhaps also (as a reference to Queen Elizabeth) pertaining to rulership of an empire (In the 1596 edition of Spenser's *Faerie Queene,* for example, Spenser refers to "The Most . . . Magnificent Empresse . . . Elizabeth . . . Queene of England, France and Ireland and of Virginia. . . ."); **vot'ress:** a woman under a vow (The word **vestal** suggests it is a vow of chastity.)
171. **bolt:** arrow
174. **love-in-idleness:** a name for the pansy or heartsease
175. **herb:** plant
177. **or . . . or:** either . . . or
180. **leviathan:** a monstrous sea creature mentioned in the Bible; **league:** approximately three miles

TITANIA
  Not for thy fairy kingdom. Fairies, away.
  We shall chide downright if I longer stay.   150
            ⌜*Titania and her fairies*⌝ *exit.*

OBERON
  Well, go thy way. Thou shalt not from this grove
  Till I torment thee for this injury.—
  My gentle Puck, come hither. Thou rememb'rest
  Since once I sat upon a promontory
  And heard a mermaid on a dolphin's back   155
  Uttering such dulcet and harmonious breath
  That the rude sea grew civil at her song
  And certain stars shot madly from their spheres
  To hear the sea-maid's music.

ROBIN   I remember.   160

OBERON
  That very time I saw (but thou couldst not),
  Flying between the cold moon and the earth,
  Cupid all armed. A certain aim he took
  At a fair vestal thronèd by ⌜the⌝ west,
  And loosed his love-shaft smartly from his bow   165
  As it should pierce a hundred thousand hearts.
  But I might see young Cupid's fiery shaft
  Quenched in the chaste beams of the wat'ry moon,
  And the imperial vot'ress passèd on
  In maiden meditation, fancy-free.   170
  Yet marked I where the bolt of Cupid fell.
  It fell upon a little western flower,
  Before, milk-white, now purple with love's wound,
  And maidens call it "love-in-idleness."
  Fetch me that flower; the herb I showed thee once.   175
  The juice of it on sleeping eyelids laid
  Will make or man or woman madly dote
  Upon the next live creature that it sees.
  Fetch me this herb, and be thou here again
  Ere the leviathan can swim a league.   180

183. **juice:** nectar from the flower
192. **page:** boy attending on a knight
197. **stay:** halt, stop; **stayeth:** arrests, holds
199. **and wood:** and mad, insane
202. **adamant:** i.e., like a magnet
203. **draw:** attract
204. **Leave you:** i.e., give up
206. **speak you fair:** i.e., speak to you civilly
208. **nor:** i.e., and

"Venus' doves." (1.1.174)
From Joannes ab Indagine, *The book of palmestry* (1666).

ROBIN
  I'll put a girdle round about the earth
  In forty minutes.   ⌈*He exits.*⌉
OBERON   Having once this juice,
  I'll watch Titania when she is asleep
  And drop the liquor of it in her eyes.   185
  The next thing then she, waking, looks upon
  (Be it on lion, bear, or wolf, or bull,
  On meddling monkey, or on busy ape)
  She shall pursue it with the soul of love.
  And ere I take this charm from off her sight   190
  (As I can take it with another herb),
  I'll make her render up her page to me.
  But who comes here? I am invisible,
  And I will overhear their conference.

    Enter Demetrius, Helena following him.

DEMETRIUS
  I love thee not; therefore pursue me not.   195
  Where is Lysander and fair Hermia?
  The one I'll stay; the other stayeth me.
  Thou told'st me they were stol'n unto this wood,
  And here am I, and wood within this wood
  Because I cannot meet my Hermia.   200
  Hence, get thee gone, and follow me no more.
HELENA
  You draw me, you hard-hearted adamant!
  But yet you draw not iron, for my heart
  Is true as steel. Leave you your power to draw,
  And I shall have no power to follow you.   205
DEMETRIUS
  Do I entice you? Do I speak you fair?
  Or rather do I not in plainest truth
  Tell you I do not, ⌈nor⌉ I cannot love you?
HELENA
  And even for that do I love you the more.

221. **impeach:** call into question, discredit; **modesty:** i.e., properly chaste female behavior

222. **To leave:** i.e., in leaving

225. **ill:** evil; **desert:** uninhabited

227. **virtue:** (1) excellence; (2) moral goodness; **privilege:** i.e., protection; **For that:** i.e., because

231. **For:** because; **in my respect:** i.e., from my perspective

234. **brakes:** thickets

238–40. **Apollo . . . tiger:** Helena gives three examples of stories that are **changed** so that the weak pursue the strong: the chaste nymph Daphne chases the god Apollo (in mythology, Daphne fled from Apollo and escaped him by being transformed into a laurel tree); the dove attacks the mythical beast called the griffin; the female deer chases the tiger. **griffin:** an animal with the head of an eagle on the body of a lion

A griffin. (2.1.239)
From Giulio Cesare Capaccio,
Delle imprese trattato . . . (1592).

I am your spaniel, and, Demetrius,   210
The more you beat me I will fawn on you.
Use me but as your spaniel: spurn me, strike me,
Neglect me, lose me; only give me leave
(Unworthy as I am) to follow you.
What worser place can I beg in your love   215
(And yet a place of high respect with me)
Than to be usèd as you use your dog?

DEMETRIUS
Tempt not too much the hatred of my spirit,
For I am sick when I do look on thee.

HELENA
And I am sick when I look not on you.   220

DEMETRIUS
You do impeach your modesty too much
To leave the city and commit yourself
Into the hands of one that loves you not,
To trust the opportunity of night
And the ill counsel of a desert place   225
With the rich worth of your virginity.

HELENA
Your virtue is my privilege. For that
It is not night when I do see your face,
Therefore I think I am not in the night.
Nor doth this wood lack worlds of company,   230
For you, in my respect, are all the world.
Then, how can it be said I am alone
When all the world is here to look on me?

DEMETRIUS
I'll run from thee and hide me in the brakes
And leave thee to the mercy of wild beasts.   235

HELENA
The wildest hath not such a heart as you.
Run when you will. The story shall be changed:
Apollo flies and Daphne holds the chase;
The dove pursues the griffin; the mild hind

240. **Bootless:** useless, fruitless
242. **stay:** i.e., stay for
243–44. **do . . . But:** i.e., you may be sure that
244, 246. **do . . . mischief:** harm
247. **my sex:** i.e., all females
251. **upon:** by
253. **fly:** flee from
257. **blows:** bursts into flower
258. **oxlips:** flowers somewhat larger than cowslips
259. **woodbine:** honeysuckle (See page 122.)
260. **eglantine:** sweetbrier
261. **sometime of:** sometimes during
263. **throws:** casts; **her:** i.e., its
264. **Weed:** garment
265. **this:** i.e., of the magic flower

Makes speed to catch the tiger. Bootless speed   240
When cowardice pursues and valor flies!

DEMETRIUS
I will not stay thy questions. Let me go,
Or if thou follow me, do not believe
But I shall do thee mischief in the wood.

HELENA
Ay, in the temple, in the town, the field,   245
You do me mischief. Fie, Demetrius!
Your wrongs do set a scandal on my sex.
We cannot fight for love as men may do.
We should be wooed and were not made to woo.
⌜*Demetrius exits.*⌝
I'll follow thee and make a heaven of hell   250
To die upon the hand I love so well.   ⌜*Helena exits.*⌝

OBERON
Fare thee well, nymph. Ere he do leave this grove,
Thou shalt fly him, and he shall seek thy love.

Enter ⌜*Robin.*⌝

Hast thou the flower there? Welcome, wanderer.

ROBIN
Ay, there it is.   255

OBERON   I pray thee give it me.
⌜*Robin gives him the flower.*⌝
I know a bank where the wild thyme blows,
Where oxlips and the nodding violet grows,
Quite overcanopied with luscious woodbine,
With sweet muskroses, and with eglantine.   260
There sleeps Titania sometime of the night,
Lulled in these flowers with dances and delight.
And there the snake throws her enameled skin,
Weed wide enough to wrap a fairy in.
And with the juice of this I'll streak her eyes   265
And make her full of hateful fantasies.
Take thou some of it, and seek through this grove.

273. **that:** i.e., so that
274. **fond on:** desperately in love with

2.2 Oberon anoints Titania's eyes as she sleeps. A weary Lysander and Hermia enter and fall asleep nearby. Robin, thinking he has found "the Athenian man," anoints the eyes of the sleeping Lysander and exits. Demetrius and Helena arrive, and he leaves her behind. Lysander awakes, sees Helena, and immediately falls in love with her. She mistakes his courtship for mockery and tries to elude him. After they exit, the abandoned Hermia awakes from a nightmare and goes in search of her beloved Lysander.

---

1. **roundel:** perhaps, a round dance; or, a song (a "roundelay")
3. **cankers:** canker worms, grubs
4. **reremice:** bats
7. **quaint:** dainty, brisk
8. **offices:** duties, responsibilities
9. **double:** forked
11. **Newts and blindworms:** species of salamanders and reptiles thought, in Shakespeare's day, to be poisonous
13. **Philomel:** the nightingale (named for Philomela, who, in classical mythology, was transformed into a nightingale after she was raped by her brother-in-law and her tongue cut out)

⌜*He gives Robin part of the flower.*⌝
A sweet Athenian lady is in love
With a disdainful youth. Anoint his eyes,
But do it when the next thing he espies   270
May be the lady. Thou shalt know the man
By the Athenian garments he hath on.
Effect it with some care, that he may prove
More fond on her than she upon her love.
And look thou meet me ere the first cock crow.   275

ROBIN
Fear not, my lord. Your servant shall do so.

They exit.

⌜Scene 2⌝
Enter Titania, Queen of Fairies, with her train.

TITANIA
Come, now a roundel and a fairy song;
Then, for the third part of a minute, hence—
Some to kill cankers in the muskrose buds,
Some war with reremice for their leathern wings
To make my small elves coats, and some keep back   5
The clamorous owl that nightly hoots and wonders
At our quaint spirits. Sing me now asleep.
Then to your offices and let me rest. ⌜*She lies down.*⌝

    Fairies sing.

⌜FIRST FAIRY⌝
        You spotted snakes with double tongue,
            Thorny hedgehogs, be not seen.   10
        Newts and blindworms, do no wrong,
            Come not near our Fairy Queen.
⌜CHORUS⌝
            Philomel, with melody
            Sing in our sweet lullaby.

36. **ounce:** lynx; **cat:** i.e., lion or tiger
37. **Pard:** leopard
38. **that:** i.e., that which

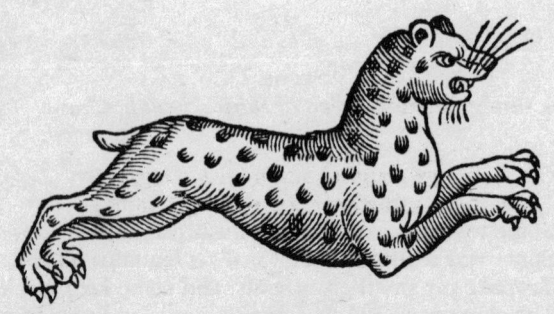

An "ounce." (2.2.36)
From Edward Topsell,
The historie of foure-footed beastes . . . (1607).

> *Lulla, lulla, lullaby, lulla, lulla, lullaby.*   15
> > *Never harm*
> > *Nor spell nor charm*
> *Come our lovely lady nigh.*
> *So good night, with lullaby.*

FIRST FAIRY
> *Weaving spiders, come not here.*   20
> > *Hence, you long-legged spinners, hence.*
> *Beetles black, approach not near.*
> > *Worm nor snail, do no offence.*

⌈CHORUS⌉
> > *Philomel, with melody*
> > *Sing in our sweet lullaby.*   25
> *Lulla, lulla, lullaby, lulla, lulla, lullaby.*
> > *Never harm*
> > *Nor spell nor charm*
> *Come our lovely lady nigh.*
> *So good night, with lullaby.*   30

⌈*Titania sleeps.*⌉

SECOND FAIRY
Hence, away! Now all is well.
One aloof stand sentinel.   ⌈*Fairies exit.*⌉

*Enter Oberon, ⌈who anoints Titania's eyelids with the
nectar.⌉*

OBERON
> What thou seest when thou dost wake,
> Do it for thy true love take.
> Love and languish for his sake.   35
> Be it ounce, or cat, or bear,
> Pard, or boar with bristled hair,
> In thy eye that shall appear
> When thou wak'st, it is thy dear.
> Wake when some vile thing is near. ⌈*He exits.*⌉   40

Enter Lysander and Hermia.

42. **troth:** truth, truly

48. **troth:** faithful vow

51. **take . . . innocence:** perhaps, understand the innocent meaning—i.e., of what I just said (In lines 53–58, Lysander explains what he meant in line 48.)

52. **Love . . . conference:** i.e., when lovers talk, it is love that hears and understands

60. **beshrew:** literally, curse (but the harshness of the word was lost through repeated use)

63. **human:** humane, civil, courteous

70. **Here:** Lysander would be some distance from where Hermia is lying.

LYSANDER
  Fair love, you faint with wand'ring in the wood.
    And, to speak troth, I have forgot our way.
  We'll rest us, Hermia, if you think it good,
    And tarry for the comfort of the day.

HERMIA
  ⌜Be⌝ it so, Lysander. Find you out a bed,   45
  For I upon this bank will rest my head.

LYSANDER
  One turf shall serve as pillow for us both;
  One heart, one bed, two bosoms, and one troth.

HERMIA
  Nay, good Lysander. For my sake, my dear,
  Lie further off yet. Do not lie so near.   50

LYSANDER
  O, take the sense, sweet, of my innocence!
  Love takes the meaning in love's conference.
  I mean that my heart unto yours ⌜is⌝ knit,
  So that but one heart we can make of it;
  Two bosoms interchainèd with an oath—   55
  So then two bosoms and a single troth.
  Then by your side no bed-room me deny,
  For lying so, Hermia, I do not lie.

HERMIA
  Lysander riddles very prettily.
  Now much beshrew my manners and my pride   60
  If Hermia meant to say Lysander lied.
  But, gentle friend, for love and courtesy,
  Lie further off in human modesty.
  Such separation, as may well be said,
  Becomes a virtuous bachelor and a maid.   65
  So far be distant; and good night, sweet friend.
  Thy love ne'er alter till thy sweet life end!

LYSANDER
  "Amen, amen" to that fair prayer, say I,
  And then end life when I end loyalty!
  Here is my bed. Sleep give thee all his rest!   70

74. **approve:** demonstrate, confirm; or, test

77. **Weeds:** garments

85. **owe:** i.e., own, possess

86–87. **let love . . . eyelid:** i.e., let love so torment you that you cannot close your eyes in sleep **forbid . . . seat:** i.e., banish from its place

91. **charge:** command

92. **darkling:** in the dark

Robin Goodfellow. (2.1.0 SD)
From Robin Good-fellow, his mad prankes . . . (1639).

HERMIA
With half that wish the wisher's eyes be pressed!
⌜*They sleep.*⌝

Enter ⌜*Robin.*⌝

ROBIN
Through the forest have I gone,
But Athenian found I none
On whose eyes I might approve
This flower's force in stirring love. 75
⌜*He sees Lysander.*⌝
Night and silence! Who is here?
Weeds of Athens he doth wear.
This is he my master said
Despisèd the Athenian maid.
And here the maiden, sleeping sound 80
On the dank and dirty ground.
Pretty soul, she durst not lie
Near this lack-love, this kill-courtesy.—
Churl, upon thy eyes I throw
All the power this charm doth owe. 85
⌜*He anoints Lysander's eyelids*
with the nectar.⌝
When thou wak'st, let love forbid
Sleep his seat on thy eyelid.
So, awake when I am gone,
For I must now to Oberon. *He exits.*

Enter Demetrius and Helena, running.

HELENA
Stay, though thou kill me, sweet Demetrius. 90
DEMETRIUS
I charge thee, hence, and do not haunt me thus.
HELENA
O, wilt thou darkling leave me? Do not so.

94. **fond:** (1) foolish; (2) infatuated
95. **grace:** favor or reward for prayer
103. **as:** i.e., as if I were
104. **glass:** mirror
105. **compare with:** i.e., rival, vie with; **sphery eyne:** perhaps, eyes belonging to the celestial spheres, like stars
110. **Transparent:** (1) radiant; (2) capable of being seen through; **Nature shows art:** In making Helena's body "transparent," so that Lysander can "see her heart," Nature acts like a magician. **art:** magic, power
121. **change:** i.e., exchange
122–29. **The will . . . book:** In this speech, Lysander attributes his sudden love for Helena to his having suddenly become mature and rational. **will:** desire

DEMETRIUS
    Stay, on thy peril. I alone will go. ⌈*Demetrius exits.*⌉
HELENA
    O, I am out of breath in this fond chase.
    The more my prayer, the lesser is my grace.   95
    Happy is Hermia, wheresoe'er she lies,
    For she hath blessèd and attractive eyes.
    How came her eyes so bright? Not with salt tears.
    If so, my eyes are oftener washed than hers.
    No, no, I am as ugly as a bear,   100
    For beasts that meet me run away for fear.
    Therefore no marvel though Demetrius
    Do as a monster fly my presence thus.
    What wicked and dissembling glass of mine
    Made me compare with Hermia's sphery eyne?   105
    But who is here? Lysander, on the ground!
    Dead or asleep? I see no blood, no wound.—
    Lysander, if you live, good sir, awake.
LYSANDER, ⌈*waking up*⌉
    And run through fire I will for thy sweet sake.
    Transparent Helena! Nature shows art,   110
    That through thy bosom makes me see thy heart.
    Where is Demetrius? O, how fit a word
    Is that vile name to perish on my sword!
HELENA
    Do not say so. Lysander, say not so.
    What though he love your Hermia? Lord, what   115
        though?
    Yet Hermia still loves you. Then be content.
LYSANDER
    Content with Hermia? No, I do repent
    The tedious minutes I with her have spent.
    Not Hermia, but Helena I love.   120
    Who will not change a raven for a dove?
    The will of man is by his reason swayed,
    And reason says you are the worthier maid.

124. **Things growing:** i.e., growing things

125. **ripe not:** i.e., did not ripen

126. **point:** i.e., the highest point; **skill:** judgment, discrimination

127. **marshal:** an officer who leads guests to their proper places

128. **o'erlook:** survey

130. **Wherefore:** why

136. **Good troth, good sooth:** i.e., in truth (mild oaths)

138. **Perforce:** of necessity

147. **of those they did deceive:** i.e., by the men who had mistakenly believed in the heresies

149. **Of:** i.e., by

Things growing are not ripe until their season;
So I, being young, till now ripe not to reason. 125
And touching now the point of human skill,
Reason becomes the marshal to my will
And leads me to your eyes, where I o'erlook
Love's stories written in love's richest book.

HELENA
Wherefore was I to this keen mockery born? 130
When at your hands did I deserve this scorn?
Is 't not enough, is 't not enough, young man,
That I did never, no, nor never can
Deserve a sweet look from Demetrius' eye,
But you must flout my insufficiency? 135
Good troth, you do me wrong, good sooth, you do,
In such disdainful manner me to woo.
But fare you well. Perforce I must confess
I thought you lord of more true gentleness.
O, that a lady of one man refused 140
Should of another therefore be abused!　*She exits.*

LYSANDER
She sees not Hermia.—Hermia, sleep thou there,
And never mayst thou come Lysander near.
For, as a surfeit of the sweetest things
The deepest loathing to the stomach brings, 145
Or as the heresies that men do leave
Are hated most of those they did deceive,
So thou, my surfeit and my heresy,
Of all be hated, but the most of me!
And, all my powers, address your love and might 150
To honor Helen and to be her knight.　*He exits.*

HERMIA, ⌈*waking up*⌉
Help me, Lysander, help me! Do thy best
To pluck this crawling serpent from my breast.
Ay me, for pity! What a dream was here!
Lysander, look how I do quake with fear. 155
Methought a serpent ate my heart away,

157. **prey:** i.e., attack
160. **an if:** i.e., if

And you sat smiling at his cruel prey.
Lysander! What, removed? Lysander, lord!
What, out of hearing? Gone? No sound, no word?
Alack, where are you? Speak, an if you hear.   160
Speak, of all loves! I swoon almost with fear.—
No? Then I well perceive you are not nigh.
Either death or you I'll find immediately.

                            She exits.

A MIDSUMMER NIGHT'S DREAM

ACT 3

3.1 The tradesmen meet in the woods to rehearse. Robin Goodfellow happens upon them and transforms Bottom's head into that of an ass. Abandoned by his terrified friends, Bottom sings. His singing awakens Titania, who, under the influence of the flower's magic, falls in love with him. She takes him away to sleep in her bower.

———————

0 SD. **Clowns:** i.e., actors who play comic roles

2. **Pat:** i.e., at exactly the right time; **marvels:** i.e., marvelously

3. **plot:** piece of ground

4. **brake:** thicket; **tiring-house:** i.e., attiring house, dressing room

8. **bully:** worthy, admirable

13. **By 'r lakin:** an oath "by our Lady"; **parlous:** perilous, terrible

15. **when all is done:** i.e., after all

⌈ACT 3⌉

⌈Scene 1⌉
⌈*With Titania still asleep onstage,*⌉ *enter the Clowns,*
⌈*Bottom, Quince, Snout, Starveling, Snug, and Flute.*⌉

BOTTOM   Are we all met?

QUINCE   Pat, pat. And here's a marvels convenient place for our rehearsal. This green plot shall be our stage, this hawthorn brake our tiring-house, and we will do it in action as we will do it before 5
the Duke.

BOTTOM   Peter Quince?

QUINCE   What sayest thou, bully Bottom?

BOTTOM   There are things in this comedy of Pyramus and Thisbe that will never please. First, Pyramus 10
must draw a sword to kill himself, which the ladies cannot abide. How answer you that?

SNOUT   By 'r lakin, a parlous fear.

STARVELING   I believe we must leave the killing out, when all is done. 15

BOTTOM   Not a whit! I have a device to make all well. Write me a prologue, and let the prologue seem to say we will do no harm with our swords, and that Pyramus is not killed indeed. And, for the more better assurance, tell them that I, Pyramus, am not 20
Pyramus, but Bottom the weaver. This will put them out of fear.

24. **eight and six:** alternating eight- and six-syllable lines (the standard ballad meter)

39. **defect:** Bottom's error for "effect"

42–43. **it were pity of my life:** i.e., I would be risking my life

QUINCE Well, we will have such a prologue, and it shall
be written in eight and six.

BOTTOM No, make it two more. Let it be written in   25
eight and eight.

SNOUT Will not the ladies be afeard of the lion?

STARVELING I fear it, I promise you.

BOTTOM Masters, you ought to consider with yourself,
to bring in (God shield us!) a lion among ladies is a   30
most dreadful thing. For there is not a more fearful
wildfowl than your lion living, and we ought to look
to 't.

SNOUT Therefore another prologue must tell he is not
a lion.   35

BOTTOM Nay, you must name his name, and half his
face must be seen through the lion's neck, and he
himself must speak through, saying thus, or to the
same defect: "Ladies," or "Fair ladies, I would
wish you," or "I would request you," or "I would   40
entreat you not to fear, not to tremble! My life for
yours. If you think I come hither as a lion, it were
pity of my life. No, I am no such thing. I am a man as
other men are." And there indeed let him name his
name and tell them plainly he is Snug the joiner.   45

QUINCE Well, it shall be so. But there is two hard
things: that is, to bring the moonlight into a chamber, for you know Pyramus and Thisbe meet by
moonlight.

SNOUT Doth the moon shine that night we play our   50
play?

BOTTOM A calendar, a calendar! Look in the almanac.
Find out moonshine, find out moonshine.
⌐*Quince takes out a book.*⌐

QUINCE Yes, it doth shine that night.

⌐BOTTOM⌐ Why, then, may you leave a casement of the   55
great chamber window, where we play, open, and
the moon may shine in at the casement.

58–59. **bush of thorns:** In legend, there is in the moon a man who carries a bundle of sticks and a lantern and who is often accompanied by his dog.

59. **disfigure:** Quince's mistake for "figure" (i.e., represent)

67–68. **plaster . . . loam . . . roughcast:** Each of these is used for plastering walls. **Plaster** is a mixture of lime, sand, and hair; **loam** is a mixture of clay, sand, and straw (it was also used for making bricks); **roughcast** is a mixture of lime and gravel.

69. **thus:** The actor playing Bottom usually, at this point, makes a "V" with his first two fingers.

76. **hempen homespuns:** i.e., country bumpkins, wearing homespun clothes woven from hemp

77. **cradle:** i.e., the bower where Titania is sleeping

78. **toward:** about to take place

QUINCE Ay, or else one must come in with a bush of
thorns and a lantern and say he comes to disfigure
or to present the person of Moonshine. Then there   60
is another thing: we must have a wall in the great
chamber, for Pyramus and Thisbe, says the story,
did talk through the chink of a wall.

SNOUT You can never bring in a wall. What say you,
Bottom?   65

BOTTOM Some man or other must present Wall. And
let him have some plaster, or some loam, or some
roughcast about him to signify wall, or let him
hold his fingers thus, and through that cranny shall
Pyramus and Thisbe whisper.   70

QUINCE If that may be, then all is well. Come, sit down,
every mother's son, and rehearse your parts. Pyramus, you begin. When you have spoken your
speech, enter into that brake, and so everyone
according to his cue.   75

Enter Robin ⌈invisible to those onstage.⌉

ROBIN, ⌈*aside*⌉
    What hempen homespuns have we swagg'ring here
    So near the cradle of the Fairy Queen?
    What, a play toward? I'll be an auditor—
    An actor too perhaps, if I see cause.

QUINCE Speak, Pyramus.—Thisbe, stand forth.   80
BOTTOM, *as Pyramus*
        Thisbe, the flowers of odious savors sweet—
QUINCE Odors, ⌈odors!⌉
BOTTOM, *as Pyramus*
                        . . . odors savors sweet.
    So hath thy breath, my dearest Thisbe dear.—
    But hark, a voice! Stay thou but here awhile,   85
    And by and by I will to thee appear.   *He exits.*
⌈ROBIN, *aside*⌉
    A stranger Pyramus than e'er played here. ⌈*He exits.*⌉

89. **marry:** i.e., indeed

92–95. **Most . . . tire:** These lines include several words that simply fill out the six-beat doggerel lines (**brisky** [rather than "brisk"], **juvenal** [rather than "youth"], **eke** [i.e., also]) and words that seem desperate attempts to rhyme (**Jew** to rhyme with **hue**, **tire** to rhyme with **brier**). Part of the comedy in the "Pyramus and Thisbe" scenes turns on the very bad "poetry" of the script. **triumphant:** splendid **brier:** wild rose bush

97. **Ninus' tomb:** In Ovid's *Metamorphoses*, the lovers meet at the tomb of Ninus, legendary founder of the city of Nineveh.

99. **part:** Actors were provided with "parts" that contained cues of two or three words, as well as their own speeches. (Flute seems not to have read "cues and all," but rather to have read two of Thisbe's speeches as if they were one.)

103 SD. **with the ass-head:** i.e., wearing the "ass head" (a stage prop)

104. **were:** i.e., would be

107. **round:** roundabout way; circle dance

111. **fire:** i.e., will-o'-the-wisp

FLUTE Must I speak now?

QUINCE Ay, marry, must you, for you must understand
    he goes but to see a noise that he heard and is to   90
    come again.

FLUTE, *as Thisbe*
    Most radiant Pyramus, most lily-white of hue,
    Of color like the red rose on triumphant brier,
    Most brisky juvenal and eke most lovely Jew,
    As true as truest horse, that yet would never tire.   95
    I'll meet thee, Pyramus, at Ninny's tomb.

QUINCE "Ninus' tomb," man! Why, you must not
    speak that yet. That you answer to Pyramus. You
    speak all your part at once, cues and all.—Pyra-
    mus, enter. Your cue is past. It is "never tire."   100

FLUTE O!
    ⌜*As Thisbe.*⌝ *As true as truest horse, that yet would never*
    tire.

    ⌜*Enter Robin, and Bottom as Pyramus with the*
            ass-head.⌝

BOTTOM, *as Pyramus*
    If I were fair, ⌜*fair*⌝ *Thisbe, I were only thine.*

QUINCE O monstrous! O strange! We are haunted. Pray,   105
    masters, fly, masters! Help!
      ⌜*Quince, Flute, Snout, Snug, and Starveling exit.*⌝

ROBIN
    I'll follow you. I'll lead you about a round,
      Through bog, through bush, through brake,
        through brier.
    Sometime a horse I'll be, sometime a hound,   110
      A hog, a headless bear, sometime a fire,
    And neigh, and bark, and grunt, and roar, and burn,
      Like horse, hound, hog, bear, fire, at every turn.
                          He exits.

BOTTOM Why do they run away? This is a knavery of
    them to make me afeard.   115

120–21. **translated:** transformed

127. **ouzel:** blackbird

129. **throstle:** thrush

130. **little quill:** i.e., small note (literally, a small musical pipe)

133. **plainsong cuckoo gray:** i.e., gray cuckoo, whose repetitive call is as simple as the early church music called **plainsong** (See page 80.)

134. **Whose . . . mark:** i.e., whose song many men hear and pay attention to (Because the cuckoo does not build nests but leaves its eggs for other birds to hatch and feed, its song of "cuckoo" is linked to "cuckold," a man whose wife is unfaithful and thus who might bear children fathered by other men. Its call was considered a mocking cry directed at married men.)

136. **who . . . foolish:** Proverbial: "Do not set your wit against a fool's." **set his wit:** use his intelligence to answer

137. **give . . . the lie:** accuse . . . of lying

138. **never so:** countless times (i.e., over and over)

140. **note:** song

142. **virtue's:** excellence's; **perforce:** i.e., whether I want to or not, willy-nilly; **move me:** persuade me; stir my emotions

Enter Snout.

SNOUT   O Bottom, thou art changed! What do I see on
   thee?

BOTTOM   What do you see? You see an ass-head of your
   own, do you?   ⌜*Snout exits.*⌝

Enter Quince.

QUINCE   Bless thee, Bottom, bless thee! Thou art trans-   120
   lated!   *He exits.*

BOTTOM   I see their knavery. This is to make an ass of
   me, to fright me, if they could. But I will not stir
   from this place, do what they can. I will walk up
   and down here, and I will sing, that they shall hear   125
   I am not afraid.
   ⌜*He sings.*⌝ *The ouzel cock, so black of hue,*
                With orange-tawny bill,
                The throstle with his note so true,
                The wren with little quill—   130

TITANIA, ⌜*waking up*⌝
   What angel wakes me from my flow'ry bed?

BOTTOM ⌜*sings*⌝
        The finch, the sparrow, and the lark,
            The plainsong cuckoo gray,
        Whose note full many a man doth mark
            And dares not answer "nay"—   135
   for, indeed, who would set his wit to so foolish a
   bird? Who would give a bird the lie though he cry
   "cuckoo" never so?

TITANIA
   I pray thee, gentle mortal, sing again.
   Mine ear is much enamored of thy note,   140
   So is mine eye enthrallèd to thy shape,
   And thy fair virtue's force perforce doth move me
   On the first view to say, to swear, I love thee.

BOTTOM   Methinks, mistress, you should have little

146. **keep little company together:** i.e., are not good friends

148. **gleek:** make a joke

156. **common:** ordinary; **rate:** value

157. **still:** always; **doth tend upon:** serves, attends; **state:** greatness, position of power

160. **deep:** ocean

162–63. **I will purge . . . go:** i.e., I will transform you into a spirit **purge:** make pure or clean **mortal:** i.e., subject to death (It has been suggested that the medical meaning of **purge** [i.e., to cleanse the body through bleedings or laxatives] should be considered here.)

164 SD. **Peaseblossom . . . Mustardseed:** Each of these names indicates something very tiny or otherwise hard to see. **Peaseblossom:** the flower of the pea plant **Mote:** speck (Since the words *mote* and *moth* were pronounced the same way, and since the character's name is spelled "moth" in the early printings of this play, the character's name might mean, instead, a small flying insect. "Mote" is an almost-silent character, not described in the dialogue as the other fairies are. Thus editors have difficulty determining whether his/its name should, in modern spelling, be "Mote" or "Moth.") **Mustardseed:** It is from tiny mustardseeds that mustard is made.

171. **gambol:** skip, leap about; **in his eyes:** in his sight

172. **apricocks:** apricots; **dewberries:** blackberries

174. **humble-bees:** bumble bees

reason for that. And yet, to say the truth, reason   145
and love keep little company together nowadays.
The more the pity that some honest neighbors will
not make them friends. Nay, I can gleek upon
occasion.

TITANIA
Thou art as wise as thou art beautiful.   150

BOTTOM   Not so neither; but if I had wit enough to get
out of this wood, I have enough to serve mine own
turn.

TITANIA
Out of this wood do not desire to go.
Thou shalt remain here whether thou wilt or no.   155
I am a spirit of no common rate.
The summer still doth tend upon my state,
And I do love thee. Therefore go with me.
I'll give thee fairies to attend on thee,
And they shall fetch thee jewels from the deep   160
And sing while thou on pressèd flowers dost sleep.
And I will purge thy mortal grossness so
That thou shalt like an airy spirit go.—
Peaseblossom, Cobweb, Mote, and Mustardseed!

Enter four Fairies: ⌜*Peaseblossom, Cobweb,*
Mote, and Mustardseed.⌝

⌜PEASEBLOSSOM⌝   Ready.   165
⌜COBWEB⌝   And I.
⌜MOTE⌝   And I.
⌜MUSTARDSEED⌝   And I.
⌜ALL⌝   Where shall we go?

TITANIA
Be kind and courteous to this gentleman.   170
Hop in his walks and gambol in his eyes;
Feed him with apricocks and dewberries,
With purple grapes, green figs, and mulberries;
The honey-bags steal from the humble-bees,

177. **have:** i.e., attend

185. **cry . . . mercy:** i.e., beg . . . pardon

189–90. **Cobweb . . . you:** Cobwebs were used to stop bleeding.

190. **honest:** honorable

192. **Squash:** an unripened pea-pod

193. **Peascod:** a ripe pea-pod

198–99. **your patience:** perhaps, referring to mustard's patience in being so often devoured; perhaps, "your Patience," as in "your Honor"

199. **ox-beef:** Mustard is often served as a condiment with beef. (Bottom is here sympathizing with Mustardseed for having lost kinsmen who have been eaten as mustard.)

207. **enforcèd chastity:** (1) chastity enforced, compelled; (2) chastity forced and destroyed, raped

A "cuckoo gray." (3.1.133)
From Konrad Gesner, . . . *Historia animalium* . . . (1585).

And for night-tapers crop their waxen thighs 175
And light them at the fiery glowworms' eyes
To have my love to bed and to arise;
And pluck the wings from painted butterflies
To fan the moonbeams from his sleeping eyes.
Nod to him, elves, and do him courtesies. 180

⌜PEASEBLOSSOM⌝ Hail, mortal!

⌜COBWEB⌝ Hail!

⌜MOTE⌝ Hail!

⌜MUSTARDSEED⌝ Hail!

BOTTOM I cry your Worships mercy, heartily.—I be- 185
seech your Worship's name.

COBWEB Cobweb.

BOTTOM I shall desire you of more acquaintance, good
Master Cobweb. If I cut my finger, I shall make
bold with you.—Your name, honest gentleman? 190

PEASEBLOSSOM Peaseblossom.

BOTTOM I pray you, commend me to Mistress Squash,
your mother, and to Master Peascod, your father.
Good Master Peaseblossom, I shall desire you of
more acquaintance, too.—Your name, I beseech 195
you, sir?

MUSTARDSEED Mustardseed.

BOTTOM Good Master Mustardseed, I know your patience well. That same cowardly, giantlike ox-beef
hath devoured many a gentleman of your house. I 200
promise you, your kindred hath made my eyes
water ere now. I desire you ⌜of⌝ more acquaintance, good Master Mustardseed.

TITANIA

Come, wait upon him. Lead him to my bower.
The moon, methinks, looks with a wat'ry eye, 205
And when she weeps, weeps every little flower,
Lamenting some enforcèd chastity.
Tie up my lover's tongue. Bring him silently.

⌜*They*⌝ *exit.*

3.2 Robin Goodfellow reports to Oberon about Titania and Bottom. When Demetrius enters wooing Hermia, Oberon discovers that Robin has anointed the eyes of the wrong Athenian. Oberon then orders Robin to fetch Helena while he anoints the eyes of the sleeping Demetrius. Helena enters pursued by Lysander vowing his love. Demetrius awakes, falls in love with Helena, and also begins to woo her. Helena believes both men are mocking her. When Hermia arrives and learns that Lysander has abandoned her for Helena, she threatens Helena, who thinks that Hermia is part of the conspiracy. Lysander and Demetrius prepare to duel to prove their right to Helena. At Oberon's command, Robin impersonates each of the two men in turn in order to lead the other astray until both, exhausted, fall asleep. Helena and Hermia also fall asleep. Robin applies nectar to Lysander's eyes to undo the spell that has drawn him to Helena.

---

3. **in extremity:** to the highest degree

5. **night-rule:** perhaps, disorder (night being associated with the irrational); **haunted:** much visited

7. **close:** hidden, secluded

8. **dull:** i.e., unconscious (because asleep)

9. **patches:** simpletons; **rude:** humble; uncivilized; **mechanicals:** workers

10. **work for bread:** i.e., earn their livings; **stalls:** booths, sheds (where cobblers, butchers, etc., worked and sold their wares)

13. **barren:** dull

14. **sport:** drama, theatrical activity

15. **scene:** stage

(continued)

⌜Scene 2⌝
Enter ⌜*Oberon,*⌝ *King of Fairies.*

OBERON
I wonder if Titania be awaked;
Then what it was that next came in her eye,
Which she must dote on in extremity.

⌜*Enter Robin Goodfellow.*⌝

Here comes my messenger. How now, mad spirit?
What night-rule now about this haunted grove?   5
ROBIN
My mistress with a monster is in love.
Near to her close and consecrated bower,
While she was in her dull and sleeping hour,
A crew of patches, rude mechanicals,
That work for bread upon Athenian stalls,   10
Were met together to rehearse a play
Intended for great Theseus' nuptial day.
The shallowest thick-skin of that barren sort,
Who Pyramus presented in their sport,
Forsook his scene and entered in a brake.   15
When I did him at this advantage take,
An ass's noll I fixèd on his head.
Anon his Thisbe must be answerèd,
And forth my ⌜mimic⌝ comes. When they him spy,
As wild geese that the creeping fowler eye,   20
Or russet-pated choughs, many in sort,
Rising and cawing at the gun's report,
Sever themselves and madly sweep the sky,
So at his sight away his fellows fly,
And, at our stamp, here o'er and o'er one falls.   25
He "Murder" cries and help from Athens calls.
Their sense thus weak, lost with their fears thus
    strong,
Made senseless things begin to do them wrong;

17. **noll:** head
18. **Anon:** soon
19. **mimic:** i.e., comic actor
20. **fowler:** one who hunts wild birds
21. **russet-pated . . . sort:** a large flock of brownish-headed jackdaws
23. **Sever themselves:** i.e., split up
25. **at our stamp:** Robin, as described in stories and ballads, has a powerful stamp. However, since his use of "our" is puzzling, it has been suggested that "at our stamp" is a misprint for "at a stump."
31–32. **from . . . catch:** perhaps, everything snatches at cowards
34. **translated:** transformed
37. **falls out:** happens
38. **latched:** snared, caught
42. **That:** i.e., so that; **of force:** of necessity (i.e., inevitably)
43. **Stand close:** an order to step aside into hiding
50. **o'er shoes:** i.e., up to your ankles
55–57. **This whole earth . . . Antipodes:** i.e., that the solid globe could be so pierced that the moon could travel through it, bringing night to the Antipodes when it should there be noon **bored:** pierced through, drilled **Her brother's:** i.e., the sun's **Antipodes:** the region on the opposite side of the globe (See page 86.)

For briers and thorns at their apparel snatch,   30
Some sleeves, some hats, from yielders all things
  catch.
I led them on in this distracted fear
And left sweet Pyramus translated there.
When in that moment, so it came to pass,   35
Titania waked and straightway loved an ass.

OBERON
This falls out better than I could devise.
But hast thou yet latched the Athenian's eyes
With the love juice, as I did bid thee do?

ROBIN
I took him sleeping—that is finished, too—   40
And the Athenian woman by his side,
That, when he waked, of force she must be eyed.

              Enter Demetrius and Hermia.

OBERON
Stand close. This is the same Athenian.

ROBIN
This is the woman, but not this the man.
                              ⌜*They step aside.*⌝

DEMETRIUS
O, why rebuke you him that loves you so?   45
Lay breath so bitter on your bitter foe!

HERMIA
Now I but chide, but I should use thee worse,
For thou, I fear, hast given me cause to curse.
If thou hast slain Lysander in his sleep,
Being o'er shoes in blood, plunge in the deep   50
And kill me too.
The sun was not so true unto the day
As he to me. Would he have stolen away
From sleeping Hermia? I'll believe as soon
This whole earth may be bored, and that the moon   55
May through the center creep and so displease

59. **dead:** (1) deadly; (2) dull; (3) deathly pale

64. **What's this to:** i.e., what does this have to do with

71. **being awake:** i.e., if Lysander were awake

73. **worm:** serpent

75. **never adder stung:** i.e., never did adder sting

76. **misprised:** mistaken; **mood:** perhaps, anger, or grief; perhaps, state of mind

80. **An if:** i.e., if; **therefor:** for it, in exchange

A map of the globe showing the Antipodes. (3.2.57)
From Macrobius, *Insomnium Scipionis exposito . . .* (1492).

Her brother's noontide with th' Antipodes.
It cannot be but thou hast murdered him.
So should a murderer look, so dead, so grim.

DEMETRIUS
So should the murdered look, and so should I,   60
Pierced through the heart with your stern cruelty.
Yet you, the murderer, look as bright, as clear,
As yonder Venus in her glimmering sphere.

HERMIA
What's this to my Lysander? Where is he?
Ah, good Demetrius, wilt thou give him me?   65

DEMETRIUS
I had rather give his carcass to my hounds.

HERMIA
Out, dog! Out, cur! Thou driv'st me past the bounds
Of maiden's patience. Hast thou slain him, then?
Henceforth be never numbered among men.
O, once tell true! Tell true, even for my sake!   70
Durst thou have looked upon him, being awake?
And hast thou killed him sleeping? O brave touch!
Could not a worm, an adder, do so much?
An adder did it, for with doubler tongue
Than thine, thou serpent, never adder stung.   75

DEMETRIUS
You spend your passion on a misprised mood.
I am not guilty of Lysander's blood,
Nor is he dead, for aught that I can tell.

HERMIA
I pray thee, tell me then that he is well.

DEMETRIUS
An if I could, what should I get therefor?   80

HERMIA
A privilege never to see me more.
And from thy hated presence part I ⌜so.⌝
See me no more, whether he be dead or no.

                    She exits.

86–89. **So sorrow's . . . stay:** Demetrius, explaining that he will now lie down and sleep, plays with two meanings of the word **heavy** (sad; sleepy). He says that sorrow grows heavier when sleep, like a bankrupt, cannot pay its debts; he lies down to wait for sleep to make him an offer (a **tender**) and pay part of its debt.

92. **Of thy misprision:** from your mistake; **perforce:** necessarily

93. **turned:** altered; changed

94–95. **Then fate . . . oath:** Robin attributes his mistake to fate, claiming that for every man who is faithful a million are fickle. **holding troth:** keeping his plighted oath **confounding:** breaking

96. **About the wood go:** i.e., go through the forest

97. **look thou:** i.e., make sure you

98. **fancy-sick:** lovesick; **cheer:** face

99. **costs . . . dear:** Sighs were thought to deplete the blood. **dear:** dearly

101. **against:** i.e., to prepare for the time

103. **Tartar's bow:** an Oriental bow, more powerful than English bows (See page 92.)

106. **apple:** i.e., the pupil

107. **his love:** i.e., Helena

109. **Venus:** the planet Venus, known as the evening star (also named above at line 63)

DEMETRIUS

There is no following her in this fierce vein.
Here, therefore, for a while I will remain.   85
So sorrow's heaviness doth heavier grow
For debt that bankrout ⌜sleep⌝ doth sorrow owe,
Which now in some slight measure it will pay,
If for his tender here I make some stay.
                    ⌜He⌝ lies down ⌜and falls asleep.⌝

OBERON, ⌜to Robin⌝

What hast thou done? Thou hast mistaken quite   90
And laid the love juice on some true-love's sight.
Of thy misprision must perforce ensue
Some true-love turned, and not a false turned true.

ROBIN

Then fate o'errules, that, one man holding troth,
A million fail, confounding oath on oath.   95

OBERON

About the wood go swifter than the wind,
And Helena of Athens look thou find.
All fancy-sick she is and pale of cheer
With sighs of love that costs the fresh blood dear.
By some illusion see thou bring her here.   100
I'll charm his eyes against she do appear.

ROBIN   I go, I go, look how I go,
Swifter than arrow from the Tartar's bow. ⌜He exits.⌝

OBERON, ⌜applying the nectar to Demetrius' eyes⌝

        Flower of this purple dye,
        Hit with Cupid's archery,   105
        Sink in apple of his eye.
        When his love he doth espy,
        Let her shine as gloriously
        As the Venus of the sky.
        When thou wak'st, if she be by,   110
        Beg of her for remedy.

            Enter ⌜*Robin.*⌝

115. **fee:** reward

116. **fond pageant:** foolish spectacle or scene

121. **needs:** necessarily, inevitably; **sport alone:** an unrivaled entertainment

126. **Look when:** whenever, all the while

129. **badge of faith:** i.e., his tears

130. **advance:** display, exhibit

131. **When truth . . . fray:** Helena argues that Lysander is using the **truth** of his present vows to kill the **truth** of his vows to Hermia, thus creating a battle that is both **devilish** (in that he is breaking his oath) and **holy** (in that it is a battle between truths).

132. **give her o'er:** abandon her

133–34. **Weigh . . . weigh:** Balance your oaths to her against your oaths to me, and (1) you will weigh "nothing," because the scales will be evenly balanced; or, (2) since they are both empty, you will be weighing nothing.

ROBIN

> Captain of our fairy band,
> Helena is here at hand,
> And the youth, mistook by me,
> Pleading for a lover's fee. 115
> Shall we their fond pageant see?
> Lord, what fools these mortals be!

OBERON

> Stand aside. The noise they make
> Will cause Demetrius to awake.

ROBIN

> Then will two at once woo one. 120
> That must needs be sport alone.
> And those things do best please me
> That befall prepost'rously.
>> ⌈*They step aside.*⌉

> *Enter Lysander and Helena.*

LYSANDER

Why should you think that I should woo in scorn?
  Scorn and derision never come in tears. 125
Look when I vow, I weep; and vows so born,
  In their nativity all truth appears.
How can these things in me seem scorn to you,
Bearing the badge of faith to prove them true?

HELENA

You do advance your cunning more and more. 130
  When truth kills truth, O devilish holy fray!
These vows are Hermia's. Will you give her o'er?
  Weigh oath with oath, and you will nothing
    weigh.
Your vows to her and me, put in two scales, 135
Will even weigh, and both as light as tales.

LYSANDER

I had no judgment when to her I swore.

HELENA

Nor none, in my mind, now you give her o'er.

141. **eyne:** eyes

142. **Crystal is muddy:** i.e., in comparison to her eyes

144. **Taurus:** a mountain range in Asia

147. **princess of pure white:** i.e., her hand; **seal:** i.e., guarantee, pledge

149. **set against:** attack

153. **join in souls:** perhaps, unite

156. **parts:** personal qualities

160. **trim:** fine (said sarcastically)

163–64. **extort . . . patience:** i.e., wring from a poor soul her patience, as if through torture   **extort:** wring out

164. **make you sport:** i.e., entertain yourselves

A Tartar's bow. (3.2.103)
From Balthasar Küchler,
Repraesentatio der fürstlichen Auffzug (1611).

LYSANDER
  Demetrius loves her, and he loves not you.
DEMETRIUS, ⌈*waking up*⌉
  O Helen, goddess, nymph, perfect, divine!   140
  To what, my love, shall I compare thine eyne?
  Crystal is muddy. O, how ripe in show
  Thy lips, those kissing cherries, tempting grow!
  That pure congealèd white, high Taurus' snow,
  Fanned with the eastern wind, turns to a crow   145
  When thou hold'st up thy hand. O, let me kiss
  This princess of pure white, this seal of bliss!
HELENA
  O spite! O hell! I see you all are bent
  To set against me for your merriment.
  If you were civil and knew courtesy,   150
  You would not do me thus much injury.
  Can you not hate me, as I know you do,
  But you must join in souls to mock me too?
  If you were men, as men you are in show,
  You would not use a gentle lady so,   155
  To vow and swear and superpraise my parts,
  When, I am sure, you hate me with your hearts.
  You both are rivals and love Hermia,
  And now both rivals to mock Helena.
  A trim exploit, a manly enterprise,   160
  To conjure tears up in a poor maid's eyes
  With your derision! None of noble sort
  Would so offend a virgin and extort
  A poor soul's patience, all to make you sport.
LYSANDER
  You are unkind, Demetrius. Be not so,   165
  For you love Hermia; this you know I know.
  And here with all goodwill, with all my heart,
  In Hermia's love I yield you up my part.
  And yours of Helena to me bequeath,
  Whom I do love and will do till my death.   170

172. **I will none:** i.e., I want none of her
174. **to her but as guest-wise sojourned:** i.e., journeyed to (or stayed with) her only as a visitor **but:** only **sojourned:** traveled; stayed
179. **aby it dear:** pay dearly for it
181. **his:** i.e., its
183. **Wherein:** i.e., in that respect (of affecting the senses) in which
188, 189. **press:** push, urge
192. **oes and eyes of light:** i.e., stars **oes:** round spangles

HELENA
  Never did mockers waste more idle breath.
DEMETRIUS
  Lysander, keep thy Hermia. I will none.
  If e'er I loved her, all that love is gone.
  My heart to her but as guest-wise sojourned,
  And now to Helen is it home returned,   175
  There to remain.
LYSANDER   Helen, it is not so.
DEMETRIUS
  Disparage not the faith thou dost not know,
  Lest to thy peril thou aby it dear.
  Look where thy love comes. Yonder is thy dear. 180

Enter Hermia.

HERMIA, ⌈*to Lysander*⌉
  Dark night, that from the eye his function takes,
  The ear more quick of apprehension makes;
  Wherein it doth impair the seeing sense,
  It pays the hearing double recompense.
  Thou art not by mine eye, Lysander, found;   185
  Mine ear, I thank it, brought me to thy sound.
  But why unkindly didst thou leave me so?
LYSANDER
  Why should he stay whom love doth press to go?
HERMIA
  What love could press Lysander from my side?
LYSANDER
  Lysander's love, that would not let him bide,   190
  Fair Helena, who more engilds the night
  Than all yon fiery oes and eyes of light.
  Why seek'st thou me? Could not this make thee
    know
  The hate I bear thee made me leave thee so?   195
HERMIA
  You speak not as you think. It cannot be.

199. **in spite of:** i.e., to spite

202. **bait:** harass, torment

205. **chid:** scolded

208. **artificial:** skillful

209. **needles:** pronounced "neeles"

211. **both in one key:** i.e., the two of us in perfect harmony

213. **incorporate:** united in one body

218–19. **Two . . . crest:** Helena here uses technical language of heraldry (**of the first, coats, crest**) to say again that she and Hermia, though in two bodies, once shared a single heart.

220. **rent:** rend, tear

223. **Our sex:** i.e., all females

225. **amazèd:** bewildered, dumbfounded (Many editions add the word "passionate" to this line, so that it reads "your passionate words"; the word is found in the Folio.)

HELENA
    Lo, she is one of this confederacy!
    Now I perceive they have conjoined all three
    To fashion this false sport in spite of me.—
    Injurious Hermia, most ungrateful maid,   200
    Have you conspired, have you with these contrived,
    To bait me with this foul derision?
    Is all the counsel that we two have shared,
    The sisters' vows, the hours that we have spent
    When we have chid the hasty-footed time   205
    For parting us—O, is all forgot?
    All schooldays' friendship, childhood innocence?
    We, Hermia, like two artificial gods,
    Have with our needles created both one flower,
    Both on one sampler, sitting on one cushion,   210
    Both warbling of one song, both in one key,
    As if our hands, our sides, voices, and minds
    Had been incorporate. So we grew together
    Like to a double cherry, seeming parted,
    But yet an union in partition,   215
    Two lovely berries molded on one stem;
    So with two seeming bodies but one heart,
    Two of the first, ⌜like⌝ coats in heraldry,
    Due but to one, and crownèd with one crest.
    And will you rent our ancient love asunder,   220
    To join with men in scorning your poor friend?
    It is not friendly; 'tis not maidenly.
    Our sex, as well as I, may chide you for it,
    Though I alone do feel the injury.

HERMIA
    I am amazèd at your words.   225
    I scorn you not. It seems that you scorn me.

HELENA
    Have you not set Lysander, as in scorn,
    To follow me and praise my eyes and face,
    And made your other love, Demetrius,

230. **spurn:** kick

232, 233. **Wherefore:** why

235. **tender:** offer; **forsooth:** in truth; a very mild oath

236. **setting on:** instigation

237. **in grace:** i.e., favored

242. **Persever:** persevere (accent on second syllable); **sad:** serious, grave

243. **Make mouths upon:** i.e., make faces at

245. **carried:** managed; **chronicled:** i.e., written up in chronicles or histories

247. **argument:** subject of contention

250. **excuse:** defense

254. **she:** i.e., Hermia; **entreat:** i.e., persuade you through her pleading

Who even but now did spurn me with his foot,   230
To call me goddess, nymph, divine and rare,
Precious, celestial? Wherefore speaks he this
To her he hates? And wherefore doth Lysander
Deny your love (so rich within his soul)
And tender me, forsooth, affection,   235
But by your setting on, by your consent?
What though I be not so in grace as you,
So hung upon with love, so fortunate,
But miserable most, to love unloved?
This you should pity rather than despise.   240

HERMIA
I understand not what you mean by this.

HELENA
Ay, do. Persever, counterfeit sad looks,
Make mouths upon me when I turn my back,
Wink each at other, hold the sweet jest up.
This sport, well carried, shall be chronicled.   245
If you have any pity, grace, or manners,
You would not make me such an argument.
But fare you well. 'Tis partly my own fault,
Which death or absence soon shall remedy.

LYSANDER
Stay, gentle Helena. Hear my excuse,   250
My love, my life, my soul, fair Helena.

HELENA
O excellent!

HERMIA, ⌈*to Lysander*⌉
Sweet, do not scorn her so.

DEMETRIUS, ⌈*to Lysander*⌉
If she cannot entreat, I can compel.

LYSANDER
Thou canst compel no more than she entreat.   255
Thy threats have no more strength than her weak
   ⌈prayers.⌉—
Helen, I love thee. By my life, I do.

259. **by that:** i.e., by my life

262. **withdraw . . . prove it:** Lysander here challenges Demetrius to prove his love in a duel.

265. **Ethiop:** Like "tawny Tartar" at line 274, this seems a reference to the dark color of Hermia's hair or complexion. (An **Ethiop** was a dark-skinned African.)

266–68. **No . . . follow:** These lines are difficult as printed in the quarto. Many editors substitute the Folio's "sir" for "he'll," thus solving the problem of the shift from "he" to "you." **Take on as:** i.e., act as if

274. **Tartar:** i.e., Gypsy

277. **sooth:** truly (a very mild oath)

278. **my word with thee:** i.e., my challenge to you

279–80. **bond . . . bond:** a quibble on **bond** as a binding legal agreement and **bond** as a fetter or chain (Hermia is the **weak bond** holding Lysander.)

I swear by that which I will lose for thee,
To prove him false that says I love thee not.   260

DEMETRIUS
I say I love thee more than he can do.

LYSANDER
If thou say so, withdraw and prove it too.

DEMETRIUS
Quick, come.

HERMIA   Lysander, whereto tends all this?
                       ⌜*She takes hold of Lysander.*⌝

LYSANDER
Away, you Ethiop!   265

DEMETRIUS, ⌜*to Hermia*⌝
                    No, no. He'll
Seem to break loose. ⌜*To Lysander.*⌝ Take on as you
    would follow,
But yet come not. You are a tame man, go!

LYSANDER, ⌜*to Hermia*⌝
Hang off, thou cat, thou burr! Vile thing, let loose,   270
Or I will shake thee from me like a serpent.

HERMIA
Why are you grown so rude? What change is this,
Sweet love?

LYSANDER   Thy love? Out, tawny Tartar, out!
Out, loathèd med'cine! O, hated potion, hence!   275

HERMIA
Do you not jest?

HELENA   Yes, sooth, and so do you.

LYSANDER
Demetrius, I will keep my word with thee.

DEMETRIUS
I would I had your bond. For I perceive
A weak bond holds you. I'll not trust your word.   280

LYSANDER
What? Should I hurt her, strike her, kill her dead?
Although I hate her, I'll not harm her so.

284. **what news:** i.e., what does this mean?

286. **erewhile:** a little while ago

296. **juggler:** trickster, deceiver; **cankerblossom:** i.e., cankerworm, a worm that destroys flower buds

306. **urged:** i.e., put forward as a recommendation

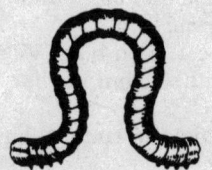

A cankerblossom. (3.2.296)
From John Johnstone, *Opera aliquot . . .* (1650–1662).

HERMIA
　　What, can you do me greater harm than hate?
　　Hate me? Wherefore? O me, what news, my love?
　　Am not I Hermia? Are not you Lysander?　　　　　285
　　I am as fair now as I was erewhile.
　　Since night you loved me; yet since night you left
　　　me.
　　Why, then, you left me—O, the gods forbid!—
　　In earnest, shall I say?　　　　　　　　　　　290
LYSANDER　　　　　　　　　Ay, by my life,
　　And never did desire to see thee more.
　　Therefore be out of hope, of question, of doubt.
　　Be certain, nothing truer, 'tis no jest
　　That I do hate thee and love Helena.　　　　　295
　　　　　　　　　　⌐*Hermia turns him loose.*⌐

HERMIA
　　O me! ⌐*To Helena.*⌐ You juggler, you cankerblossom,
　　You thief of love! What, have you come by night
　　And stol'n my love's heart from him?
HELENA　　　　　　　　　　　Fine, i' faith.
　　Have you no modesty, no maiden shame,　　　　300
　　No touch of bashfulness? What, will you tear
　　Impatient answers from my gentle tongue?
　　Fie, fie, you counterfeit, you puppet, you!
HERMIA
　　"Puppet"? Why so? Ay, that way goes the game.
　　Now I perceive that she hath made compare　　　305
　　Between our statures; she hath urged her height,
　　And with her personage, her tall personage,
　　Her height, forsooth, she hath prevailed with him.
　　And are you grown so high in his esteem
　　Because I am so dwarfish and so low?　　　　　310
　　How low am I, thou painted maypole? Speak!
　　How low am I? I am not yet so low
　　But that my nails can reach unto thine eyes.

315, 316. **curst, shrewishness:** These words (like **shrewd** at 3.2.340) were used to describe women who were considered quarrelsome, talkative, or sharp-tongued.

317. **a right maid:** i.e., a girl indeed, a real sissy

319. **something:** i.e., somewhat

328. **chid me hence:** i.e., tried to drive me away through scolding

330. **so:** i.e., if

333. **fond:** foolish; or, doting

339. **she:** i.e., Hermia; **her:** i.e., Helena's

340. **keen:** cruel, fierce; **shrewd:** i.e., shrewish

HELENA
  I pray you, though you mock me, ⌈gentlemen,⌉
  Let her not hurt me. I was never curst;   315
  I have no gift at all in shrewishness.
  I am a right maid for my cowardice.
  Let her not strike me. You perhaps may think,
  Because she is something lower than myself,
  That I can match her.   320
HERMIA   "Lower"? Hark, again!
HELENA
  Good Hermia, do not be so bitter with me.
  I evermore did love you, Hermia,
  Did ever keep your counsels, never wronged you—
  Save that, in love unto Demetrius,   325
  I told him of your stealth unto this wood.
  He followed you; for love, I followed him.
  But he hath chid me hence and threatened me
  To strike me, spurn me, nay, to kill me too.
  And now, so you will let me quiet go,   330
  To Athens will I bear my folly back
  And follow you no further. Let me go.
  You see how simple and how fond I am.
HERMIA
  Why, get you gone. Who is 't that hinders you?
HELENA
  A foolish heart that I leave here behind.   335
HERMIA
  What, with Lysander?
HELENA   With Demetrius.
LYSANDER
  Be not afraid. She shall not harm thee, Helena.
DEMETRIUS
  No, sir, she shall not, though you take her part.
HELENA
  O, when she is angry, she is keen and shrewd.   340
  She was a vixen when she went to school,
  And though she be but little, she is fierce.

344. **suffer:** allow

345. **come to her:** i.e., get at her

347. **minimus:** i.e., tiniest of creatures; **knotgrass:** a weed that was thought to stunt growth

354. **aby:** pay for

356–57. **whose right . . . is most in:** i.e., who has the most right to

359. **coil:** turmoil; **is long of:** i.e., is because of

365. **amazed:** astounded (as if lost in a maze)

366. **Still thou:** i.e., you always, you continue to

368. **shadows:** illusions, spirits; also, darkness

HERMIA
  "Little" again? Nothing ⌜but⌝ "low" and "little"?
  Why will you suffer her to flout me thus?
  Let me come to her.   345
LYSANDER   Get you gone, you dwarf,
  You minimus of hind'ring knotgrass made,
  You bead, you acorn—
DEMETRIUS   You are too officious
  In her behalf that scorns your services.   350
  Let her alone. Speak not of Helena.
  Take not her part. For if thou dost intend
  Never so little show of love to her,
  Thou shalt aby it.
LYSANDER   Now she holds me not.   355
  Now follow, if thou dar'st, to try whose right,
  Of thine or mine, is most in Helena.
DEMETRIUS
  "Follow"? Nay, I'll go with thee, cheek by jowl.
                  ⌜*Demetrius and Lysander exit.*⌝
HERMIA
  You, mistress, all this coil is long of you.
                     ⌜*Helena retreats.*⌝
  Nay, go not back.   360
HELENA   I will not trust you, I,
  Nor longer stay in your curst company.
  Your hands than mine are quicker for a fray.
  My legs are longer though, to run away. ⌜*She exits.*⌝
HERMIA
  I am amazed and know not what to say. ⌜*She exits.*⌝ 365
OBERON, ⌜*to Robin*⌝
  This is thy negligence. Still thou mistak'st,
  Or else committ'st thy knaveries willfully.
ROBIN
  Believe me, king of shadows, I mistook.
  Did not you tell me I should know the man
  By the Athenian garments he had on?   370

373. **it so did sort:** i.e., that it happened this way
374. **As:** since
376. **Hie:** hurry
377. **welkin:** sky; **anon:** immediately
378. **Acheron:** i.e., hell (literally, one of the four rivers of the classical underworld, Hades)
380. **As one come:** i.e., so that one comes
384. **from:** i.e., away from
386. **batty:** batlike
387. **herb:** plant, flower
388. **liquor:** juice; **virtuous property:** potent power
389. **his might:** i.e., its strength
390. **wonted sight:** i.e., usual (normal) vision
392. **fruitless:** idle, empty
394. **With league . . . end:** i.e., united in a compact that will last until death   **date:** duration, term
397. **charmèd:** bewitched
400. **night's swift dragons:** Night is here presented as driving across the sky in a chariot drawn by dragons.
401. **Aurora's harbinger:** i.e., Venus, the morning star, announcing the approach of dawn (**Aurora**)

And so far blameless proves my enterprise
That I have 'nointed an Athenian's eyes;
And so far am I glad it so did sort,
As this their jangling I esteem a sport.

OBERON

Thou seest these lovers seek a place to fight.   375
Hie, therefore, Robin, overcast the night;
The starry welkin cover thou anon
With drooping fog as black as Acheron,
And lead these testy rivals so astray
As one come not within another's way.   380
Like to Lysander sometime frame thy tongue;
Then stir Demetrius up with bitter wrong.
And sometime rail thou like Demetrius.
And from each other look thou lead them thus,
Till o'er their brows death-counterfeiting sleep   385
With leaden legs and batty wings doth creep.
Then crush this herb into Lysander's eye,
⌜*He gives the flower to Robin.*⌝
Whose liquor hath this virtuous property,
To take from thence all error with his might
And make his eyeballs roll with wonted sight.   390
When they next wake, all this derision
Shall seem a dream and fruitless vision.
And back to Athens shall the lovers wend,
With league whose date till death shall never end.
Whiles I in this affair do thee employ,   395
I'll to my queen and beg her Indian boy;
And then I will her charmèd eye release
From monster's view, and all things shall be peace.

ROBIN

My fairy lord, this must be done with haste,
For night's swift dragons cut the clouds full fast,   400
And yonder shines Aurora's harbinger,
At whose approach, ghosts wand'ring here and
    there

405. in crossways . . . burial: i.e., those not buried in sacred ground **crossways:** i.e., crossroads, where the bodies of suicides were buried

409. for aye: i.e., forever

411–15. I . . . streams: i.e., I do not have to flee the daylight (as do the ghosts of the damned) **the Morning's love:** perhaps, Aurora herself **the eastern gate:** i.e., where the sun rises **Neptune:** i.e., the ocean

421. Goblin: i.e., hobgoblin (another name for Robin Goodfellow)

424. drawn: i.e., with my sword out

425. straight: straightway, immediately

427. plainer: flatter, more level

Neptune, god of the sea. (2.1.130)
From Johann Basilius Herold, *Heydenweldt* . . . (1554).

Troop home to churchyards. Damnèd spirits all,
That in crossways and floods have burial, 405
Already to their wormy beds are gone.
For fear lest day should look their shames upon,
They willfully themselves exile from light
And must for aye consort with black-browed night.

OBERON
But we are spirits of another sort. 410
I with the Morning's love have oft made sport
And, like a forester, the groves may tread
Even till the eastern gate, all fiery red,
Opening on Neptune with fair blessèd beams,
Turns into yellow gold his salt-green streams. 415
But notwithstanding, haste! Make no delay.
We may effect this business yet ere day. ⌈*He exits.*⌉

ROBIN
　　　　Up and down, up and down,
　　　　I will lead them up and down.
　　　　I am feared in field and town. 420
　　　　Goblin, lead them up and down.
Here comes one.

Enter Lysander.

LYSANDER
Where art thou, proud Demetrius? Speak thou now.
ROBIN, ⌈*in Demetrius' voice*⌉
Here, villain, drawn and ready. Where art thou?
LYSANDER　I will be with thee straight. 425
ROBIN, ⌈*in Demetrius' voice*⌉　Follow me, then, to
　　plainer ground.　　　　　　　⌈*Lysander exits.*⌉

Enter Demetrius.

DEMETRIUS　Lysander, speak again.
Thou runaway, thou coward, art thou fled?
Speak! In some bush? Where dost thou hide thy 430
　head?

434. **recreant:** coward

436. **rod:** a stick used to whip a child; **defiled:** i.e., because Demetrius is such a coward, it would be shameful to fight him like a man

439. **try no manhood:** i.e., have no test of our courage

440. **still:** continually

444. **That:** i.e., so that; **in:** i.e., into a

449. **Abide me:** i.e., wait for me; **wot:** know

454–55. **buy this dear:** i.e., pay dearly for this

ROBIN, ⌜*in Lysander's voice*⌝
   Thou coward, art thou bragging to the stars,
   Telling the bushes that thou look'st for wars,
   And wilt not come? Come, recreant! Come, thou
      child!   435
   I'll whip thee with a rod. He is defiled
   That draws a sword on thee.
DEMETRIUS   Yea, art thou there?
ROBIN, ⌜*in Lysander's voice*⌝
   Follow my voice. We'll try no manhood here.
                                        ⌜*They exit.*⌝

                  ⌜*Enter Lysander.*⌝

LYSANDER
   He goes before me and still dares me on.   440
   When I come where he calls, then he is gone.
   The villain is much lighter-heeled than I.
   I followed fast, but faster he did fly,
   That fallen am I in dark uneven way,
   And here will rest me. Come, thou gentle day,   445
   For if but once thou show me thy gray light,
   I'll find Demetrius and revenge this spite.
                          ⌜*He lies down and sleeps.*⌝

            ⌜*Enter*⌝ Robin and Demetrius.

ROBIN, ⌜*in Lysander's voice*⌝
   Ho, ho, ho! Coward, why com'st thou not?
DEMETRIUS
   Abide me, if thou dar'st, for well I wot
   Thou runn'st before me, shifting every place,   450
   And dar'st not stand nor look me in the face.
   Where art thou now?
ROBIN, ⌜*in Lysander's voice*⌝
                          Come hither. I am here.
DEMETRIUS
   Nay, then, thou mock'st me. Thou shalt buy this
      dear   455

458. **this cold bed:** i.e., the ground
459. **By day's approach:** i.e., as soon as day breaks
461. **Abate:** cut short
468. **curst:** angry
476. **mean:** i.e., intend to have

"Winged Cupid." (1.1.241)
From Henry Peacham, *Minerua Britanna* (1612).

If ever I thy face by daylight see.
Now go thy way. Faintness constraineth me
To measure out my length on this cold bed.
By day's approach look to be visited.
⌈*He lies down and sleeps.*⌉

Enter Helena.

HELENA
O weary night, O long and tedious night,   460
    Abate thy hours! Shine, comforts, from the east,
That I may back to Athens by daylight
    From these that my poor company detest.
And sleep, that sometimes shuts up sorrow's eye,
Steal me awhile from mine own company.   465
⌈*She lies down and*⌉ *sleeps.*

ROBIN
        Yet but three? Come one more.
        Two of both kinds makes up four.
        Here she comes, curst and sad.
        Cupid is a knavish lad
        Thus to make poor females mad.   470

⌈*Enter Hermia.*⌉

HERMIA
Never so weary, never so in woe,
    Bedabbled with the dew and torn with briers,
I can no further crawl, no further go.
    My legs can keep no pace with my desires.
Here will I rest me till the break of day.   475
Heavens shield Lysander if they mean a fray!
⌈*She lies down and sleeps.*⌉

ROBIN
            On the ground
            Sleep sound.
            I'll apply
            ⌈To⌉ your eye,   480
        Gentle lover, remedy.

⌜*Robin applies the nectar
to Lysander's eyes.*⌝

When thou wak'st,
Thou tak'st
True delight
In the sight   485
Of thy former lady's eye.
And the country proverb known,
That every man should take his own,
In your waking shall be shown.
Jack shall have Jill;   490
Naught shall go ill;
The man shall have his mare again, and all shall be
well.
⌜*He exits.*⌝

A MIDSUMMER NIGHT'S DREAM

ACT 4

4.1 Titania and her attendants pamper Bottom, who falls asleep with her. Oberon, watching them, tells Robin that Titania has given him the Indian boy and thus they can now remove the spells from Titania and Bottom. Reunited, Titania and Oberon use music to charm Bottom and the four lovers into a deep sleep, and then exit.

Theseus and Hippolyta, accompanied by Egeus and others, have come to the woods to celebrate May Day. They discover the four lovers asleep and wake them. Lysander now loves Hermia again, and Demetrius loves Helena. When Lysander reveals how he and Hermia fled Athens, Egeus begs Theseus to punish him. But when Demetrius announces that he now loves Helena, Theseus overrides Egeus and decrees that Lysander will marry Hermia and Demetrius Helena when Theseus himself weds Hippolyta. As the lovers depart for Athens, Bottom awakes and attempts to recall his night's experience, which seems to him now a dream.

---

2. **amiable:** charming, lovable; **coy:** caress
16. **overflown with:** submerged in

⌜Scene 1⌝
⌜*With the four lovers still asleep onstage,*⌝ *enter*
⌜*Titania,*⌝ *Queen of Fairies, and* ⌜*Bottom*⌝ *and Fairies,*
and ⌜*Oberon,*⌝ *the King, behind them* ⌜*unseen by those*
onstage.⌝

TITANIA
Come, sit thee down upon this flow'ry bed,
    While I thy amiable cheeks do coy,
And stick muskroses in thy sleek smooth head,
    And kiss thy fair large ears, my gentle joy.

BOTTOM Where's Peaseblossom? 5

PEASEBLOSSOM Ready.

BOTTOM Scratch my head, Peaseblossom. Where's Monsieur Cobweb?

COBWEB Ready.

BOTTOM Monsieur Cobweb, good monsieur, get you 10
your weapons in your hand and kill me a red-hipped
humble-bee on the top of a thistle, and, good
monsieur, bring me the honey-bag. Do not fret
yourself too much in the action, monsieur, and,
good monsieur, have a care the honey-bag break 15
not; I would be loath to have you overflown with a
honey-bag, signior. ⌜*Cobweb exits.*⌝ Where's Monsieur Mustardseed?

MUSTARDSEED Ready.

20. **neaf:** fist

21. **leave your courtesy:** i.e., perhaps, stop bowing

23–24. **Cavalery:** i.e., Cavalier

24. **Cobweb:** Cobweb has been sent off already, and so this reference is considered an error by many editors. Some suggest "Peaseblossom" should be substituted for "Cobweb," but it is impossible to know how exactly to correct the "error."

25. **marvels:** i.e., marvelously

30. **the tongs and the bones:** instruments used in burlesque or rustic music (**Tongs** were played by hitting pieces of metal, like a modern triangle. **Bones** were pieces of bone clicked together.)

32. **provender:** hay, food for cattle

34. **bottle:** bundle

35. **fellow:** equal

40. **exposition of:** Bottom's error for "disposition to"

42. **all ways:** i.e., in every direction

Woodbine. (4.1.43)
From John Gerard, *The herball or generall historie of plantes* (1597).

BOTTOM   Give me your neaf, Monsieur Mustardseed.   20
   Pray you, leave your courtesy, good monsieur.
MUSTARDSEED   What's your will?
BOTTOM   Nothing, good monsieur, but to help Cava-
   lery Cobweb to scratch. I must to the barber's,
   monsieur, for methinks I am marvels hairy about   25
   the face. And I am such a tender ass, if my hair do
   but tickle me, I must scratch.
TITANIA
   What, wilt thou hear some music, my sweet love?
BOTTOM   I have a reasonable good ear in music. Let's
   have the tongs and the bones.   30
TITANIA
   Or say, sweet love, what thou desirest to eat.
BOTTOM   Truly, a peck of provender. I could munch
   your good dry oats. Methinks I have a great desire
   to a bottle of hay. Good hay, sweet hay, hath no
   fellow.   35
TITANIA
   I have a venturous fairy that shall seek
   The squirrel's hoard and fetch thee new nuts.
BOTTOM   I had rather have a handful or two of dried
   peas. But, I pray you, let none of your people stir
   me; I have an exposition of sleep come upon me.   40
TITANIA
   Sleep thou, and I will wind thee in my arms.—
   Fairies, begone, and be all ways away.
                              ⌈*Fairies exit.*⌉
   So doth the woodbine the sweet honeysuckle
   Gently entwist; the female ivy so
   Enrings the barky fingers of the elm.   45
   O, how I love thee! How I dote on thee!
                       ⌈*Bottom and Titania sleep.*⌉

               Enter Robin Goodfellow.

OBERON
   Welcome, good Robin. Seest thou this sweet sight?

48. **dotage:** infatuation
54. **sometime:** formerly
55. **orient:** bright, lustrous
56. **flouriets:** i.e., little flowers
61. **straight:** straightway, immediately
67. **other:** i.e., others
68. **May:** i.e., they may; **repair:** go, travel
69. **accidents:** incidents, events
72. **wast wont to:** i.e., used to
74–75. **Dian's bud . . . power:** Oberon earlier explains (at 2.1.191 and 3.2.387–92) that he has in his possession a second flower that can undo the effect of the flower he calls "love-in-idleness." Here, as he applies the juice to Titania's eyes, he links the curative flower to Diana (**Dian's bud**), the goddess of chastity, and love-in-idleness to Cupid, god of love.
81. **visage:** appearance, face

Her dotage now I do begin to pity.
For, meeting her of late behind the wood,
Seeking sweet favors for this hateful fool,   50
I did upbraid her and fall out with her.
For she his hairy temples then had rounded
With coronet of fresh and fragrant flowers;
And that same dew, which sometime on the buds
Was wont to swell like round and orient pearls,   55
Stood now within the pretty flouriets' eyes,
Like tears that did their own disgrace bewail.
When I had at my pleasure taunted her,
And she in mild terms begged my patience,
I then did ask of her her changeling child,   60
Which straight she gave me, and her fairy sent
To bear him to my bower in Fairyland.
And now I have the boy, I will undo
This hateful imperfection of her eyes.
And, gentle Puck, take this transformèd scalp   65
From off the head of this Athenian swain,
That he, awaking when the other do,
May all to Athens back again repair
And think no more of this night's accidents
But as the fierce vexation of a dream.   70
But first I will release the Fairy Queen.
                    ⌈*He applies the nectar to her eyes.*⌉
          Be as thou wast wont to be.
          See as thou wast wont to see.
          Dian's bud o'er Cupid's flower
          Hath such force and blessèd power.   75
     Now, my Titania, wake you, my sweet queen.
TITANIA, ⌈*waking*⌉
     My Oberon, what visions have I seen!
     Methought I was enamored of an ass.
OBERON
     There lies your love.
TITANIA   How came these things to pass?   80
     O, how mine eyes do loathe his visage now!

84. **these five:** i.e., Bottom and the four lovers
92. **solemnly:** ceremoniously
93. **triumphantly:** festively
97. **attend and mark:** i.e., pay attention, notice
99. **sad:** serious
106 SD. **Wind horn:** i.e., one or more hunting horns are blown

OBERON
  Silence awhile.—Robin, take off this head.—
  Titania, music call; and strike more dead
  Than common sleep of all these ⌜five⌝ the sense.

TITANIA
  Music, ho, music such as charmeth sleep!   85

ROBIN, ⌜*removing the ass-head from Bottom*⌝
  Now, when thou wak'st, with thine own fool's eyes
    peep.

OBERON
  Sound music.   ⌜*Music.*⌝
              Come, my queen, take hands with me,
  And rock the ground whereon these sleepers be.   90
             ⌜*Titania and Oberon dance.*⌝
  Now thou and I are new in amity,
  And will tomorrow midnight solemnly
  Dance in Duke Theseus' house triumphantly,
  And bless it to all fair prosperity.
  There shall the pairs of faithful lovers be   95
  Wedded, with Theseus, all in jollity.

ROBIN
          Fairy king, attend and mark.
          I do hear the morning lark.

OBERON
          Then, my queen, in silence sad
          Trip we after night's shade.   100
          We the globe can compass soon,
          Swifter than the wand'ring moon.

TITANIA
          Come, my lord, and in our flight
          Tell me how it came this night
          That I sleeping here was found   105
          With these mortals on the ground.
              ⌜*Oberon, Robin, and Titania*⌝ *exit.*

Wind horn. Enter Theseus and all his train,
        ⌜*Hippolyta, Egeus.*⌝

107. **Forester:** the official in charge of the forest land and responsible for the wild animals of the forest

108. **our observation:** i.e., our observance of May Day rites

109. **since . . . day:** i.e., since it is still early **vaward:** vanguard

110. **music of my hounds:** The cry of a pack of hounds in pursuit of hunted animals was compared to orchestral or vocal music, and its sound was much prized. At line 127, Theseus suggests that his hounds' music is more important to him than their speed.

111. **Uncouple:** i.e., unleash the hounds

114–15. **mark . . . conjunction:** i.e., listen to the sound created by the coming together of the cry of the hounds and its echo from the mountains

116. **Hercules:** a hero in Greek and Roman mythology; **Cadmus:** legendary founder of the city of Thebes

117. **bayed:** i.e., brought to bay

118. **hounds of Sparta:** Spartan hounds, celebrated for their hunting abilities

119. **chiding:** i.e., barking

124. **So:** i.e., like those of Sparta; **flewed:** with large folds of flesh about the mouth; **sanded:** i.e., sandy-colored

126. **dewlapped:** i.e., with folds of skin under their necks

127–28. **matched . . . each:** i.e., their cry was like a set of bells, each voice chiming in tune with the others **Each under each:** i.e., like notes on a scale

128. **cry:** pack; **tunable:** i.e., tuneful

131. **soft:** i.e., stop a minute

136. **of:** i.e., at

THESEUS
Go, one of you, find out the Forester.
For now our observation is performed,
And, since we have the vaward of the day,
My love shall hear the music of my hounds.   110
Uncouple in the western valley; let them go.
Dispatch, I say, and find the Forester.
⌈*A Servant exits.*⌉
We will, fair queen, up to the mountain's top
And mark the musical confusion
Of hounds and echo in conjunction.   115

HIPPOLYTA
I was with Hercules and Cadmus once,
When in a wood of Crete they bayed the bear
With hounds of Sparta. Never did I hear
Such gallant chiding, for, besides the groves,
The skies, the fountains, every region near   120
⌈Seemed⌉ all one mutual cry. I never heard
So musical a discord, such sweet thunder.

THESEUS
My hounds are bred out of the Spartan kind,
So flewed, so sanded; and their heads are hung
With ears that sweep away the morning dew;   125
Crook-kneed, and dewlapped like Thessalian bulls;
Slow in pursuit, but matched in mouth like bells,
Each under each. A cry more tunable
Was never holloed to, nor cheered with horn,
In Crete, in Sparta, nor in Thessaly.   130
Judge when you hear.—But soft! What nymphs are
these?

EGEUS
My lord, this ⌈is⌉ my daughter here asleep,
And this Lysander; this Demetrius is,
This Helena, old Nedar's Helena.   135
I wonder of their being here together.

137–38. **observe / The rite of May:** i.e., celebrate May Day

139. **grace:** honor; **solemnity:** observance (i.e., of May Day rites)

144. **Saint Valentine:** i.e., Valentine's Day (when birds proverbially chose their mates)

150. **jealousy:** suspicion, mistrust

152. **amazèdly:** i.e., in a state of bewilderment (as if lost in a maze)

155. **truly . . . speak:** i.e., I wish to speak the truth

159. **Without:** outside of, beyond

A hound. (4.1.118)
From George Turberville, *The noble arte of venerie or hunting* (1611).

THESEUS
  No doubt they rose up early to observe
  The rite of May, and hearing our intent,
  Came here in grace of our solemnity.
  But speak, Egeus. Is not this the day   140
  That Hermia should give answer of her choice?
EGEUS   It is, my lord.
THESEUS
  Go, bid the huntsmen wake them with their horns.
                       ⌐*A Servant exits.*⌐
            Shout within. Wind horns. They all start up.

THESEUS
  Good morrow, friends. Saint Valentine is past.
  Begin these woodbirds but to couple now?   145
     ⌐*Demetrius, Helena, Hermia, and Lysander kneel.*⌐
LYSANDER
  Pardon, my lord.
THESEUS   I pray you all, stand up.
                                    ⌐*They rise.*⌐

  I know you two are rival enemies.
  How comes this gentle concord in the world,
  That hatred is so far from jealousy   150
  To sleep by hate and fear no enmity?
LYSANDER
  My lord, I shall reply amazèdly,
  Half sleep, half waking. But as yet, I swear,
  I cannot truly say how I came here.
  But, as I think—for truly would I speak,   155
  And now I do bethink me, so it is:
  I came with Hermia hither. Our intent
  Was to be gone from Athens, where we might,
  Without the peril of the Athenian law—
EGEUS
  Enough, enough!—My lord, you have enough.   160
  I beg the law, the law, upon his head.
  They would have stol'n away.—They would,
    Demetrius,

168. **hither:** i.e., to come here
169. **hither:** here
170. **in fancy:** i.e., drawn by her love
171. **wot:** know
174. **idle gaud:** worthless trinket
176. **virtue:** power
180. **like a sickness:** i.e., like one who is sick
186. **overbear:** i.e., overrule
189. **for:** i.e., because; **something:** i.e., somewhat
192. **in great solemnity:** i.e., with great ceremony

A mermaid. (2.1.155)
From August Casimir Redel,
Apophtegmata symbolica . . . (n.d.).

Thereby to have defeated you and me:
You of your wife and me of my consent,   165
Of my consent that she should be your wife.

DEMETRIUS
My lord, fair Helen told me of their stealth,
Of this their purpose hither to this wood,
And I in fury hither followed them,
Fair Helena in fancy following me.   170
But, my good lord, I wot not by what power
(But by some power it is) my love to Hermia,
Melted as the snow, seems to me now
As the remembrance of an idle gaud
Which in my childhood I did dote upon,   175
And all the faith, the virtue of my heart,
The object and the pleasure of mine eye,
Is only Helena. To her, my lord,
Was I betrothed ere I ⌜saw⌝ Hermia.
But like a sickness did I loathe this food.   180
But, as in health, come to my natural taste,
Now I do wish it, love it, long for it,
And will forevermore be true to it.

THESEUS
Fair lovers, you are fortunately met.
Of this discourse we more will hear anon.—   185
Egeus, I will overbear your will,
For in the temple by and by, with us,
These couples shall eternally be knit.—
And, for the morning now is something worn,
Our purposed hunting shall be set aside.   190
Away with us to Athens. Three and three,
We'll hold a feast in great solemnity.
Come, Hippolyta.
                        ⌜*Theseus and his train,*
              including Hippolyta and Egeus, exit.⌝

DEMETRIUS
These things seem small and undistinguishable,
Like far-off mountains turnèd into clouds.   195

196. **parted:** divided (i.e., out of focus)

199–200. **like a jewel . . . own:** i.e., as if I had found a jewel whom someone else might claim

211. **My next:** i.e., my next line

212. **Hey-ho!:** This may signal either a call or a big yawn.

213. **God's:** i.e., perhaps, may God save

216. **go about:** i.e., try

219. **patched:** i.e., dressed in motley, such as a professional fool would wear

220–24. **The eye . . . dream was:** This seems to be Bottom's confused memory of 1 Corinthians 2.9, where St. Paul writes: "The eye hath not seen, and the ear hath not heard, neither have entered into the heart of man, the things which God hath prepared for them that love him" (as translated in the Bishops' Bible [1568]).

225–26. **because it hath no bottom:** St. Paul's letter to the Corinthians continues (1 Corinthians 2.10): ". . . the spirit searcheth all things, yea the deep things of God," words that again may be confusingly echoed in Bottom's reflection on the bottomlessness of his vision.

HERMIA
  Methinks I see these things with parted eye,
  When everything seems double.
HELENA   So methinks.
  And I have found Demetrius like a jewel,
  Mine own and not mine own.   200
DEMETRIUS   Are you sure
  That we are awake? It seems to me
  That yet we sleep, we dream. Do not you think
  The Duke was here and bid us follow him?
HERMIA
  Yea, and my father.   205
HELENA   And Hippolyta.
LYSANDER
  And he did bid us follow to the temple.
DEMETRIUS
  Why, then, we are awake. Let's follow him,
  And by the way let ⌜us⌝ recount our dreams.
                            ⌜*Lovers exit.*⌝
BOTTOM, ⌜*waking up*⌝ When my cue comes, call me,   210
  and I will answer. My next is "Most fair Pyramus."
  Hey-ho! Peter Quince! Flute the bellows-mender!
  Snout the tinker! Starveling! God's my life! Stolen
  hence and left me asleep! I have had a most rare
  vision. I have had a dream past the wit of man to say   215
  what dream it was. Man is but an ass if he go about
  ⌜to⌝ expound this dream. Methought I was—there
  is no man can tell what. Methought I was and
  methought I had—but man is but ⌜a patched⌝ fool if
  he will offer to say what methought I had. The eye of   220
  man hath not heard, the ear of man hath not seen,
  man's hand is not able to taste, his tongue to
  conceive, nor his heart to report what my dream
  was. I will get Peter Quince to write a ballad of this
  dream. It shall be called "Bottom's Dream" be-   225
  cause it hath no bottom; and I will sing it in the

227–29. **a play . . . her death:** It has been suggested that the vagueness here about "a play" and "her death" are signs that Bottom is still half asleep.

4.2 The tradesmen regret, for their own sakes and for Bottom's, the loss of their opportunity to perform the play, since Bottom is irreplaceable. Bottom arrives and announces that their play has been chosen by Theseus for performance that night.

3. **Out of doubt:** i.e., surely
4. **transported:** i.e., transformed; carried away
5–6. **It goes . . . doth it?:** i.e., it won't go on, will it?
8. **discharge:** i.e., play, perform
11. **person:** personage, appearance
14. **thing of naught:** an evil thing
17–18. **we . . . men:** i.e., our fortunes would have been made
19–20. **six pence . . . life:** Such a daily pension would have been very grand.
21. **An:** if

latter end of a play, before the Duke. Peradventure,
to make it the more gracious, I shall sing it at her
death.

⌜*He exits.*⌝

⌜*Scene 2*⌝
Enter Quince, Flute, ⌜*Snout, and Starveling.*⌝

QUINCE Have you sent to Bottom's house? Is he come
home yet?

⌜STARVELING⌝ He cannot be heard of. Out of doubt he
is transported.

FLUTE If he come not, then the play is marred. It goes   5
not forward, doth it?

QUINCE It is not possible. You have not a man in all
Athens able to discharge Pyramus but he.

FLUTE No, he hath simply the best wit of any handi-
craftman in Athens.   10

QUINCE Yea, and the best person too, and he is a very
paramour for a sweet voice.

FLUTE You must say "paragon." A "paramour" is (God
bless us) a thing of naught.

Enter Snug the joiner.

SNUG Masters, the Duke is coming from the temple,   15
and there is two or three lords and ladies more
married. If our sport had gone forward, we had all
been made men.

FLUTE O, sweet bully Bottom! Thus hath he lost six
pence a day during his life. He could not have   20
'scaped six pence a day. An the Duke had not given
him six pence a day for playing Pyramus, I'll be
hanged. He would have deserved it. Six pence a day
in Pyramus, or nothing!

Enter Bottom.

26. **hearts:** hearties, good fellows

31–32. **right . . . fell out:** just . . . happened

34. **of me:** i.e., from me

36. **strings to your beards:** i.e., strings to tie on your false beards

36–37. **ribbons to your pumps:** i.e., ribbons to decorate your fancy shoes

37. **presently:** right away

39. **preferred:** recommended

BOTTOM Where are these lads? Where are these   25
hearts?

QUINCE Bottom! O most courageous day! O most happy hour!

BOTTOM Masters, I am to discourse wonders. But ask
me not what; for, if I tell you, I am not true   30
Athenian. I will tell you everything right as it fell
out.

QUINCE Let us hear, sweet Bottom.

BOTTOM Not a word of me. All that I will tell you is that
the Duke hath dined. Get your apparel together,   35
good strings to your beards, new ribbons to your
pumps. Meet presently at the palace. Every man
look o'er his part. For the short and the long is, our
play is preferred. In any case, let Thisbe have clean
linen, and let not him that plays the lion pare his   40
nails, for they shall hang out for the lion's claws.
And, most dear actors, eat no onions nor garlic, for
we are to utter sweet breath, and I do not doubt but
to hear them say it is a sweet comedy. No more
words. Away! Go, away!   45

⌜*They exit.*⌝

A MIDSUMMER NIGHT'S DREAM

ACT 5

5.1 Theseus dismisses as imaginary the lovers' account of their night's experience, and then chooses "Pyramus and Thisbe" for the night's entertainment. The play is so ridiculous and the performance so bad that the courtly audience find pleasure in mocking them. When the play is over and the newly married couples have retired to bed, the fairies enter, led by Titania and Oberon, to bless the three marriages. Robin Goodfellow asks the audience to think of the play as if it were a dream.

---

1. **that:** i.e., that which, what
2. **may:** i.e., can
3. **antique fables:** (1) old stories; (2) fantastic tales; **fairy toys:** i.e., foolish tales (**toys**) about fairies
5. **shaping fantasies:** i.e., creative imaginations; **apprehend:** conceive, imagine
6. **comprehends:** grasps, understands
8. **of imagination all compact:** i.e., made up entirely of imagination
10. **all as frantic:** i.e., just as insane
11. **Helen's beauty:** i.e., the beauty of the legendary Helen of Troy; **a brow of Egypt:** i.e., a Gypsy-like face (another allusion to the supposed unattractiveness of women with darker coloring)

⌜ACT 5⌝

⌜Scene 1⌝

Enter Theseus, Hippolyta, and Philostrate, ⌜Lords, and
Attendants.⌝

HIPPOLYTA
'Tis strange, my Theseus, that these lovers speak of.
THESEUS
More strange than true. I never may believe
These antique fables, nor these fairy toys.
Lovers and madmen have such seething brains,
Such shaping fantasies, that apprehend   5
More than cool reason ever comprehends.
The lunatic, the lover, and the poet
Are of imagination all compact.
One sees more devils than vast hell can hold:
That is the madman. The lover, all as frantic,   10
Sees Helen's beauty in a brow of Egypt.
The poet's eye, in a fine frenzy rolling,
Doth glance from heaven to earth, from earth to
    heaven,
And as imagination bodies forth   15
The forms of things unknown, the poet's pen
Turns them to shapes and gives to airy nothing
A local habitation and a name.
Such tricks hath strong imagination
That, if it would but apprehend some joy,   20

143

21. **comprehends:** includes (as a part of its conception of the joy); **some bringer of:** i.e., someone or something that brings

25. **all . . . together:** i.e., their minds all suffering the same transformation

26. **More witnesseth than fancy's images:** i.e., attests to more than imaginary delusions

27. **constancy:** consistency, unchangingness

28. **howsoever:** i.e., in any case; **admirable:** i.e., worthy of wonder

32. **More:** i.e., more joy

33. **Wait . . . your board:** i.e., await you . . . your table

34. **masques:** like **revels** (line 39), a name for courtly entertainment

37. **after-supper:** a light meal or dessert served after the main supper

43. **abridgment:** i.e., pastime (to abridge or shorten the evening)

46. **brief:** i.e., list, short account; **sports:** diversions; **ripe:** ready, prepared

It comprehends some bringer of that joy.
Or in the night, imagining some fear,
How easy is a bush supposed a bear!

HIPPOLYTA
But all the story of the night told over,
And all their minds transfigured so together,   25
More witnesseth than fancy's images
And grows to something of great constancy,
But, howsoever, strange and admirable.

Enter Lovers: Lysander, Demetrius, Hermia, and Helena.

THESEUS
Here come the lovers full of joy and mirth.—
Joy, gentle friends! Joy and fresh days of love   30
Accompany your hearts!

LYSANDER   More than to us
Wait in your royal walks, your board, your bed!

THESEUS
Come now, what masques, what dances shall we
   have   35
To wear away this long age of three hours
Between ⌜our⌝ after-supper and bedtime?
Where is our usual manager of mirth?
What revels are in hand? Is there no play
To ease the anguish of a torturing hour?   40
Call Philostrate.

PHILOSTRATE, ⌜*coming forward*⌝
                    Here, mighty Theseus.

THESEUS
Say what abridgment have you for this evening,
What masque, what music? How shall we beguile
The lazy time if not with some delight?   45

PHILOSTRATE, ⌜*giving Theseus a paper*⌝
There is a brief how many sports are ripe.
Make choice of which your Highness will see first.

48. **battle with the Centaurs:** a famous incident in the life of Hercules

50. **We'll none:** i.e., we'll have none

51. **my kinsman:** Plutarch's "Life of Theseus" says that Hercules was Theseus's cousin.

52–53. **The riot . . . rage:** This would be the story of Orpheus (**the Thracian singer**) who was torn to pieces by women who worshiped Bacchus.

54. **device:** show, entertainment

56–57. **The thrice . . . beggary:** presumably a satirical play about the neglect of scholarship and learning. **thrice-three Muses:** The nine muses presided over literature, arts, and sciences. (See page 164.)

58. **critical:** judgmental

59. **sorting with:** i.e., suitable for, appropriate to

74. **passion of loud laughter:** i.e., intense or vehement laughter

78. **toiled:** fatigued, worn out; **unbreathed:** i.e., unexercised

79. **against:** i.e., in time for

THESEUS
  "The battle with the Centaurs, to be sung
  By an Athenian eunuch to the harp."
  We'll none of that. That have I told my love   50
  In glory of my kinsman Hercules.
  "The riot of the tipsy Bacchanals,
  Tearing the Thracian singer in their rage."
  That is an old device, and it was played
  When I from Thebes came last a conqueror.   55
  "The thrice-three Muses mourning for the death
  Of learning, late deceased in beggary."
  That is some satire, keen and critical,
  Not sorting with a nuptial ceremony.
  "A tedious brief scene of young Pyramus   60
  And his love Thisbe, very tragical mirth."
  "Merry" and "tragical"? "Tedious" and "brief"?
  That is hot ice and wondrous strange snow!
  How shall we find the concord of this discord?
PHILOSTRATE
  A play there is, my lord, some ten words long   65
  (Which is as brief as I have known a play),
  But by ten words, my lord, it is too long,
  Which makes it tedious; for in all the play,
  There is not one word apt, one player fitted.
  And tragical, my noble lord, it is.   70
  For Pyramus therein doth kill himself,
  Which, when I saw rehearsed, I must confess,
  Made mine eyes water; but more merry tears
  The passion of loud laughter never shed.
THESEUS
  What are they that do play it?   75
PHILOSTRATE
  Hard-handed men that work in Athens here,
  Which never labored in their minds till now,
  And now have toiled their unbreathed memories
  With this same play, against your nuptial.

85. **conned:** memorized

89. **simpleness:** sincerity; lack of sophistication

91. **wretchedness:** i.e., poor wretches; **o'er-charged:** overburdened

92. **his:** i.e., its

96. **take:** accept

97. **noble respect:** i.e., a generous regard or consideration

98. **Takes . . . merit:** i.e., perhaps, considers the effort, not the effect

99. **come:** i.e., journeyed; **clerks:** scholars

100. **premeditated:** previously designed

102. **periods:** i.e., stops

103. **their practiced accent:** i.e., the emphasis they had rehearsed

104. **dumbly:** silently

107. **fearful:** frightened

THESEUS
And we will hear it. 80
PHILOSTRATE   No, my noble lord,
It is not for you. I have heard it over,
And it is nothing, nothing in the world,
Unless you can find sport in their intents,
Extremely stretched and conned with cruel pain 85
To do you service.
THESEUS   I will hear that play,
For never anything can be amiss
When simpleness and duty tender it.
Go, bring them in—and take your places, ladies. 90
⌐*Philostrate exits.*¬

HIPPOLYTA
I love not to see wretchedness o'ercharged,
And duty in his service perishing.
THESEUS
Why, gentle sweet, you shall see no such thing.
HIPPOLYTA
He says they can do nothing in this kind.
THESEUS
The kinder we, to give them thanks for nothing. 95
Our sport shall be to take what they mistake;
And what poor duty cannot do, noble respect
Takes it in might, not merit.
Where I have come, great clerks have purposèd
To greet me with premeditated welcomes, 100
Where I have seen them shiver and look pale,
Make periods in the midst of sentences,
Throttle their practiced accent in their fears,
And in conclusion dumbly have broke off,
Not paying me a welcome. Trust me, sweet, 105
Out of this silence yet I picked a welcome,
And in the modesty of fearful duty,
I read as much as from the rattling tongue
Of saucy and audacious eloquence.

111. **to my capacity:** perhaps, in my opinion
112. **addressed:** ready
114–24. **If . . . know:** The comic effect of this prologue depends on its being delivered with the major pauses in the wrong places, in just the way that Theseus had earlier described.
117. **end:** aim, purpose
119. **minding:** i.e., intending
125. **stand upon points:** (1) is not a stickler for detail; (2) pays no attention to punctuation
126. **rid:** i.e., ridden; **rough:** i.e., untrained
127. **stop:** (1) signal to stop; (2) punctuation mark
130. **recorder:** a flutelike musical instrument
130–31. **in government:** i.e., controlled
132–33. **nothing:** not at all

Love, therefore, and tongue-tied simplicity 110
In least speak most, to my capacity.

⌐*Enter Philostrate.*⌐

PHILOSTRATE
So please your Grace, the Prologue is addressed.
THESEUS Let him approach.

Enter the Prologue.

PROLOGUE
If we offend, it is with our goodwill.
That you should think we come not to offend, 115
But with goodwill. To show our simple skill,
That is the true beginning of our end.
Consider, then, we come but in despite.
We do not come, as minding to content you,
Our true intent is. All for your delight 120
We are not here. That you should here repent
you,
The actors are at hand, and, by their show,
You shall know all that you are like to know.
⌐*Prologue exits.*⌐

THESEUS This fellow doth not stand upon points. 125
LYSANDER He hath rid his prologue like a rough colt;
he knows not the stop. A good moral, my lord: it is
not enough to speak, but to speak true.
HIPPOLYTA Indeed he hath played on this prologue like
a child on a recorder—a sound, but not in govern- 130
ment.
THESEUS His speech was like a tangled chain—nothing impaired, but all disordered. Who is next?

*Enter Pyramus ⌐(Bottom),⌐ and Thisbe ⌐(Flute),⌐ and
Wall ⌐(Snout),⌐ and Moonshine ⌐(Starveling),⌐ and Lion
⌐(Snug),⌐⌐ and Prologue (Quince).⌐*

QUINCE, *as Prologue*
Gentles, perchance you wonder at this show.

148. **hight:** is called
151. **fall:** i.e., drop
153. **tall:** brave
156. **broached:** i.e., stabbed (with a comic allusion to "broaching [i.e., tapping] a keg of beer or wine")
160. **At large:** i.e., at length

Pyramus and Thisbe. (5.1.136–37)
From Ovid, *Le metamorphosi* . . . (1538).

But wonder on, till truth make all things plain.   135
This man is Pyramus, if you would know.
  This beauteous lady Thisbe is certain.
This man with lime and roughcast doth present
  "Wall," that vile wall which did these lovers
    sunder;   140
And through Wall's chink, poor souls, they are
    content
  To whisper, at the which let no man wonder.
This man, with lantern, dog, and bush of thorn,
  Presenteth "Moonshine," for, if you will know,   145
By moonshine did these lovers think no scorn
  To meet at Ninus' tomb, there, there to woo.
This grisly beast (which "Lion" hight by name)
  The trusty Thisbe coming first by night
Did ⌜scare⌝ away, or rather did affright;   150
And, as she fled, her mantle she did fall,
  Which Lion vile with bloody mouth did stain.
Anon comes Pyramus, sweet youth and tall,
  And finds his trusty Thisbe's mantle slain.
Whereat, with blade, with bloody blameful blade,   155
  He bravely broached his boiling bloody breast.
And Thisbe, tarrying in mulberry shade,
  His dagger drew, and died. For all the rest,
Let Lion, Moonshine, Wall, and lovers twain
At large discourse, while here they do remain.   160
THESEUS   I wonder if the lion be to speak.
DEMETRIUS   No wonder, my lord. One lion may when
    many asses do.
        Lion, Thisbe, Moonshine, ⌜and Prologue⌝ exit.
SNOUT, *as Wall*
  In this same interlude it doth befall
That I, one ⌜Snout⌝ by name, present a wall;   165
And such a wall as I would have you think
That had in it a crannied hole or chink,
Through which the lovers, Pyramus and Thisbe,

172. **sinister:** left (Here, in performance, "Wall" usually makes a "cranny" by holding his fingers in the shape of a V.)

174. **lime and hair:** the materials that make up roughcast

176. **wittiest:** most intelligent

188. **eyne:** i.e., eyes

189. **Thanks:** in response to Wall's gesture of showing the cranny; **Jove shield thee:** i.e., God reward you

194. **being sensible:** i.e., having senses

195. **curse again:** i.e., return the curse

198–99. **fall pat:** i.e., happen exactly

Did whisper often, very secretly.
This loam, this roughcast, and this stone doth show   170
That I am that same wall. The truth is so.
And this the cranny is, right and sinister,
Through which the fearful lovers are to whisper.

THESEUS   Would you desire lime and hair to speak
better?   175

DEMETRIUS   It is the wittiest partition that ever I heard
discourse, my lord.

THESEUS   Pyramus draws near the wall. Silence.

BOTTOM, *as Pyramus*
O grim-looked night! O night with hue so black!
O night, which ever art when day is not!   180
O night! O night! Alack, alack, alack!
I fear my Thisbe's promise is forgot.
And thou, O wall, O sweet, O lovely wall,
That stand'st between her father's ground and
mine,   185
Thou wall, O wall, O sweet and lovely wall,
Show me thy chink to blink through with mine
eyne.
Thanks, courteous wall. Jove shield thee well for
this.   190
But what see I? No Thisbe do I see.
O wicked wall, through whom I see no bliss,
Cursed be thy stones for thus deceiving me!

THESEUS   The wall, methinks, being sensible, should
curse again.   195

BOTTOM   No, in truth, sir, he should not. "Deceiving
me" is Thisbe's cue. She is to enter now, and I am
to spy her through the wall. You shall see it will fall
pat as I told you. Yonder she comes.

Enter Thisbe ⌈(Flute).⌉

FLUTE, *as Thisbe*
O wall, full often hast thou heard my moans   200

205. **an:** if

209. **Limander:** no doubt "Leander," a famous lover

210. **Helen:** perhaps, Helen of Troy (One would think that the name here should have been Hero, Leander's love.)

211. **Shafalus, Procrus:** no doubt Cephalus and Procris, famous tragic lovers

215. **Ninny's tomb:** i.e., Ninus's tomb (See page 74, note to line 97.)

216. **'Tide . . . death:** i.e., come life or death **'Tide:** betide

217. **dischargèd:** performed

222. **to:** i.e., as to

224. **in this kind:** i.e., plays and/or players; **shadows:** illusions, fictions

    For parting my fair Pyramus and me.
My cherry lips have often kissed thy stones,
    Thy stones with lime and hair knit ⌈up in thee.⌉

BOTTOM, *as Pyramus*
  I see a voice! Now will I to the chink
    To spy an I can hear my Thisbe's face.   205
  Thisbe?

FLUTE, *as Thisbe*
       My love! Thou art my love, I think.

BOTTOM, *as Pyramus*
    Think what thou wilt, I am thy lover's grace,
And, like Limander, am I trusty still.

FLUTE, *as Thisbe*
  And I like Helen, till the Fates me kill.   210

BOTTOM, *as Pyramus*
  Not Shafalus to Procrus was so true.

FLUTE, *as Thisbe*
  As Shafalus to Procrus, I to you.

BOTTOM, *as Pyramus*
  O kiss me through the hole of this vile wall.

FLUTE, *as Thisbe*
  I kiss the wall's hole, not your lips at all.

BOTTOM, *as Pyramus*
  Wilt thou at Ninny's tomb meet me straightway?   215

FLUTE, *as Thisbe*
  'Tide life, 'tide death, I come without delay.
                ⌈*Bottom and Flute exit.*⌉

SNOUT, *as Wall*
  Thus have I, Wall, my part dischargèd so,
And, being done, thus Wall away doth go. ⌈*He exits.*⌉

THESEUS Now is the ⌈wall down⌉ between the two
    neighbors.   220

DEMETRIUS No remedy, my lord, when walls are so
    willful to hear without warning.

HIPPOLYTA This is the silliest stuff that ever I heard.

THESEUS The best in this kind are but shadows, and

238. **A lion . . . dam:** perhaps, am neither a lion nor a lioness   **fell:** fierce   **dam:** mother

254–55. **horns . . . head:** a reference to the cuckold

256. **no crescent:** i.e., not a crescent (waxing, growing) moon

A ''horned man,'' or cuckold. (5.1.254–55)
From *Bagford Ballads* (printed in 1878).

the worst are no worse, if imagination amend   225
them.

HIPPOLYTA   It must be your imagination, then, and not
theirs.

THESEUS   If we imagine no worse of them than they of
themselves, they may pass for excellent men. Here   230
come two noble beasts in, a man and a lion.

Enter Lion ⌈(Snug)⌉ and Moonshine ⌈(Starveling).⌉

SNUG, *as Lion*
You ladies, you whose gentle hearts do fear
   The smallest monstrous mouse that creeps on
      floor,
May now perchance both quake and tremble here,   235
   When lion rough in wildest rage doth roar.
Then know that I, as Snug the joiner, am
A lion fell, nor else no lion's dam;
For if I should as lion come in strife
Into this place, 'twere pity on my life.   240

THESEUS   A very gentle beast, and of a good conscience.

DEMETRIUS   The very best at a beast, my lord, that e'er I
saw.

LYSANDER   This lion is a very fox for his valor.   245

THESEUS   True, and a goose for his discretion.

DEMETRIUS   Not so, my lord, for his valor cannot carry
his discretion, and the fox carries the goose.

THESEUS   His discretion, I am sure, cannot carry his
valor, for the goose carries not the fox. It is well.   250
Leave it to his discretion, and let us listen to the
Moon.

STARVELING, *as Moonshine*
This lanthorn doth the hornèd moon present.

DEMETRIUS   He should have worn the horns on his
head.   255

THESEUS   He is no crescent, and his horns are invisible
within the circumference.

263. **for the candle:** i.e., for fear of the candle

264. **in snuff:** i.e., (1) in need of having its wick trimmed; (2) angry

269. **stay:** wait for

284. **moused:** torn or shaken (as a cat with a mouse)

STARVELING, *as Moonshine*
  This lanthorn doth the hornèd moon present.
    Myself the man i' th' moon do seem to be.

THESEUS This is the greatest error of all the rest; the   260
    man should be put into the lanthorn. How is it else
    "the man i' th' moon"?

DEMETRIUS He dares not come there for the candle,
    for you see, it is already in snuff.

HIPPOLYTA I am aweary of this moon. Would he would   265
    change.

THESEUS It appears by his small light of discretion that
    he is in the wane; but yet, in courtesy, in all reason,
    we must stay the time.

LYSANDER Proceed, Moon.   270

STARVELING, *as Moonshine* All that I have to say is to tell
    you that the lanthorn is the moon, I the man i' th'
    moon, this thornbush my thornbush, and this dog
    my dog.

DEMETRIUS Why, all these should be in the lanthorn,   275
    for all these are in the moon. But silence. Here
    comes Thisbe.

Enter Thisbe ⌐(Flute).¬

FLUTE, *as Thisbe*
  This is old Ninny's tomb. Where is my love?

SNUG, *as Lion* O!

                  ⌐*The Lion roars. Thisbe runs off,*
                            dropping her mantle.¬

DEMETRIUS Well roared, Lion.   280

THESEUS Well run, Thisbe.

HIPPOLYTA Well shone, Moon. Truly, the Moon shines
    with a good grace.

                        ⌐*Lion worries the mantle.*¬

THESEUS Well moused, Lion.

Enter Pyramus ⌐(Bottom).¬

293. **dole:** sorrow

299. **Furies:** the Erinys, mythological beings who punished those who offended against natural and moral laws; **fell:** fierce

300. **Fates:** In Greek mythology, the three Fates wove one's life and brought about one's death by cutting life's thread.

301. **thread and thrum:** i.e., the whole thread of my life **thrum:** the tufted end of the warp

302. **Quail:** overcome; **quell:** kill

303. **passion:** i.e., staging of strong emotion

305. **Beshrew:** i.e., curse

306. **wherefore:** why

307. **deflowered:** a malapropism, or verbal confusion, perhaps for "devoured"

309–10. **with cheer:** i.e., with her face; also, perhaps, cheerfully

311. **confound:** destroy

313. **pap:** breast (usually used to refer to the nipple or breast of a woman or the teat of an animal)

DEMETRIUS   And then came Pyramus.   285
⌈*Lion exits.*⌉

LYSANDER   And so the lion vanished.

BOTTOM, *as Pyramus*
  Sweet Moon, I thank thee for thy sunny beams.
    I thank thee, Moon, for shining now so bright,
  For by thy gracious, golden, glittering ⌈gleams,⌉
    I trust to take of truest Thisbe sight.—   290
      But stay! O spite!
      But mark, poor knight,
    What dreadful dole is here!
      Eyes, do you see!
      How can it be!   295
    O dainty duck! O dear!
      Thy mantle good—
      What, stained with blood?
    Approach, ye Furies fell!
      O Fates, come, come,   300
      Cut thread and thrum,
    Quail, crush, conclude, and quell!

THESEUS   This passion, and the death of a dear friend,
    would go near to make a man look sad.

HIPPOLYTA   Beshrew my heart but I pity the man.   305

BOTTOM, *as Pyramus*
  O, wherefore, Nature, didst thou lions frame,
  Since lion vile hath here deflowered my dear,
  Which is—no, no—which was the fairest dame
  That lived, that loved, that liked, that looked with
    cheer?   310
      Come, tears, confound!
      Out, sword, and wound
    The pap of Pyramus;
      Ay, that left pap,
      Where heart doth hop. ⌈*Pyramus stabs himself.*⌉   315
    Thus die I, thus, thus, thus.
      Now am I dead;

323. **die:** one of a pair of dice   **ace:** a one-spot on a die

328. **ass:** perhaps a pun on the earlier **ace**

329. **How chance Moonshine is:** i.e., why has Moonshine

340. **means:** (1) moans, laments; (2) lodges a formal complaint; **videlicet:** to wit, as follows

344. **dumb:** silent

"The thrice-three Muses." (5.1.56)
From Natale Conti, *Natalis Comitis Mythologiae* . . . (1616).

    Now am I fled;
My soul is in the sky.
    Tongue, lose thy light!   320
    Moon, take thy flight!   ⌜*Moonshine exits.*⌝
Now die, die, die, die, die.   ⌜*Pyramus falls.*⌝

DEMETRIUS No die, but an ace, for him, for he is but
one.

LYSANDER Less than an ace, man, for he is dead, he is   325
nothing.

THESEUS With the help of a surgeon he might yet
recover and yet prove an ass.

HIPPOLYTA How chance Moonshine is gone before
Thisbe comes back and finds her lover?   330

THESEUS She will find him by starlight.

      ⌜*Enter Thisbe (Flute).*⌝

Here she comes, and her passion ends the play.

HIPPOLYTA Methinks she should not use a long one for
such a Pyramus. I hope she will be brief.

DEMETRIUS A mote will turn the balance, which Pyra-   335
mus, which Thisbe, is the better: he for a man, God
warrant us; she for a woman, God bless us.

LYSANDER She hath spied him already with those
sweet eyes.

DEMETRIUS And thus she means, *videlicet*—   340

FLUTE, *as Thisbe*
        Asleep, my love?
        What, dead, my dove?
      O Pyramus, arise!
        Speak, speak. Quite dumb?
        Dead? Dead? A tomb   345
      Must cover thy sweet eyes.
        These lily lips,
        This cherry nose,
      These yellow cowslip cheeks
        Are gone, are gone!   350

353. **Sisters Three:** i.e., the Fates

357. **shore:** i.e., shorn, cut (phrased to rhyme with **gore**)

358. **thread of silk:** i.e., the thread of his life (phrased to rhyme with **milk**)

361. **imbrue:** drench with blood

369–70. **see . . . hear:** Once again, Bottom confuses the senses of seeing and hearing.

370. **Bergomask dance:** a rustic dance

377–78. **discharged:** performed

380. **iron tongue of midnight:** i.e., the midnight bell (with its iron clapper) **told:** counted out

381. **fairy time:** i.e., the time between midnight and dawn

382. **outsleep:** i.e., sleep past, oversleep

383. **overwatched:** i.e., stayed up so late

Lovers, make moan;
His eyes were green as leeks.
    O Sisters Three,
    Come, come to me
With hands as pale as milk.   355
    Lay them in gore,
    Since you have shore
With shears his thread of silk.
    Tongue, not a word!
    Come, trusty sword,   360
Come, blade, my breast imbrue!
                                ⌜*Thisbe stabs herself.*⌝
    And farewell, friends.
    Thus Thisbe ends.
    Adieu, adieu, adieu.   ⌜*Thisbe falls.*⌝
THESEUS Moonshine and Lion are left to bury the   365
    dead.
DEMETRIUS Ay, and Wall too.
                        ⌜*Bottom and Flute arise.*⌝
⌜BOTTOM⌝ No, I assure you, the wall is down that
    parted their fathers. Will it please you to see the
    Epilogue or to hear a Bergomask dance between   370
    two of our company?
THESEUS No epilogue, I pray you. For your play needs
    no excuse. Never excuse. For when the players are
    all dead, there need none to be blamed. Marry, if
    he that writ it had played Pyramus and hanged   375
    himself in Thisbe's garter, it would have been a fine
    tragedy; and so it is, truly, and very notably dis-
    charged. But, come, your Bergomask. Let your
    epilogue alone.
                    ⌜*Dance, and the players exit.*⌝
The iron tongue of midnight hath told twelve.   380
Lovers, to bed! 'Tis almost fairy time.
I fear we shall outsleep the coming morn
As much as we this night have overwatched.

384. **palpable-gross:** i.e., obviously dull

385. **heavy gait:** slow pace

386. **solemnity:** festive celebration

390. **heavy:** sleepy

391. **fordone:** exhausted

392. **wasted brands:** burned-up logs

394–95. **Puts . . . In remembrance of:** causes . . . to think

398. **his:** i.e., its

401. **triple Hecate:** The goddess Hecate had three forms (Luna, the moon, in the sky, Diana on earth, and Proserpina in the underworld).

404. **frolic:** frolicsome, merry

This palpable-gross play hath well beguiled
The heavy gait of night. Sweet friends, to bed.   385
A fortnight hold we this solemnity
In nightly revels and new jollity.   *They exit.*

        Enter ⌐Robin Goodfellow.⌐

ROBIN
        Now the hungry ⌐lion⌐ roars,
            And the wolf ⌐behowls⌐ the moon,
        Whilst the heavy plowman snores,   390
            All with weary task fordone.
        Now the wasted brands do glow,
            Whilst the screech-owl, screeching loud,
        Puts the wretch that lies in woe
            In remembrance of a shroud.   395
        Now it is the time of night
            That the graves, all gaping wide,
        Every one lets forth his sprite
            In the church-way paths to glide.
        And we fairies, that do run   400
            By the triple Hecate's team
        From the presence of the sun,
            Following darkness like a dream,
        Now are frolic. Not a mouse
        Shall disturb this hallowed house.   405
        I am sent with broom before,
        To sweep the dust behind the door.

Enter ⌐Oberon and Titania,⌐ King and Queen of Fairies,
                with all their train.

OBERON
        Through the house give glimmering light,
            By the dead and drowsy fire.
        Every elf and fairy sprite,   410
            Hop as light as bird from brier,
        And this ditty after me,
            Sing and dance it trippingly.

420. **will we:** i.e., Titania and I will go
422. **there create:** i.e., created there
426. **the blots of Nature's hand:** i.e., deformities
427. **in their issue stand:** appear in their offspring
429. **prodigious:** ominous; abnormal
432. **field-dew consecrate:** i.e., consecrated dew
434. **several:** separate, individual
440. **shadows:** illusions; actors
444. **idle:** trivial

TITANIA

> First rehearse your song by rote,
> To each word a warbling note. 415
> Hand in hand, with fairy grace,
> Will we sing and bless this place.
> ⌜*Oberon leads the Fairies in song and dance.*⌝

OBERON

> Now, until the break of day,
> Through this house each fairy stray.
> To the best bride-bed will we, 420
> Which by us shall blessèd be,
> And the issue there create
> Ever shall be fortunate.
> So shall all the couples three
> Ever true in loving be, 425
> And the blots of Nature's hand
> Shall not in their issue stand.
> Never mole, harelip, nor scar,
> Nor mark prodigious, such as are
> Despisèd in nativity, 430
> Shall upon their children be.
> With this field-dew consecrate
> Every fairy take his gait,
> And each several chamber bless,
> Through this palace, with sweet peace. 435
> And the owner of it blest,
> Ever shall in safety rest.
> Trip away. Make no stay.
> Meet me all by break of day.
> ⌜*All but Robin*⌝ *exit.*

ROBIN

> If we shadows have offended, 440
> Think but this and all is mended:
> That you have but slumbered here
> While these visions did appear.
> And this weak and idle theme,

445. **No . . . dream:** i.e., producing no more than a dream

447. **mend:** improve

450. **serpent's tongue:** i.e., hisses (from the audience)

454. **Give me your hands:** i.e., applaud

No more yielding but a dream,   445
Gentles, do not reprehend.
If you pardon, we will mend.
And, as I am an honest Puck,
If we have unearnèd luck
Now to 'scape the serpent's tongue,   450
We will make amends ere long.
Else the Puck a liar call.
So good night unto you all.
Give me your hands, if we be friends,
And Robin shall restore amends.   455

⌜*He exits.*⌝

Textual Notes

The reading of the present text appears to the left of the square bracket. The earliest sources of readings not in **Q1,** the quarto of 1600, upon which this edition is based, are indicated as follows: **Q2** is the quarto of 1619; **Qq** is "Q1 and Q2"; **F** is the Shakespeare First Folio of 1623, in which *A Midsummer Night's Dream* is a slightly edited reprint of Q2. **Ed.** is an earlier editor of Shakespeare, from the editor of the Second Folio of 1632 to the present. No sources are given for emendations of punctuation or for correction of obvious typographical errors, such as turned letters that produce no known word. **SD** means stage direction; **SP** means speech heading; ~ refers to a word already quoted; ⌃ indicates the omission of a punctuation mark.

1.1	4. wanes] Q2, F; waues Q1
	10. New] Ed.; Now Qq, F
	20. SD *Lysander and*] F; Lysander *and* Helena, *and* Qq
	25, 27. Stand forth, Demetrius . . . Stand forth, Lysander] Ed.; *set as stage directions in* Qq, F
	138. low] Ed.; loue Qq, F
	154. patience] patienee Q1
	190. Yours would] Ed.; Your words Qq, F
	195. I'd] Ed.; ile Qq, F
	221. sweet] Ed.; sweld Qq, F
	224. stranger companies] Ed.; strange companions Qq, F
	229. SD *1 line earlier in* Qq, F
1.2	1. SP QUINCE] *Qnin.* Q1
	26. rest.—Yet] ~ ⌃ ~ , Qq, F
	28–29. split: / *The*] Ed.; split the Qq, F

43. SP FLUTE] *Fla.* Q1

2.1   63   *and hereafter throughout Act 2.* SP TI-
TANIA] Ed.; *Qu.* Qq, F

63. Fairies] Ed.; Fairy Qq, F

71. steep] Q1 (steppe)

81. Perigouna] Ed.; *Perigenia* Qq, F

82. Aegles] Ed.; *Eagles* Qq, F

112. thin] Ed.; chinne Qq, F

158. certain] cettain Q1

160   *and hereafter in Act 2.* SP ROBIN] Ed.;
Puck. Qq, F

164. the] F; *omit* Q

190. off] Q (of)

201. thee] Q (the)

208. not, nor] F; not, not Qq

253. SD *Robin*] Ed.; *Pucke* Qq, F; SD *1 line
later in* Qq, F

2.2   9. SP FIRST FAIRY] Ed.; *omit* Qq, F

13, 24. SP CHORUS] Ed.; *omit* Qq, F

24–30. *Philomel . . . lullaby*] Ed.; *Philomele* with
melody, &c. Qq, F

44. comfort] comfor Q1

45. Be] Q2, F; Bet Q1

49. good] Q1 (god)

53. is] Q2, F; it Q1

71. SD *Robin*] Ed.; *Pucke* Qq, F

156. Methought] Me thoughr Q1

3.1   8. SP QUINCE] *Qnin.* Q1

50. SP SNOUT] Q1 (*Sn.*)

55. SP BOTTOM] Q2, F; *Cet.* Q1

73. your] yonr Q1

81, 83, 104. SP BOTTOM, *as Pyramus*] Ed.; *Pyra.* Qq, F

82. odors] F; odorous Qq

87. SP ROBIN.] F (*Puck*); *Quin.* Qq

88. SP FLUTE] Ed.; *Thys.* Qq, F

92. SP FLUTE, *as Thisbe*] Ed.; *Thys.* Qq, F

101. SP FLUTE] Ed.; *Thys.* Qq, F
103. SD *after line 113 in F "Enter Piramus with the Asse head"; omit* Q1
104. fair Thisbe] Ed.; *Thysby* Qq, F
106. SD *Quince ... exit.] omit* Qq; *The Clownes all Exit.* F
164. SD *Enter foure Fairyes.* Qq; *Enter Peaseblossome, Cobweb, Moth, Mustardseede, and foure Fairies.* F
165. SP PEASEBLOSSOM] Ed.; *Fairies.* Qq, F
166. SP COBWEB] Ed.; *omit* Qq, F
167. SP MOTE] Ed.; *omit* Qq, F
168. SP MUSTARDSEED] Ed.; *omit* Qq, F
169. SP ALL] Ed.; *omit* Qq, F
181. SP PEASEBLOSSOM] Ed.; *1. Fai.* Qq, F
182. SP COBWEB] Ed.; *omit* Qq, F
183. SP MOTE] Ed.; *2. Fai.* Qq, F
184. SP MUSTARDSEED] Ed.; *3.Fai.* Qq, F
202. of] Ed.; *omit* Qq, F

3.2
0. SD *Enter ... Fairies.*] F (*adding "solus"*); Qq (*adding "and* Robin goodfellow."*)
3. SD *Enter ... Goodfellow.*] F (*Enter Pucke.*); *omit* Qq
6. SP ROBIN] Ed.; *Puck* Qq, F
6–7. love. . . . bower,] ~, . . . ~. Q1; ~, . . . ~, Q2, F
19. mimic] F; Minnick Q1; Minnock Q2
54. From] Frow Q1
82. so] Ed.; *omit* Qq, F
86. grow] ~. Q1
87. sleep] Ed.; slippe Qq, F
111. SD *Robin*] Puck Qq, F
112. *and hereafter until line 418.* SP ROBIN] Puck Qq, F
140. *waking up*] F (*Awa.*) *after* 1. 139; *omit* Qq

162. derision! None] Ed.; ~ ˌ ~ Q1; ~,~ Q2,
     ~;~ F
218. first, like] Ed.; first life Qq, F
244. sweet] sweeete Q1
257. prayers] Ed.; praise Qq, F
270. off] Q1 (of)
293. Therefore] Thefore Q1
314. gentlemen] Q2, F; gentleman Q1
343. but] Q2, F; hut Q1
365. SD *She exits.*] *Exeunt.* Qq; *omit* F
369. should] shoud Q1
416. notwithstanding] notwiststanding Q1
430. Speak!] Ed.; ~ ˌ Qq, F
454. shalt] shat Q1
470. SD *1 line earlier in* F
480. To] Ed.; *omit* Qq, F

4.1   0. SD *Bottom*] Ed.; *Clowne* Qq, F. *At the
        end of Act 3* F *reads* "They sleepe all the
        Act."
     5 *and throughout scene.* SP BOTTOM] Ed.;
        Clown. Qq, F
    30. F *prints* SD "Musicke Tongs, Rurall Mu-
        sicke."
    42. all ways] Q1 (alwaies)
    74. o'er] Q1 (or)
    84. sleep ˌ . . . these five] Ed.; sleepe: . . .
        these, fine Qq, F
    85. F *prints* SD "Musick still."
   105. F *prints* SD "Sleepers Lye still."
   106. SD *Oberon . . . Egeus.*] *Exeunt. Enter
        Theseus and all his traine. Winde
        horne.* Qq; *Exeunt. Winde Hornes. En-
        ter Theseus, Egeus, Hippolita and all
        his traine.* F
   121. Seemed] Ed.; Seeme Qq, F
   133. is] Q2, F; *omit* Q1
   138. rite] Q1 (right)

143. SD *Shout . . . up.*] *Shoute within: they all start vp. Winde hornes.* Qq; *Hornes and they wake. Shout within, they all start vp.* F
179. saw] Ed.; *see* Qq, F
193. SD *Theseus . . . exit.*] *Exit Duke and Lords.* F
199. found] Q1 (fonnd)
209. let us] Q2, F; *lets* Q1
210. SD *waking up*] F (*"Bottome wakes." after line 209*)
217. to] Q2, F; *omit* Q1
219. a patched] F; *patcht a* Qq

4.2

0. SD *Enter . . . Starveling.*] *Enter Quince, Flute, Thisby and the rabble.* Qq; *Enter Quince, Flute, Thisbie, Snout, and Starueling.* F
3. SP STARVELING] F; *Flut.* Qq
5 *and throughout scene.* SP FLUTE] Ed.; *Thys*[be] Qq, F

5.1

0. SD *Enter . . . Attendants.*] Q1; *Enter Theseus, Hippolita, Egeus and his Lords.* F
37. our] F; *Or* Qq
113. SP THESEUS] Ed.; *Duk.* Qq, F
113. SD F *begins with "Flor. Trum."*
133. SD F *begins with "Tawyer with a Trumpet before them."*
133. SD *Prologue (Quince)*] F *at 113 SD has "Prologue. Quince."*
134. SP QUINCE, *as Prologue*] Ed.; *Prologue* Qq, F
137. Thisbe] *Thsby* Q1
150. scare] Ed.; *scarre* Qq, F
163. SD *Lion . . . exit.*] Qq; *Exit all but Wall.* F, *3 lines earlier*
164 *and hereafter.* SP SNOUT, *as Wall*] Ed.; *Wall.* Qq, F

165. Snout] F; *Flute* Qq
178. F *prints "Enter Pyramus."*
179 *and hereafter.* SP BOTTOM, *as Pyramus*
     Py. Qq, F
196. SP BOTTOM] Ed.; *Pyr.* Qq, F
200 *and hereafter.* SP FLUTE, *as Thisbe*] Ed.;
     This. Qq, F
203. hair] hayire Q1
203. up in thee] F; now againe Qq
218. SD *He exits.*] Exit Clow. F
219 *and hereafter.* SP THESEUS] Ed.; *Duk.* Qq
     F
219. wall down] Ed.; morall downe F; Moo:
     vsed Qq
223 *and hereafter.* SP HIPPOLYTA] Ed.; *Dutch*
     Qq, F
231. beasts. in,] ~, ~. Qq, F
232 *and hereafter.* SP SNUG, *as Lion*] Ed.; *Lyon*
     Qq, F
253 *and hereafter.* SP STARVELING, *as Moon*
     shine] Ed.; *Moone.* Qq, F
278, 345. tomb] Q1 (tumbe)
279. SD *The . . . off*] F; *omit* Q1
284. SD *2 lines later in Q1*
289. gleams] Ed.; beames Qq, F
329-30. before. Thisbe] ~? ~ Qq, F
331. SD *1 line earlier in F*
337. warrant] Q1 (warnd)
368. SP BOTTOM] F; *Lyon* Qq
387. SD *Robin Goodfellow*] Ed.; Pucke Qq, F
388. SP ROBIN] Ed.; *Puck* Qq, F
388. lion] Ed.; Lyons Qq, F
389. behowls] Ed.; beholds Qq, F
418. SP OBERON] Qq; *The Song.* F
436-37. *lines transposed in Qq, F*
439. SD *All . . . exit.*] Ed.; *Exeunt.* Qq; *omit* F

A Midsummer Night's Dream:
A Modern Perspective

Catherine Belsey

When Bottom wakes up, near the end of *A Midsummer Night's Dream,* after spending a night of love with the queen of the fairies, this formerly masterful and garrulous figure is suddenly very nearly inarticulate. What could he say that would do justice to the experience? "I have had a most rare vision. I have had a dream past the wit of man to say what dream it was. Man is but an ass if he go about to expound this dream" (4.1.214–17). Bottom's name, and his transformation—an event that clarifies more than it changes his identity—invite the audience to associate him with the least poetic aspects of life, and yet, even as an ass, Bottom has been touched by something special but mysterious, a power that he finds unusually hard to define. In quest of a way of talking about what has happened to him, Bottom reaches for the language of the Bible, St. Paul's account of the future glory that God has prepared for human beings (1 Corinthians 2.9), though of course, being Bottom, he gets it wrong: "The eye of man hath not heard, the ear of man hath not seen, man's hand is not able to taste, his tongue to conceive, nor his heart to report what my dream was" (4.1.220–24). In the end he concludes that the solution is for Peter Quince to write a ballad of his dream. Evidently only the lyricism of popular poetry seems to Bottom adequate to define the experience of love.

We do not have Peter Quince's ballad, but—if we assume that Quince wrote "Pyramus and Thisbe," in which Bottom plays the romantic hero—we do have his play, and we also have Shakespeare's play, which is its

181

setting. *A Midsummer Night's Dream* is a play about love. It proposes that love is a dream, or perhaps a vision; that it is absurd, irrational, a delusion, or, perhaps, on the other hand, a transfiguration; that it is doomed to be momentary ("So quick bright things come to confusion" [1.1.151]), and that it constitutes at the same time the proper foundation for lifelong marriage. Possibly Bottom is right, the play suggests, not to pin down anything so multiple, not to encapsulate love in a neat definition that would encourage us to measure our own and other people's experience and find it normal or abnormal, mature or immature, wise or foolish. The play's device, on the contrary, is to dramatize the plurality of love by characterizing it differently in a range of distinct voices.

As soon as Hermia and Lysander are left alone together on the stage for the first time, they discuss their predicament in a series of elegant and elaborate exchanges:

LYSANDER
  How now, my love? Why is your cheek so pale?
  How chance the roses there do fade so fast?
HERMIA
  Belike for want of rain, which I could well
  Beteem them from the tempest of mine eyes.
                    (1.1.130–33)

Since the lovers and the audience have both heard Theseus tell Hermia that she must die or go into a convent if she refuses to marry another man, it is hardly necessary for Lysander to ask why she is pale, or for her to tell him that she thinks she might be going to cry. But the poetic image of the roses in her cheeks legitimates the conceit that follows: the roses are short of water, which Hermia is about to supply. The exchange has the effect of distancing the threat to Hermia, and putting before the audience instead what is delicate, lyrical, and witty in romance. Lysander's next utterance explains the way all four lovers tend to talk to each other:

> Ay me! For aught that I could ever read,
> Could ever hear by tale or history . . .
> > (1.1.134–35)

How else, after all, do people learn to talk about love in the first instance, except by reading love stories? No wonder the four lovers are virtually indistinguishable. Romantic love is in this sense oddly impersonal. Because of love's power to idealize, the object of desire seems unique, even though in the event it turns out that Hermia and Helena are interchangeable. But the ways of idealizing, of investing the other person with the special beauty or magnetism that justifies desire, are drawn in the first place from the culture in which people learn about love.

Meanwhile Theseus, we are to understand, in contrast to the young lovers, has been around. The stories of his many loves and betrayals would have been well known, at least to those members of the audience who had been to school, and Oberon alludes to them in the course of his quarrel with Titania (2.1.81–83). Theseus himself talks quite differently about love:

> Now, fair Hippolyta, our nuptial hour
> Draws on apace. Four happy days bring in
> Another moon. But, O, methinks how slow
> This old moon wanes! She lingers my desires
> Like to a stepdame or a dowager
> Long withering out a young man's revenue.
> > (1.1.1–6)

Theseus acknowledges that he has desires, and they are urgent and imperative. He is impatient with the moon, that conventional poetic symbol of romance, and the comparison he invokes is anything but lyrical. The moon that is delaying his marriage is like an old woman who refuses to die and so prevents her young heir from getting his hands on his inheritance. Paradoxically, the love that is voiced by Theseus seems more insistent to the degree that it is more prosaic, literally more like prose, since the speech rhythms do not coincide with the line endings, but run directly across them. The Amazon Hippolyta, whose comments so often counterpoint those of Theseus, immediately supplies the missing romance by reinvesting with its customary lyricism "the moon, like to a silver bow / New-bent in heaven" (1.1.9–10).[1]

The young lovers perfectly reproduce the conventional idealizing imagery of the period:

> O Helen, goddess, nymph, perfect, divine!
> To what, my love, shall I compare thine eyne?
> Crystal is muddy. O, how ripe in show
> Thy lips, those kissing cherries, tempting grow!
> That pure congealèd white, high Taurus' snow,
> Fanned with the eastern wind, turns to a crow
> When thou hold'st up thy hand.
>
> (3.2.140–46)

Eyes like crystals, lips like cherries, hands white as snow—this is engaging to the degree that it is lyrical. It is also delightfully absurd, when we bear in mind that it is the instant effect of Robin Goodfellow's love-juice, and represents a vision of Helena that Demetrius was quite unable to see before his sight was bewitched. But as Helena herself explains earlier in the play, love does not necessarily see what is there:

> Things base and vile, holding no quantity,
> Love can transpose to form and dignity.
> Love looks not with the eyes but with the mind;
> And therefore is winged Cupid painted blind.
>   (1.1.238–41)

Helena's words might equally constitute a commentary on Titania's first response to Bottom braying in his ass's head: "What angel wakes me from my flow'ry bed?" (3.1.131). The fairy queen's temporary devotion to a donkey is the play's clearest and funniest indication of love's arbitrary nature.

One reason why the lovers seem comic is that their changes of preference do not appear arbitrary to them. As Lysander solemnly explains to his new love, Helena, "The will of man is by his reason swayed, / And reason says you are the worthier maid" (2.2.122–23). The element of absurdity is compounded when we recognize (though they do not) a parody of their idealizing vision in Thisbe's lament for the dead Pyramus:

> These lily lips,
> This cherry nose,
> These yellow cowslip cheeks
> Are gone, are gone!
> Lovers, make moan;
> His eyes were green as leeks.
>   (5.1.347–52)

The king and queen of the fairies are old (or, rather, ageless) married lovers, and they are quarreling. The play does not ignore the trace of violence that exists within love when the other person fails to conform to the lover's idealized image. The quarrel between Oberon and Titania has upset the proper sequence of the seasons, which is a serious problem in a society based on agriculture, though it is hard for the audience to feel great anxiety about this when the fairies quarrel so musically:

> These are the forgeries of jealousy;
> And never, since the middle summer's spring,
> Met we on hill, in dale, forest, or mead,
> By pavèd fountain or by rushy brook,
> Or in the beachèd margent of the sea,
> To dance our ringlets to the whistling wind,
> But with thy brawls thou hast disturbed our sport.
>   (2.1.84–90)

The brawls are not mentioned until the verse has quite distracted us from the substance of the quarrel through its evocation of imaginary landscapes, so lacking in specific detail that they seem the settings of half-remembered legends and tales of adventure. No wonder Oberon and Titania are finally reconciled. In a similar way, lyricism and comedy distance the passionate quarrels between Demetrius and Lysander, Hermia and Helena. Conversely, if the play of "Pyramus and Thisbe" evokes tears of laughter rather than sorrow (5.1.73–74), it alludes, nevertheless, to the tragic possibilities of a conflict between love and parental opposition. *A Midsummer Night's Dream* does not let its audience forget that love entails confusion and danger as well as grace, although it never entirely separates these contraries.

None of the distinct voices in the play—romantic, lyrical, or urgent—seems to exhaust the character of love; none of them can be identified with "true" love as opposed to false. Nor does any of them summarize the nature of love; and when Theseus tries to do so, what he says seems quite inadequate. "I never may believe," he insists, "These antique fables, nor these fairy toys" (5.1.2–3). "Antique" implies both "ancient" and "antic" (theatrical), and ironically Theseus himself is both. He is a fictional hero of classical legend and a figure on a stage in the most theatrical of plays. As for the fairy stories he repudiates, we have seen them enacted in the course of the play, and we are therefore in no position to share his entirely rational dismissal of lovers, along with lunatics and poets (5.1.7). Hippolyta seems more to the point when she answers him, but she is considerably less than specific. The separate stories of the night, she affirms, grow "to something of great constancy [consistency], / But, howsoever, strange and admirable [eliciting wonder]" (5.1.27–28). In talking about love, as perhaps in love itself, there is commonly a sense of a quality that cannot be made present, cannot be presented, or represented. In the most exhaustive analysis, the most effusive declaration, or the most lyrical poem, something slips away, and it is that elusiveness that sustains desire itself, as well as the desire to talk about it.

And this, perhaps, is a clue to the nature of the pleasure *A Midsummer Night's Dream* offers its audience. It constructs for the spectators something of the desire it also puts on display. In one sense comedy produces the wishes it then goes on to fulfill. The play invites us to sympathize with the young lovers. In consequence, we want Hermia to marry the man she loves, in spite of the opposition of her ridiculous father, who supposes that serenades and love tokens are forms of witchcraft. And we want Helena to be happy with Demetrius in spite of his initial rejection of her love. The enigma that enlists the desire of the audience centers on whether the play will bring about the happy ending we hope for, and if so, how. The pleasure of this dramatic form is familiar from Roman comedy to Neil Simon, and its familiarity is precisely part of the enjoyment we are invited to experience.

But *A Midsummer Night's Dream* does not always do

exactly what we might expect, and in this way it keeps its audience guessing, continually reoffering itself in the process as an object of our desire. The play begins with the longing of Theseus and Hippolyta to consummate their love, and the action that follows occupies the intervening space, so that at the end of Act 5 the newly married lovers go off to bed together. Desire constitutes the frame of the play itself. In the meantime, Theseus dispatches the master of the revels, who is responsible for entertainment at court, in search of "merriments" and "reveling" (1.1.13, 20), and at once an old man comes in with his daughter and her two rival suitors. Egeus is appropriately stagy ("Stand forth, Demetrius . . . Stand forth, Lysander" [1.1.25, 27]), and the audience might be expected to recognize the pattern of Roman comedy, familiar from the plays of Plautus and Terence and widely imitated in Elizabethan drama. The conventional poetry and the extravagance of the lovers intensifies the sense that we are watching the first of the revels that Theseus has sent for, a play within a play.

But Roman comedy does not characteristically include fairies, and it is the mischief-making Robin Goodfellow, a supernatural figure from English folklore, who largely motivates the plot of this inset play. The genres are mixed, with the effect that the audience is never quite sure whether the conventions in operation at any specific moment are those of comedy or folktale. At the same time, Robin Goodfellow (Puck) both is and is not a native English replica of the blind, irrational, overhasty, and Continental Cupid that Helena describes. The play teases the audience with glimpses of familiar forms and figures, and then deflects our attention onto something unexpected. In consequence, the delight it invites the spectators to experience is entirely distinct from the comfortable feeling of recognition other plays rely on.

The plot leads up to the marriages of the lovers, but it does not quite confirm the distinction we might expect it to identify between true love on the one hand and arbitrary passion induced by magic on the other. Demetrius still has the love-juice on his eyes, and yet the play gives no indication of a difference between this marriage and the others. If marriage is a serious social institution, it seems to rest on a remarkably precarious base. But the imperatives of fiction require that the comedy of love end in marriage, and Demetrius marries the partner he has when the action comes to a stop.

If the story leads up to marriage, however, it does not quite end there. Many critical accounts of the play depend on an opposition between its two locations, the house of Theseus in Athens and the wildwood under the control of the fairies. The Athenian court represents the world of reconciliation and rationality, of social institutions and communal order, while the wood outside Athens is the location of night and bewildering passions, a place of anarchy and anxiety, where behavior becomes unpredictable and individual identity is transformed. On this reading, the fairies, who are by no means the sugary creatures of Victorian fantasy, represent the quintessence of all that is turbulent and uncontrolled in human experience, and in particular the traces of instability and violence that inhabit desire.

At the end of the play, however, when the couples, now properly distributed and legitimately married, have gone to bed, the fairies come in from the wood and take possession of the palace: "Through the house give glimmering light, / By the dead and drowsy fire . . ." (5.1.408–9). Though their purpose, we are to understand, is benevolent, they also bring with them the uncanny resonances of the dreamworld that seemed to have been left behind in the wood:

> . . . we fairies, that do run
>   By the triple Hecate's team
> From the presence of the sun,
>   Following darkness like a dream
> Now are frolic.
>
>   (5.1.400–4)

Hecate is the queen of the night, and the team the fairies run with are the dragons who draw her chariot. Their unexpected presence within the house, therefore, implies the invasion of elements of the turbulent, the magical, and the unearthly into the social and domestic proprieties of marriage.

How could it be otherwise? This is, after all, a wedding night. But by handing over the conclusion to the fairies, the play displaces the apparent closure, the celebration of restored identity and the return to community it has duly delivered. Instead, it goes on to re-create what is most mysterious and elusive in the world it has portrayed, and gives the stage back to the representatives of all that is unaccountable and still unrecounted in the experience of love. In this way *A Midsummer Night's Dream* offers to leave its audience in a state of mind that bears some resemblance to Bottom's when he wakes up from *his* dream: exalted, perhaps, but a little less assured, less confident, and altogether less knowing than before.

---

1. It is possible, of course, that the new-bent bow is not merely lyrical. As an Amazon, Hippolyta would have carried a bow as a weapon against Theseus and his army. See James Calderwood's *"A Midsummer Night's Dream:* Anamorphism and Theseus' Dream," *Shakespeare Quarterly* 42 (1991): 409–30, esp. p. 413, for a discussion of Elizabethan attitudes toward Amazons.

Further Reading

A Midsummer Night's Dream

Barber, C. L. "May Games and Metamorphoses on a Midsummer Night." In *Shakespeare's Festive Comedy*, pp. 119–62. Princeton: Princeton University Press, 1959.

Barber proposes that Shakespeare's *Dream* involves a "complex fusion of pageantry and popular games." Mixed with the kind of pageantry usually presented at aristocratic weddings are the more popular rituals of May Day—a combination Shakespeare exploits to fashion the town-grove-town movement the play follows. By structuring the play around oppositions—everyday/holiday, town/grove, day/night—Shakespeare confidently separates "shadow" from "substance" and provides an environment of "unshadowed gaiety."

Barkan, Leonard. "Ovid Translated." In *The Gods Made Flesh: Metamorphosis and the Pursuit of Paganism*, pp. 251–70. New Haven: Yale University Press, 1986.

Focusing on Theseus's fifth-act dismissal of the lovers' stories as "antique fables," Barkan explores *Dream*'s self-conscious awareness of the classical myths that inspire much of *Dream*'s action. Specifically, Barkan examines Shakespeare's "translation" of Ovid's *Metamorphoses* into his own "mythic language." Barkan concludes that Shakespeare views antiquity through the eyes of Ovid and therefore constructs an Athens where "gods, mortals and heroes live in democratic proximity, intermingling via the perils and delights of love."

Bristol, Michael. "Wedding Feast and Charivari." In *Carnival and Theater: Plebeian Culture and the Structure*

191

of Authority in Renaissance England, pp. 162–78. New York and London: Methuen, 1985.

In Elizabethan England, marriage was a largely public matter, with questions of preference and personal desire open to public scrutiny. Bristol therefore reads "Pyramus and Thisby" as an inadvertent social critique of the wedding of Theseus and Hippolyta, in that the farce's admonitory effects do not depend on the unwitting company's knowledge. The burlesque counterfestivity of the drama—which invokes a complex fusion of festive customs—reveals the insubstantiality of social identity by ridiculing the desires and behaviors of the drama's upper-class audience.

Calderwood, James L. *"A Midsummer Night's Dream:* Anamorphism and Theseus' Dream." *Shakespeare Quarterly* 42 (1991): 409–30.

Calderwood explores the broader implications of doubling in *Dream,* i.e., assigning to a single actor the parts of both Titania and Hippolyta and assigning to another the parts of both Theseus and Oberon, a widespread practice in recent productions. With wonderfully comic results, Calderwood speculates that the scenes in the woods may be read as "Theseus' dream," in which the anxieties and desires that he feels on the occasion of his imminent wedding to the Amazon Hippolyta are played out with Theseus and Hippolyta as the Fairy King and Queen.

Girard, René. "Myth and Ritual in Shakespeare: *A Midsummer Night's Dream.*" In *Textual Strategies: Perspectives in Post-Structuralist Criticism,* ed. Josué V. Harari, pp. 29–45. Ithaca, N.Y.: Cornell University Press, 1979.

Girard disentangles the relationship(s) among the four young lovers, finding the only constant to be the convergence of more than one desire on a single object, as if rivalry were more important than love. Girard determines that the driving desire is the absolute seductive dominance that each character in turn appears to embody in the eyes of the others. Their frantic attempt to "translate" themselves into the figure that, for the moment, possesses this sexual quality ultimately causes their differences to disintegrate and their identities to collapse.

Greer, Germaine. "Love and the Law." In *Politics, Power, and Shakespeare*, ed. Frances McNeely Leonard, pp. 29–45. Arlington, Texas: Texas Humanities Research Center, 1981.
   Greer sets out the underlying conundrum of *Dream:* how to "civilize love," which is by nature "anarchic." Love and law meet, Greer writes, in marriage, and she therefore explores the unreliability of sexual passion as a basis for a lasting marriage as it is manifested in *Dream*. Rather than concluding with a "starry-eyed statement about living happily ever after," Shakespeare provides a pragmatic answer to *Dream*'s riddle in his appeal to "simple human dignity," in the persons of the mechanicals, and the responsibility of child rearing, as expressed in the play's marriage poem.

Leggatt, Alexander. *"A Midsummer Night's Dream."* In *Shakespeare's Comedy of Love*, pp. 89–115. London: Methuen, 1974.
   Leggatt reads the play as a constant process of exorcism as each possible threat to the comic world is driven away. The slender separation between the comic world of the play and the darker world of "passion, terror and chaos" is maintained by the audience's empathy for the seemingly "trivial" concerns of the lovers. By taking the illusions of art and love as reality, the audience plays a vital part in *Dream*'s total harmony.

Marcus, Leah. *The Politics of Mirth: Jonson, Herrick, Milton, Marvell, and the Defense of Old Holiday Pastimes*. Chicago: University of Chicago Press, 1986.

Marcus traces the political struggle over the traditional pastimes of May Day and morris dances (both mentioned in *Dream*) that took place among Shakespeare's contemporaries and successors. She places the festive rituals associated with seasonal holidays within the context of royal support for festive observances and specific literary practice. The literature of festival, according to Marcus, attempted to meld art and life and hence destroy its perceived separateness.

Miller, Ronald F. *"A Midsummer Night's Dream:* The Fairies, Bottom, and the Mystery of Things." *Shakespeare Quarterly* 26 (1975): 254–68.

Dream, for Miller, is a study of the nature and validity of the imagination. The indefiniteness of the fairies themselves calls into question the nature of love in *Dream*, for if the fairies, who in Theseus's analysis are the bringers of joy, are delusions, love is a delusion. Ultimately, however, Bottom's speech upon waking from his transformation—which echoes St. Paul's paradox that faith is both folly and the highest wisdom—establishes the fairies' ambiguous existence within the framework of a play that simultaneously encourages credulity and skepticism.

Mowat, Barbara. "'A local habitation and a name': Shakespeare's Text as Construct," *Style* 23 (1989): 335–51.

Mowat examines Shakespeare's construction of Theseus as an example of the construction of Shakespearean dramatic character in general. She finds that rather than being a unitary character "created in a flash of poetic frenzy," Theseus is "woven from texts [of Ovid, Chaucer, and Reginald Scot] not only various but rhetorically and ideologically at odds." His speeches are constructed "within a massive field" of printed discourse, including texts "expressing both sides of a contemporary (and heated) debate" on the imagination and witchcraft.

Nashe, Thomas. *Summer's Last Will and Testament* (1592). In *Thomas Nashe*, ed. Stanley Wells, pp. 91–143. Stratford-upon-Avon Library. London: Edward Arnold, 1964.
    Nashe's allegorical play on the theme of summer represents a dramatic style from the early 1590s. In his influential study of Shakespearean comedy, C. L. Barber reads Nashe's drama as analogous to Shakespeare's *Dream*.

Ovid. *The Metamorphoses* (1567). Translated by Arthur Golding. London: Centaur Press, 1961.
    Among the direct sources of Shakespeare's works, after North's *Plutarch* and Holinshed's *Chronicles*, probably the most influential was Ovid. In Shakespeare's *Dream* in particular, Ovid's *Metamorphoses* is evident both in the transformation of Bottom and in the play-within-the-play "Pyramus and Thisby." Shakespeare seems to have known Ovid's work in the original Latin and in Arthur Golding's 1567 translation.

Riemer, A. P. *Antic Fables: Patterns of Evasion in Shakespeare's Comedies.* Manchester: Manchester University Press, 1980.
    Riemer maintains that modern critical efforts to bring Shakespeare's comedies into line with the dominant tradition of European comedy misunderstands their essential nature. Shakespeare's comic ends, dismissed frequently as too cavalier to be sincere, are for Riemer an assertion that art exists "for the sake of its own conceit [i.e., conception of itself]," and not to castigate folly or correct the manners of the age.

Slights, William W. E. "The Changeling in *A Dream*." *Studies in English Literature* 28 (1988): 259–72.

The disputed changeling boy at the center of Oberon and Titania's custody battle illustrates, for Slights, a principle of indeterminacy evident in many parts of the play. Indeterminacy—that is, contending and conflicted meanings—is the essential condition of people in love, Slight argues. As a figure of indeterminacy, the changeling boy skirts the boundaries between human and other worlds and propels the play into the "uncharted territory on the fringes or 'margins' of society" where rules of power collapse, leading to liberating and amusing results.

Shakespeare's Language

Abbott, E. A. *A Shakespearian Grammar*. New York: Haskell House, 1972.

This compact reference book, first published in 1870, helps with many difficulties in Shakespeare's language. It systematically accounts for a host of differences between Shakespeare's usage and sentence structure and our own.

Blake, Norman. *Shakespeare's Language: An Introduction*. New York: St. Martin's Press, 1983.

This general introduction to Elizabethan English discusses various aspects of the language of Shakespeare and his contemporaries, offering possible meanings for hundreds of ambiguous constructions.

Dobson, E. J. *English Pronunciation, 1500–1700*. 2 vols. Oxford: Clarendon Press, 1968.

This long and technical work includes chapters on spelling (and its reformation), phonetics, stressed vowels, and consonants in early modern English.

Houston, John. *Shakespearean Sentences: A Study in Style and Syntax*. Baton Rouge: Louisiana State University Press, 1988.

Houston studies Shakespeare's stylistic choices, considering matters such as sentence length and the relative positions of subject, verb, and direct object. Examining plays throughout the canon in a roughly chronological, developmental order, he analyzes how sentence structure is used in setting tone, in characterization, and for other dramatic purposes.

Onions, C. T. *A Shakespeare Glossary*. Oxford: Clarendon Press, 1986.
This revised edition updates Onions's standard, selective glossary of words and phrases in Shakespeare's plays that are now obsolete, archaic, or obscure.

Partridge, Eric. *Shakespeare's Bawdy*. London: Routledge & Kegan Paul, 1955.
After an introductory essay, "The Sexual, the Homosexual, and Non-Sexual Bawdy in Shakespeare," Partridge provides a comprehensive glossary of "bawdy" phrases and words from the plays.

Robinson, Randal. *Unlocking Shakespeare's Language: Help for the Teacher and Student*. Urbana, Ill.: National Council of Teachers of English and the ERIC Clearinghouse on Reading and Communication Skills, 1989.
Specifically designed for the high-school and undergraduate college teacher and student, Robinson's book addresses the problems that most often hinder present-day readers of Shakespeare. Through work with his own students, Robinson found that many readers today are particularly puzzled by such stylistic characteristics as subject-verb inversion, interrupted structures, and compression. He shows how our own colloquial language contains comparable structures, and thus helps students recognize such structures when they find them in Shakespeare's plays. This book supplies worksheets—with examples from major plays—to illu-

minate and remedy such problems as unusual sequences of words and the separation of related parts of sentences.

Shakespeare's Life

Baldwin, T. W. *William Shakspere's Petty School*. Urbana: University of Illinois Press, 1943.

Baldwin here investigates the theory and practice of the petty school, the first level of education in Elizabethan England. He focuses on that educational system primarily as it is reflected in Shakespeare's art.

Baldwin, T. W. *William Shakspere's Small Latine and Lesse Greeke*. 2 vols. Urbana: University of Illinois Press, 1944.

Baldwin attacks the view that Shakespeare was an uneducated genius—a view that had been dominant among Shakespeareans since the eighteenth century. Instead, Baldwin shows, the educational system of Shakespeare's time would have given the playwright a strong background in the classics, and there is much in the plays that shows how Shakespeare benefited from such an education.

Beier, A. L., and Roger Finlay, eds. *London 1500–1800: The Making of the Metropolis*. New York: Longman, 1986.

Focusing on the economic and social history of early modern London, these collected essays probe aspects of metropolitan life, including "Population and Disease," "Commerce and Manufacture," and "Society and Change."

Bentley, G. E. *Shakespeare's Life: A Biographical Handbook*. New Haven: Yale University Press, 1961.

This "just-the-facts" account presents the surviving documents of Shakespeare's life against an Elizabethan background.

Chambers, E. K. *William Shakespeare: A Study of Facts and Problems*. 2 vols. Oxford: Clarendon Press, 1930.
Analyzing in great detail the scant historical data, Chambers's complex, scholarly study considers the nature of the texts in which Shakespeare's work is preserved.

Cressy, David. *Education in Tudor and Stuart England*. London: Edward Arnold, 1975.
This volume collects sixteenth-, seventeenth-, and early-eighteenth-century documents detailing aspects of formal education in England, such as the curriculum, the control and organization of education, and the education of women.

Dutton, Richard. *William Shakespeare: A Literary Life*. New York: St. Martin's Press, 1989.
Not a biography in the traditional sense, Dutton's very readable work nevertheless "follows the contours of Shakespeare's life" as he examines Shakespeare's career as playwright and poet, with consideration of his patrons, theatrical associations, and audience.

Fraser, Russell. *Young Shakespeare*. New York: Columbia University Press, 1988.
Fraser focuses on Shakespeare's first thirty years, paying attention simultaneously to his life and art.

De Grazia, Margreta. *Shakespeare Verbatim: The Reproduction of Authenticity and the Apparatus of 1790*. Oxford: Clarendon Press, 1991.
De Grazia traces and discusses the development of

such editorial criteria as authenticity, historical periodization, factual biography, chronological developments, and close reading, locating as the point of origin Edmond Malone's 1790 edition of Shakespeare's works. There are interesting chapters on the First Folio and on the "legendary" versus the "documented" Shakespeare.

Schoenbaum, S. *William Shakespeare: A Compact Documentary Life*. New York: Oxford University Press, 1977.
This standard biography economically presents the essential documents from Shakespeare's time in an accessible narrative account of the playwright's life.

Shakespeare's Theater

Bentley, G. E. *The Profession of Player in Shakespeare's Time, 1590–1642*. Princeton: Princeton University Press, 1984.
Bentley readably sets forth a wealth of evidence about performance in Shakespeare's time, with special attention to the relations between player and company, and the business of casting, managing, and touring.

Berry, Herbert. *Shakespeare's Playhouses*. New York: AMS Press, 1987.
Berry's six essays collected here discuss (with illustrations) varying aspects of the four playhouses in which Shakespeare had a financial stake: the Theatre in Shoreditch, the Blackfriars, and the first and second Globe.

Cook, Ann Jennalie. *The Privileged Playgoers of Shakespeare's London*. Princeton: Princeton University Press, 1981.

Cook's work argues, on the basis of sociological, economic, and documentary evidence, that Shakespeare's audience—and the audience for English Renaissance drama generally—consisted mainly of the "privileged."

Greg, W. W. *Dramatic Documents from the Elizabethan Playhouses*. 2 vols. Oxford: Clarendon Press, 1931.
Greg itemizes and briefly describes almost all the play manuscripts that survive from the period 1590 to around 1660, including, among other things, players' parts. His second volume offers facsimiles of selected manuscripts.

Gurr, Andrew. *Playgoing in Shakespeare's London*. Cambridge: Cambridge University Press, 1987.
Gurr charts how the theatrical enterprise developed from its modest beginnings in the late 1560s to become a thriving institution in the 1600s. He argues that there were important changes over the period 1567–1644 in the playhouses, the audience, and the plays.

Harbage, Alfred. *Shakespeare's Audience*. New York: Columbia University Press, 1941.
Harbage investigates the fragmentary surviving evidence to interpret the size, composition, and behavior of Shakespeare's audience.

Hattaway, Michael. *Elizabethan Popular Theatre: Plays in Performance*. London: Routledge & Kegan Paul, 1982.
Beginning with a study of the popular drama of the late Elizabethan age—a description of the stages, performance conditions, and acting of the period—this volume concludes with an analysis of five well-known plays of the 1590s, one of them (*Titus Andronicus*) by Shakespeare.

Shapiro, Michael. *Children of the Revels: The Boy Companies of Shakespeare's Time and Their Plays*. New York: Columbia University Press, 1977.

Shapiro chronicles the history of the amateur and quasi-professional child companies that flourished in London at the end of Elizabeth's reign and the beginning of James's.

The Publication of Shakespeare's Plays

Blayney, Peter. *The First Folio of Shakespeare*. Hanover, Md.: Folger, 1991.

Blayney's accessible account of the printing and later life of the First Folio—an amply illustrated catalogue to a 1991 Folger Shakespeare Library exhibition—analyzes the mechanical production of the First Folio, describing how the Folio was made, by whom and for whom, how much it cost, and its ups and downs (or, rather, downs and ups) since its printing in 1623.

Hinman, Charlton. *The Printing and Proof-Reading of the First Folio of Shakespeare*. 2 vols. Oxford: Clarendon Press, 1963.

In the most arduous study of a single book ever undertaken, Hinman attempts to reconstruct how the Shakespeare First Folio of 1623 was set into type and run off the press, sheet by sheet. He also provides almost all the known variations in readings from copy to copy.

Hinman, Charlton. *The Norton Facsimile: The First Folio of Shakespeare*. New York: W. W. Norton, 1968.

This facsimile presents a photographic reproduction of an "ideal" copy of the First Folio of Shakespeare; Hinman attempts to represent each page in its most fully corrected state.

Key To
Famous Lines and Phrases

The course of true love never did run smooth.
[Lysander—1.1.136]

Over hill, over dale . . .   [Fairy—2.1.2 ff.]

Ill met by moonlight, proud Titania. [Oberon—2.1.62]

. . . a fair vestal thronèd by the west
[Oberon—2.1.164]

In maiden meditation, fancy-free   [Oberon—2.1.170]

I'll put a girdle round about the earth . . .
[Robin—2.1.181]

I know a bank where the wild thyme blows . . .
[Oberon—2.1.257]

You spotted snakes with double tongue . . .
[First Fairy—2.2.9 ff.]

Lord, what fools these mortals be!   [Robin—3.2.117]

I was with Hercules and Cadmus once,
When in a wood of Crete they bayed the bear . . .
[Hippolyta—4.1.116–17]

The lunatic, the lover, and the poet
Are of imagination all compact.   [Theseus—5.1.7–8]

The lover . . .
Sees Helen's beauty in a brow of Egypt.
                              [Theseus—5.1.10–11]

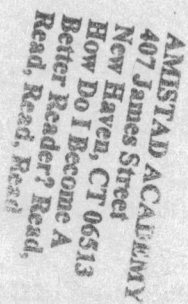
AMISTAD ACADEMY
407 James Street
New Haven, CT 06513
How Do I Become A
Better Reader? Read,
Read, Read, Read

P9-CLO-384

Praise for

THE EXTRAORDINARY ADVENTURES OF ALFRED KROPP

A *Publishers Weekly* Best Book of the Year
A Book Sense Pick
A BookBrowse Recommendation
A Texas Lone Star Reading List Selection

★ "The high-speed car chases, spectacularly gory deaths and Arthurian echoes seem tailor-made for a Hollywood action flick, but it's Alfred's naiveté and basic good nature that make this page-turner stand out in the crowded fantasy adventure genre. . . . This story of a 'big-headed loser' is as funny as it is scary." —*Publishers Weekly*, starred review

★ "Yancey has hit one out of the park with this original, engaging and sequel-worthy read. . . . The expertly paced plot will keep action-adventure fans entertained, and those interested in all things Camelot will get a kick out of watching this funny, self-deprecating teenager save the world."
—*Kirkus Reviews*, starred review

"By merging the modern with the medieval, Yancey shoves the historical adventure story into a new realm of endless plot turns. . . . At the center is the funny, self-deprecating, self-doubting and guilt-ridden Alfred, who is not allowed to cross the line into herodom until he has paid dearly for the privilege. Yancey builds him carefully into an unforgettable character, who, in the end, is far more than anyone imagined."
—*The San Diego Union-Tribune*

"Inventive and delightfully original, this fast-paced tale plants ancient legend in a modern world filled with speeding Ferraris and knights in business suits. 'Artemis Fowl' fans will eat it up." —*Seattle Post-Intelligencer*

"A fast-paced thriller of a tale told by an unlikely hero who gets involved with loyal knights, deadly assassins on Suzukis, helicopter gunships, a Ferrari Enzo, and—oh, yeah—a plot to take over the world with King Arthur's sword, Excalibur. . . . It's great to find such good, fun writing." —Jon Scieszka, author of *Guys Write for Guys Read*

"What an utterly splendid book! *Alfred Kropp* grabbed me and held me so thoroughly that I read as I used to when I was a kid, totally engrossed and utterly unwilling to leave the world of the story. I want more!" —Bruce Coville, author of *Jeremy Thatcher, Dragon Hatcher*

"Strap on your sword and prepare for big adventure. . . . From fast cars to ancient legend, a skyscraper to a wizard's cave, a boy with a big heart takes on the meanest, baddest bad guys who wield swords and daggers without conscience. . . . Don't miss it." —Ridley Pearson, coauthor of *Peter and the Starcatchers*

THE EXTRAORDINARY ADVENTURES OF

ALFRED KROPP

RICK YANCEY

Property of
Tyngsborough Public Library
25 Bryants Lane
Tyngsborough, MA 01879
(978) 649-7361

BLOOMSBURY

YA.
SERIES
Alfred

To Sandy

And—naturally—for the boys,
Jonathan, Joshua & Jacob

Copyright © 2005 by Rick Yancey
First published by Bloomsbury U.S.A. Children's Books in 2005
Trade paperback edition published in 2007
Mass market edition published in 2008

All rights reserved. No part of this book may be used or reproduced
in any manner whatsoever without written permission from the publisher,
except in the case of brief quotations embodied in critical articles or reviews.

Published by Bloomsbury U.S.A. Children's Books
175 Fifth Avenue, New York, New York 10010

Excerpt from "Ash Wednesday" from COLLECTED POEMS 1909–1962 by
T. S. Eliot, copyright 1936 by Harcourt, Inc., copyright © 1930 and renewed 1958
by T. S. Eliot, reprinted by permission of the publisher.

The Library of Congress has cataloged the hardcover edition as follows:
Yancey, Richard.
The extraordinary adventures of Alfred Kropp / by Rick Yancey. —1st U.S. ed.
p.   cm.
Summary: Through a series of dangerous and violent misadventures, teenage loser
Alfred Kropp rescues King Arthur's legendary sword Excalibur from the forces of evil.
ISBN-13: 978-1-58234-693-9 • ISBN-10: 1-58234-693-3 (hardcover)
[1. Adventure and adventurers—Fiction. 2. Arthur, King—Fiction.
3. Orphans—Fiction.] I. Title.
PZ7.Y19197Ext 2005   [Fic]—dc22   2005013044

ISBN-13: 978-1-59990-283-8 • ISBN-10: 1-59990-283-4 (mass market)

Typeset by Westchester Book Composition
Printed in the U.S.A. by Quebecor World Buffalo
3 5 7 9 10 8 6 4 2

All papers used by Bloomsbury U.S.A. are natural, recyclable products made from
wood grown in well-managed forests. The manufacturing processes conform to the
environmental regulations of the country of origin.

If you purchased this book without a cover, you should be aware that this book is
stolen property. It was reported as "unsold and destroyed" to the publisher, and neither
the author nor the publisher has received any payment for this "stripped book."

The silent sister veiled in white and blue
Between the yews, behind the garden god,
Whose flute is breathless, bent her head
   and sighed but spoke no word

T. S. Eliot, ASH WEDNESDAY

1

I never thought I would save the world—or die saving it. I never believed in angels or miracles either, and I sure didn't think of myself as a hero. Nobody would have, including you, if you had known me before I took the world's most powerful weapon and let it fall into the hands of a lunatic. Maybe after you hear my story you won't think I'm much of a hero anyway, since most of my heroics (if you want to call them that) resulted from my being a screwup. A lot of people died because of *me*—including *me*—but I guess I'm getting ahead of myself and I'd better start from the beginning.

It began with my uncle Farrell wanting to be rich. He never had much money growing up and, by the time Mr. Arthur Myers came along with his once-in-a-lifetime deal, my uncle was forty years old and sick of being poor. Being poor isn't one of those things you get used to, even if being poor is all you've ever been. So when Mr. Myers flashed the cash, all other considerations—like if any of it was legal, for instance—were forgotten. Of course, Uncle Farrell had no way of knowing who Mr. Arthur Myers actually was, or that his name wasn't even Arthur Myers.

But I'm getting ahead of myself again. Maybe I should just start with me.

I was born in Salina, Ohio, the first and last child of Annabelle Kropp. I never knew my dad. He took off before I was born.

Mom's pregnancy was difficult and very long. She was almost ten and a half months along when the doctor decided to get me the heck out of there before I exploded from her stomach like some kind of alien hatchling.

I was born big and just kept getting bigger. At birth, I weighed over twelve pounds and my head was about the size of a watermelon. Okay, maybe not the size of a watermelon, but definitely as big as a cantaloupe—one of those South American cantaloupes, which is a lot bigger than your California variety.

By the time I was five, I weighed over ninety pounds and stood four feet tall. At ten, I hit six feet and two hundred pounds. I was off the pediatrician's growth chart. Mom was pretty worried by that point. She put me on special diets and started me on an exercise program.

Because of my large head, big hands and feet, and my general shyness, a lot of people assumed I was mentally handicapped. Mom must have been worried about that too, because she had my IQ tested. She never told me the results. When I asked her, she said I most definitely was not. "You're just a big boy meant for big things," she said.

I believed her. Not the part about being meant for big things, but the part about me not being retarded, since I never saw my scores and it was one of those things where you have to believe that your parent isn't lying.

We lived in a little apartment near the supermarket where she worked as an assistant manager. Mom never got married, though occasionally a boyfriend came around. She took a second job keeping the books for a couple of mom-and-pop stores. I remember going to bed most nights with the sounds of her calculator snapping in the kitchen.

Then, when I was twelve, she died of cancer.

One morning she had found a tender spot on her left temple. Four months later, she was dead and I was alone.

I spent a couple of years shuttling between foster homes, until Mom's brother, my uncle Farrell, volunteered to take me in, to his place in Knoxville, Tennessee. I had just turned fifteen.

I didn't see much of Uncle Farrell: He worked as a night watchman at an office building in downtown Knoxville and slept most of the day. He wore a black uniform with an embroidered gold shield on the shoulder. He didn't carry a gun, but he did have a nightstick, and he thought he was very important.

I spent a lot of time in my bedroom, listening to music or reading. This bothered Uncle Farrell because he considered himself a man of action, despite the fact that he sat on his butt for eight hours every night doing nothing but staring at surveillance monitors. Finally, he asked me if I wanted to talk about my mom's death. I told him I didn't. I just wanted to be left alone.

"Alfred," he said. "Look around you. Look at the movers and shakers of this world. Do you think they got to be where they are by lying around all day reading books and listening to rap music?"

"I don't know how they got to be where they are," I said. "So I guess they could have."

He didn't like my answer, so he sent me to see the school psychologist, Dr. Francine Peddicott. She was very old and had a very long, sharp nose, and her office smelled like vanilla. Dr. Peddicott liked to ask questions. In fact, I can't remember anything she said that *wasn't* a question besides "Hello, Alfred," and "Good-bye, Alfred."

"Do you miss your mother?" she asked on my first visit, after asking me if I wanted to sit or lie on the sofa. I chose to sit.

"Sure. She was my mom."

"What do you miss most about her?"

"She was a great cook."

"Really? You miss her cooking the most?"

"Well, I don't know. You asked what I missed most and that's the first thing that popped into my head. Maybe because it's almost dinnertime. Also, Uncle Farrell can't cook. I mean, he cooks, but what he cooks I wouldn't feed to a starving dog. Mostly we have frozen dinners and stuff out of a can."

She scribbled for a minute in her little notebook.

"But your mother—she was a good cook?"

"She was a great cook."

She sighed heavily. Maybe I wasn't giving the kind of answers she was looking for. "Do you hate her sometimes?"

"Hate her for what?"

"Do you hate your mother for dying?"

"Oh, jeez, that wasn't her fault."

"But you get mad at her sometimes, right? For leaving you?"

"I get mad at the cancer for killing her. I get mad at the doctors and . . . you know, how it's been around for centuries and we still can't get rid of it. Cancer, I mean. And I think, what if we put all the money we spend on these wasteful government projects toward cancer research. You know, stuff like that."

"What about your father?"

"What about him?"

"Do you hate him?"

"I don't even know him."

"Do you hate him for leaving you and your mom?"

She was making me feel freaky, like she was trying to get me to hate my father, a guy I didn't even know, and even like she was trying to get me to hate my dead mother.

"I guess so, but I don't know all the facts," I said.

"Your mother didn't tell you?"

"She just said he couldn't commit."

"And how does that make you feel?"

"Like he didn't want a kid."

"Like he didn't want—who?"

"Me. Me, I guess. Of course me."

I wondered what the next thing I was supposed to hate was.

"How do you like school?"

"I hate it."

"Why?"

"I don't know anyone."

"You don't have any friends?"

"They call me Frankenstein."

"Who does?"

"Kids at school. You know, because of my size. My big head."

"What about girls?" she asked.

"Girls calling me Frankenstein?"

"Do you have a girlfriend?"

Well, there *was* this one girl—her name was Amy Pouchard, and she sat two seats over from me in math. She had long blond hair and very dark eyes. One day during my first week, I thought she might have smiled at me. She could have been smiling at the guy on my left, or even not smiling at all, and I just projected a smile onto a nonsmiling face.

"No. No girlfriends," I said.

Uncle Farrell talked to Dr. Peddicott for a long time afterwards. He told me she was referring me to a psychiatrist who could prescribe some antidepressants because Dr. Peddicott believed I was severely depressed and recommended I get involved with something other than TV and music, in addition to seeing a shrink and taking anti-crazy drugs. Uncle Farrell's idea was football, which wasn't too surprising given my size, but football was the last thing I wanted to do.

"Uncle Farrell," I told him, "I don't want to play football."

"You're high-risk, Al," Uncle Farrell answered. "You're running around with all the risk factors for a major psychotic episode. One, you got no dad. Two, you got no mom. Three, you're living with an absentee caretaker—me—and four, you're in a strange town with no friends.

"There was another one too . . . Oh, yeah. And five, you're fifteen."

"I want to get my license," I told him.

"Your license for what?"

"For driving. I want my learner's permit."

"I'm telling you that you're about to go off the deep end and you want to talk about getting your learner's permit?"

"That reminded me, the fact that I'm fifteen."

"Dr. Peddicott thought it was a great idea," Uncle Farrell said.

"A learner's permit?"

"No! Going out for the football team. One, you need some kind of activity. Two, it's a great way to build confidence and make friends. And three, look at you! For the love of the Blessed Virgin, you're some kinda force of nature! Any coach would love to have you on his team."

"I don't like football," I said.

"You don't like football? How can you not like football? What kind of kid are you? What kind of American kid doesn't like football? I suppose next you're going to say you want to take dancing lessons!"

"I don't want to take dancing lessons."

"That's good, Al. That's real good. Because if you said you wanted to take dancing lessons, I don't know what I'd do. Throw myself over a cliff or something."

"I don't like pain."

"Ah, come on. They'll bounce off you like—like—pygmies! Gnats! Little pygmy gnats!"

"Uncle Farrell, I cry if I get a splinter. I faint at the sight of blood. And I bruise very easily. I'm a very easy bruiser."

But Uncle Farrell wouldn't take no for an answer. He ended up bribing me. He wouldn't take me to get my learner's permit unless I tried out for the football team. And if I didn't try out for the team, he promised he would put me on so much antidepressant dope, I wouldn't remember to sit when I crapped. Uncle Farrell could be gross like that.

I really wanted my permit—I also didn't want to be so doped up, I couldn't remember how to crap—so I went out for the team.

2

I made the team as a second-string right guard, which basically meant I was a practice dummy for the first-string defense.

Coach Harvey was a short round guy with a gut that hung over his pants, and calves about the size of my head, which, as I mentioned, was large. Like a lot of coaches, Coach Harvey liked to scream. He especially liked to scream at me.

One afternoon, about a month before Uncle Farrell struck his deal with the chief Agent of Darkness, I saw how much screaming he could do. I had just let a linebacker blow by me and cream the starting quarterback, the most popular kid in school, Barry Lancaster. I didn't mean for this to happen, but I was having trouble memorizing the playbook. It seemed very complicated, especially seeing it was a document intended for big jocks, most of whom could barely read. Anyway, I thought Barry had called a Dog Right, but actually he had said "Hog Right." That one letter makes a huge difference and left Barry on the turf, writhing in agony.

Coach Harvey charged from the sidelines, silver whistle clamped between his fat lips, screaming around the hysterical screeches of the whistle as he ran.

"Kropp!" *Tweet!* "Kropp!" *Tweet!* "KROPP!"

"Sorry, Coach," I told him. "I heard 'dog,' not 'hog.'"

"Dog, not hog?" He turned his head toward Barry, still twisting on the ground. He kept his body turned toward me. "Lancaster! Are you hurt?"

"I'm okay, Coach," Barry gasped. But he didn't look okay to me. His face was as white as the hash marks on the field.

"What play was that, Kropp?" Coach Harvey snapped at me.

"Um, Dog Right?" I said.

"Dog! Dog! You thought hog was dog? How is dog like hog, Kropp? Huh? Tell me!"

The whole team had gathered around us by this point, like gawkers at the scene of a terrible accident.

Coach Harvey reached up and slapped my helmet with the palm of his hand.

"What's the matter with you, boy?" He slapped me

again. He proceeded to punctuate his questions with a hard slap against the side of my head.

"Are you stupid?" Slap.

"Are you stupid, Kropp?" Slap.

"Are you thick, is that it, Kropp?" Slap-slap.

"No, sir, I'm not."

"No, sir, I'm not *what*?"

"Stupid, sir."

"Are you sure you're not stupid, Kropp? Because you act stupid. You play stupid. You even talk stupid. So are you absolutely sure, Kropp, that you are not stupid?" *Slap-slap-slap*.

"No, sir, I know I'm not!"

He slapped me again. I yelled, "My mother had my IQ tested and I'm not stupid! Sir!"

That cracked everybody up, and they kept laughing for the next three weeks. I heard it everywhere—"My mommy had my IQ tested and I'm not stupid!"—and not just in the locker room (where I heard it plenty). It spread over the whole school. Strangers would pass me in the hallway and squeal, "My mommy had my IQ tested!" It was horrible.

That night after the practice, Uncle Farrell asked how it was going.

"I don't want to play football anymore," I said.

"You're playing football, Alfred."

"It's not just about me, Uncle Farrell. Other people can get hurt too."

"You're playing football," he said. "Or you're not getting your license."

"I don't see the point of this," I said. "What's wrong with not playing football? I think it's pretty narrow-minded to assume just because I'm big, I should be playing football."

"Okay, Alfred," he said. "Then you tell me. What do you want to do? You want to go out for the marching band?"

"I don't play an instrument."

"It's a high school band, Alfred, not the New York Philharmonic."

"Still, you probably need to have some kind of basic understanding of music, reading notes, that kind of thing."

"Well, you're not going to lie around in your room all day listening to music and daydreaming. I'm tired of coming up with suggestions, so you tell me: What are your skills? What do you like to do?"

"Lie in my room and listen to music."

"I'm talking about skills, Mr. Wisenheimer, gifts, special attributes—you know, the thing that separates you from the average Joe."

I tried to think of a skill I had. I couldn't.

"Jeez, Al, everybody has something they're good at," Uncle Farrell said.

"What's so wrong about being average? Aren't most people?"

"Is that it? Is that all you expect from yourself, Alfred?" he asked, growing red in the face. I expected him to launch into one of his lectures about the movers and shakers or how anybody could be a success with a little luck and the right mindset.

But he didn't do that. Instead he ordered me into the car and we drove downtown.

"Where are we going?" I asked.

"I'm taking you on a magical journey, Alfred."

"A magical journey? Where to?"

"The future."

We crossed a bridge and I could see a huge glass building towering over everything around it. The glass was dark tinted, and against the night sky it looked like a fat, glittering black thumb pointing up.

"Do you know what that is?" Uncle Farrell asked. "That's where I work, Alfred, Samson Towers. Thirty-three stories high and three city blocks wide. Take a good look at it, Alfred."

"Uncle Farrell, I've seen big buildings before."

He didn't say anything. There was an angry expression on his thin face. Uncle Farrell was forty and as small and scrawny as I was big and meaty, though he had a large head like me. When he put on his security guard uniform, he reminded me of Barney Fife from that old *Andy Griffith Show*, or rather of a Pez dispenser of Barney Fife, because of the oversized head and skinny body. It made me feel guilty thinking of him as a goofy screwup like Barney Fife, but I couldn't help it. He even had those wet, flappy lips like Barney.

He pulled into the entrance of the underground parking lot and slid a plastic card into a machine. The gate opened and he drove slowly into the nearly empty lot.

"Who owns Samson Towers, Alfred?" he asked.

"A guy named Samson?" I guessed.

"A guy named Bernard Samson," he said. "You don't know anything about him, but let me tell you. Bernard Samson is a self-made millionaire many times over, Alfred. Came to Knoxville at the age of sixteen with nothing in his pockets and now he's one of the richest men in America. You want to know how he got there?"

"He invented the iPod?"

"He worked hard, Alfred. Hard work and something you are sorely lacking in: fortitude, guts, vision, passion. Because let me tell you something, the world doesn't belong to the smartest or the most talented. There are plenty of smart, talented losers in this world. You wanna know who the world belongs to, Alfred?"

"Microsoft?"

"That's it, smarty-pants, make jokes. No. The world belongs to people who don't give up. Who get knocked down and keep coming back for more."

"Okay, Uncle Farrell," I said. "I get your point. But what about the future?"

"That's right," he said. "The future! Come on, Alfred. You won't find the future in this garage."

We took the elevator to the lobby. Uncle Farrell led me to his horseshoe-shaped desk that faced the two-story atrium. About halfway between the security desk and the front doors was a waterfall that fell over these huge rocks that Uncle Farrell told me had been hauled down at great expense from the Pigeon River in the Smokies.

"Funny thing about life is you never know where it's going to take you," Uncle Farrell told me. "I'm working at the auto body shop when in strolls Bernard Samson. He strikes up a conversation, and next thing I know here I am making double what I pulled in at the shop. And for sitting—for nothing! *Double* for *nothing*, just because the richest man in Knoxville decides to give *me* a job!"

Mounted on the desktop were dozens of closed-circuit monitors set up to survey every nook and cranny of Samson Towers.

"This system is state-of-the-art, Alfred. I mean, this place is tighter than Fort Knox. Laser sensors, sound detectors, you name it."

"That's pretty cool, Uncle Farrell."

"Pretty cool," he echoed. "You betcha. And this is where I sit, eight hours a day, six nights a week, in front of these monitors, staring. Watching. What do you think I'm watching, Alfred?"

"Didn't you just say you were watching the monitors?"

"I am watching nothing, Alfred. Eight hours a day, six nights a week, I sit in this little chair right here, watching nothing."

He leaned very close to me, so close, I could smell his breath, which did not smell very good.

"This is the future, Alfred. *Your* future, or something like it, if you don't find your passion. If you don't figure out what you're here for. A lifetime of watching nothing."

3

I studied hard for my driver's test, but I flunked it. So I took it a second time and flunked again, but I didn't miss as many questions, so at least I was improving as a failure. Uncle Farrell pointed to my scores as proof I lacked the guts to achieve even something as simple as a learner's permit.

Things were not much better at school. Barry Lancaster's wrist was still badly sprained, which meant he was now a bench player just like me. Barry wasn't happy about this. He went around telling everybody how he was going to "get Kropp," so I spent my days looking over my shoulder, waiting for the getting to start. I became jumpy; every loud noise, like the slamming of a locker door, was enough to make me nearly wet my pants.

One afternoon in early spring, I came home to find Uncle Farrell already out of bed.

"What is it?" I asked.

"What's what?"

"Why are you out of bed?"

"Aren't you the king of Twenty Questions."

"That was only two questions, Uncle Farrell, and they were kind of related, so that probably would only count as one and a half."

"You know, Alfred, people who think they're funny rarely really are."

"I don't think I'm funny. I think I'm too tall, too fat, too slow, and too much of a screwup, but I don't think I'm funny. Why are you out of bed, Uncle Farrell?"

"We have company coming," he said, wetting his big lips.

"We do?" We never had anyone over. "Who's coming?"

"Somebody very important, Alfred. Put on some clean clothes and come into the kitchen. We're eating early."

I changed my clothes and found my Salisbury steak frozen dinner fresh from the microwave sitting at my spot on the kitchen table. Uncle Farrell was drinking a beer, which was unusual. He never drank beer at dinner.

"Alfred, how'd you like to move out of this dump and live in one of those huge mansions in Sequoia Hills?"

"Huh?"

"You know, where all the rich people live."

I thought about it. "That'd be great, Uncle Farrell. But when did we get rich?"

"We're not rich. But we might be. Someday." He was smiling a mysterious smile while he chewed his Salisbury steak.

"And you'll be taking your driving test again next week—how'd you like a Ferrari Enzo for your first car?"

"Oh, boy, that'd be great, Uncle Farrell," I said. He got like this sometimes. It's no big secret that it's lousy being poor. But there's poor and then there's really poor, and we weren't really poor. I mean, I never went to bed hungry, and the lights always stayed on, but I guess it wasn't easy working a lonely night job for the richest man in Knoxville. He wasn't getting much sleep lately either, and that can make you a little loopy. "But I'd rather have a Hummer."

"Okay, a Hummer. Whatever. The kind of car doesn't matter, Al. This guy who's coming tonight—he's a very rich man and he's got this proposition that . . . well, if it works out the way I hope, you and me, we'll never have to worry about money again."

"Honestly, Uncle Farrell, I didn't know we worried about it now."

"His name is Arthur Myers and he owns Tintagel International. You ever hear of Tintagel International?"

"No."

"Well, it's one of the biggest international conglomerates there is, maybe bigger than Samson Industries."

"Okay."

"So here's the deal, Al. One night I'm on my shift and it's just like any other night, nobody but me at the desk, doing nothing, when all of a sudden the phone rings and guess who's on the other end."

"Mr. Myers."

"Right!"

"What's a conglomerate?"

"It's a business that owns businesses, or something like that. That really isn't the point. Alfred, you need to stop interrupting me and focus a little, okay?"

"I'll try, Uncle Farrell."

"So anyway, Mr. Arthur Myers says he's got a business proposition for me."

"The owner of one of the biggest conglomerates in the world had a business proposition for you?" I asked.

"It's crazy!"

"It sure sounds crazy."

"That's what I thought!" Uncle Farrell tapped his fork on the plate and started talking really fast. "Who am I but this lowly little night watchman? But I met with him and it turns out he's the real McCoy, and he needs my help. Our help, Alfred."

"Our help?" The more he talked about this funny deal, the funnier I felt.

"See, Myers and Bernard Samson go way back. Good buds from, I don't know, the old country or something. Anyway, Myers convinced Samson to invest in this big business deal—I'm not sure of all the ins and outs but apparently there was a lot of money involved and it went bad. It went real bad. Samson lost a lot of money and he blamed Myers for it."

"Why did he blame Myers?"

"I don't know. Now listen, and stop interrupting, Alfred. We don't have much time."

"Why don't we have much time?"

"I'm getting to that."

"To what?"

"The reason we don't have much time!"

He took a deep breath.

"Mr. Samson blamed Mr. Myers for this deal that went bad. He took it pretty hard, Samson did, and so he did a terrible thing."

"What did he do?"

"He stole something."

"From Mr. Myers?"

"No, from the Louvre in Paris. Of course from Myers! Samson stole it and locked it away in his office."

I started to get it. "His office in Samson Towers?"

"That's right. Now you're getting it. Samson Towers, the night watchman of which happens to be yours truly."

"And Myers wants you to get it back for him."

"Right. That's right, and—"

"What is it?"

"What's what?"

"The thing Samson stole."

"Oh. I don't know."

"You don't know?"

Uncle Farrell slowly shook his head. "I have no idea."

"Uncle Farrell, how are you going to get it if you don't know what it is?"

"That's a detail, Alfred. Just a detail. The point is—"

"A pretty big detail if you ask me."

"Do you want to know what the point is?"

"Sure."

His mouth was moving but no sound was coming out.

"You interrupt me and every thought in my head just flies away! Whoosh! Right out the window! Where was I?"

"You were going to tell me the point."

"The point? Oh. Yeah! The point is he's paying me one million dollars to get it."

I stared at him. "Did you say one million dollars?" I asked.

"Well, I didn't say one million pesos, that's for sure!"

I thought about it. "This is illegal."

"No, it isn't illegal."

"But if Mr. Samson stole it, why doesn't Mr. Myers go to the police?"

Uncle Farrell wet his lips. "He said he didn't want the police involved."

"How come?"

"He said he wanted to keep everything real quiet. He doesn't want to press charges because the papers and the TV would pick it up and he doesn't want that."

"Maybe this thing belongs to Mr. Samson and Mr. Myers is lying. Maybe he's just using you because you're the guy with the keys."

"Well, I am the guy with the keys—that's why he needs me—but I'm no thief, Al. Look, I didn't bring this up to get your permission. I brought this up to ask for your help."

"My help?"

"That's right," Uncle Farrell said. "I can't do it alone, Al. And I figured who'd be better to help me than you, since you stand to gain in this operation too. One million dollars! Think about it, Al, because you're only fifteen; you haven't lived very long, not as long as me, and things like this, these kinds of opportunities, they're once-in-a-lifetime!"

"I'll have to think about it," I said.

He stopped chomping his microwave steak, his mouth hanging open a little so I could see the food.

"What do you mean you'll have to think about it? Think about what? I'm your uncle. I'm all the family you got left since your good-for-nothing father abandoned you and your mother died of cancer, God rest her soul. This could be the sweetest deal ever to come down the pike, one million smackers for an hour's work, and you're telling me you got to *think* about it?"

"It's just a lot to think about, Uncle Farrell."

He snorted. "Well, you better think quick, Alfred, because—"

The doorbell rang. Uncle Farrell gave a little jump, then forced a smile. Uncle Farrell had very large teeth.

"That's him; he's here."

"Who's here?"

"Myers! I told you we didn't have much time."

"Mr. Myers is here?"

"You know something, Alfred? You would think, with a head the size of yours, you'd be able to think a little bit quicker. Clear off the plates and meet us in the living room, will ya? You don't keep a man like Arthur Myers waiting."

He hurried from the kitchen. I heard the front door open and Uncle Farrell say, "Hey, Mr. Myers! Right on time. Come on in, make yourself at home. Alfred! Alfred is the kid I told you about."

I heard the sound of a man's voice talking, but I couldn't understand the words, he was speaking so softly. I carried the plates to the sink and wiped down the kitchen table.

In the living room, I heard Uncle Farrell say, "Would you like something to drink, Mr. Myers?" And then he yelled to me, "Alfred! Make some coffee, will ya?"

So I got the coffee going, and then I stood there by the sink, chewing on a thumbnail. I knew he wanted me in there to meet this Arthur Myers, but for some reason I was scared. The whole thing struck me as some shady deal. Why would someone as rich and powerful as Arthur Myers give Uncle Farrell a million dollars to pull a "recovery" job for him? What was in Samson Towers that was so valuable?

But my biggest question was what would happen to me if Uncle Farrell got caught breaking into Bernard Samson's office. If he was in jail, it was back to the foster home for me.

I waited until the pot was finished brewing, then poured two cups and carried them into the living room.

Uncle Farrell was sitting on the edge of the sofa, leaning toward the chair in which Arthur Myers sat. I noticed a large leather satchel with gold clasps sitting on the floor beside him.

Arthur Myers was thin, with long brown hair pulled into a ponytail hanging halfway down his back. His silk suit was a funny color, almost multicolored, and when he moved, the light played off the material and made it shimmer, first blue, then white, then red. But the most noticeable thing about him were his eyes, set very deep into his head under a jutting brow. They were so brown, they almost looked black. And when he turned those eyes toward me for the first time, I shivered, as if I'd walked over a grave.

"Alfred!" Uncle Farrell said. "Coffee! Great! How do you like your coffee, Mr. Myers?"

"Black, thank you," Mr. Myers said. He took the cup from me. He had an accent that sounded kind of French but kind of not; I don't know, I'm no good with accents.

"So you are Alfred Kropp," he said. "Your uncle thinks a great deal of you."

"He does?" I turned to Uncle Farrell. "Cream and two scoops of sugar," I said, and handed him his cup.

"Indeed he does," Mr. Myers said. "But he failed to mention your impressive . . . proportions. Tell me, do you play football in your school?"

"I went out for the team," I said. "I made second-string

right guard. Coach wouldn't put me in much because I couldn't remember the plays. But if we got ahead by twenty points he put me in. I blew a play in practice and our star quarterback got hurt. I may have ruined his only chance to get into college and I think he's going to kill me for it."

"Come here, Al, and take a load off," Uncle Farrell said, patting the couch. He was wetting his lips. He turned to Mr. Myers. "I've filled Al in on most of the details of the operation."

"I had my reservations, as I told you," Mr. Myers answered. "But I understand the necessity for an accomplice. As long as he can be trusted."

"Oh," Uncle Farrell said. "You bet."

"I'm not sure I can," I said. Both men stared at me. "I mean, I'm not too quick on the uptake—I can't even memorize a football playbook—and this whole thing smells fishy to me."

Arthur Myers crossed his long legs, rested his elbows on the armrests, steepled his thin fingers together, and said, "In what way does it 'smell fishy' to you, Mr. Kropp?"

"Well, Mr. Myers, for one thing you just used the word 'accomplice.' That kind of implies you're putting Uncle Farrell up to no good."

"An unfortunate choice of words, then. How is 'partner'? Would you prefer that word?"

"Hey, I think that's a great word," Uncle Farrell said.

"The other thing is," I said, "how do we know this whatchamacallit in Mr. Samson's office is really yours?

Maybe it belongs to Mr. Samson and you're making this story up to get us to steal it for you."

"Alfred!" Uncle Farrell cried. He mouthed to me, "Ix-nay on the ealing-stay."

Mr. Myers raised his hand. "That is quite all right, Mr. Kropp. The boy has a sense of honor. All in all, not a bad thing, particularly in one so young." Then he turned those dark eyes right on me and I felt a pressure in my chest, as if a huge fist was squeezing me. "What would you like, Alfred Kropp? Testimonials? Eyewitness accounts? A certificate of authenticity or proof of purchase, as from a cereal box? It is a family heirloom, a treasure that has been handed down from generation to generation. Bernard Samson took it from me in retaliation for a business deal gone awry, an unfortunate occurrence that was nevertheless not my fault. If you know anything about the man, you understand why he took it."

"I don't know anything about him," I said. "I've never even met him. Why did he take it?"

"For revenge."

"Have you asked him to give it back, whatever it is?"

Mr. Myers stared at me for a second before Uncle Farrell said, "Yeah, that's a good point, Mr. Myers. I mean, what exactly *is* it you need recovered?"

"This," Mr. Myers said, pulling a long manila envelope from his pocket and handing it to Uncle Farrell. He was still looking at me.

"I was just thinking maybe you don't need to shell out a

million dollars to get it back," I said. "Maybe you and Mr. Samson should just make up and then he'll give it back."

"Really, Mr. Kropp?" He was smiling at me. My face felt hot, but I barreled on.

"Well, I'm not pretending to know how things work in the world of big business and conglomerations, but if I had a fight with a friend or he borrowed something and wouldn't give it back, I'd invite him over to hang out, maybe play some video games, or you would probably have martinis, and I'd schmooze a little and then I'd ask for whatever it was back. I'd say, 'Hey, Bernie (or Bernard or whatever you call him), I know you're pretty sore, but that thing you took means a lot to me, been in my family for generations, and maybe we could work something out, because I'd hate to get the cops involved,' or something along those lines. Have you thought about doing that?"

"You're correct, Mr. Kropp," Mr. Myers said, the same stiff smile frozen on his lips. "You do not know how 'conglomerations' work. Are you and your uncle turning down the job? Time is of the essence."

"How come?" I asked.

"My, Mr. Kropp," Arthur Myers said to Uncle Farrell. "How proud you must be of this boy. So direct! So thoughtful. So . . . inquisitive."

"I'm all the family he's got left," Uncle Farrell said. "Plus he spends a lot of time alone, you know, because I'm sleeping during the day and away all night. It's a miracle he isn't in juvie hall, if you ask me."

Uncle Farrell had opened the envelope and pulled out an eight-by-ten glossy photograph that he now held out to me.

I looked at the picture.

"It's a sword," I said.

"Yes." Mr. Myers laughed for some reason. "And the Great Pyramid is just a headstone."

It was mounted in a glass case, like a museum piece. A dull silvery color with a fancy handle. But "handle" wasn't the right word. There was a word for the handle of a sword. I bit my lip, trying to think of the word. There was some kind of writing on the flat part of the blade, or maybe just a fancy design, I couldn't tell.

"I took that picture years ago," Mr. Myers was saying as I stared at the picture. "For insurance purposes. Samson was fascinated by our family heirloom from the moment he saw it. He offered to buy it from me at a fantastic price, but of course I refused. It is hardly worth what he offered, but its sentimental value is astronomical."

"I know how that is," Uncle Farrell said. "I've got a baseball from the 1932 Cubs that—"

"I *have* asked for it back," Mr. Myers said. "I have even offered him money, all to no avail. I do not see that I have any recourse now but to seize it."

"I say the old so-and-so has it coming," Uncle Farrell said.

"I cannot do it myself, of course. And I understand I am putting your uncle's very job in jeopardy. That is why I'm offering this bounty. Speaking of which . . ." He slid the leather case toward Uncle Farrell. "The down payment. I will pay the balance upon delivery of the sword."

Uncle Farrell's fingers were shaking as he undid the gold clasps. Inside were bundles of twenty-dollar bills.

"Oh, my sweet aunt Matilda!" Uncle Farrell whispered.

"Five hundred thousand dollars," Mr. Myers said softly. "You may count it if you wish."

"Oh, I trust you, Mr. Myers," Uncle Farrell said. "You bet I do! Look at this, Alfred!"

But I wasn't looking at the money. I was looking at the picture of the sword in its glass case. I had a hundred questions racing through my mind, but they were whirling so fast, I couldn't get a grip on one.

Then Mr. Myers said, "As I told your uncle, Mr. Kropp, I need someone to retrieve the sword for me. A man of consummate skill and discretion. A man who is incorruptible, untouched by the temptations of evil men. I need someone who is indefatigable, Mr. Kropp. A man who will not give up or falter when all odds are against him. In short, I need someone who will lay down his life to recover a treasure that is beyond any value mortal men may place on it."

" 'Lay down his life'?" I asked. "Uncle Farrell, he's saying you might have to lay down your life."

"He's just trying to make a point, Alfred. Some people exaggerate to get across what they're saying. You know, to get your attention. He doesn't mean literally lay down your life. Right, Mr. Myers? Huh? Not literally lay down our lives." Mr. Myers didn't say anything. Uncle Farrell wet his big lips and said to me, "You should listen to Mr. Myers. You can learn a lot from a guy like him."

Mr. Myers said, "I could turn to more . . . ruthless men for my purpose. I know such men, but I do not trust them. For the very quality that makes them ruthless makes them untrustworthy. I need someone I can trust. Someone who will not betray me."

"Well, you've come to the right place, Mr. Myers!" Uncle Farrell said. "You can trust us. You can consider your fancy sword as good as returned."

"Excellent," Mr. Myers said. "As I mentioned, time is of the essence. Samson leaves for Europe tonight and will return in two days."

"We're going in tonight," Uncle Farrell said firmly. "Or tomorrow night. Tonight or tomorrow, either one, but maybe Al has homework, I don't know." He looked at me. "Anyway, very soon, one of the two nights. Tonight or tomorrow night, right, Al?"

"How do you know the sword's in his office?" I asked Mr. Myers.

"I don't know for certain, but I do know for certain it isn't in his home."

"We don't need to know how you know that," Uncle Farrell said. "Right, Alfred?"

"What happens if it isn't there?" I asked. "Do we have to give back the five hundred thousand?"

"Hey," Uncle Farrell said. "That's a pretty good question!" He was clutching the satchel to his chest as if he were afraid Mr. Myers might reach over and yank it away.

"Of course you may keep it," Mr. Myers said. "That money is for your trouble. The rest is for the sword."

We had a big fight after Mr. Myers left. Despite the money sitting there on the sofa that was ours to keep whether we found the sword or not, I still felt really weird about doing this. It just felt wrong. Maybe Mr. Samson really did take the sword and hide it in his office, but that didn't make stealing it back the right thing to do.

"It's not like he's asking us to knock somebody off or do something really evil. And it's a million dollars, Alfred. We could do anything we wanted, live anywhere we wanted, have anything we wanted!"

It didn't matter how many objections I raised. To Uncle Farrell, money trumped everything.

He even said, "You do what you want, Al, but maybe I need to rethink this whole arrangement of ours—I mean, maybe you're too much for me to handle . . . Maybe I should send you back to the foster care . . ."

That ended the fight. He knew I didn't want to go back to foster care.

4

The very next day my math teacher informed me I was flunking. That was bad enough, but not as bad as being assigned a tutor to save my grade, because my tutor turned out to be Amy Pouchard.

We met for thirty minutes after school, just me—Alfred Kropp—and Amy Pouchard, she of the long golden hair and dark eyes. Sitting right next to her I could smell her perfume.

"Where are you from?" she asked me in that twangy east Tennessee accent. "You talk funny."

"Ohio," I said.

"Are you a resource student?" Resource students were

either mentally challenged or from a really bad background, or both. I guess some people would say I was both.

"No, I just suck at math."

"Hey," she said. "Kropp! You're the guy who had his IQ tested!"

"Something like that."

"And you broke Barry Lancaster's wrist."

"It isn't broken and I didn't actually do it. Somebody else did, but it was my fault, which I guess is practically the same thing."

"I hate tutoring," she said.

"Then why do you do it?"

"Because I get extra credit."

"Well," I said, "I really appreciate it. It's hard for me— math, I mean—and it's been hard too getting used to a new place, a new school, and things like that."

She put a piece of gum in her mouth and the spearmint warred with the musk of her perfume.

"I'm going to a shrink," I admitted, at the same time not really sure why I was admitting it. "Not that I want to go, but my uncle is making me. She's about a thousand years old and she wanted to know if I had a girlfriend."

She smacked her gum and stared at me. She couldn't have cared less. She was tapping the end of her pencil on the desktop, and her whole being was in a state of couldn't-care-less-ness.

"So I told her I didn't . . . have a girlfriend. Because a new school is hard, um, in terms of meeting them. Girls. Plus the fact that I'm shy and I'm pretty self-conscious of my size."

"You are pretty big," she said around her wad of gum. "Maybe we better work on some problems."

"Like, I was wondering," I said, my mouth now so bone-dry, I would have mugged her for a stick of her gum. "About your ideas on dating somebody my size."

"I have a boyfriend."

"I was just searching out your ideas, really."

"Barry Lancaster."

"Barry Lancaster is your boyfriend?"

She flipped her hair over her right shoulder and nodded, and the gum went click-click-click in her mouth.

"Some guys have all the luck," I said, meaning Barry Lancaster and in a funny way, me too.

Uncle Farrell had to pick me up that afternoon, since I missed the bus. We drove straight to the driver's license place and I took my test for the third time. This time I passed, missing four questions, one less than the maximum allowable. To celebrate, I drove us to IHOP for dinner. I ordered the Rooty Tooty Fresh and Fruity. Uncle Farrell had the patty melt. He was wearing his black uniform and wetting his lips more than usual.

"So, what have you decided, Alfred?"

"About what?"

"About this operation for Mr. Myers."

"I think it's incredibly unfair of you to threaten me with a foster home to make me do it."

"Forget unfair. Is it fair that you won't help your only flesh and blood?"

"You just told me to forget fair and then you ask me if something's fair."

"So?"

"That isn't fair."

"Sometimes I think you're toying with me, Alfred, which is incredibly cheeky for a kid in your position. Final time, last chance, do-or-die: Are you going to help me tonight?"

"Tonight? You're doing it tonight?"

He nodded. He was on about his third cup of coffee and his nod was quick and sharp, like a bobble-head's. "I have to. Samson is out of town and Myers wants his sword back ASAP. It's now-or-never time. Fourth quarter, ten seconds left."

"So you're going to do it whether I help you or not?"

"I gave my word, Alfred. I made a promise," he said pointedly, as if reminding me I should keep mine, although I couldn't remember actually making any promises. "So the only question left is . . . are you going to help me?"

When I didn't answer right away, he leaned in close and whispered, "You think I won't do it? You think I won't send you back to foster care?"

I wiped my cheek with my napkin, which was sticky with syrup, and I felt the stickiness on my cheek.

"Maybe if you try, I'll tell the police you stole the sword."

"Keep your voice down, will ya? I'm not stealing anything.

I'm recovering it for the victim. I'm doing a good deed, Al. Now, last time I'm going to ask. Are you going to help me?"

I dabbed my cheeks again with my sticky napkin, and for some reason I thought about Amy Pouchard and the fact that Barry Lancaster was probably going to kill me when he found out she was tutoring me in math, and then I thought about my mom who died and the dad I never knew. The only person I had left was sitting across the table from me, slugging down coffee, nervously wetting his lips and drumming his fingers on the table.

"Okay," I said. "But I'm a minor, so whatever happens up there they'll blame you for it."

"Whatever happens up there," he said, "it's gonna change both our lives forever."

I would remember those words when Uncle Farrell turned to me and whispered my name, *Alfred*, right before he died.

5

In the car on the way to the Towers, I asked him, "Uncle Farrell, have you thought about how you're gonna do this?"

"Do what?"

"Get the sword. What about all the security cameras?"

"We're going to cut the power."

"To the whole building?"

"No, just the power to the security system. Power goes out every now and then."

"There's no backup?"

"You can override it. If it stays down over ten minutes, though, a call automatically goes to police headquarters."

I thought about it. "Okay, so we have ten minutes from the time you cut the power till the cops know."

"Yeah. But it's maybe another five, ten minutes before a cop gets there."

"How do you know?"

"We've run drills before, Alfred." He sighed, and his head went shake-shake-shake again.

"Okay. Let's say a terminal window of no more than fifteen minutes."

" 'Terminal window'? You've been watching too many movies, Alfred."

"What if someone shows up downstairs while we're in Mr. Samson's office?"

"While *you're* in Samson's office."

"Me?"

"Well, I can't do it, Alfred. Why do you think you're here? I've got to provide cover downstairs. I'll get you in, you get the sword, and then we get out. Then I call Myers and we swap the sword for another cool half-mil."

We drove in silence for a while. Samson Towers loomed ahead, silhouetted against the night sky.

Uncle Farrell said, "Now, stay right here in the car, Alfred." He pulled into the underground parking lot. "I'll come back and get you once the shift's changed."

So he left me there, hunkered in the front seat. My watch read 10:45. I have to admit, even though this deal seemed awfully fishy to me, I was excited. It was kind of like a spy movie, only we weren't spies and this wasn't a movie. So maybe it wasn't like a spy movie but more like a fifteen-year-old kid and his uncle trying to steal a sword that may or may not belong to a guy who was paying them a truckload of money to steal it.

Uncle Farrell came back downstairs and I got out of the car.

"All clear," he whispered. "I've already cut the power to the system. Hurry, Alfred!"

He popped the trunk and pulled out a beat-up old duffel bag.

"What's that for?" I whispered. The garage was empty and I wasn't sure why we were whispering.

"You want to be seen lugging a big sword into our apartment building, do you? Here." He handed the bag to me.

We took the elevator from the garage to the main floor, where the fountain spattered and gurgled and our footfalls echoed eerily in the great empty space.

I followed him to the guard station with the bank of surveillance monitors. They were all dark. I noticed tiny dots of sweat beaded on his forehead.

"Okay, Alfred, let's go."

We got into the elevator and Uncle Farrell pulled out the key for the executive suite. He was sweating pretty bad by that point. I was sweating too, and my tongue felt very thick in my mouth. We didn't say anything. Secretly I was hoping our quest would come up a big fat zero. That way we could tell Mr. Myers we couldn't find it and be half a million dollars richer without actually taking anything that wasn't ours and that might not even be his.

The elevator doors opened and we stepped out. I could feel my heart slamming in my chest and it actually hurt to breathe. I inhaled shallower and shallower, to lessen the pain.

The double doors leading into Mr. Samson's office suite were directly ahead of us. Uncle Farrell looked at his watch. I had already checked mine.

"Okay, four minutes down; we're fine," he said.

He slipped the key into the lock and the doors opened silently. I felt for the light switch.

"No lights," Uncle Farrell hissed. He pulled the flashlight from his belt.

"Somebody could see that too," I said.

"Well, gee, Alfred, I left my infrared night-vision goggles at home, so I guess we don't have much choice."

He clicked on the flashlight and the beam of light glanced off the dark mahogany of the secretary's desk.

"Where is it?" I asked.

"I don't know."

"You don't know?"

"But I don't think it would be out here."

He pulled a pair of rubber gloves from his pocket.

"Aren't those for washing dishes?" I asked.

"I got 'em from the janitor's closet. Here, put them on."

"Where are yours?" I asked.

"I work here, Al," he reminded me. "My fingerprints won't mean anything."

"But won't the cops wonder why your fingerprints are all over Mr. Samson's things?"

He stared at me for a second. "We only got one pair."

I pulled off the left glove and handed it to him.

"I'm right-handed," he said.

"So am I," I said.

We stared at each other for a second.

"What?" he asked. "I can't be expected to think of *everything*."

I sighed, and put the glove back on. He swung his flashlight toward the left, where it glinted on the gold-plated doorknob of the door leading to Samson's office.

"If it's anywhere in this place," he breathed, "it would be in there. Hold the light, Al."

I shone the flashlight on Uncle Farrell's key ring as his shaking fingers searched for the right key. I tried to check my watch, but it was too dark and Uncle Farrell needed the light.

He found a key he thought was the right one, but it wasn't. He cursed and started over.

He tried another key. This one slid right in and we stepped into Mr. Samson's inner office. There was a massive desk facing the door, a leather sofa along the wall beside it, and bookcases lining three sides of the room. The place was huge, about twice the size of Uncle Farrell's apartment. Against the far wall, to the left of the desk, was another door.

"Okay," Farrell said. "Where would it be?"

I thought about it. "Well, it's a sword, and it must be pretty big. He can't just hide it anywhere."

"Maybe those bookcases open to a secret chamber or somethin'," Uncle Farrell said. "Saw that on *Scooby-Doo*."

"You watch *Scooby-Doo*?"

"When I was a kid. Al, that show's been around forever."

"If this was *Scooby-Doo*, you'd be the bad guy," I said. "The bad guy was always the janitor or the night watchman."

"What a relief it is, Al, that it's not."

The far wall was one big window, all glass, commanding a view of the downtown below. Just enough light came through that Uncle Farrell could switch off the flashlight and still see. He went to the other door and disappeared inside. I heard him gasp. "Jeez Louise!" He stepped back into the room.

"Bathroom. I think the faucet's made of solid gold."

I looked at my watch. "Nine minutes into the window. We got to hurry."

I didn't know where to look in the big, sparse office. All I could see were bookcases, filled mostly with knickknacks and pictures, a potted palm tree, a sofa, a coffee table, the desk and chair, and that was about it. I pulled on a drawer handle in the desk, but it was locked. Of course, he couldn't fit a full-length sword into a desk drawer. Maybe Uncle Farrell was right, and we should look for a secret hiding place somewhere. Maybe a safe behind that big watercolor over the sofa. You saw that all the time in the movies. Uncle Farrell stood by the door leading to the reception area, his cool completely gone.

"Why are you just standing there?" Uncle Farrell snapped at me.

"I don't know where to look," I admitted. "Maybe Mr. Myers was wrong. Maybe it isn't here."

"It's here," he insisted.

"How do you know?"

"I don't know. I just know."

"You don't know but you just know?"

"Shut up, Alfred. I'm trying to think."

I sat down in Mr. Samson's leather chair. I had never sat in a more comfortable chair in my whole life. It felt like the chair was hugging me. I wondered how much a chair like this cost.

"What are you doing now?"

"I'm thinking," I said.

"Alfred, we don't got that kinda time."

Bernard Samson kept a clean desk. His blotter was bare. On one corner sat a framed photograph of a man with a big white dog that looked like a cross between a wolf and a Saint Bernard. I wondered if the man was Mr. Samson—maybe he got that kind of dog because his name was Bernard too. Other than the picture, there was a penholder and a nameplate, in case somebody forgot when they walked in who was sitting in the big fat hugging chair. I looked at the picture again. The man was broad-shouldered, with a large head and a mass of golden brown hair that he wore swept back from his high forehead, like a lion's mane.

I lifted the blotter an inch or two, which isn't an easy thing to do when you're wearing Playtex rubber gloves; sometimes guys hid things under their blotters.

"Uncle Farrell, if you had a priceless sword, where would you hide it?"

"In my priceless patooty." He peeked into the other office, as if he was waiting for the cops to storm in any second. Uncle Farrell had gone twitchy all over.

"Maybe it's behind that picture over the sofa," I said.

"'Maybe it's behind that picture over the sofa,'" he mocked me, but he kneeled on the center cushion and gingerly lifted the bottom of the frame. I knew the answer before he said it.

"Nothing." He flopped onto the sofa and rubbed his forehead.

I pulled the chair closer to the desk and rested my elbows on the blotter.

"I don't think it's here," I said.

"Shut up. I'm trying to think, Al."

"Or maybe it was here and Mr. Samson moved it."

"Why would he move it?"

"Maybe somebody told him what Mr. Myers was up to."

"Maybe, maybe, maybe," Uncle Farrell said. "If maybes were pickles we could have a picnic."

"Maybe he's too smart for us," I said, meaning Mr. Samson.

"Smart?" Uncle Farrell raised his head and glared at me from across the room.

"What did I tell you about that?" he asked. "Being smart doesn't matter as much as people think. You want to know what matters more than smarts? Stubbornness. Stubbornness and *energy*, Alfred. *That's* what gets you ahead in this world."

He dropped to his knees and shone his flashlight under the sofa. I looked at my watch. The terminal window had passed.

"Uncle Farrell, we have to go."

"I'm not going."

"We're going to get caught."

"I'm not walking out on half a million dollars!"

I pushed myself up, and somehow my belt buckle caught under the edge of the desk. It got stuck there, so when I stood, it pulled up, and the top of the desk hitched about half an inch. My buckle slipped free and the desktop smacked back down.

From across the room, Uncle Farrell was still on his knees, staring at me. "Well, I'll be jiggered," he whispered.

6

"It's heavy," I told him. "Take that side." I had cleared everything off, putting it all on the bookshelves behind me.

"Jeez Louise, I guess it is heavy." He puffed out his cheeks as we lifted. "Quick now, Alfred. I got to get downstairs to meet the cops. You stay up here till they're gone."

That made me nervous. I didn't want to be alone in the dark, but I couldn't think of any way around it.

The desktop was hinged on the front side, like the lid to the biggest music box ever made. Uncle Farrell took a deep breath as we both leaned over to peer inside.

"Holy nut-buckets!" he breathed. "Wouldn't you know?"

Inside the hidden cavity was a silver keyboard, like the pad of an ATM or calculator, built into the desk itself.

"There's a code," I said. "You punch in a code and that opens something."

"What's the code?" he asked. He looked like he was about to cry.

"I don't know," I answered.

"Well, of course you don't know, Alfred! I wasn't asking the question because I thought you knew!" He looked at his watch and chewed on his big bottom lip.

"Okay, Al, this is okay," he said in that false-positive tone adults sometimes take with kids. "I'll get on downstairs to meet the cops and you stay up here."

"Stay up here and what?"

"Break the code."

He gave me an encouraging pat on the back and headed for the door.

"Uncle Farrell!" I called after him, but he ignored me. I heard the elevator bell go *ding*, and then there was the loudest silence I had ever heard.

I stared at the pad. The PIN was probably Mr. Samson's birthday, or the year he founded the company, or maybe just some random number that had nothing to do with anything. Since I didn't know any of those numbers, I just started punching digits at random. Nothing happened, and it occurred to me I could punch numbers from now until doomsday and nothing might work.

I gave up, lowered myself back into the chair, and looked

at my watch. What if the cops demanded to see the suite and he was leading them up here right now? Part of the plan should have included walkie-talkies.

Being nervous and bored at the same time is an odd combination; I couldn't sit still, so I leaned forward and peered into the interior of the secret compartment. A little voice inside my head whispered "*telephone*," then whispered it again, "*telephone*," and I wondered why my little voice was whispering "*telephone*" like that.

Then it hit me. "Letters," I whispered.

Mr. Samson's phone sat on the floor beside the desk. I picked it up and set it on my lap. Like most phones, each key had three letters that corresponded to each number, like ABC was the number 2.

So I started punching in some numbers.

7-2-6-7-6-6 = SAMSON. Nothing. 2-3-7-6-2-7-3 = BERNARD. Nothing. What was the name of the dog in the picture? I punched in 9-6-5-3 (WOLF) on a hunch.

Nothing happened.

I sighed and looked at my watch. Uncle Farrell had been gone for five minutes. He had said being smart didn't matter so much, but right then it sure would have helped. More out of desperation than anything else, I punched in the first thing that popped into my head: 2-5-3-7-3-3.

From beneath my feet came a whining sound, like a motor revving up, and the floor began to shake. I pushed back from the desk with a little yelp as the desk itself began to rise, like an invisible magician was levitating it.

A huge silver metal pole rose slowly from the carpeting, until the top of the desk was about two inches from the ceiling.

The pole had an opening on the side facing me, and inside the hollow space, hung on two silver spikes, blade facing down, was the sword.

I had brought the picture, just to make sure I got the right sword, but I didn't need the picture to know this was the one. In the bluish glow from the city lights outside the window, it seemed to shimmer, like the surface of a lake on a cloudy day.

I took a deep breath and grasped the sword handle. It practically flew out of the column; I didn't expect it to feel so light. I thought it would weigh a ton, but it felt no heavier than a ballpoint pen. It sounds funny, but right away it felt like a part of me, a five-foot extension of my right arm. Grinning like a kid playing pirate, I swung it around a few times. It hissed as it cut the empty air. I held it up to the streetlights, turning it so the ambient light glittered off the edges.

I ran my left thumb along the blade. Immediately, a thin line of blood began to seep out of the wound. I hadn't even felt it. The blood brought me to my senses, though. I stuffed the sword into the duffel bag. Then I stuck my thumb in my mouth: I didn't want to drip my DNA all over Mr. Samson's office during my getaway.

I trotted to the door and stopped—what if the cops demanded to see Mr. Samson's office for some reason? Should I hide somewhere till Uncle Farrell came back up? I hesitated in the doorway, hugging the duffel against my chest while I sucked nervously on my thumb, the taste of blood in my mouth. I didn't know how to lower the desk, so I left it and stepped out into the hallway.

I closed the door, checked the lock, and headed straight for the elevator to wait for Uncle Farrell.

I leaned against the wall, my heart still pounding hard, sweat trickling down the middle of my back and my chest. The duffel bag felt very heavy all of a sudden. I pulled my thumb out of my mouth. The bleeding had stopped, but my thumb tingled, like it had fallen asleep. I panicked for a second, thinking maybe the blade was poisoned and I would die in this semidark hallway.

Then I heard the elevator coming. It must have taken a long time for Uncle Farrell to get rid of the cops, I thought as I pushed myself away from the wall. I still felt a little dizzy, but the duffel didn't feel as heavy.

The doors slid open and I was saying, "What took so long, Uncle Farrell?" when two big brown shapes stepped out. I backed down the hall, toward the emergency exit door that opened onto the stairwell. Two big men dressed in flowing brown robes, like monks, stepped out of the elevator, their hoods pulled low to cover their faces.

One stepped ahead of the other and said softly, so softly, I could barely hear him, "We don't want to hurt you. We just want the sword." He held out his hand.

His tone was so nice and reasonable, I almost handed him the sword. I might have too, but at that moment, the one behind him made a snarling sound and rushed me, his right hand coming out of the folds of his robe, and in that hand was a long saber, thin as a pool cue, black and double-bladed.

The first monk made a move to hold him back, but he was too late. Before I even had a chance to think, I jammed my hand into the duffel bag and whipped out the sword. My attacker hesitated, but only for a split second. He was nearly on top of me when I felt the sword in my hand whistle over my head—I don't even remember lifting my arm—and then I watched as my arm brought it down, aimed right at the guy's forehead.

He cried out and brought his sword up at the last second. The sound of the swords smashing into each other reverberated like thunder in the tiny hallway. He fell back a little, stunned by the blow.

The tingling in my thumb had spread to my arm, and I brought the sword around again as the first monk gave up trying to negotiate and rushed me.

His partner fell back, gripping the wrist of his blade hand. I fell back too. This taller monk moved more slowly than his buddy, but it was a thoughtful kind of slowness. I backpedaled until I bumped the stairwell door.

"Surrender the sword," came the voice beneath the brown hood. A pale hand reached for me as another raised the black tapered blade.

I reached for the handle of the door with my left hand, shoved it down, then kicked at it with my foot. At the same time, my sword was whistling toward his left ear. He blocked the swing with the black-bladed sword. I grabbed his left wrist and yanked hard, stepping to my right at the same instant, and that sent him flying past me into the stairwell. I heard him cry out in pain as he tumbled down the stairs.

The smaller monk had recovered and now he rushed me, swinging his weapon so fast, it was just a dark blur in front of my eyes—but my sword was blocking every thrust, parrying every blow, like it had a mind of its own. I didn't know how I was fighting this guy, who obviously knew what *he* was doing when it came to swordplay.

The sword in my hand seemed to weigh nothing at all, and everything started to slow down to a dreamlike dance: I could see his sword coming from a mile away.

He made one more desperate lunge at me. I turned his blade easily and brought my left fist down hard against the side of his head. He sank to his knees.

"Sorry," I said. "I don't want to hurt anybody. I'm just trying to help my uncle so he won't send me to a foster home. Who are you?"

Before he could answer, a hand grabbed me from behind and yanked me into the stairwell. It was the bigger man, the one who had first spoken. He swung me around and slammed his body hard into mine, forcing me back against the wall. He clutched my right wrist and held it against the concrete; the blade of my sword clinked against it. He took the tip of that black-bladed sword and pressed it against my Adam's apple.

"Drop the sword if you want to live," he whispered.

"Okay."

I dropped the sword. For a second neither one of us moved; I think we were both surprised I dropped it. Then, without even thinking about it, I brought my knee up as hard as I could into his crotch. He fell straight down and didn't move.

I hopped over his body, grabbed the sword, and met the other one coming through the door. He saw his fallen companion and gave a little cry. I grabbed him by the front of the robe and flung him behind me.

"Stop him!" the leader choked out from the floor.

I sprinted down the hall, the tip of the sword tapping against the carpeting as I ran. I punched the down button at the elevator. If no one had hit the call button since my attackers came out, it should be waiting for me.

The doors slid open, and Uncle Farrell was standing inside with a third monk in a brown robe, also holding a black-bladed sword, which was pressed across Uncle Farrell's neck.

7

"Alfred!" Uncle Farrell squeaked at me.

"Throw down the sword," the new monk said. "Throw it down or he dies."

"Uh, Alfred," Uncle Farrell gasped. "I think you better do what he says."

I heard the stairway door open behind me. I glanced over my shoulder and saw the first two monks coming toward me, the taller one—the one I had kneed—limping a few steps behind his partner.

"There is no escape," the tall monk said. "If you give us the sword now, you still may live."

"If you kill my uncle," I said to the monk in the elevator,

"I'll kill all of you." I sounded a lot braver than I felt. There was no way I could kill anyone, but these monks didn't know that.

"We don't want to hurt anyone," the tall monk said. "We want only the sword."

"So give it to them, Al," Farrell said. "Stop screwin' around!"

Right then the smaller monk behind me lost patience, I guess, because he leaped forward with a cry, bringing his black blade over his head. The tall monk cried, "*No!*" as he came for me. I blocked his downward thrust with an upper-cut (if that's the word for it; I don't know fencing talk) of my bigger sword. I heard a loud screech of metal hitting metal. It sounded just like a car wreck.

His smaller blade shattered on impact. I grabbed his wrist and swung him into the elevator, pieces of glittering black metal raining down on us.

He fell into Uncle Farrell and the third monk, knocking both off balance. I reached into the elevator, grabbed Uncle Farrell by the hand, and pulled him out. I dragged him a couple of steps toward the stairs, but there was still the tall monk standing between us and the exit.

"Upon my honor," he said. "All we want is the sword. Please. You know not what you are doing."

He held out his hand. "Give me the sword and you will not be harmed. You have my word."

I walked toward him, dragging Uncle Farrell with me, the tip of the sword pointed at the tall monk's stomach. I didn't know what I was doing, but I was doing it pretty well up to this point.

"Step out of the way," I told him. "We're leaving."

"You will not get far," he promised.

From beneath the hood, I swear I could see his eyes glowing, not red, like a demon or something, but a gentle bluish light, like the glow of a night-light.

"You cannot keep it long," he said. "We know who you are."

Then the tall monk did something that took me totally by surprise: He stepped out of the way.

Behind me, one of the other monks cried out, and the head monk raised his hand. His hand was very pale and his fingers long and delicate, almost like a woman's.

"No," he said quietly. Then he said to me, "We will meet again."

We hit the stairs, and the large door slammed shut behind us, echoing like a gunshot.

8

I took the steps two at a time, dragging Uncle Farrell behind me. I went down two flights, then paused at the landing, listening, but heard nothing.

"Twenty-seven floors to go," I said. "Can you make it?"

"The freight elevator—we can take that," Uncle Farrell gasped.

I pushed open the stairway door and pushed Uncle Farrell too, down the dark hall to the freight elevator. He fumbled with his keys, fussing at me the whole time. What was the matter with me, taking on a bunch of saber-shaking monks? He said I had screwed up everything, particularly his life. I was thinking about the duffel bag I had left in the hall outside Samson's office. I think I read somewhere that the cops can pull fingerprints off fabric.

Uncle Farrell was right: I had screwed up everything, his life and mine too.

He finally found the right key and when the elevator doors opened, we fell inside and he hit the lobby button. We leaned against the back wall of the elevator and tried to catch our breaths.

The doors opened onto the lobby. "Mr. Myers was right," I said. "This isn't your ordinary sword."

We stepped into the lobby.

"Where'd you learn to swing a sword like that?" he asked. He didn't wait for an answer, which was a good thing, because I didn't have one.

"You broke the code?" he asked.

I nodded.

"Well, you're just a young man of many hidden talents, aren't you? What was the code?"

"Two-five-three-seven-three-three."

"What's that?"

"That," I said, "is my name."

He stared at me. I said, "It also could be 'Alepee,' but that doesn't make much sense."

"Neither do you. Somebody ratted us out, Alfred."

"Or maybe the desktop was wired," I said.

"Right. Alarm goes off in the monastery and the monks break from vespers and scramble for battle."

The lobby was eerily quiet, except for the splashing of the water in the fountain.

"What happened to the cops?" I asked.

"That's what I'd like to know," he growled. "It's true. Never one around when you need one." He told me the third monk was waiting for him in the lobby when he stepped out of the elevator. He put a sword to his throat and took Uncle Farrell straight back to the penthouse.

Uncle Farrell stopped at his desk and hit the switches. The monitors flickered back to life. The hall on the top floor was empty. I looked at the wall behind the desk where the red indicator lights showed the location of all six elevators. The express elevator was still on the top floor.

"They took the stairs," I said.

"What do we do now?" Uncle Farrell asked. It was as if holding the sword put me in charge.

I thought about it. "Call the cops."

"Huh?"

"Maybe the monks or whoever they are intercepted the automatic emergency call. Call the cops, Uncle Farrell."

"And tell them *what*?"

"Tell them you've got three guys, maybe more, running around with swords." I reached around him again and hit a button that was labeled "Alarm." A red light began to flash on the panel.

"Okay, and while I'm waiting for the cops I think I'll whip up a snack for me and the monks when they get here. What are you talking about, Alfred?"

"They don't want you," I said, meaning the brown-robed monk men. "They want the sword, and the sword isn't going to be here."

"You're leaving? Al, you can't leave."

"Sure I can, Uncle Farrell. Give me your car keys."

"You can't have my car!"

"You'll get fired if you leave."

"Alfred, I'm about to be a millionaire—do you really think I care if they fire me? We're getting outta here!"

We took the access stairs to the underground lot. Uncle Farrell drove while I sat in the backseat, the sword across my lap. Three cop cars roared past us in the direction of Samson Towers, sirens wailing.

Once we were safely away, my own panic and fear started to set in. I broke out in a cold sweat and fought back tears. "Okay, Uncle Farrell, you've got to tell me what's really going on here."

"I don't know."

"Where'd those guys come from?"

"I don't know."

"How'd they get into the building?"

"I don't know."

"Why is my name the code to the secret chamber?"

"I don't know."

Apparently, there wasn't much Uncle Farrell did know. That made it even worse, the thought that I was the real brains of the operation.

He drove straight to our apartment. He doubled-parked

on the street. It was almost three a.m.; we didn't see anybody going up the stairs. Uncle Farrell went in first so I could check out the hall one last time.

Then I stepped into the dark room and asked, "Uncle Farrell, is everything all right?"

I flipped the switch and heard Uncle Farrell gasp. He was standing about ten feet away, by the sofa. Behind him stood Arthur Myers, his forearm across Uncle Farrell's throat.

"Of course it's all right, Mr. Kropp," Arthur Myers said.

9

"Alfred," Uncle Farrell wheezed. "I can't breathe."

"He's having some difficulty breathing, Mr. Kropp," Mr. Myers said. "Drop the sword and step away, please."

I dropped the sword. It made a dull clang as it hit the floor.

"Very good. Step away, toward the window, please."

I sidestepped to the window, keeping my eye on them.

Mr. Myers let Uncle Farrell go, stepped around him as he fell back onto the sofa, and strode quickly to the sword. He picked it up and turned it from side to side.

"All right," I said. "You have the sword. You can go now, Mr. Myers."

"Wait a minute," Uncle Farrell said, rubbing his throat. "I want some answers first. What in the name of Jehoshaphat is this sword and who were those guys in the funny robes trying to take it?"

"They weren't trying to take it," Mr. Myers said. He was staring at the sword with a weird expression. "They were trying to stop you from taking it." He leveled his eyes at me and something dark passed over his face.

"You have done me a great service, Mr. Kropp," he said to Uncle Farrell, but he was still staring at me. "So I will pay you in kind."

"That's good," Uncle Farrell said. "We had a deal, and I almost got killed getting it."

"Oh, yes. They certainly would have killed you for the sword. They are sworn to protect it at all costs. They are ruthless men of iron will, Mr. Kropp. Ruthlessness has gotten a bad reputation over the years, but there is honor in ruthlessness, a purity to it, would you not agree?"

Mr. Myers had the sword now, but he was getting at something important, something he wanted us to understand before he left.

"They are my enemies, in a way, since we work at cross-purposes, but I admire them," Mr. Myers said. "They have much to teach us about the importance of the will." He turned to me. He was smiling. It was the kind of smile that could give smiling a bad name.

"You see, Alfred Kropp, the will of most men is weak. It buckles at the slightest challenge. It crumbles at the first sign of resistance. It does not listen to the dictates of necessity. Are you following me, Mr. Kropp?"

"Not really," I said. "You've got the sword, Mr. Myers. Can we have the money now?"

"I'm going to give you something much more valuable than money, Mr. Kropp. I am going to give you an important life lesson. I am going to teach you what happens when your will conflicts with one that is stronger."

In two strides, he was in front of the sofa, and I could do nothing but watch as he drove the sword into my uncle's chest, burying the blade into the cushions behind him. Uncle Farrell's eyes slid in my direction and he whispered, "*Alfred*," before he died.

10

Myers came toward me. I froze, waiting for him to slam the sword into my chest, but instead he put a finger to my lips and whispered, "Shhhhh." Then he left without another word.

I realized right away that this was the time to get some adults involved and, since Uncle Farrell was the only adult in the room and he happened to be dead, I dialed 911.

The police came. First a couple in uniforms, then the detectives, who wore rumpled jackets and crooked ties. A photographer came to snap pictures of my dead uncle, and a lady from the coroner's office. Then another lady showed up who said she was a counselor from social services. I told her instead of some counseling I could really use a glass of water. One of the policemen brought me a glass of water.

I told them everything, from the night Mr. Myers gave Uncle Farrell the down payment to get the sword, to my fight with the brown-robed sword-fighting monks, to Mr. Myers stabbing Uncle Farrell and how he promised to kill me too if I didn't keep my mouth shut.

Nobody acted like they believed me.

Then they put Uncle Farrell in a black plastic bag and carried him into the hall, where all the neighbors were standing around, gawking. One of the detectives asked me to describe Mr. Myers, so I did. I told him about the long hair drawn back in a ponytail and the shimmering suit.

One of the detectives took a call on his cell phone and he talked in a whisper for a long time. I don't know what time it was, but it must have been close to dawn when the door opened and a big man with a lion's mane of golden blond hair stepped into the room, followed by two tall men in dark suits.

"Are you done?" one of the men in dark suits asked a detective.

"We're done."

They left us alone, and the two guys in dark suits took positions on either side of the door and stared at nothing.

The big man with the golden hair sat beside me by the window. The rising sun shone through the window, glinting off the ends of his hair. He put a hand on my forearm.

"Do you know who I am?" His voice was kind and very deep.

"Are you Bernard Samson? You look like the guy in the picture."

"Yes, I am Bernard Samson, Alfred," he said softly.

"How do you know my name?" I asked.

He smiled. "What I know might surprise you."

"Are you going to explain what's going on, Mr. Samson?"

"Yes, Alfred, I am," he said in that same soft voice. "Would you like anything?"

"One of the cops gave me a glass of water," I said. "So that's taken care of. I could use some sleep. I haven't slept in twenty-four hours. Plus I'm hungry, but I'm afraid if I eat anything, I'll puke. Mostly what I'd like, though, is some answers."

He smiled. "Ask."

"Who are those guys?" I asked, nodding toward the men by the door.

"They are agents."

"Agents of what?"

"Agents of an organization that you have never heard of, that very few people have heard of, actually. They belong to an agency specifically trained to deal with emergencies such as this one."

"This is an emergency?"

"More of a crisis. You see, Alfred, what has been lost is very important."

"You mean the sword?"

He nodded.

"It doesn't really belong to Arthur Myers, does it?" I asked.

"No."

"I knew it," I said. "I tried to tell Uncle Farrell that, but he wouldn't listen."

"Yes," was all he said.

"Who is Arthur Myers?" I asked.

"He is many things."

"You're answering my questions, but you're not giving me any answers, Mr. Samson. I thought you were in Europe."

"My flight just got in."

He patted my arm again and stood up. He began to pace around the living room, his hands behind his back.

"Who is Arthur Myers?" he said. "I had never heard that name before today. But I know the man. He has gone by many names and many guises in many lands. Bartholomew in England. Vandenburg in Germany. Lutsky in Russia. Who knows what his true name is? To my friends here"—he nodded toward the men by the door—"he is known by his code name, *Dragon*. The name he used when I first met him, though, years ago, in Paris, was Mogart, so to me he has been and always will be Mogart."

Mr. Samson gave a little shake of his enormous head and laughed bitterly.

"Mogart! What can I tell you about Mogart? He is many things, and yet nothing. Mercenary, provocateur, assassin, a destroyer and murderer, but I don't need to tell you that. A lover of darkness. Yes! Of darkness. For if a man may be defined by what he does, you may think of him as simply an agent, Alfred. An agent of darkness."

His cell phone rang. I jumped a little. I don't know if it was my jumping or the ringing of the phone, but one of the men by the door jammed his hand inside his coat pocket, then slowly took it out again when Mr. Samson began to talk.

"Yes. . . . When? . . . Are you certain?" He listened for a long time. In the early-morning light his face looked old, with deep shadow-filled creases. I wondered how old Bernard Samson was. I wondered if he was telling me the truth. I wondered what exactly he was telling me.

"Very well," he said into the phone, and flipped it closed. He sat next to me again.

"I'm afraid I haven't much time, Alfred. Things are moving very quickly and time is our enemy now. We've tapped every resource at our disposal, but he has had time, too much time, to slip through the net. The rest of your questions, quickly."

"I just want to know what's so special about this sword; why three guys dressed like monks with black swords tried to kill me for it; and most of all I want to know why my uncle is dead."

"Your uncle died to send a message, Alfred. To me. To you. To those men you met last night. He died as a warning and a promise that more will die should we oppose Mogart.

I'm afraid we can fully trust that message, Alfred: More people *will* die before this is over."

"Before *what* is over? Why don't you just talk plain to me, Mr. Samson? I'm really tired and I feel really bad. I felt bad from the first about this deal and I tried to talk Uncle Farrell out of it, but he wouldn't listen, and now I feel really bad."

He patted my hand, looked at his watch, and then said, "The sword you took from my office, did you notice anything unusual about it?"

I didn't say anything.

"You fought those men with it. Have you ever fought with a sword, Alfred?"

"Not a real one. A play one, when I was a kid."

"Yet, despite your total lack of expertise, you were able to best three very accomplished swordsmen, were you not?"

"Yes. Who were they? They don't work for Mr. Myers— or Mogart, or whatever his name is, do they?"

"No."

"So they work for you."

"They work for no man, Alfred. They are part of an ancient and secret order, bound by a sacred vow to keep safe the sword until its master comes to claim it. Yes, they should have killed you for refusing to give it to them, but they are not murderers or thieves."

"No, I guess that would be Mr. Mogart and me."

"They are knights, Alfred, or at least that's what we would call them, if there were such things in this dark age."

"Mr. Samson, are you ever going to tell me what this is all about? I thought you had to go." I felt like I was shrinking to the size of a pencil lead, which wasn't a very comfortable feeling for someone my size.

"Long ago, Alfred," Mr. Samson said. "Long ago there was a man who united the greatest kingdom the world had ever known. This kingdom was not great in lands or armies, but great in the vision it gave humankind, that justice, honor, and truth were within our grasp, not in some world to come, but here, in the world of mortal men. That king departed, but his vision remained. We are the guardians of that vision, for what we guard is the last physical embodiment of it."

"You mean the sword?"

"The sword is *in* this world, Alfred, but it is not *of* this world. Forged before the foundations of the earth, not by mortal hands, it is the True Sword, Alfred, the Sword of Kings. In another time it was known as Caliburn. You may know it by its other name, the sword Excalibur."

"You're talking about King Arthur, right?"

"Yes, King Arthur."

"That's just a legend, a story, Mr. Samson."

"I don't have the time to convince you of anything, Alfred. You held it tonight. In your inexperienced hands, the Sword bested three of the finest swordsmen in the world. Yet that is only a fraction of its power. The Sword of Kings contains the power of heaven itself, Alfred, the power to create as well as to destroy. All the mortal arts of weaponry are powerless against it, but more than this, the *will* of ordinary men cannot withstand its might."

I thought of the tall monk stepping aside to let me and Uncle Farrell pass, as I held the Sword, telling him to move. *The will of ordinary men cannot withstand its might.*

Mr. Samson's eyes were shining with a faraway look, as if he was seeing things I could not see, great battles and men in gleaming armor on horseback, thundering across rolling fields.

"You asked who those men in the Towers were. Only twelve of us are left now, but they—and I—are the descendents of King Arthur's Knights of the Round Table. The Sword has been in our care for centuries and, as far as I know, this is the first time we have failed to keep it from the hands of evil men."

"You're a knight," I said, slowly shaking my head. "You're telling me you guys are knights like King Arthur–type knights?"

"Not those men, no," Mr. Samson said, gesturing toward the two gray suits still at attention by the door. "Their organization did not even know of the Sword's existence before tonight. Circumstances now demand the use of every tool at our disposal. You see, Monsieur Mogart has many powerful friends, Alfred, friends who would pay any price for a weapon against which there is no defense. And Mogart's friends are no friends of humanity. They are despots and dictators who would pay anything to possess the Sword. Do you begin to understand? There is no weapon devised by man, no army or combination of armies, no nation or alliance of nations on earth that can resist the power of the Sword."

"Mr. Myers paid my uncle to steal the Sword so he could sell it to somebody?"

"To the highest bidder, and you can guess how high those bids will go."

He touched my arm again, and I was surprised to see tears shining in his hazel eyes.

"And what kinds of men will bid on it. Alfred," he said, "an army with the Sword at its head would be invincible."

11

"It is a prize beyond any price, Alfred," Mr. Samson said. "But Mogart can expect billions for it. Tens of billions. And if we do not find him before the Sword passes into the hands of evil men, the world will plunge into an age of unimaginable cruelty and terror. Envision the horrors of Nazi Germany or the Russia of the Stalinists, multiply them tenfold, and then you will begin to understand the magnitude of this loss."

The rising sun was shining now through the window on his sharp features.

"We must retrieve the Sword before this can happen. He

may yet decide to keep it for his own use, but that result would not be much better."

"You know where he is?" I asked.

"I know where he is going. He has been preparing a long time for this day. Right now he is crossing the Atlantic, making for his keep in Játiva." He saw my confused expression and gave a little laugh. "In Spain, Alfred." He smiled at me again. "You have a thousand more questions, but I've stayed too long; I must go."

"Don't go yet," I begged. "Don't leave me alone."

He patted my hand and his smile faded. "That seems to be my doom—and yours, Alfred."

He turned and went to the door. I jumped up and followed him.

"There's gotta be something I can do," I said. "Take me with you; I could help. I'm the one who lost it; I should help get it back."

I expected him to say something like "I think you've done quite enough already." Instead, he leaned toward me and whispered, "Pray."

He started down the hall and I called out after him, "Just one more question, Mr. Samson! Why didn't he kill me too?"

He paused, then turned back to me, smiling that same sad smile. "Two reasons, I think. First, it is crueler to kill your uncle and let you live. Second, there is such a thing as honor among thieves."

He disappeared into the stairwell, followed by the two agents. Nothing he could have said would have made me feel worse than calling me a thief. I don't think he meant to hurt my feelings, though. My feelings were the least of his worries.

12

With Uncle Farrell gone, I was now a ward of the state. A couple named Horace and Betty Tuttle volunteered to take me in, pending the unlikely event of somebody adopting me.

The Tuttles lived in a tiny house on the near north side of Knoxville. Five other foster kids lived crammed into that little house. I never saw Horace Tuttle go to work, and I knew they received all sorts of checks from the state and the federal government for each kid, so I think we were how he made a living.

Horace Tuttle was a short, round little guy, always making remarks about my size, particularly my head. I think I scared him or he resented how big I was, I mean, because he was awfully small. Betty, his wife, was short and round like him, with the same conical-shaped head. They reminded me of turtles, kind of like their name, Tuttle. Maybe some people come to resemble their names, the way some people come to resemble their dogs.

I shared a bedroom with two of the other foster kids. The very first night the older one threatened to kill me in my sleep. I was feeling so low and lousy, I told him that would be fine with me.

I usually had trouble concentrating in school, but try concentrating when your uncle has just been murdered right before your eyes and you know the world is about to end. Try studying when you know World War III is about to start and it's all your fault.

I still met with Amy Pouchard twice a week. She asked why I had missed the past couple of weeks and I told her.

"My uncle was murdered."

"Oh, my God!" she exclaimed. "Who killed him?"

I thought about my answer. "An agent of darkness."

"So they caught him?"

"They're trying."

"Hey, isn't your mom dead too?"

"She died of cancer."

"You must be the unluckiest person on earth," she said, and scooted away from me a little, probably without realizing she was doing it. "I mean, your mom and now your uncle and what you did to Barry and everything."

"I've been trying to tell myself all those things had nothing to do with me, that I'm okay and everything," I said. "But it's getting harder and harder."

I was Uncle Farrell's sole heir, so I got all his things, but I only kept his TV and VCR, which I set up in my bedroom. The main thing I didn't get was the $500,000. I didn't remember Mogart leaving with the brown leather satchel, but it wasn't under Uncle Farrell's bed where he stashed it, and the police never found it, probably because I didn't tell them about it. That cash would be hard to explain and would probably get me in more trouble than I already was in, but I started wishing I still had that money. If I did, I would have taken it and run. I didn't know where I'd run, but anywhere seemed better than the Tuttles and the delinquents who lived with them.

Over the next couple of days, I would grab Horace's newspaper and take it to school and, instead of studying, I read the newspaper from front page to last, looking for anything that might give me a clue as to what was happening with Mr. Samson's quest. I wondered what good a billion dollars was in a world of unimaginable cruelty and terror, but men like Mogart have imaginations different than mine. For example, if I had been Mogart, it would have never occurred to me to hire somebody like my uncle Farrell to steal the most powerful weapon that ever existed.

I missed Uncle Farrell. I missed the little apartment and the frozen dinners. I missed the way he wet his big lips and even all his lectures about getting ahead in the world. He was just trying to help me, to show me I didn't have to end up like him. It hit me that he loved me, and I was the only family *he* had left.

To take my mind off things, I checked out a book from the library called *The Once and Future King,* about King Arthur and the Knights of the Round Table. I couldn't get through it, so I rented this old movie called *Excalibur* with a bunch of English actors I had never heard of.

Arthur was this kind of goofy kid, actually, a squire to his brother Kay, toting around his sword and taking care of Kay's horse and his armor, kind of his lackey, not even a knight. Nobody believed this kid could actually pull the Sword from the Stone, until Arthur did it and told them, "If you would be knights and follow a king, then follow me!"

Then he became king, built Camelot, and gathered his knights around the Round Table. Everything was great until his best knight, Lancelot, got together with his queen, Guinevere, and Arthur's bastard son, Mordred, came to take everything over.

There's a big, bloody battle at the end. Arthur kills Mordred, who sort of kills Arthur too, but it's confusing because they show Arthur being taken over the sea by three angel-looking women in white robes. One of the knights picks up Excalibur and throws it into this big lake, where the Lady of the Lake kind of floats up to grab it.

That last part confused me. I wondered how Mr. Samson and his knights ended up with the sword if the Lady took it after Arthur left. If I ever saw Mr. Samson again, I was going to ask him about that.

I don't know if it was that movie, which I saw about forty-nine times, that made me have the dreams. I always fell asleep while the credits rolled, and I would dream of a gleaming white castle on a mountainside, and from its rampart flew triangular flags of black and gold, and inside its outer wall a thousand knights were mustered in full armor. They carried long black swords and their faces were painted black and their expressions were terrible as they fought some guys who had breached the outer wall, men with flowing hair in brown robes, and their faces were covered with mud and grimly set. The men in robes followed a man with golden hair and somehow I knew this man was Mr. Samson, though in my dream he looked different than I remembered him. They were about ten against a thousand, they had no hope, but they fought until the last man fell, and this last man was the knight with the golden hair.

I woke after that dream with the word "Játiva" on my lips. I went to the school library and found Játiva in the atlas. It was a town in Spain, like Mr. Samson said, right at this mountain called Monte Bernisa.

I had another dream too, a terrible dream, the kind that makes you wish you could wake up. I was far above a great plain or field and saw a vast army, row upon row of blank-faced soldiers marching, stretching as far as I could see, a million or more men, and the tramp of their feet was like thunder. Warplanes screamed overhead, lines of tanks rumbled over the field, and the night sky was lit up from the concussions of long-range missiles. Before this army, on a dark horse, rode a big man holding Excalibur, his face hidden in shadow, and as the jets screamed overhead, he raised the Sword in defiance, and from the army behind him came a cry that drowned out the sound of the bombs.

The man leaped from the horse, brought the Sword high over his head, and slammed it into the ground. Brilliant white light exploded from that spot and planes fell burning from the sky, tanks erupted into flame, and whole divisions of his foes were consumed in fire or fled screaming from the flood of light.

The light slowly died away, and then I was walking in a wasteland of broken concrete, uprooted, leafless trees, crushed and twisted cars with their hazard lights blinking. Ash floated everywhere, clinging to my hair and making me cough. I was looking for someone, calling a name, but I couldn't hear who I was calling for. I was desperate to find whoever it was; if I could just find them, everything would be all right. But I always woke up without finding them.

13

After Mogart took the Sword, my life followed the same pattern. I would stay up late watching the news or *Excalibur*, stumble off to school after two or three hours of sleep filled with bad dreams, read the newspaper in class, then come home and go straight to my room to wait for the beginning of the end of the world.

At supper, the Tuttles would start in on me.

"Look at you!" Horace shouted one night. "You don't sleep, you don't eat, you mope around all day with your nose glued to the television screen or the newspaper—what's the matter with you, you big-headed palooka?"

"Oh, I don't know," I said. "Maybe it has something to do with my uncle dying."

"Dear," Betty said to Horace. "Maybe you shouldn't bring up little Alfred's uncle."

"First of all, this kid is anything but little, and second of all, I didn't bring up his uncle, he did!"

And he yelled, his pinched face puckered with rage: "Your problem is self-pity! You think you're the only person on earth who's ever lost somebody? The world is full of pain, Alfred, pain and big losers, and you've got to make up your mind to be a winner!"

"Like you?" I asked.

"Oh," Betty gasped. "Oh, oh, oh!"

"That's your other problem!" Horace screamed. "No gratitude! At least you've got a roof over your head and food for your big self! A lot of people in this world don't even have that!"

And I couldn't take any more. I left him sitting there, his thin lips moving silently, and locked myself in the bedroom. This got my roomies going, a thirteen-year-old greasy-haired thug named Dexter and his ten-year-old brother, Lester, who was also a thug, only not registering as high as Dexter on the thug-o-meter. They pounded on the door and yelled that it was their room too. I just turned the volume up on the news and pretended I didn't hear them. Then Dexter began to shout he was going to cut me; he was going to cut me bad; and that reminded me of the scar on my thumb, which was an inch long and white as dental floss. Sometimes it ached and sometimes it burned and sometimes it just throbbed and tingled. I developed this nervous habit of running my index finger along it, feeling the little indent in my flesh, especially when I was nervous or thought I was going crazy.

I started skipping school. I didn't see much point in an education when the world was about to end. I left in the mornings as if I was going to the bus stop, then cut through a side street to Broadway and walked all the way to the Old City, the historic section of downtown Knoxville. I hung out in the coffeehouses and used-book shops or paced up and down Jackson Street, looking at the homeless people or the long-haired college kids lounging in the sidewalk cafés.

Then, late one afternoon, I decided I just couldn't go back and face the Tuttles, so I ate an early dinner at a place called McCallister's. It was about five o'clock and the dinner crowd hadn't arrived yet, so I had the place mostly to myself.

Mostly, but not all. Across the room sat a tall man with long snow-white hair. He ate very slowly, carving his steak into razor-thin slices and chewing real slow. Every once in a while he lifted his eyes toward me. He looked familiar, but I couldn't remember where I had seen him before. His fingers wrapped around his wineglass were long and delicate. He had big hands, like a basketball player or a pianist.

He stood up and that's when I saw how tall he was. He pulled a white handkerchief from his breast pocket as he sneezed loudly. Then he walked out of the room without looking in my direction, and I wondered why some old guy having dinner was making me so paranoid.

I was feeling guilty at about this point because now it was past six and the Tuttles were probably sitting down to dinner and Horace was probably shouting, "Where is that Kropp? Where is that big-headed palooka?" So I called their house from a pay phone.

Betty answered. "Oh, Alfred, where have you been? Where are you now? We've been worried sick! We were about to call the police or 911, though Horace has been telling me we shouldn't call 911 except in the case of an emergency and he doesn't feel this qualifies since you're nearly sixteen and old enough to look after yourself, but I told him you're just a boy despite your larger-than-normal size, but we have been worried *sick*."

"Don't be worried, Betty," I said. "I'm okay."

"Where are you?"

"I'm going to be a while longer. I just wanted to tell you I was okay."

"Oh, Alfred," she said. "Alfred, please come home." She was crying.

"I don't have a home anymore," I said, and I hung up.

There was somebody else I wanted to call, but it took me a long time to work up the nerve to do it. I got her number from the operator and almost hung up when a guy who sounded like he might be her dad answered the phone. But I didn't.

"Is Amy there?" I asked.

After what seemed like a couple of years, I heard her twangy voice.

"Who is this?" she asked.

"Me. Alfred. Alfred Kropp."

"Who?"

"The guy you're tutoring in math."

"Oh! The dead-uncle guy," she said.

"Yeah," I said. "The dead-uncle guy. Look, I just wanted to say—"

"I knew it wasn't somebody I know," she said. "Because you called this number. People I know call me on my cell phone."

"Right," I said. "Look, the reason I called. I—I don't think I'll be at tutoring tomorrow. Or ever. I don't think I'm coming back."

There was silence. I said, to break it, "I said I don't think I'm coming back."

"I heard you. Look, I know you must be really messed up right now. I know what that's like. When I was twelve my big brother ran over my dog. I couldn't get out of bed for a *week*."

Why did I think she cared? Why was I thinking anybody cared? My own father hadn't even cared. I was an accident everybody had to suffer from, like Barry with his sprained wrist.

I said good-bye to Amy Pouchard and started to walk. It was getting dark now, and there were a lot of people about, couples mostly, walking arm in arm, and I watched them as I walked. Something made me turn around at one point and I saw him, the tall guy with the white hair, about half a block down. He was standing by a newspaper rack, pretending to read. I walked to the intersection of Western and Central, turned left, and walked half a block to Ye Olde Coffee House, right next to the old JFG coffee plant.

I went in and ordered a grande with extra cream and sugar, and sat at the long counter against the window, watching the couples pass outside.

Halfway through my grande I saw him sit down at the very end of the bar, next to the bathroom. I picked up my coffee and walked over to sit down next to him.

We drank our coffee in silence for a moment. The end of his nose was red and runny; he had a cold. He pulled out the white handkerchief. It had a design of a horse and rider on it. The rider was a knight carrying a red banner. That clinched it for me.

"How is Mr. Samson?" I asked him.

"Dead."

I thought about my dream and asked, "When did that happen?"

"Two days ago."

"Mr. Mogart—he killed him?"

"Do not say that name." He folded the handkerchief into a perfect square and tucked it back into his breast pocket.

"Who're you?" I asked.

"Call me Bennacio."

"I'm Alfred Kropp."

"I know who you are."

"We've met before," I said. "At Samson Towers. I didn't

recognize you at first without your robe. But I recognize your hands. And your voice."

He nodded. "The man you know as Bernard Samson was killed two nights ago in Játiva, on the slopes of Monte Bernisa in Spain." He sipped his coffee. He had taken off the lid and I could see he drank it black. "I was given instructions to find you in the event of his fall."

I thought about that. It didn't make much sense to me, but, since Mom died and I went to live with Uncle Farrell, almost everything had stopped making sense. "Why?"

"To tell you of his fate."

"That's important—telling me?"

He shrugged, like he really couldn't make a judgment on the importance of keeping Alfred Kropp in the loop.

"What happened in Spain?"

Bennacio kept looking out the window. "He fell. Four of our Order fell with him. I alone have escaped to bring this news to you, Kropp. It was his dying wish that you should know."

He sipped his coffee. He had a sharp nose and dark, deep-set eyes beneath thick salt-and-pepper brows. His white hair was swept back from his high forehead.

"Two of the Order fell in Toronto," Bennacio said. "They were the first, dispatched by Samson to stop the enemy before he could flee North America. Another in London. Two in Pau, before the rest of us arrived."

I did the math. Mr. Samson had told me there were twelve knights left. "That leaves just two of you."

Bennacio shook his head. "Windimar fell near Bayonne, the night before we discovered the enemy in Játiva. I am the last of my Order."

He didn't say anything for a while. We finished our coffee. Finally, I said, "I'm sorry, Mr. Bennacio."

"Just Bennacio," he said. I don't think it really mattered to him if I was sorry.

I went on. "But there's a lot of other people in on this, right? Mr. Samson brought in this secret agency, some kind of spies, I guess, or mercenaries; I don't know what you'd call them . . ."

"You are speaking of oy-pep."

"I am?"

He nodded. "O-I-P-E-P. Oy-pep." He made a face like saying the word left a bad taste in his mouth.

"What's OIPEP?"

"Did you not just say Samson told you?"

"Well, like a lot of things he told me, he kind of did but he kind of didn't. But I'm not exactly what you might call quick on the uptake. What exactly *is* OIPEP?"

He glanced around the coffee shop. "We should not talk about OIPEP here, Kropp."

He stood up. I don't know why, but I stood up too. I followed him to the door and into the night. The late-spring air was soft and warm. He took out his white handkerchief again and blew his nose.

"It is a fool's hope," he said with a little laugh.

"What is?" I asked.

He didn't give me a direct answer, sort of like Mr. Samson never gave direct answers. Maybe that was part of being a knight. "For Mogart cannot be stopped, not while he wields the Sword. Yet while I live, I must try to stop him." He turned and looked right at me for the first time. His dark eyes were sad.

"Now is the hour," he said softly. "Our doom is upon us."

He walked away without saying anything else and I watched him cross the street. Then I saw two big men step out of the doorway of an antique store and follow him. Both wore long gray cloaks that were too heavy for the warm weather.

Bennacio didn't seem to notice them; he walked with his head bowed, like he was deep in thought. A little voice inside my head said, "*Go home, Alfred.*" But I didn't have a home anymore. Now Mr. Samson was dead and all the other knights except this Bennacio guy, and it was all my fault. I could have—*should have*—told Uncle Farrell no, I wasn't going to help him get the Sword. I knew it was wrong at the time, and if I had stood my ground everybody would still be alive and I would have a home. I had hated that little apartment with the worn-out furniture and its old fishy smell. I had wished every day that my mom hadn't died and my uncle was somebody more like Donald Trump than Farrell Kropp, but now that sounded like heaven to me. I would have given anything to have it back.

Bennacio was walking north on Central, the men keeping pace a few feet behind him.

And for some reason I have never understood, I followed them.

When I turned the corner, they had Bennacio against the wall and were taking turns slugging him, one guy holding him up while the other one slammed his big fists into his gut. They were too busy pounding the crap out of him to notice me.

One of them turned to his buddy and said with a foreign accent, "Finish him." The second man pulled something long and black from the folds of his gray cloak.

"Hey!" I shouted.

They looked over at me. None of us moved for a second; then the guy holding the dagger jammed it into Bennacio's side, the other one let him go and, as Bennacio slid slowly down the brick wall, they took off east along the railroad tracks.

I ran over to Bennacio. His eyes were open and he was breathing. He was clutching that white handkerchief in both hands. I put my hand on his side and it came away covered in his blood.

"Leave me," he said.

I hauled him up, pulling his arm over my shoulder, and kind of dragged him back to Central.

"You're hurt," I said. "I'm taking you to the hospital."

"No hospital. No hospital," he gasped.

I spotted a Yellow Cab parked on the corner. I shoved Bennacio into the backseat.

"Where to?" the driver asked.

"Where to?" I asked Bennacio.

"The Marriott . . ." Bennacio gasped.

"Take us to the Marriott," I told the driver.

Bennacio leaned against me, and I tugged the handkerchief from his hands and pressed it against the badly bleeding wound in his side.

"Oh, boy," I whispered. "Oh, jeez, you're bleeding pretty bad, Bennacio."

"Hey," the cabbie said, staring at us in his rearview mirror. "Your friend okay, kid?"

"No hospital, no hospital," Bennacio kept whispering. His face was very pale and his eyes were rolling in his head as he leaned against me. I guessed he was dying.

14

I managed to get Bennacio out of the cab and into the lobby of the hotel, with him leaning against me. The clerk behind the desk gave me a look.

"My uncle," I told the clerk. "Little too much wine."

Bennacio told me his room number and somehow I got him into the elevator, up to the sixth floor, and into his room. I laid him on the bed.

His eyes were closed and he was breathing in short, hard gasps. I opened his jacket and unbuttoned his white shirt to expose the wound, a gash just below his ribs on the left side. I got some towels from the bathroom and pressed one into his side, watching the blood soak into it. I threw that towel on the floor and replaced it with another. He wouldn't stop bleeding.

"I don't know what I'm doing," I told him. "You're gonna bleed to death if we don't get you to a doctor."

He opened his eyes and looked at me. "The blade was poisoned," he said. "The bleeding will not stop." Then he raised his head a little and looked at my hand holding the towel against his side.

He must have seen the scar on my thumb, because he whispered, "You have been wounded by the Sword."

"Yeah."

"In the bathroom," he gasped. "My straight razor. Bring it to me."

I found it in a little black leather bag on the vanity. The razor had a long retractable blade that slipped into the handle. I didn't think anybody used a straight razor anymore. How did I know this Bennacio wasn't lying—that he wasn't really a goon for Mogart, come to kill me? But even if he was lying, even if he was a bad guy, who was I to let him slowly bleed to death?

I brought the razor back to him. He sat forward a little, groaning with the effort, grabbed my wrist, and held it tight.

"Hey," I said. "What are you doing?"

He grabbed the razor, placing the edge along my scar, and made a shallow cut just shallow enough to draw blood.

"Oh, my God!" I yelped, trying to pull my hand away.

He tossed the towel aside with his other hand, then

brought my bleeding thumb to his side and pressed it into the wound.

"What are you doing?" I asked.

"The Sword has the power to heal as well as to rend," he said. After a few minutes he let go of my wrist. I picked up the towel and put it back on the wound, but already the bleeding had slowed.

Bennacio closed his eyes. His breathing became easier, and for a second I thought he had fallen asleep.

"Who were those men, Bennacio?" I asked, clutching my throbbing thumb.

"Servants of the enemy . . . following me since my return to America."

Which meant he got stabbed because of me. Why had Mr. Samson sent him to me? Like telling Alfred Kropp about it was going to help them get the Sword back.

I sat beside him and felt like crying, but I didn't want to cry in front of Bennacio. Everybody around me lately was dying. All because I took something I shouldn't have. I was like some lumbering, awkward, big-headed Angel of Death.

"You want anything, Bennacio?" I asked. He didn't answer. "I don't know what to do. I mean, I'm really scared right now. Why did Mr. Samson send you here? What's going to happen now that all the knights are dead? I'm not going to live, am I? None of us are. You said our doom was upon us. I'm thirsty. You want a drink of water?"

He didn't answer. This time he had really fallen asleep.

15

I watched him sleep for a long time, un-til I started feeling sleepy myself. There was sofa in the outer room, and I lay on that for a while, but it made me nervous because I couldn't keep an eye on him.

So I went back into his room and sat on the bed. I must have finally passed out, because I woke up at dawn curled at the foot of the bed, like a big, faithful dog.

When I woke up he was still asleep, so I ordered room service, a plain bagel (since I didn't know how he liked them), a bagel with everything, a pot of coffee, and an or-ange juice.

I answered the door to get the food. When I came back,

he was awake. I helped him sit up so he could eat. He took the bagel with everything, the one I wanted, but he was the guy with the stab wound, so I didn't say anything.

"What happened in Játiva?" I asked.

"Samson believed our only hope lay in attacking the enemy in force. I argued against it, but he was the head of our Order, and in the end I acquiesced. We had tracked Mogart to his keep in Játiva, an ancient castle overlooking the city, rebuilt and refortified in preparation for this day. Samson planted a story in one of the British dailies that he was actually in London, attending a conference of foreign business leaders. He had hoped this would lull Mogart into relaxing his vigilance."

"I guess it didn't."

"They waited until we had reached the inner courtyard of Mogart's castle—and then ambushed us. Fifty men at least. Bellot fell, then Cambon, yet even so we might have succeeded. We bested the front guard and had taken the grounds, when fate turned against us and Mogart appeared with the Sword."

He took a deep breath. "And, as we fell, one by one, the angels themselves wailed and beat upon their breasts. The Sword was not meant for such work, was never forged to spill the blood of its protectors. We fell back, our hearts filled with dread, but another contingent of the enemy had formed behind us, cutting off our escape."

"He killed—he killed everyone?"

"It was a slaughter, Kropp. I fell by the gate, wounded,

though not mortally, and thus became the sole surviving witness to Mogart's ultimate treachery, the killing of our captain, the man you call Bernard Samson. What Mogart did to him I will not say here—but it was terrible, Kropp. Terrible! Yet still Samson found strength before he died to tell me to take the message to you, that he had fallen and the Sword is still not safe. In short, that the Knights of the Order of the Sacred Sword are no more."

I set down my half-eaten bagel. All of a sudden, I wasn't hungry anymore. I remembered my dream, of the brave men outnumbered in a gray castle, and the man with the golden hair falling.

"For hours I lay half dead in the blood-soaked mud of Mogart's keep," Bennacio went on. "Finally darkness fell and I deemed it safe to slip away. I was spotted, of course, and pursued here to America, though I thought I had lost my pursuers. Apparently, I have not."

He set down his cup and put his plate with the uneaten bagel on the bedside table.

"Nor will they stop until I am dead. For I am the last knight, the sole hope for the Sword's retrieval. These others, the outsiders Samson enlisted to our cause, this . . . *OIPEP* cannot prevail against Mogart. Only a Knight of the Order has any prayer of retrieving the Sword. And Mogart knows this."

He rolled to the edge of the bed, holding his side, wincing from the pain.

"What are you doing?" I asked.

"Leaving."

"You can't leave, Bennacio. You lost a lot of blood. You gotta rest for a couple—"

"Listen!" he said sharply. "They will not stop hunting me, Kropp. Even as we speak, they may be in this building. Now that my final oath to Samson is fulfilled, I must return to Europe and pick up Mogart's trail before the calamity strikes, before he or anyone else can use the Sword to an evil end."

He pushed himself from the bed, swayed a second on his feet, and fell back. I caught him and eased him back down as he gulped in air.

"I am the last knight," he gasped. "I am bound by my sacred oath to recover what should never have been lost."

I don't know if those words were aimed at me, *what should never have been lost,* but I took it like they were.

"What can I do?" I asked.

He cocked one of those thick eyebrows in my direction and I felt about the size of pencil lead again.

"Please, Bennacio, let me do something. Let me help. I didn't realize I was doing it until now, but I've run away. I'm not going back to the Tuttles' ever again. So if I'm not going back, then I've got nowhere to go and I can't go nowhere, I've got to go somewhere. All this—it's my fault. Well, it's also my uncle's fault, but if I had said no then none of this would have happened. He couldn't have done it without me. But he's dead now, so I'm the only one who can do anything about it, about letting Mogart get his hands on the Sword. I don't know what I can do, but you're in pretty rough shape; maybe you could use me. Please. Please, use me, Bennacio."

He almost smiled. Almost. He held on to his side, wincing. "Can you drive a car, Kropp?"

16

I told him, you bet, I could drive a car, but I had just started and didn't have much experience. That didn't seem to bother him. I helped him get dressed and he leaned on me as we walked to the parking lot. He directed me to a brand-new silver Mercedes parked near the exit.

"This is your car?" I asked.

"Yes."

"Cool car."

I helped him into the passenger seat. After I slid behind the wheel, he handed me the keys.

"This is a really nice car, Bennacio," I said. "You sure it's okay if I drive it?"

"Did you not say in the room you could drive?"

"Sure, but I only got my learner's permit six months ago and I don't have that much experience behind the wheel."

He gave a little wave of his hand, a gesture that struck me as very European. "We must use the instruments given us, Kropp."

"Oh," I said. "You bet."

The engine purred to life and I felt my scalp tingle. If things weren't so serious, I would have been thrilled.

Bennacio directed me to the interstate. I asked him where we were going, thinking I was just giving him a quick lift to the airport, but all he said was "North," which was the opposite direction of Knoxville's airport. I didn't know where we were going, only that somehow I was along for the ride. I kept checking the rearview mirror, but didn't see anything suspicious, just cars and big semis. What would a suspicious car look like anyway? Since I didn't know, *all* the cars around us started to look suspicious. It's hard enough being a novice driver tooling down the interstate in heavy traffic; try adding covert pursuit by quasi-medieval bad guys to the list.

I was about an hour out of the city when Bennacio asked, "Why did you take the Sword?"

"That was my uncle's idea," I said. "Well, I guess it was his idea by way of Mr. Myers's—I mean Mogart's idea."

"And why did your uncle take it?"

"Mogart gave him five hundred thousand dollars."

"So you took it for money." He said the word "money" like it was dirty.

"No. Not the money, really. I'm not greedy, if that's what you're thinking."

"Then why?"

"Look, Bennacio, I didn't know who Mr. Samson really was or what the Sword really was. How could I? I was just helping out Uncle Farrell. Plus he threatened to send me back to foster care if I said no. I told him we shouldn't. I told him I had a bad feeling about it and it was wrong, but he's my uncle. I'm a kid. And I ended up in foster care anyway."

But I was just making excuses. Once you're about ten, maybe eleven tops, "I'm just a kid" doesn't cut it when it comes to your core ideas like the difference between right and wrong.

We didn't say anything for a while. He was staring at the road, not looking at me.

"Where am I taking you, Bennacio?" I asked.

He didn't answer. I glanced over at him. He was still staring at the road.

"How are you going to find Mogart and the Sword once you get to Europe?"

He didn't answer. I took a deep breath and let it out very slowly. Then I tried again.

"Mr. Samson told me you guys were all descended from the original Knights of the Round Table," I said. "Which one did you come from?"

He waited before answering. Maybe he wasn't allowed to tell.

"Bedivere," he said finally.

"Hey, wasn't he the one who found the Holy Grail?"

"No, Galahad found the Grail."

"Oh. I've been watching this movie, *Excalibur*. You ever seen it?"

He didn't answer.

"I've seen it about fifty times. But a couple of parts have been confusing me. Like at the end Percival takes the Sword and throws it into this big lake and the Lady grabs it."

"Arthur did not give the Sword to Percival. The Sword was given to Bedivere."

"Well, in the movie it's Percival."

He cocked an eyebrow at me. I cleared my throat.

"So . . . the Sword belongs to you?" I asked.

"The Sword *belongs* to no man." He sighed. "Upon the fields of Salisbury Plain, Arthur fell, mortally wounded, in the last battle against the armies of Mordred. Before he drew his last breath, Arthur entrusted the Sword to my forebear, Bedivere, who was meant to return it to the waters from which it came, lest the very calamity which has now happened should befall it."

"Well, in the movie it was Percival and he *did* throw it into the lake. So if that's true, how did Samson end up with it?"

He said, "It is a movie, Kropp."

"Did Arthur really die?"

"All men die."

"Mr. Samson said you guys were keeping the Sword until its master comes to claim it. Who's the master if Arthur's dead?"

"The master is the one who claims it," Bennacio said.

"And who would that be?" I asked.

"The master of the Sword," he said

"Do you know who that is?" I asked.

"I do not need to know."

"How come?"

"The Sword knows," he said. "The Sword chose Arthur."

"How does a sword choose somebody?"

He didn't say anything.

"How do you know the Sword didn't choose Mogart?" I asked.

He leaned his head back and closed his eyes, I guess to let me know he was still angry at me or he didn't feel like talking or his side still hurt.

I pulled off the interstate around noon to get some gas and something to eat. All I'd had that day was half a bagel, and Bennacio hadn't even touched his breakfast.

I paid for my gas and bought two corn dogs, a bag of chips, and a couple of fountain drinks. Back in the car, I handed one of the corn dogs to Bennacio.

"What is this?" he asked.

"A corn dog."

"A corn dog?"

"It's a wiener wrapped in corn bread."

"Why is it skewered?"

"It's a kind of handle."

He looked at the corn dog suspiciously. I pulled to the far side of the building and parked near the air hose.

"What are you doing, Kropp?"

"I need to check your side. Pull up your shirt, Bennacio."

"My side is fine. We need to keep driving."

I just looked at him. He sighed, laid the corn dog still in its yellow wrapping on his lap, and lifted up his shirt. I pulled the dressing aside and saw the wound had already closed. I'm no doctor, but it looked almost healed.

"Let's go, Kropp," Bennacio said crisply, pulling down his shirt.

I got back on the interstate. Bennacio didn't eat his corn dog; it lay on his lap for another twenty miles as he stared out his window.

"Your corn dog's getting cold," I told him. He ignored me. I reached over, took it off his lap, pulled off the wrapping, and ate it. It occurred to me I hadn't seen Bennacio eat since the restaurant the night before.

"Maybe I should have asked before I bought you the corn dog," I said. "But I figured, who doesn't like corn dogs?"

"I am not hungry."

"You gotta eat, Bennacio. Tell me what you want and I'll stop again."

"No, no. Keep driving."

"Where am I going, exactly?"

"Canada."

I looked over at him. "Canada?"

He sighed. "To Halifax, in Nova Scotia. I have friends there."

"Jeez, Bennacio, I had no idea I was driving you all the way to Canada! Wouldn't it have been easier just to fly to Spain?"

"The airports will be watched."

"Won't they be in Halifax too? I mean, wouldn't they think of that?"

I wondered where exactly Halifax was in Nova Scotia. I wondered where Nova Scotia was. I didn't ask him, though. He had a way of talking to me that sounded like he didn't want to talk to me, like he was just being polite.

"Who are these friends in Halifax? The what-do-ya-call-'ems, OIPEP guys?"

"OIPEP is not my friend," he said.

"Then what is it? What does OIPEP stand for, anyway?" He didn't say anything, so my mind tried to fill in the blanks: *Organization of Interested Parties in Evolutionary Psychiatry*. But that didn't make any sense.

"The knights were not the only ones who knew of the Sword's existence," Bennacio said. "We were its protectors, Kropp, but the Sword itself has many friends."

"Oh. Well, that's good. It's good to have friends. I left my best friend behind in Salina, where I grew up. His name is Nick. So what happens once we get to Halifax? Are you crossing the Atlantic by boat?"

He didn't say anything.

"What?" I asked. "Too slow? You guys probably have supersonic jets or something at your disposal."

After driving in silence a while—that seemed to be the method Bennacio preferred—we hit some rain. Bennacio sipped his fountain drink, holding the tip of the straw against his lower lip with his upper, the straw pressing against his chin, not sucking but delicately drawing up the soda into his mouth. There was the gentle hissing of the rain and Bennacio slurping his drink, and those were the only two sounds for miles. It started to get to me.

"I was wondering," I said, "who Mr. Samson was descended from."

Bennacio sighed. "Lancelot," he said wearily.

I decided not to worry if I was bugging him. I was getting tired of his Old World superior act and the way he talked to me like I was a little kid or somebody with a mental condition. And I was getting sleepy. And though it was a truly awesome car, I wasn't used to driving long distances. I wasn't used to driving, period.

"That's the guy who stole Guinevere from King Arthur," I said, like Bennacio might not know that little detail. "I guess none of this would have happened if he had controlled himself. Are you married, Bennacio?"

"No. Many of us marry in secret or not at all, thus our numbers have dwindled over the years."

"How come?"

"Remember, Kropp, we are sworn to protect the Sword.

To love another, to be bound by blood to another, that is to invite blackmail—or worse, betrayal. You mention Lancelot. Samson himself never wed because he could not bear the thought of endangering another human being."

"There was something else I was wondering," I said. "How did Mogart know about the Sword in the first place?"

"All Knights of the Sacred Order know."

I looked over at him. He was staring at the rain smacking against the glass and his face was expressionless.

"Mogart was a knight?"

"Once."

"What happened?"

"Samson expelled him." He sighed. "Mogart did not take banishment well, as one might imagine."

"Then why did Mr. Samson expel him?"

Bennacio hesitated before answering. "That was between Samson and Mogart." He glanced over at me and then looked away. "It was only a matter of time until a man like Mogart appeared among us. We were fortunate over the centuries, but the ancient bloodlines became diluted over time. Our blood intermingled with that of lesser men, our valor has been tarnished by the desires of this world. The voices of the angels have faded and into the void the voice of corruption rushes."

"What angels?"

"There were some in my Order, Kropp, who believed the Sword is actually the blade of the Archangel Michael, given to Arthur to unite mankind."

I remembered Mr. Samson telling me that the Sword was not made by human hands.

"That didn't turn out too good, did it?" I asked.

"It is certainly not the first time we have disappointed heaven," Bennacio answered.

17

I stopped just outside of a little town in the Shenandoah Valley called Edinburg to pee and to find Bennacio something other than a corn dog to eat. The rain had slackened to a gray mist and the temperature had dropped at least ten degrees. I had left Knoxville with just the clothes on my back, no jacket, no umbrella, and both would probably come in handy, especially in Nova Scotia, which I pictured as rainy and windswept and desolate.

I wondered if the Tuttles were looking for me back in Knoxville or if they even cared to look for me. I thought about missing school and about Amy Pouchard, and all of that—the Tuttles and Amy and school—felt to me like it had happened to somebody else, like the memories weren't my memories but the hijacked memories of another kid. It was as if I left more than the little I had back in Knoxville. Somehow, I had left the me that made me *me*.

We ducked into a McDonald's and Bennacio ordered a Big Mac and a Coke. He asked for some plasticware, and I wondered how he planned to eat a Big Mac with a plastic fork. I ordered a large Coke to keep me awake on the road and a fish sandwich. I waited in the car with the food while Bennacio used the pay phone outside the restaurant. He talked for about five minutes. His gait was thrown off by his wound and he moved slowly, as if each step cost him something.

He sat down, closed the door, and said, "Lock the doors, Kropp."

I was about to ask him why, when the back doors opened and two big men slid into the backseat.

"Too late," Bennacio said.

Something sharp pressed into the side of my neck. A voice behind me whispered, "Drive."

I backed out of the space using the rearview, where I could see the side of someone's square-shaped head and the large hand pressing the black dagger against my neck. The skin over every inch of my body was tingling. The other guy was sitting back in his seat, looking like he didn't have a care in the world.

"Turn right."

I pulled out of the parking lot and turned right, away from the on-ramp.

"Where am I going?" I asked.

"Where do you think?" the guy behind me cracked. I guessed he was saying I was going to my grave or to hell, probably to hell for all the people dead because of me.

Bennacio said, "Think carefully about what you are doing. I do not wish to kill you."

"Shut up," the man sitting behind him said.

"There is still time," Bennacio said. "If you repent now, heaven may still receive you."

The guy holding the dagger to my throat laughed.

"Whatever Mogart has offered you—is it worth the price of your immortal soul?" Bennacio asked calmly. He might have been talking about the weather.

The guy behind me said something to his buddy. It sounded like French. His buddy grunted and said, "Repos!"

"Think of your wives, your children," Bennacio said. "Would you have them widowed, fatherless? If you do not value your own lives, can you not consider theirs?"

"Speak again and the fat kid dies," the guy behind me said. I glanced into the rearview mirror and saw his hand was shaking slightly. Bennacio was getting to him. I thought about what Mogart told me, about the will of most men being weak. I also was thinking that just because a guy has an oversized head and a big body, you shouldn't call him fat.

We drove a few miles until we passed a sign that said "George Washington National Forest." I was directed onto this access road marked "Rangers Only" that narrowed to a skinny one-lane, winding deep into the woods.

"Here," the guy with the dagger to my throat said. "Stop here."

"I will kill you both," Bennacio said, still in that weird, calm voice. "First you with the knife. I will turn your own hand upon your throat and use it to sever your head from your body." He nodded to the guy behind him. "Then you I shall gut as a hog in a slaughterhouse, and I shall spread your steaming entrails on the ground for the carrion to feast upon."

This guy said something to the guy behind me. I don't know what he said, but it sounded pretty urgent. *"Fou!"* the guy with the dagger hissed back.

"You guys oughtta listen to Bennacio," I said. "He's a knight and those guys never lie."

"Get out," the guy with the dagger said.

"Ave Maria, gratia plena . . ." Bennacio began to pray. The guy behind him got out of the car, opened Bennacio's door, and yanked him out.

"Get out," the man behind me said. I got out. They dragged us into the trees. *Dominus tecum. Bendicta tu in milieribus. . . .* The ground was carpeted with pine needles and dead leaves, and there was a mist in the air and no sound, not even a bird singing. I looked over to Bennacio, now on his knees, with his arms hanging loosely at his sides. *Et benedictus fructus ventris tui, Iesus.* His eyes were half closed. The man standing before the kneeling Bennacio was heavy and broad-shouldered, with short-cropped black hair and a jutting brow. My guy was slighter and shorter, though

I probably had at least ten pounds on him. He had shaggy blond hair and an ugly scar running from beneath his right eye, down his cheek, to his jawline.

I got a good look at the dagger too. It was about two feet long, black, double-bladed, with the image of a dragon's head carved into its hilt. It looked like a miniature version of the swords Bennacio and the other knights used in Samson Towers. All these guys must go the same outfitters.

Santa Maria, Mater Dei, ora pro nobis peccatoribus, nunc, et in hora mortis nostrae.

"I want to pray too," I said. I don't know why I said that, but Bennacio was praying and he seemed like the kind of guy who always did just the right thing in a crisis. I went to my knees, bowed my head, and started the Hail Mary, only in English, but when I got to the "pray for us sinners" part I stopped because I heard a scream and a loud snap like the sound of a branch breaking. That's it, I thought. Bennacio's bought it.

Then I looked to my right and saw Bennacio coming in a blur for the guy in front of me. The man raised his dagger.

He was moving in slow motion, though. Bennacio wasn't.

Bennacio grabbed his wrist and I heard another snapping sound, not quite as loud as the first, and with his other hand Bennacio grabbed the guy by his shaggy hair while he forced the dagger back toward his throat. I didn't want to see what was going to happen next, so I stood up and kind of stumbled through the trees and undergrowth, passing the bigger man, who lay twisting on the ground. I heard a soft thud behind me and I knew without looking that Bennacio had kept the first part of the promise he made in the car. Then I heard the pleading tone in the bigger man's voice as Bennacio walked back to him, and I knew he was going to keep the second part too.

I went behind a tree and threw up. I was still bent over when I heard Bennacio call softly behind me.

"Kropp! Alfred! Come!"

Don't look; don't look, just keep your head up and your eyes on Bennacio, I told myself as I walked back to the car. He was already sitting in the passenger seat. He had taken the Big Mac apart and was eating the patty, holding it in the palm of his large hand, using a napkin as a plate, cutting the meat with the side of his plastic fork. *Don't look, don't look,* I told myself, but I had to look because I didn't want to trip on any body parts on the way to the car. So I looked and saw Bennacio had kept both his promises.

18

I drove toward the interstate. Bennacio told me to turn into the McDonald's parking lot. At first I thought he wanted to wash up, but I couldn't see any blood on his clothes, not a speck anywhere. He had me cruise around the building once, then pull onto the road again and turn left into the parking lot of the gas station on the interstate side of the McDonald's.

"There it is. Stop, Kropp."

I pulled beside a car parked behind the station. Bennacio dabbed both corners of his mouth with a napkin and got out while I sat there and watched him through his open door. He pulled a set of keys from his pocket and pressed the remote button, unlocking the other car. I got out then and joined him.

"Hey," I said. "This is a Ferrari Enzo."

Bennacio didn't answer. He was searching the car. He checked the center console, over the visors, under the seats and floor mats. He opened the glove box and pulled out a sleek black cell phone.

I said, "You know, it's funny. Somebody once promised I would have one of these cars." All of a sudden I felt like crying.

"Park the car, Kropp," he said, with a little jerk of his head toward the Mercedes. "Over there." He pointed to the far corner of the lot. I parked, walked back to the Ferrari, and when I got there, Bennacio was going through the trunk. He threw the keys to the Ferrari at me.

"What, we're taking this?" I asked.

"Hurry, Kropp," he said. "They know where we are now and where we're going. There will be more."

I slid into the driver's seat of the Ferrari and said to Bennacio, "You knights sure like to travel in style."

Bennacio said, "Drive, Kropp."

I got back on the highway and the Ferrari sped up to seventy-five like it was cruising a neighborhood street. Bennacio told me to go faster. At ninety he told me to go faster again. At 110 I told him I wasn't going any faster because if I drove any faster, my stomach would come out of my mouth. He didn't say anything after that.

I wished I could put the top down. I had always wanted a

convertible and to take it onto the open road like in a commercial and go a hundred miles an hour with the top down.

After an hour, the black cell phone rang. Bennacio flipped it open, listened for a second, then said, "It is too late. They are dead." He snapped it closed and tossed it out the window.

He leaned back in his seat, closed his eyes, and said, "I must rest now. Wake me when you are tired and I will drive."

"I don't get it," I said. I was pretty upset. There had been more blood flying around than in a horror movie. I had somehow found myself in an R-rated movie when all I wanted was PG-13. "There's a whole lot I don't get, Bennacio, like why we're driving in a hot car to Nova Scotia; why people are trying to kill us; what the heck OIPEP is and how it fits into all this; how Mogart or anybody else could use a sword no matter how powerful to take over the whole world; and why any of this had to happen to me in the first place. But what I *really* don't get is why you had to slaughter those guys like that."

"They would have slaughtered us."

"But how's that make you any different from them?"

"They are servants of the enemy—"

"So?"

"—thralls of the Dragon. Would you have them live to pursue us to our end?"

"I just don't get it, that's all. Chopping off people's heads and cutting out their guts . . ."

"You would not pity them if you knew them as I do."

"I don't know anybody who deserves something like that."

"You are afraid. I understand." His eyes were still closed. He spoke kindly to me, like a father would, or how I imagined a father would, since I never knew my father.

"You may pull off and find the nearest bus terminal if you wish, Kropp. I will give you the money for a ticket. I am well enough now to drive the rest of the way."

I thought about it. I thought about it hard. His offer was tempting, but really, where would I go? I didn't want to live with the Tuttles, and if I went back to Knoxville I wouldn't have a choice. Then all of a sudden I thought about that little beach town in Florida where Mom used to take me every summer. Maybe I could go there and get a job and live on the beach until the world ended. There were a lot worse places you could wait for the end of the world.

And, really, what did I think I was doing—me, Alfred Kropp of all people—driving a hundred miles an hour in a Ferrari Enzo with a modern-day knight by my side? Who the heck did I think I was?

"It was because of what Mogart did to Mr. Samson, wasn't it?" I asked finally. "The reason you mutilated those guys."

"Samson was my captain, Kropp," Bennacio said. "And there are some debts that cry to heaven to be repaid."

19

We were about twenty-five miles north of Harrisburg, Pennsylvania, when Bennacio told me to take the next exit. We had been on the road for over sixteen hours and maybe he noticed how much I was yawning and rubbing my eyes. We hadn't stopped since Edinburg except to fill up on gas and use the john.

I started to turn into a Super 8 just off the exit, but Bennacio told me to keep driving. I drove west on Highway 501, which hugged the edge of Swatara State Park. Trees crowded both sides of the road and there were no streetlights; it felt as if we were driving through a tunnel. I thought maybe the idea was to park somewhere in the woods and sleep in the car. We passed a sign that said "Suedberg 2 mi."

About a mile past the sign, Bennacio told me to turn onto a little dirt lane that wound up a hill, then through a dense group of trees. On the other side of the trees was a bridge that spanned a little creek, and after the bridge the road narrowed until it ended at a house set back in the woods. It reminded me of the houses from those old scary children's stories, like the witch's house in *Hansel and Gretel*.

Maybe this was like a safe house for the knights, a refuge for when they were in the area, cavorting about on an adventure.

I stopped the car and Bennacio said, "Kropp, you must stay here for a moment."

He got out of the car and I called to him before he shut the door. "How come?"

"I don't know how you will be received."

He mounted the steps. The front door opened, and a dark shape was silhouetted in the light from inside. This person wore a dress, so I figured it was a woman. She hugged Bennacio, rising on her toes to kiss both his cheeks. She bent her head while he whispered in her ear. Then her head came up and she looked at me.

Maybe she said something to Bennacio, because he waved his hand toward me, and the two of them disappeared inside.

I got out and locked the car: The place was isolated and

you never know what might be lurking in the woods. I was still pretty shaken up by our encounter with Mogart's henchmen back in Edinburg, and every shadow seemed to be holding a two-foot-long black dagger. I was finding out the hard way that the world is always more dangerous than you think it is.

They had closed the door behind them and I hesitated for a second before going in. Was I supposed to knock? Maybe Bennacio's wave didn't mean *Come on in, Kropp*. Maybe it meant *Stay in the car or forfeit your life!* Then I smelled bread fresh from the oven and my stomach decided for me; I hadn't eaten anything since the corn dog.

I opened the door after a quick little knock, a sort of compromise between knocking and not knocking, and stepped inside.

The front parlor was empty, but I could hear voices coming from down the hall, which also seemed to be where the bread smell was coming from. I stepped into the parlor. A small fire was going in here, and in one corner was a little wooden stand where a candle was burning. There was a picture displayed there of a guy about my age, with long blond hair and large, bright blue eyes, wearing a purple tunic and looking grimly at the camera, a silver headband across his forehead. A single white rose lay in front of the picture. It was some kind of shrine, I guessed, and I was sure without knowing exactly *how* I was sure that I was looking at a picture of one of Mr. Samson's knights.

"Kropp."

Bennacio was standing in the entry. I pointed at the picture.

"A knight?" I asked.

He nodded. "Windimar."

"This is his house?"

"This is the house of his mother. We shall stay here for the night."

"I thought we were in a hurry."

"We are, but even knights must eat and rest, and I desire her counsel. Miriam is a soothsayer, Kropp."

"Really? Wow. What's a soothsayer?"

"She has the gift of sight."

"You mean she can see the future?"

He didn't answer. I followed him down the hall to the kitchen, where a large oak table took up most of the space. The table was one of those sturdy, rough-hewn jobs, with thick legs and a top about five inches thick. It was covered with steaming dishes: a stew in an earthenware bowl, pots of potatoes and vegetables, fruit in a big wooden bowl, and five loaves of freshly baked bread on a cutting board in the shape of a fish.

Windimar's mother moved around the table, setting out the plates and these huge mugs that reminded me of pirate movies and grog. I stood there because Bennacio was standing, feeling big and awkward, like I was taking up too much space, light-headed from hunger, and nervous for some reason. Maybe it was because nobody was talking and she had a grim look on her face as she set out the plates. She was wearing a black full-length dress and her steel gray hair was pulled into a bun so tight, it looked painful. Her eyes were the same bright sky blue as her son's, her nose perfectly straight, her lips slightly oversized for someone her age, and the only wrinkles I saw were around the corners of her eyes, which were swollen slightly, I guessed from crying.

She set places for two, one on either side of the table. Bennacio sat down at one and, relieved, I sat at the other. He muttered something that sounded like Latin over the food and we set in while she stood at the sink washing up the cookery.

It was one of the best meals I ever had. The stew was beef-based, very thick and hot, the bread so buttery, it practically dissolved on my tongue, and even my drink had substance to it, kind of sweet-tasting, like honey, warm like hot apple cider, but not apple-based . . . I don't know what the heck it was, but it was good.

Miriam stacked the pots in the drainer to dry and sat down next to Bennacio. They spoke in low voices in a language I didn't understand. It sounded not quite French and not quite Spanish and it definitely wasn't German. Maybe it was Latin or whatever language they spoke in Arthur's day, like Celtic.

I was on my third helping of stew and second loaf of bread when their conversation got intense; I guessed they were having an argument about something and I guessed too that the something was me, because she kept glancing at me and at one point jabbed a finger in my direction. I was pretty uncomfortable, them talking about me while I sat right in front of them, and I think Bennacio knew that, because he switched to English.

"Do not forget," he said to her. "Without him I would not be here."

She answered in a thick accent, "And you forget, Lord Bennacio, without him my son would be here."

So it was about me taking the Sword, which got the knights, including her son, killed. I dropped my spoon into the bowl. I wasn't hungry anymore.

"Windimar did not die for anything Kropp did; he perished keeping a vow he made to heaven, Miriam."

"Yet his vow would not have been put to the test if not for him." Again she jabbed her finger at me.

"Perhaps. At last to our generation the test has come, whether born of the divine or the diabolical who can say? Yet we must take comfort, Miriam, in the fact that heaven has used odder instruments."

"He is an instrument of destruction," she spat back at him. "At the critical hour he will fail you, Bennacio. He will stand aside while you fall."

"Now that just isn't true!" I said. "Ma'am." I couldn't keep quiet anymore. "I screwed up, big time, but ever since I've been trying to do the right thing. Maybe you don't know this, but Mogart killed my uncle. Maybe it's true I'm partly responsible for all this mess, for the Sword being lost and all the knights . . . and what happened to the knights. So that's, um, true, and the only way I can make up for it is by helping Bennacio here."

"No," she said. "I have seen it. You will fail him, and the last knight will fall." Her eyes narrowed and somehow the room narrowed too. She was staring at me at the other end of a long, darkening tunnel, her crooked finger pointed at my nose. "And you too shall perish, Alfred Kropp, alone in the dark, where neither day breaks nor night falls. The Dark One will pierce your heart and—upon his command—you will die."

20

Bennacio and I sat in the parlor after dinner. It was half past one in the morning and Bennacio said we had to leave at dawn, but neither of us felt sleepy. My seat was right next to Windimar's shrine, and his big blue eyes stared at me like a rebuke.

Bennacio wasn't in a talkative mood. He sat with his elbows on the armrests, his long fingers laced together, staring at the fire.

Miriam's words were still echoing in my head, and his silence wasn't helping my creepy mood any. So I asked, "How do you become a knight? I mean, I know you have to come from one of the original knights, but you guys aren't born knowing how to handle a sword and all that stuff. What do you do, go to knight school?"

If he got the joke, he didn't let on. "We are trained by our fathers. In some cases, we apprentice under another knight, if the father is unable."

"What about Windimar's dad?" He was young enough for his father to still be alive, judging by his picture in the gilded frame beside me.

"His father died before he could complete the training."

"You completed Windimar's training, didn't you, Bennacio?"

He didn't say anything. Miriam came into the room with a big brandy snifter for Bennacio. She asked me if I wanted anything and I could tell that took a lot out of her, being gracious to me, but I told her no.

She said something in that funny-sounding language and Bennacio shook his head, but she came back at him pretty insistently, and he finally shrugged and shook his head, waving his hand at her as if to say, *Whatever, I'm too tired to argue.* She left the room.

"How'd his father die?" I asked, expecting to hear a story about a jousting tournament gone bad.

"His riding lawn mower flipped over on him."

"You're kidding."

"Even knights are not immune to absurd ends, Kropp."

Miriam came into the room again, this time carrying a long black case that looked like a musical instrument carrier.

Maybe she expected Bennacio to play a dirge on an oboe or something. She laid it at his feet, fussing at him in that strange tongue, until he finally said, in English, "Very well, Miriam."

"He would want you to have it." She couldn't seem to let the argument go.

"And I shall take it, in his memory. I pray I will not have to use it."

"You *will* use it, Lord Bennacio, before the sun sets on the morrow."

She left us alone. I cleared my throat. "Do her visions always come true?" I asked, because who wants to die alone in the dark, where no days break or nights fall, pierced in the heart by the Dark One?

He said, "I have never questioned her gift. But you must understand, Kropp, she is nearly overcome by grief, and grief always clouds our insight, even the insight of the gifted. From his birth, Miriam has known Windimar would die a bloody death. Imagine that if you can."

"I guess it could mess you up. I remember when my mom first told me she was dying from cancer . . ." I couldn't go on. Bennacio nodded as if he understood I couldn't, and patted my arm.

After he finished his brandy, Bennacio announced it was time we got some sleep because he planned to drive straight through to Canada. There was another long discussion or argument with Miriam about sleeping arrangements, I guess, and I wasn't sure who won, but I figured it was Bennacio by her fierce expression and the way she stomped down the hall, leading me to a room.

It was Windimar's old room. There was no bathroom, but there was an antique washstand with a bowl set in a hollowed-out shelf and a pitcher of steaming water. I washed my face and brushed my teeth in the warm water from the pitcher, and then I looked around the room.

A rocking chair sat beside a small fireplace on the wall opposite the bed, where a silver and gold crucifix was hung over the headboard. On that side was a tapestry that looked very old but couldn't have been that old, because there was Mr. Samson mounted on a great white horse in full armor and around him eleven men dressed in purple and holding shields painted with a horse and rider. At least it looked like Mr. Samson—there was the same large head and flowing golden hair, and I picked out a tall knight that could have been Bennacio and a knight with bright blue thread for eyes, Windimar, I guessed, staring right at me, and he was one good-looking guy; he looked a little like Brad Pitt, except for those bright blue eyes. Jealousy never did anybody any good and I wasn't really the jealous type, but this guy was learning swordplay and how to ride a horse and pledging his sacred honor to die for a noble cause when I was sitting by my mom's hospital bed watching her die and getting the stuffing beaten out of me at football practice.

I opened the closet door and inside was a full suit of armor, shined to a mirror finish, with a six-foot lance leaning against the wall beside it. It was fully assembled and I gave a little yelp when I opened the door, thinking I was the victim of a medieval ambush.

I stared at that suit of armor for a long time. It was polished so bright, I could see little shards of myself reflected in the metal, twenty-five Kropps at least, distorted like funhouse images. Shaggy brown hair, brown eyes, average-sized nose, chin, ears, teeth. If there was one trait these knights in the tapestry shared, it was that none of them looked average. Not all were as pretty as Windimar, as noble-looking as Samson, or as intense as Bennacio, but there was a set to their jaw, a certain look in the eyes they all had in common. I wondered if I put on the armor in the closet something like that might happen to me, the way even the geekiest guy in school looked macho in his ROTC uniform. I had this nutty urge to pull the armor off its stand and put it on. Then I thought that would be the ultimate gesture of disrespect, donning the armor of the knight who died because of me. I closed the closet door.

I turned out the light and crawled into the bed fully dressed and it bothered me, Christ hanging right over me, looking down like, *What the heck are* you *doing here?* that it took a long time for me to fall asleep. It didn't help that I could hear Miriam crying down the hallway, a low moaning sort of weeping. For a crazy second I thought about finding her and telling her I was sorry, which I kind of did already but not really in the kitchen. But Miriam didn't want to hear about me being sorry; she wanted her son back. Probably if I went in there she'd find the nearest heavy object and bash me over the head with it.

Her crying went on for a long time. I had cried for my mom when she died, but not the way Miriam was crying for Windimar. It was while I listened to her cry that I realized what I did went beyond Uncle Farrell, Mr. Samson and the knights, Bennacio and Windimar. What I did was slamming people I didn't even know about, like Miriam, the shock waves of my boneheadedness spreading out in ever widening circles, like a boulder the size of Montana landing in the ocean or that huge asteroid that hit the earth millions of years ago, wiping out the dinosaurs.

I finally fell asleep and dreamed I was scrambling up this rocky slope, not exactly a mountain, more like a slag heap of broken rock and tiny glittering shards of quartz or maybe those crystals you see growing inside of caves, sparkling like big wet teeth in the moonlight. I kept slipping and sliding as I tried to reach the top. The palms of my hands and my knees were all cut up and bleeding. Every time I gained a couple feet, I lost one, but it seemed very important I get to the top. I caught ahold of a big boulder near the summit and pulled myself up.

I rested awhile, looking at the shimmering shards littering the hill beneath me, feeling kind of proud of myself that I made it at least this far.

Finally I stood up, turned, and jumped the rest of the way. The top was perfectly flat and covered with long grasses whose tips reached up and caressed my aching legs as I walked toward this yew tree.

Under the tree sat a lady wearing a white robe, and her hair was long and dark, and her face almost as pale as her dress.

I don't know why, but she seemed familiar to me, and when I got close she lifted her head and smiled.

She looked at me with her sad, dark eyes, as if she knew me, and something I had done or failed to do had disappointed her. Then she asked me a question and I woke up.

"You have been dreaming," a voice said.

I scooted up in the bed and saw Bennacio sitting in the rocker by the fireplace.

I brought my hand to my face and it came away wet. I'd been crying.

"There was this . . . lady," I said. I cleared my throat. "All in white, with dark hair."

"Did she speak to you?"

"Yes."

"What did she say?"

"She asked me a question." I didn't want to talk about it. Bennacio had a bemused expression on his face, as if he knew what I'd been dreaming.

"What was the question?" he asked.

"She asked me . . . she asked me where the master of the Sword was."

"And what was your answer?"

"I didn't have an answer."

"Hmmm." He was smiling at me. Not a big, wide smile, but a secret little smile, like he knew what my answer should have been and that maybe I knew it too, and all that was holding me back was my reluctance to think things through.

"Who was she, Bennacio?"

"That is not for me to say."

"How come?"

"She came to your dream, Alfred."

I remembered him talking about angels as if they were real and wondered if the Lady in White was one. But why would an angel talk to me?

"I never believed in angels and saints or even God, much," I told Bennacio.

"That hardly matters," he said. "Fortunately for us, the angels do not require our consent in order to exist."

Everything about this Bennacio guy reminded me of my own insignificance. I didn't think he was trying to put me down, though. He had stepped up to a different level long before he met me. It wasn't his fault I was still scrubbing around at the bottom of the slag heap.

"I never really gave much thought to stuff like that," I said. "I guess one of my biggest problems is I don't take the time to think things through. If I did, the Sword would still be under Mr. Samson's desk and Uncle Farrell would be alive. Everybody would be alive and Miriam wouldn't be crying but maybe sewing on a tapestry. Did she make that? It must have taken her a very long time. What happened to Windimar, Bennacio?"

"I have told you. He fell near Bayonne."

"No, I mean, what happened to him?"

"Do you really wish to know?" He studied me for a minute, and I wondered why he had come in here while I slept. It was like he knew I would be waking up and he wanted to be there when I did.

"Very well. He was traveling by rail to Barcelona, the rendezvous point for our assault upon Mogart in Játiva, when he was set upon by seven of the Dragon's thralls. He might have escaped, but he chose to fight.

"He was the youngest of our Order, impetuous, idealistic—and vain. He never believed that our cause might fail. His pride undid him, Alfred. For though he fought well and bravely, besting five before he was overcome, in the end the two that remained mutilated him while he still drew breath."

His voice had dropped to a whisper. He wasn't looking at me anymore, but at some point over my head.

"He was found with no eyes, Alfred. They killed him, and then they cut out his eyes."

His gray eyes turned to me then, and they were hard. "The enemy has been gathering such men to himself for two years now, Alfred, since Samson expelled him from our Order. You have not lived very long, but surely you have heard of such men. Alas, the world is full of them. Men without conscience, their hearts corrupted by greed and the lust for power, their minds twisted past all human recognition. They have forgotten love, pity, remorse, honor, dignity, grace. They have fallen, mere shadows of men, their humanity a distant memory. Mogart has promised them riches beyond human imagining, and in their lust they have descended to barbarity beyond divine imagining. Remember that before you judge me for what I did in Edinburg. Remember Játiva. Remember Windimar's eyes, and then you may judge me."

21

At sunrise the next morning I stumbled into the kitchen, where Miriam had laid out blueberry muffins and these little buttery rolls that melted in my mouth like cotton candy. I wouldn't have stayed to eat—Bennacio was nowhere to be seen and Miriam acted as if I were this large empty space, like a bubble, floating around her kitchen—but those rolls were delicious and the muffins were about the size of my fist. Finally I couldn't stand it any longer and I said, "Where's Bennacio?" because he had made such a big deal about getting an early start. Loudly too because I was nervous around her and she wasn't too good with English and, like a lot of people, I spoke louder to people who did not share my native tongue. She jerked her head toward the little window over the sink, so I figured he had gone outside and in another instant I leaped to the conclusion he wasn't out on his morning constitutional but had actually taken off without me. I ran out the front door and was relieved to see the Ferrari still parked outside.

A heavy fog had rolled in during the night, and the early-morning sunlight was red and ghostly in the wispy moisture around the dark tree trunks of the woods around Miriam's house. I heard a thudding sound in the trees off to my right, and I turned toward it as it became louder. I think I knew what was coming before it came bursting through the trees, and I fought the impulse to dash back inside.

Bennacio exploded from the woods astride a huge white horse, bending low over its massive neck, both hands gripping its halter because there were no reins or bit.

They drew up beside me. The horse's dark nostrils flared and its tail slapped its flanks as Bennacio smiled down at me.

"We're riding horses to Canada?" I asked.

"Wouldn't that be grand?" he laughed. "The hour darkens, and we must make haste now, but I could not resist one last ride." He held out his hand.

"I'm scared of horses," I told him.

"Fortunately, I am not," he said, and he grabbed me by the forearm and swung my big self onto that horse's broad back as easily as if he were throwing a coat over his shoulder. Then he leaned over and whispered something into the horse's ear and we were off.

Just a few hours before, I had been racing down the interstate at a hundred miles an hour, but that seemed like crawling next to that horse ride through the Pennsylvania countryside. The trees whistled by my ears as I wrapped my arms around Bennacio's chest, my face pressed against his back, my eyes clenched shut. I slipped right and left on the horse's back, and I pressed my teeth together because I was terrified I might bite my tongue in two.

I don't know how long we rode before I felt this lessening of pressure in my chest and a light-headedness that made me crack my eyes open and sit back a little, my death grip loosening around Bennacio's middle—maybe fifteen minutes, but it seemed like an hour or two. I leaned farther back and opened my eyes wide, and the spring air was sweet and swift against my face, the trees blurs of brown and bright green, and the sound of this steed's hooves was like muffled thunder in my ears. I actually started to laugh out loud, whooping it up like a kid on a carnival ride, while Bennacio spurred on our mount. Bennacio, the Last Knight of the Round Table, astride a white stallion, riding to the rescue of the whole darn world, with Alfred Kropp hanging on for dear life behind him, shouting and crying at the same time, glad just to be along for the ride.

22

After we returned to the house, I waited by the Ferrari while Miriam said good-bye to Bennacio on the front steps. Her hair was down and she looked even younger that way. She took Bennacio's hands in hers and was talking urgently, and whatever she was saying was getting to him. He kept shaking his head, *No, no,* and I could tell, despite not spending a lot of time around the two of them, that they had a complicated relationship. She stood on her tiptoes and kissed both his cheeks, then took his head in both hands and looked at him without saying anything for a long time.

Bennacio came down the steps, holding out his hand.

"The keys, Kropp. I shall drive now. We must reach the border at Saint Stephen before dark."

I handed the keys to him and slid into the passenger seat. Bennacio tossed the black case Miriam had given him into the backseat and slid behind the wheel. About the only thing I was looking forward to was driving that Ferrari, but I didn't argue with him about it.

"Don't you think this car's been reported stolen and we'll be arrested?" I asked after we reached the interstate.

"I had not considered it."

"Maybe you should."

"We shall see."

I had lost track of the days, but I think it was Saturday. The interstate was practically deserted, except for a few big semis that Bennacio sailed past as if they were standing still.

We were somewhere between Hazelton and Scranton in Pennsylvania.

"Was that Windimar's horse?" I asked. He didn't answer, I guess because it was a stupid question. If you acknowledge a stupid question, you're just encouraging more of them. I made a resolution to evaluate the quality of my questions before I asked.

"Do you travel a lot in the knight business, Bennacio?" I asked.

"At times."

"That's something I've been wondering. I mean, I know your main job is to protect the Sword, but is that all you do? Do you have adventures?"

"Probably not in the sense that you mean. But we are knights nevertheless, sworn to protect the weak and defend the innocent."

"So that's a yes, right?"

"Is it so important, Kropp? For me, it has always been enough, that I should be charged with the protection of the Holy Sword."

"So I guess you're saying it's mostly just a lot of sitting around."

He didn't answer. I went on. "Sounds like my life. Only I wasn't protecting anything holy. Just sitting around eating Bugles, drinking Coke, and listening to music. I bet this baby's got a heck of a sound system. Want to try it out? What kind of music do you like? I bet it's Gregorian chants or something like that. Sinatra maybe. Though Sinatra was no monk. I thought you were a monk in the Towers the night I stole the Sword. My mom loved Sinatra. Am I talking too much? I think my brain is on overload, trying to process everything. You know, it's a lot to process. Sacred swords and modern-day knights and the world teetering on the brink of total annihilation. I think I'm doing pretty good, considering.

"I don't travel much either, not since my mom died, anyway. Every summer she took me to the beach in Florida and we wouldn't be four miles down the road before I had to eat something. What's in the case back there, by the way?"

"A gift."

"Oh, I was hoping maybe that Miriam lady packed us a

couple of sandwiches for the road. Anyway, I always got these cravings for some pecan logs or those bags of boiled peanuts they sell from the roadside stands."

"What is a pecan log?"

"You know, pecan-encrusted nuggety things. On our Florida trips Mom would stop at these stores along the highway called Stuckey's. Stuckey's pecan logs and also turtles—not real turtles, but that's the name for this chocolate candy with pecans. I really don't know what that nugget in a pecan roll was made out of; it's sort of like candy or maybe like congealed pie filling. Sort of vanilla-y, but real sweet. When you put the crunchy pecans with it, it's really good."

"One might have it with a bread-wrapped wiener."

"Corn dog."

"Corn dog, yes."

His eyes had been flicking between the road, the rearview mirrors, and me.

Suddenly he slammed the accelerator to the floor and my head popped back against the seat. A few seconds later, when we reached 120, he hit the cruise-control button and said, "Take the wheel, Alfred."

"Huh?"

"Drive for a moment."

He let go of the wheel and I grabbed it with my left hand as he twisted around to fumble with the latches of the black carrying case.

"Bennacio . . . !"

He sat back down and said, "Keep your hand on the wheel. If we run off the road at this speed we will not survive."

He pulled two curved pieces of wood from the black case, fitting one piece into the other, the curves going in the same direction. He was having some trouble with it because together they were about five feet long. I glanced in the rearview mirror and saw sunlight sparking off a mass of black metal and chrome that took up both lanes, coming up fast.

"What are those things behind us, Bennacio?"

"Suzuki Hayabusas."

"They're gaining on us."

"I have no doubt," he said. "They are the fastest motorcycles in the world."

He had pulled a long white cord from the case. The cord had a hook on each end. He threw one hook over the little metal eye at one end of the stick, flipped the staff around, and his neck muscles stood out as he pressed on the curved part of the other end, bending the whole thing so he could hook the cord.

"What you are doing?" I asked.

He answered in that same calm voice, "I am stringing my bow, Kropp." He rolled down the window and wind tore into the car, whipping his hair into a white tornado.

I looked in the rearview mirror again and saw that the riders—*dragon thralls*, Bennacio had called them—had separated and were gaining fast. I counted six, but I had to count quickly or risk running off the road.

"Keep us in the lane, Alfred!" Bennacio shouted. "Steer with your right hand and hold on to me with your left!" He reached back and pulled a quiver full of arrows from the case.

"I don't think I can do that!"

"You have no choice!"

He threw the quiver over his back and scooted backwards through the open window until he was sitting on the door, leaving only half his butt and his long legs inside the car. I grabbed a fistful of his pants leg with my left hand.

Now I could hear the harsh, throaty screaming of the motorcycles' engines as five of them swarmed past the car like enraged wasps. The sixth stayed a few car-lengths behind us.

The riders were dressed all in black. Even the visors on the helmets were black. As they roared past, Bennacio let fly the arrows. I heard the shhh-*phut* of the arrow leaving the bow and saw the lead bike spin out of control: Bennacio had shot the arrow into the right side of the rider's neck, a nice shot, considering he was firing against the wind in a Ferrari Enzo going 120 miles an hour. Two of the bikes couldn't avoid hitting the leader as he went down. Both struck him with their front tires and both bikes jackknifed, throwing the thralls forward, their bodies already limp as rag dolls when they hit the pavement.

That left two plus the one behind us, and now I could hear explosions coming from our left. The guns they fired at us were pretty big, but I couldn't see what kind because

Bennacio was blocking my line of vision and besides, I had to watch the road.

We took a hit near the left bumper and I figured they were aiming for the tires or the gas tank or maybe both. The impact slung us to the right and I nearly lost control, but I overcompensated for the skid and now we were straddling the centerline.

That gave me an idea and I gently eased the wheel to the left as Bennacio let fly the arrows, one after the other, shhh-*phut*-shhh-*phut*-shhh-*phut,* shooting, reloading (or whatever archers call it), and firing faster than you could blink. I kept edging into the left lane; the riders had to choose now between dropping back and passing us before I forced them into the median.

Out of the corner of my eye I saw one of the Suzukis leap ten feet into the air with a terrific explosion—Bennacio probably got his tire. You puncture a tire with an arrow at 120 miles an hour and that's what will happen.

One rider remained on our left, and he accelerated till he was even with the front bumper, and then I could see they had been shooting at us with sawed-off shotguns. As Bennacio twisted around, I wondered why we were using a bunch of arrows against six shotgun-toting madmen on Suzuki Hayabusas.

I glanced in the rearview mirror and saw the last rider coming up with the butt of a sawed-off shotgun resting in his lap, the black barrel pointing up and gleaming in the rising sun.

The guy pacing us managed to hold his course while he twisted to his right to fire. I saw an orange flash of light and the windshield exploded, showering us with glass. I think I might have screamed, but any sound I made was drowned out by the wind howling through the busted windshield.

Suddenly I was in a very small, very powerful wind tunnel, and tears rolled straight back from the corners of my eyes and ran into my ears.

The rider to our left eased off the gas and drifted toward us. Before I could react he leaped from the bike onto the hood of the Ferrari, his abandoned bike careening to the left and into the median strip. His black outfit whipped and snapped around his body. He still held the shotgun in his right hand.

Bennacio's thigh tensed below my fist as he leaned over the hood to get off a shot before the rider blew my head off. He was too late. I saw another dull orange flash, and the rear window exploded.

I whipped the wheel hard to the right, catching the rider off guard—he flew off the hood and his scream was abruptly cut off as he hit the pavement.

Bennacio fell back into the driver's seat, his hands empty; he must have tossed his bow onto the road. Maybe his quiver was empty or maybe bows and arrows against guns just wasn't quite challenging enough for him. I fell back into my seat and tried to catch my breath, but there was no catching it and I wondered if I had wet my pants. There were shards of glass everywhere, in my lap, down my shirt, in my hair. I twisted to my left and looked behind us.

"What happened to him?" I shouted in Bennacio's ear.

"Duck, Kropp."

I just stared stupidly at him, not moving until his hand shot out and pushed my head down. The window beside me exploded inward, raining glass on my back and legs, and I sat back up without thinking, turned, and saw the end of the shotgun about a foot away.

I grabbed it with both hands and screamed out the broken window at the guy on the bike, "Let go!" like he would if only I told him to. He didn't let go.

I yanked as hard as I could before he could fire a second time and he had to choose between losing control and letting go of the shotgun. He let go and faded toward the emergency lane.

"Lean back, Kropp," Bennacio said. His voice was loud but calm, as if we were still discussing corn dogs. He picked up the gun from my lap and pointed it at the biker out my window. I yelped and threw myself back against the seat as the gun exploded practically beside my nose.

The shell went through the window and landed in the gas tank of the Suzuki Hayabusa. I felt the heat of the fireball against my face, and the concussion from the blast shook the Ferrari so hard, Bennacio had to drop the shotgun onto my lap and grab the steering wheel with both hands to keep us from spinning out of control.

"I think I'm going to be sick!" I shouted against the howling wind.

He didn't say anything. He was smiling, and I don't think it was because I told him I was going to be sick.

23

Bennacio slowed to a more comfortable eighty, but the wind was still blowing fiercely in my face, so I scrunched down in the seat. I covered my eyes and wondered when the reinforcements would arrive.

I don't know how long I sat there like that, shivering in the cold blasts of air, my knees actually knocking together and my teeth chattering in my head, but it seemed like a very long time. Then I heard the motor winding down and the wind dwindling. I took my hand away and saw Bennacio was pulling into the emergency lane. A tractor-trailer was coming up fast behind us, laying on its horn, and Bennacio gave the trucker a friendly little wave as he rumbled past.

"What's the matter?" I asked.

"We're out of gasoline," he answered as the car slowly rolled to a stop.

"You're kidding, right?"

"I am not. Come, Kropp, we must walk now."

"Walk?"

"We have no choice."

"You keep saying that. How come we never have a choice?"

"Sometimes it is easier not to have one."

We got out of the car and stood for a moment looking at it. It didn't look cool anymore. I reached through the window and grabbed the shotgun.

"No, leave it, Kropp."

I sighed and dropped it back onto the seat.

"Lemme ask you something, Bennacio. What's with the swords and daggers and bows and arrows and medieval stuff like that? Aren't you knights allowed to carry guns?"

"There's nothing that prohibits us."

"Then why don't you?"

"It is mostly a matter of pride. You may think otherwise, but guns are far more barbaric than swords. There is no elegance to a firearm, Alfred."

He smiled. "Besides, our way is more fun."

We started to walk. We hadn't gone very far, maybe a quarter of a mile, when I stopped walking. Bennacio, his head bowed, deep in thought, kept walking for several yards before noticing I wasn't beside him. He stopped and watched as I sat down and wrapped my arms around my knees.

It had turned into a nice day, with just a few wisps of cloud and a light breeze from the south. I lifted my face to the sun. Bennacio came back to me and sat down.

"I'll be honest with you, Bennacio. I'm pretty shaken up right now. I know this sort of thing must be normal for a knight, but what happened back there freaked me out a little. No. Not a little. A lot. You go to the movies and you watch these guys in car chases and shoot-outs and you think, hey, I could do that. I mean, you sit there in the dark theater and you kind of wish it was you up there taking out the bad guys. But it isn't like that in real life, though this whole thing is starting to feel more like a movie than real life—which is weird, because I'm starting to miss my real life, even though it sucked. I'm not sure how much farther I can go."

"I see." He sighed. There was a sad look in his eyes. "Unfortunately, we cannot stay here long, Alfred. The police will be here soon—and perhaps worse."

"More AODs?"

"AODs?"

"Agents of darkness."

He smiled. "Yes. AODs. Quite so."

"I don't want to hold you up, Bennacio. You've got an important job to do—saving the world and everything, and it's kind of selfish of me to tag along. Especially when I'm not even sure I *want* to be tagging along."

"You do not give yourself enough credit, Alfred. Without you, I would not have survived this morning."

He obviously said it to make me feel better, but I didn't think he didn't believe it.

"Broadway," he said suddenly.

"Huh?"

He was smiling. "You asked what kind of music I like. I love show tunes."

I don't know why, but I laughed out loud.

"I am particularly fond of Lerner and Loewe. *Camelot*. Have you heard of it?" He sang softly. " 'In short there's simply not/A more congenial spot/For happy-ever-aftering than here in/Camelot!' Predictable, I know."

I cracked up. It helped. "We gotta get a ride somehow, Bennacio," I said after I caught my breath. "We can't walk the whole way to Halifax."

Bennacio stood up. "No, we cannot. Get up, Kropp, and stand with your hands by your sides."

He was staring down the road, and I stood up and looked with him. I heard the siren before I saw the car and the flashing lights.

"Great," I said. "Cops."

The patrol car pulled into the emergency lane, cut the siren, but left the blue-and-reds spinning. The patrolman stepped out of the car, his hand on the butt of his pistol.

"Get on your knees with your hands behind your head!" he shouted at us. "Now!"

"Do as he says," Bennacio said quietly, and we kneeled

on the pavement and I laced my fingers behind my head. The patrolman's shoes went *scrape-scrape* against the concrete as he came toward us.

"You fellows know anything about what happened back there?" he asked.

"We ran out of gas," Bennacio said.

"Looks like you did more than that," the cop said. He stopped a couple of feet from Bennacio, his gun drawn now and aimed at Bennacio's high forehead.

"I have a gun," Bennacio said calmly, as if he were remarking on the weather. "Behind my back."

"Don't move!" the cop said, and he wet his lips. He wasn't much older than me, maybe nineteen or twenty, looking kind of silly in his tall brown hat, like a kid playing dress-up. He crouched down, the gun's muzzle about four inches from Bennacio's nose, and reached around his back to find the weapon that wasn't there.

Bennacio's right hand shot straight up, his index and middle finger extended from his fist, into the kid's neck. He fell straight down and lay still.

"You killed him," I said. "Jeez, Bennacio!"

"He is not dead," Bennacio said. "Come, Alfred."

He was already on his feet and walking rapidly toward the patrol car.

"We're taking his car?"

"Yes."

"Because we've got no choice."

"Yes."

"I want to go home, Bennacio."

He turned at the door. "What home, Alfred?"

He wasn't trying to be mean. He just didn't know what I meant by "home." What did I mean by "home"? The Tuttles'? Knoxville? He didn't know and I sure didn't know. I had no real home anymore.

I got in the car.

24

He cut the spinning red and blue lights, hit the gas pedal, and the Crown Victoria was soon up to 105. Cars pulled out of our way as we approached because we were obviously on some pretty important police business. I rode shotgun, next to the cop's actual shotgun, and thought if we were attacked again it was all up to me because we were out of arrows and something like a shotgun wasn't elegant enough for Bennacio.

We were in the Wyoming Valley, and to my right I could see the Poconos rising. I had never been on a road trip before, if you didn't count the trips to Florida with my mom, which you couldn't count, since that was a family thing. But you really couldn't count this as a road trip either, since the one thing all road trips have in common is they're supposed to be fun.

Bennacio turned on the scanner and listened to the chatter, but there wasn't anything about a stolen cruiser—not yet, anyway, though we both knew it wouldn't be long.

"What now?" I asked.

"We must find another means of transportation."

"Lemme guess," I said. "White stallions?"

"I was thinking more along the lines of a very fast cat," he said. He turned on the flashing red-and-blues. The car directly in front of us changed into the right lane and Bennacio followed it, coming up close on his bumper.

"A Jaguar," I said. "Fast cat, I get it, very funny, but how is carjacking part of the code of chivalry?"

He didn't answer, but reached for the button that operated the siren.

"Hey, can I?" I asked.

"If you wish."

I hit the button, the siren wailed, and Bennacio proceeded to flash his headlights at the Jaguar. It eased into the emergency lane. Bennacio stopped about ten yards behind it. Then he unhooked the shotgun from its holder and pressed it into my hand.

"I thought these were barbaric."

"Just so, but you are not a knight."

"I'm not shooting anyone, Bennacio."

"I don't think that will be necessary."

He reached into his breast pocket and pulled out a long, thin leather-bound folder. A checkbook. On the face of the top check, embossed in gold letters, were the words "Samson Industries." He flipped it open and signed a blank check.

"To answer your question: No, we do not steal; we do not 'jack cars,' but sometimes there are those who refuse to sell. Come, Kropp."

He was outside the car and walking up to the Jag before I could say anything. I heaved myself out of the cop car and followed him, holding the gun across my body. A big guy in a tan overcoat was stuffed behind the wheel of the little sports car. It was pretty clear from his expression that Bennacio and I weren't what he was expecting after being pulled over by the Highway Patrol.

"What's up?" he said.

"Don't be alarmed," Bennacio said. He motioned to me and, as soon as I stepped forward, Bennacio ripped the shotgun out of my hand and pointed at the big guy's nose.

"Sure looks like I should be!" the big guy cried out, instinctively bringing his hands up.

"Step out of the car, please," Bennacio said.

"Sure. You bet. Don't shoot me."

He had some trouble getting his bulk out of the car, but being nervous probably wasn't helping his coordination.

"This is for your trouble," Bennacio said, shoving the check at him. "I place it upon your honor to fill in an amount you feel is reasonable. Come, Kropp," he said, and he tossed the shotgun at me. I caught it and halfheartedly pointed it at the incredulous guy, who didn't know what to look at by that point: Bennacio getting behind the wheel of his Jag, me holding the shotgun, or the blank check in his trembling hand. I walked around him to the passenger side and said, to be helpful, "We left the keys in the ignition"—motioning toward the cop car—"but it probably wouldn't be a good idea to follow us."

I climbed into the car and Bennacio floored the gas before I could even get my seat belt fastened.

"You're awful trusting, Bennacio," I said after a few miles had rolled by and it was clear the guy wasn't going to follow us in the borrowed cop car. "How do you know he won't write himself a check for a million dollars?"

"Most people are honest, Kropp. Most are good and will choose right when given a choice. If we did not believe this, what point would there be in being a knight?"

Then he reached across the seat, grabbed the shotgun out of my lap, and tossed it out the open window.

25

Through the rest of Pennsylvania, up into
New York, Massachusetts, onto 95 up the New England
coast, into New Hampshire and then crossing the border
into Maine, we stopped only for gas (the Jag gulped it) and
to pee, and once to pick up a lobster sandwich at the Mc-
Donald's drive-thru. I had no idea McDonald's served lobster sandwiches. I kept looking behind us expecting to see a
dozen cop cars bearing down on us—or more AODs, maybe
on Harleys this time, sacrificing speed for muscle.

Twenty miles from the Canadian border, hitting 115
along State Road 9, I noticed we had the northbound lane

practically to ourselves, but the southbound lane was backed up for miles.

"Something's wrong," I said. "Everybody's fleeing Canada." It was hard to imagine, though, Armageddon starting in Canada.

"Most likely the border has been closed."

"What'll we do?"

"We have no choice. We must cross."

I pictured us flying through the barricades at 110 with the Royal Mounted Police racing after us. Right as I was picturing this, the first set of blue-and-reds shot out of the dark behind us. Soon there were three or four sets of them and I could hear the sirens from inside the car. Bennacio responded by speeding up, the needle hovering around 120. We roared past an electronic sign that was flashing: "Border Closed."

"Look, this is bad, Bennacio," I told him. "We gotta ditch the Jag and find a place to cross on foot." It wasn't the brightest suggestion, given we were being chased by half the patrol cars in Maine.

Bennacio didn't answer. He kept our speed up until he saw the battalion of National Guardsmen with their assault rifles manning the crossing. The first line of soldiers had already gone to its knees and had taken aim at us.

He slammed on the brakes and we skidded about fifty feet to a stop. Then he said, "Get out of the car, Alfred. Make sure they can see your hands."

I stepped out of the patrol car, my hands in the air, as somebody screamed into a bullhorn, "STEP OUT OF THE

CAR—NOW! KEEP YOUR HANDS WHERE WE CAN SEE THEM!"

Behind us the cop cars rolled in, lights blazing, and a dozen brown uniforms took positions behind their open doors. I wondered how Bennacio was going to get out of this one.

"ON YOUR STOMACH WITH YOUR HANDS OVER YOUR HEAD, FINGERS LACED!"

Bennacio nodded to me and we lay on the ground, side by side. These last few feet of America were very cold. Somebody came and stood right over us, and I could see my reflection in the bright finish of his black shoe.

"Hi. This is the point where I ask what your business in Canada is tonight," the wearer of the shiny shoe said.

"There is a card in my jacket pocket," Bennacio said. "Before you do anything rash, I suggest you contact the person on that card."

I couldn't see if Mr. Shiny Shoes got the card or not, but he walked away and was gone for some time.

"What's going on, Bennacio?" I whispered.

"I am calling in a favor."

"I'm cold," I said. Bennacio didn't say anything.

Somebody grabbed me by the collar and hauled me up. A guy in a blue Windbreaker, the owner of the polished shoes, handed Bennacio the card and said, "This is your lucky day."

"It isn't luck," Bennacio answered. "It is necessity."

We climbed back into the Jag. The guy in the blue Windbreaker and the very nicely shined shoes waved to the border guard. He hit the code to open the gate. The guy in the Windbreaker stepped back and waved us through.

"Good luck!" he called, as we roared through the gate into Canada.

"Necessity," Bennacio muttered.

26

I had never been to Canada, but I didn't see much of it because it was dark and Bennacio took secondary two-lane roads. He drove through the night like the hounds of hell were after us. I knew Halifax was on the coast and probably he had a plane waiting there for him, but what good would it do if all flights were grounded? I tried to sleep, but you try sleeping in a Jaguar going 120 miles an hour in a strange country.

We crossed a long bridge at three a.m. and Bennacio told me we were in Nova Scotia. We may as well have been on the dark side of the moon for all I could tell. We drove in silence until a faint orange glow appeared on the horizon. At first I thought it was the sun rising, then remembered it was three a.m.

"We may be too late," Bennacio said.

He slowed down to a leisurely eighty and, coming up on a huge fire, I saw we were at a private airstrip. There was some kind of wreckage burning on the runway.

Bennacio pulled into an access road that led directly to the airstrip. Three guys were standing at the end of it, next to a tan Chevy Suburban, wearing long brown robes like the one Bennacio wore the first time we met.

"I thought you were the last knight," I said.

"I am," he said. "And I believe I have told you, Alfred, that the Sword has many friends."

He stopped the car and we got out. A light, freezing rain was falling. I could hear the ocean and taste the salt on my tongue. Bennacio left the headlights on and we gathered in front of the car. The air seemed to sparkle as the light danced in the tiny droplets of rain.

One of the guys came toward Bennacio. They kissed each other on both cheeks, and then the guy gave him a big hug and looked at me.

"Cabiri, this is Kropp," Bennacio said.

"He is a Friend?" Cabiri asked, studying me.

"A Friend and a Wielder."

"Indeed! Then he is my friend," Cabiri said, and he kissed both my cheeks and wrapped me in the same tight bear hug.

He turned to Bennacio. "We had a little trouble, as you

can see." He nodded toward the burning wreckage. "They came on foot, apparently, and that took us by surprise. We expected an aerial assault. They used this."

He nodded to one of the guys standing behind him. He was toting what looked like an oversized bazooka, but I figured it was probably a rocket launcher.

"Derieux?" Bennacio asked.

"He was inside the plane, Lord Bennacio."

Bennacio closed his eyes. I saw the other two brown-robed guys staring at me and I looked away.

"*Diabli!*" Bennacio muttered. "Did they escape?"

Cabiri smiled grimly. He jerked his head toward the burning plane. "Come, I will show you."

We followed him across the tarmac, past the twisted, burning husk of the plane, where the rain hissed and spat and smoke billowed upward, to the other side of the airstrip. Three men in black robes lay there faceup, staring blankly straight up into the rain. Bennacio pulled the hoods away from their faces and studied each one for a long time. He gestured toward the one lying in the middle, the biggest of the three, with a large, flattened nose and black slits for eyes.

"This is Kaczmarczyk," he said. "The other two I do not recognize."

Cabiri turned his head and spat. "Local fishermen, I suspect, recruited by Kaczmarczyk."

"Perhaps." Bennacio turned from the bodies and stared at the burning plane, and the light of the fire danced in his gray eyes.

"We cannot stay here, Bennacio," Cabiri said. "More will come when Kaczmarczyk fails to report. Many more, I fear, than the four of us can manage." Actually, five of us stood there, but I guess Cabiri wasn't counting me. "Come, my house is not far from here. You may rest and we will decide our course."

"Our pilot Derieux is dead," Bennacio said. "Even if we can find another plane, we have no one to fly it."

Cabiri placed one of his large hands on Bennacio's shoulder. "Come, Lord Bennacio," he said softly. His eyes were filled with tears, though his tone was jovial. "A hot meal, a warm bed, and things will look brighter in the morning."

He glanced at the other two guys. "And there is someone who would very much like to see you."

27

We left the bodies lying there. Bennacio covered the faces of the men he did not recognize, but left Kaczmarczyk's exposed to the rain. I wasn't sure why, but thought maybe he was getting at something symbolical.

We climbed into the Suburban. We left the Jaguar sitting on the runway and nobody said anything about it.

Bennacio, me, and the guy with the bazooka, Jules, sat in the back of the Suburban, with Cabiri and the other brown-robed guy, Milo, up front. Jules had a funny smell, like black liquorish, and a very long nose with a turned-under tip. Milo had long blond hair that he wore in a ponytail, and piercing blue eyes, like Windimar's. Thinking of Windimar reminded me of the painful fact that I wasn't Windimar, but Alfred Kropp, and I had no business hanging with these bazooka-wielding warriors.

We drove in silence for a few minutes, then Cabiri said, "The outsiders stormed Mogart's keep in Játiva yesterday. Of course, they found nothing."

"Where is Mogart?" Bennacio asked.

Cabiri shook his head. "I don't know. We've heard nothing, Lord Bennacio."

His whole attitude toward Bennacio was tender and respectful, like it was a great honor just to be around him. If he had known I was responsible for this whole mess, he probably would have directed Jules to take me out with the bazooka.

"And now there is no way to cross the Atlantic," Bennacio went on.

"They closed the border and yet you crossed. Do not despair, Lord Bennacio. I know you loathe them, but I see no choice now. We must use what tools we have."

Bennacio sighed. "I will consider it."

I wondered who Bennacio loathed.

"Who are the outsiders?" I asked. "OIPEP?"

"OIPEP!" Cabiri sneered, and he made a spitting sound.

"What *is* OIPEP anyway?" I asked. "The best I could come up with was 'Operatives Investigating Powerful Evil Persons.'"

"Ha ha!" Cabiri shouted. "You have found a witty one, Lord Bennacio!"

Nobody said anything for the rest of the drive, which lasted about thirty minutes. We ended up in this little hamlet with Cape Cod–type houses lining these narrow, twisty streets. It might have been Halifax or it might not; I didn't know how big a town Halifax was or how far it was from the airstrip.

We went inside a house painted blue with white shutters. There was a fire snapping and popping in the fireplace and kerosene lamps set on tables, and I wondered why they didn't have electricity. Maybe these servants of the Sword had to operate on a tight budget. But Bennacio handed that guy a blank check from Samson Industries. Maybe the knights had an expense account but the Friends didn't. Or maybe it was a lifestyle choice, like those reenactors you see on TV.

"We are safe here, Lord Bennacio," Cabiri said. "At least for a few hours. Jules, find Lord Bennacio something to eat." He didn't tell Jules to find me something to eat. "Milo, tell her Lord Bennacio has arrived." He smiled at Bennacio. "She has been quite concerned."

Bennacio didn't answer. He sank into the chair closest to the fire and pressed his fingertips against his eyelids. I didn't know what to do with myself, so I sat on a stool next to Bennacio and wished I had some dry socks; the bottoms of my feet were starting to itch. I wondered if it would be rude to take off my shoes.

Cabiri slipped off his brown robe. Underneath he wore a flannel shirt and Wrangler jeans. He had short-cropped, very curly hair, like a poodle. He looked like the guy on the Brawny paper towels.

Jules carried in a tray loaded down with smoked salmon, big chunks of cheese, bundles of fat grapes, and lumps of little black greasy-looking balls on thin crackers that I guessed was caviar. I had never tasted caviar and didn't want to try anything new on an empty stomach, so I helped myself to some salmon and cheese. The grapes were good, with very tight skin, so when I bit into one the juice exploded in my mouth. Jules left and came back with a bottle of wine and some glasses, but I'm not a wine drinker, so I ate a lot of grapes for their juice. Maybe they'd have the cash for electricity, I thought, if they didn't blow it on caviar and expensive French wine. Cabiri was a big guy like me with an appetite to match, and between us the tray didn't stay full for long.

"You must call them," Cabiri told Bennacio.

"The thought galls me," Bennacio answered.

Just then a girl came into the room, and Cabiri got up and Jules got up and so I got up, and all the crumbs in my lap fell on the throw rug. She was tall, almost six feet, barefoot, wearing a sleeveless green dress that trailed the floor. Her auburn hair was pulled back from her face and her pale skin glowed in the firelight. She was the most beautiful girl I had ever seen.

She went directly to Bennacio, who stood up as she came toward him, and she took his hand and kissed it, then pressed it against her cheek. "My lord," she said softly.

He touched her cheek with his free hand and said, "Natalia, you should not be here."

"Nor should you," she said.

He was turned three-quarters from the firelight, so his face was in shadow and I couldn't see his expression when he said, "I have no choice," but he sounded sad, the same way he'd sounded when he said "Our doom is upon us" back in Knoxville.

He turned toward me and said, "This is Alfred Kropp."

"I know who Kropp is," Natalia said, and she didn't look at me. Her voice had a very clear tone, like the ringing of bells in the distance, so even though she spoke softly, you could hear her across the room.

"He saved my life," Bennacio added. I'm not sure why. Maybe to get her to like me. I could see that was going to be a hard sell.

"That you might sacrifice it," she said to Bennacio.

"That I might keep my promise."

I looked at Cabiri, who was studying the way the light played on his wineglass, and at Milo, who was standing by the front door, like a soldier on watch. I didn't know what had happened to Jules. Bennacio and Natalia were talking like they were the only people in the room, and I was very uncomfortable.

"Your promise!" she said. "No, not *your* promise, my lord, but another's, the promise of a myth, made a thousand years ago to one whose bones have long since crumbled to dust. You trust the word of the dead above the vows of the living."

"I trust the purity of my Order."

"Your precious Order is no more, my lord. The knights have departed."

"All but one."

"And soon you too will fall and I will be alone."

"Is this why you came?" Bennacio asked. "To torment me in this way? I cannot abandon my oath for any human being, no matter who she may be. I cannot sacrifice the world for the sake of one person."

"The world is not worth saving, if not for the sake of one person," she said.

He touched her cheek. "I love you before all things, and I would perish rather than see you suffer. But you do not understand what you are asking, Natalia. I cannot turn my back on heaven. I will not damn myself, even for love."

"You're the one who does not understand," she shot back. Then her shoulders slumped and all the fight went out of her. She leaned against him, and he took her in his arms and held her as she cried softly into his shoulder. He murmured her name into her hair as he looked at me. Our eyes met and I looked away. I couldn't take the look in those eyes.

28

"The hour grows late," Cabiri said. "You must decide, Bennacio. We have lost both plane and pilot. You did not hesitate to use the outsiders to cross the border. You *must* call them now."

Before Bennacio could answer, Milo said, "Someone is here."

The window beside him exploded inward, and glass flew across the room. Something landed in the entryway and rolled toward us, bumping against Cabiri's leg before coming to a stop.

It was Jules's head.

"The lights!" Cabiri cried. He and Milo rushed around,

blowing out the kerosene lamps. Bennacio shoved Natalia toward me, picked up a bucket that was sitting by the fireplace, and threw water onto the logs. There was an angry hiss and a plume of white smoke.

"Down the hall, Alfred," Bennacio said. "Last door on the left. Hurry!"

I grabbed Natalia and pulled her down the hall, feeling my way along the wall with my right hand. She wasn't making it any easier in the pitch dark by trying to pull free. She was a tall girl and strong for someone so thin. Behind us, I could hear the sounds of a pretty terrific fight going on, breaking glass, shouting, the clump of feet, and the sharp crack of furniture breaking.

I reached the end of the hall and found the door, pushing Natalia into the room and slamming the door closed behind us. What were we supposed to do now? Duck in the closet? Hide under the bed? A roaring sound moved directly overhead now, the steady *thumpa-thumpa-thumpa* of a helicopter, and then the *pop-pop-pop* of gunfire and men screaming.

I let go of her wrist. "Maybe we should—" I started to say, but she didn't let me finish. Out of the dark a knee landed right in my crotch and I dropped straight down and curled into a ball on the floor. When you take a hit like that, there's nothing you can do but curl up around the pain and hug it till it fades.

"That is for taking the Sword and sentencing him to death," she hissed at me. Through my tears I saw the door open and her shape silhouetted in the lighter dark of the hallway. She held a tapered dagger in her right hand. Then she was gone and my pain and I were alone together.

I grabbed on to the edge of the bed and pulled myself up. I was swaying there by the foot of the bed, the pain keeping tempo with the beat of my heart, when the beam from a large flashlight stabbed into the room. I just rushed the guy without thinking about it, lowering my shoulder and slamming into his chest, forcing him out the doorway and into the hall. He lost the flashlight when I hit him. I started pounding his middle with both fists, till he grabbed my right wrist, twisted my hand behind my back, swung me around, and forced me to the floor, putting his knee in the small of my back and bringing my wrist up so the tips of my fingers were touching my neck. It felt like he was pulling my arm out of its socket. Then I felt something cold press behind my ear.

All of a sudden it was very quiet. The guy holding me down was breathing hard, but that and the slow *whump-whump* of the helicopter blades turning outside were the only things I could hear.

Then I heard Bennacio call out, "No! He is with us!"

The guy got off me and picked up the flashlight. He kicked me onto my back and shone the light right in my eyes.

"Who are you?" he demanded.

"Alfred Kropp!"

"Alfred Kropp! Hey, my mistake, but you bushwhacked me, kid."

A hand came out of the dark and pulled me to my feet. I

could smell his cologne and hear him working on a piece of gum. Bennacio joined us, carrying a kerosene lamp.

The guy with the flashlight pumped my hand twice, very hard. He was wearing Dockers and a polo shirt beneath a blue Windbreaker. He couldn't have been older than twenty-five or thirty. His hair was shoulder-length and slicked back with some kind of gel.

"Mike Arnold," he said. "How ya doin'?" He turned to Bennacio. "Close call, Benny, huh? You can thank me later. Right now we gotta get the heck outta Dodge. There's more baddies on the way."

He herded us down the hall into the main room. Cabiri stood near the fireplace, a couple of black-robed bodies lying at his feet. Another guy in a black robe was sprawled face-down on the kitchen floor, blood pooling under his head. Natalia stood over him, breathing heavily, the dagger glistening in her hand.

"Milo?" Bennacio asked Cabiri, who slowly shook his head and motioned toward the sofa. I didn't want to look at Milo, but I looked anyway and then was sorry I had looked.

"We all here?" Mike Arnold asked. "All accounted for? That's terrific. That's just jim-dandy. Leave the mess; we'll send somebody over to clean up."

"How did you find us?" Bennacio asked him.

"No time for that now. Grab whatever gear you have and let's go." Mike strode to the front door and flung it open. There was a large black helicopter sitting on the street, whipping cold air into the house.

Cabiri stepped up to Bennacio and said softly, as if he didn't want Mike to hear, "Come, Lord Bennacio. The choice has been made for us. Trust this turn of fortune."

"Oh yeah, you gotta trust it when fortune turns," Mike Arnold said, snapping his gum, and I wondered who the heck Mike Arnold was.

29

We piled into the helicopter, which was one of those big military types that sat seven with room for gunners on both sides. I sat next to Bennacio and Natalia in the seat at the back. My butt was hardly on the cushion when we were airborne, dipping hard to the left as we climbed, and I could taste soured cheese as my stomach came up toward my throat. Natalia was still barefoot and I thought her feet must be freezing in the swirling air inside the open hold. Cabiri and Mike Arnold sat across from us, and Mike was smiling at me with very large white teeth that the gum-smacking made easy to notice.

He leaned forward and shouted in my face, "So you're

Alfred Kropp, huh! Hey, what a boner, taking the Sword like that! You're our century's Pandora! You study Greek mythology in school? Pandora's Box? You must be like, 'Holy moley, what the hell was I *thinking*?' " He laughed and his gum went *smack-smack-smack*. He chewed gum like he was angry at it.

He looked at Natalia. "Don't think we've met. Mike Arnold, how ya doin'?"

Natalia just stared at him. He didn't let it faze him, though. He gave her a wink and turned to Bennacio.

"So anyway, you were asking how I found you. Of course, we knew when and where you crossed the border. Then a couple hours ago we got the intel on the little number you guys did on Kaczmarczyk, so it wasn't brain surgery figuring you were probably gone to ground with Cabiri."

"Your arrival was most . . . fortuitous," Bennacio said.

"Like the cavalry, huh?"

"Where are you taking us?" Bennacio asked.

"We're giving you a ride across the pond, Benny. See, there's been a development."

"What development?"

He glanced at me, then said, "That's classified."

"Mogart has contacted you," Bennacio said. It wasn't a question.

"That's classified, Benny. Class-i-fied." He flashed a meaningless smile in my direction.

"You have made an offer to buy the Sword and he has accepted."

"I'm beginning to think we have a communication problem here," Mike shouted at him over the roar of the engine. "We've taken full jurisdiction over this little matter and I'm not authorized to tell you anything else!"

Cabiri turned his head and pretended to spit. I had seen him make that gesture once before, and as I stared at Mike Arnold it hit me I was looking at an agent of OIPEP.

We were in the air only about twenty minutes when the helicopter made a wide loop and started to descend. Mike looked at his watch, pulled a gun from his Windbreaker pocket, and held it loosely in his lap. He noticed me staring at it.

"A nine-millimeter Glock! Wanna hold it?" he asked me. I shook my head. He smiled, smacking on the gum. Mike Arnold clearly didn't share Bennacio's opinion that guns were barbaric. I got the feeling Mike Arnold liked guns—a lot.

The morning sun was just visible below the cloud cover that was pulled across the sky as we touched down. It felt cold enough to snow, and the wind was kicking up. We were at another airfield. About a hundred yards away was a military cargo plane parked on the runway, its huge back door open to a blackness like the inside of a gigantic mouth.

I followed Mike and Cabiri out of the helicopter, but Bennacio stayed inside with Natalia. It looked like they were having another argument, and Natalia's eyes were shining with tears. Bennacio tried to get up, but she put a hand on his arm and it was pretty clear to me she was pleading with him not to go. He shook his head and kissed her cheek before joining us in the tornado beneath the helicopter's spinning blades.

"All set then?" Mike asked. "Great!" He started across the tarmac toward the cargo plane, but nobody followed him. Bennacio turned to Cabiri.

"I am coming with you!" Cabiri shouted at him.

"No. You must stay with Natalia. While I live she is in danger. Keep her safe, Cabiri!"

He turned to me. "I will say good-bye to you now, Kropp. Though not himself a knight, Cabiri is a Friend of the Sword and will help you home if that is what you wish."

Deep shadows crept along his mouth and under his deepset gray eyes. He looked very old, and tired. "My path is dark and only heaven knows its end. Pray for me, Alfred. Good-bye."

He squeezed my shoulder, then turned and walked quickly toward where Mike was waiting by the rear of the cargo plane door. I watched until Bennacio had almost reached the plane, and then I took off after him, yelling, "Bennacio! Bennacio! Wait! Wait for me, Bennacio!

"Bennacio!" I stopped by the gangplank, gasping for air. It was a hard run; I was big and not used to it, and besides, I had just taken a hard one between the thighs. "Take me with you."

"You do not know what you ask," he said.

"I could help. I could . . ." I had no idea what I could do. "I could be your squire or lackey, whatever it's called. Please don't leave me here, Bennacio. I've got to—you gotta give me a chance to make up for what I've done."

He glanced at Mike, who was smiling at me like a preppie Buddha. Then Bennacio said quietly, "And what have you done, Alfred?"

"Took the Sword," I stammered. Again he was like the stern father and I was like the little kid who just got caught with his hand in the cookie jar. "And that got Uncle Farrell killed, and Mr. Samson and all the rest of the Knights, Jules and Milo now, and God knows who else is gonna die just because I didn't want to live in a foster home. So I can't go back now, Bennacio, don'cha understand? I can't go back."

"Maybe that's so," Mike Arnold said. "But you can't come with us. You don't have clearance and I've got no authorization."

I ignored him. "You owe me," I told Bennacio. "I saved your life and you owe me."

"I saved yours," Bennacio reminded me.

"Look, Mr. Samson sent you all the way back here just to tell me what happened," I said. "Why do you think he did that? There's got to be a reason. I don't know what it is, but he thought it was important enough to have you drop everything just to tell me. You know he would have said I could come. You know that, Bennacio."

He didn't say anything. He turned and walked up the ramp into the plane.

"Gee, what a tough break, Al," Mike said. "But you really should count yourself lucky you made it this far."

He hit a button and the ramp started to rise. Something caught his eye over my shoulder and all of a sudden he said, "Great! Company!"

He reached down, grabbed my wrist, and heaved me into the cargo bay. I turned around and saw three dark shapes on the edge of the sky coming in fast, either helicopters or low-flying planes. Mike pushed me out of the way and ran toward the front of the plane, shouting into a walkie-talkie, "This is Mother Goose, we've laid the egg and we have three baby dragons heading for the nest. Repeat, we are still on the nest! Request immediate air support!" He slammed into the cockpit at the front of the plane. The bay door was still closing as the plane lurched forward, throwing me backwards. I would have fallen if Bennacio hadn't caught me. We both peered out the shrinking opening as the black shapes got closer—they looked like the attack helicopters that brought us here. I looked over and saw ours taking off and one of the baby dragons, as Mike called them, peel away from the other two and head after it.

Then the bay door closed and I couldn't see anymore. Bennacio reached around me, swung the locking mechanism down, and said, "Come, then, Alfred." I followed him to a small bench against the hull and we sat down as the plane accelerated for takeoff.

"There's no safety belts!" I yelled at him over the roar of the engines. He ignored me and flipped up the plastic shade of the small window behind us. He craned his neck but snorted with frustration because he couldn't see anything, I guess.

Then we were off the ground and banking sharply to the right. Bennacio had turned from the window and was sitting with his eyes closed. Maybe he had a fear of flying, like me. I looked out the window and saw two helicopters, one chasing the other, but they were identical, so I couldn't tell which was ours and which was theirs. Little explosions of bright light were coming from the chasing helicopter as the other one rose and dipped, banked hard right, then left, trying to avoid the fire. We kept gaining altitude, until they were about the size of my thumbnail below us, and then I saw a fireball and a great cloud of billowing black smoke. I wondered where the other two baby dragons were and if our plane was armored and how, if it wasn't, it ought to be.

I looked at Bennacio and he still had his eyes closed. I looked out the window again and this time, maybe a thousand or so feet beneath us, saw what looked like fighter jets, maybe F-16s or their Canadian equivalents. The jets were chasing down two of the helicopters. I couldn't see the third one, so maybe the one that blew up wasn't the one with Cabiri and Natalia on board. I hoped so. I looked at Bennacio again to tell him what I'd seen, but he had fallen asleep.

30

Bennacio and I were alone in the cargo bay. His eyes were still closed. He must know something I don't, I thought. If it were me, I'd be beside myself with worry. Were Cabiri and Natalia alive? Did they make it? I looked at his thin fingers folded in his lap. He wasn't wearing a wedding ring, but that didn't mean he wasn't married. Still, she seemed awfully young for him. I had the impression that a lot of these Old World types take younger brides, but like most impressions I had, this one didn't come from firsthand experience. Bennacio was a knight, very up on tradition— maybe it was an arranged marriage. But Natalia loved him, you could tell that. If she didn't, she wouldn't have kneed me in the groin.

I rested my head against the hard shell of the plane. Between the droning of the engines and Bennacio's soft snoring beside me, soon I was asleep too.

I dreamed I was on that plateau atop the same slag heap, under the yew tree, and my head was lying in the lap of the Lady in White. She was stroking my forehead and a light, warm breeze stirred the dark ends of her hair. She was singing something, though I couldn't make out the words, or they were in another language. I interrupted her song to ask her where I was.

Do you not know? she asked. *Have you not been here before?*

"Once, but I didn't know what it was then either."

What do you think it is, Alfred?

"Heaven?"

She smiled like I had said something cute.

And what am I?

"An angel?"

I am the one who waits. And this is the place of waiting.

"What are you waiting for?"

You know what I am waiting for.

I would have guessed she was the Lady of the Lake from the Arthur stories—only there wasn't a lake anywhere in this dream—and that she was waiting for us humans to stop mucking around with Excalibur and give it back.

Lying with my head in her lap, I was looking straight up

at the yew tree, and the leaves were fluttering in the wind you couldn't feel, and I noticed something funny about them: The leaves of the tree were multicolored, red and black and white, and then I saw the branches were bare and it wasn't leaves fluttering at all, but the wings of thousands of butterflies beating uselessly in the air, because each butterfly was pinned to the branch by a long silver needle. That kind of freaked me a little, and I started to pull a needle free to let the butterfly go, but the Lady slowly pushed my hand down.

It is not time.

"Time for what?"

She had a sad, faraway look in her eyes, which were as dark as her hair and shone like she was about to cry.

When the master comes, he will free them.

"The master," I said. "Who is the master?"

The one who remembers.

"Remembers what?"

What has been forgotten.

I stared at the butterflies fluttering helplessly above my head and thought that was my problem: I wanted to forget everything. I wanted to forget, but I couldn't.

"What's been forgotten?" I asked.

She leaned over and pressed her cool lips against my forehead. I caught a whiff of jasmine.

When the hour comes, you will remember.

31

I woke up, rubbing the back of my neck. These military cargo planes were not built for comfort. Bennacio was awake, staring out the window.

"You were dreaming of her again, weren't you?" he asked.

"Is she the Lady of the Lake?"

"I do not know. She is important, whoever she is, if only to you."

"It was one of those dreams where you never want to wake up. You don't think she's kind of the ghost of my mother, do you? She's dead, you know."

"I cannot answer that, Kropp."

"Only my mother was never that pretty, even when she was young. I don't think it was heaven. I mean, you don't picture heaven being on top of a slag heap. Where are we?"

"About an hour from our destination, I would guess. You have slept a very long time."

"What is our destination?"

"France."

"I've never been to France," I said. "I don't have a visa or a passport or anything."

"That will not matter."

"Is Mogart in France now?"

He shook his head. "I do not know. It appears Mogart has offered to sell the sword to OIPEP itself. OIPEP operates a safe house in France, where we will wait for Mogart's final instructions on the delivery of the cash."

"Bennacio, it's none of my business, but whose plane is this? Who's that guy Mike?"

"Surely you have guessed the answer by now, Kropp."

He reached into his breast pocket and handed me the same business card he had showed the guard at the border. Mike Arnold's name was on the card. Above the name was the acronym, in bold type, OIPEP. There was an 800 number beneath Mike's name.

"Bennacio, are you ever going to tell me what OIPEP is?"

He smiled at me. "What do you think it is?"

"Mr. Samson said it was some kind of supersecret spy outfit. You don't trust them, do you?"

"I do not trust outsiders to resist the temptation of obtaining the ultimate weapon."

"So that's the deal? Mogart's offering the Sword to OIPEP?"

"Perhaps."

"You seem awful calm about it, Bennacio."

"I am a man of faith, Alfred."

"What's that supposed to mean?"

"There is a purpose to all things."

"Maybe," I said. "But I don't get it."

"Not many do, when the test comes."

"I think I failed that test."

"Do you? Perhaps you have. Yet it is also possible that the true test has not yet come. Who can say? I have given much thought to your words in Halifax. Indeed, Samson did think it important you knew of our fall."

"Maybe he just wanted me to know what a mess I made of everything."

"Have you learned so little of us, Kropp, that you would believe such a thing? This mess, as you say, does not belong to you, any more than it belongs to me. Do not concern yourself so much with guilt and grief, Alfred. No battle was ever won, no great deed ever accomplished, by wallowing in guilt and grief."

He patted my hand and stood up. "Excuse me, I must speak with Mr. Arnold for a moment."

He disappeared into the cockpit. I yawned. I looked out

the little window and saw nothing but a lot of sky, a lot of water, and something glinting in the fading sunlight off our wing. Probably an F-16. I yawned again. I had slept for hours and I still felt sleepy.

Bennacio was gone a long time. When he came back he was smiling.

"What?" I asked.

"She lives," he said simply, and sat down beside me.

"That's great," I said. "I should apologize, Bennacio. I was supposed to keep her in that back room, but she kneed me in the crotch." My face got hot telling him that. Some kind of squire I was turning out to be.

He gave a little wave of his hand. I didn't know what that meant.

I said, "Is she your wife?"

"She is my daughter."

"Oh." I didn't know what else to say, so I added, "She's, um, pretty."

He didn't answer. He was peering out the window again. "It appears we are making our final approach, Kropp. Say nothing of what you know about the Sword to Mike."

"That won't be hard because there's not a lot I know."

"He is our ally in this quest, but we are strange bedfellows."

"How's that?"

"Surely it has occurred to you that evil men are not alone in their desire for the Sword. It is the ultimate weapon. There is no defense against it."

"I was thinking about that," I said. "Mr. Samson told me an army with the Sword at its head would be invincible, but couldn't somebody just drop a nuke on it?"

"It is impervious to any device of man," Bennacio said, "no matter how terrible. I do not know precisely what would happen, Alfred. All I know is the Sword cannot be defeated or destroyed."

"After Uncle Farrell died, I had this dream. Well, more of a nightmare than a dream." I told him about the faceless army and the rider of the black horse, how he slammed the Sword into the smoking ground, how planes fell and tanks blew up, how the soldiers screamed and ran from the blinding light of the Sword.

Bennacio stared at me for a long time after I finished.

"What interesting dreams you have, Alfred Kropp," he said. "Let us pray they are not prophetic."

32

Two cars waited for us on the edge of the private airstrip when we touched down in France. Three men in dark suits and dark sunglasses stood beside two black cars parked by the runway. I looked up as we walked down the stairs and saw the two F-16s scream by overhead.

"You guys must be wiped out," Mike said. "Come on. It isn't far from here, I promise."

He opened the rear door of one of the black cars. I looked at Bennacio. He nodded and I slid in. He sat down beside me and one of the dark-suited guys got behind the wheel. Mike sat beside him up front and we started to drive. The other two guys followed us in the second black car.

Mike opened the glove box and pulled out something black. It looked like a rag.

"Al," he said to me. "I really hate to do this, but it's a secure location, you know?"

He reached over the seat and, before I could put my hands up, he had slipped the cloth over my head. I couldn't see a thing. I started to yank it off, but felt a hand on my arm. Bennacio. He patted me as if to say, *It's going to be all right.*

"Hope you guys are hungry," Mike was saying. "Jeff joined us from Istanbul yesterday and he is one *heck* of a cook. We'll grab some grub, and then you can take a shower and change your clothes. Al, you especially look like somebody's chewed you up and spit you out."

"Where is Mogart?" Bennacio asked.

"No idea, man." He didn't sound too concerned about it, but that may have come from the gum-chewing. "We know where he *isn't,* which is Játiva. Our folks went in yesterday, took out the whole compound, but he and his boys had already cleared out. Found Samson. Or what was left of him. Man, talk about freaky. You guys operate on a whole different level, don't you? What in the dickens was *that* about?"

Bennacio didn't say anything. I wondered what Mike was talking about. What did Mogart do to Samson that was "freaky"?

I was having a hard time breathing inside my hood. It took everything inside me not to pull it off. I wondered what Mike would do if I did. Maybe shoot me. Casually, though, the way he talked and smacked the gum, like it was a summer afternoon and all he was doing was watching a baseball game. My voice was muffled by the cloth when I said, "Samson was Bennacio's captain; you shouldn't talk about him like that."

He ignored me. "We think he may have slipped into Morocco or maybe even Algeria. Anyway, every border in the free world's been locked down, but that's a lot of square footage to cover and not everybody's a friend of truth, justice, and the American way, if you know what I mean. Anyway, yesterday we get the call he's ready to deal. Tells us to sit tight and he'll be back in touch with the final figure and location of the exchange. Don't know where it'll be or what the final price tag is—they don't tell us much at our level, but we've got a pool going if you want in on it. The rumor is—and this is unconfirmed and classified, by the way—the rumor is one hundred billion dollars. That's *billion* with a capital *B*, man. You wanna know my personal opinion? I think he did all this just to make the Forbes list."

I heard a cell phone ringing and then Mike talking quietly. It seemed like we had been driving for a long time, but it was hard to tell with the hood over my face; time passes differently when you can't see. We went fast, then slow, then fast again, like we were hitting highways, then getting off again onto lesser roads. Then the engine revved as we climbed up a steep incline. Once we leveled off, I heard the engine stop, and my door opened. A hand reached in, grabbed my right arm, and pulled me out.

Somebody said, "Watch your head," and guided me by the elbow along a rocky path. The rocks or gravel crunched under my feet and I thought about my dream and scrambling up the slag heap to find the Lady in White with her long black hair and dark eyes staring sadly into space, waiting for the Master to come.

"Step up," the same voice said, and now I was walking on wooden planks. I shivered in the cold. The air around me suddenly got warmer; I was inside. Somebody pulled the hood off. I squinted in the light, though it wasn't really that bright inside.

We were standing in a little entryway to a cabin, or maybe in France you call it a château. Wooden floors, a cathedral ceiling, and a huge fireplace. About a dozen guys milled about and I could smell bacon frying. Suddenly I was the hungriest I had ever been in my life. My knees were actually weak.

"So what would you guys like? Shower first, or breakfast?"

"Alfred needs to eat," Bennacio said.

"All I had was some cheese and grapes," I said to no one in particular. No one in particular seemed to be listening.

33

An agent named Jeff laid out ham and bacon, biscuits, eggs, sugary things somebody said was *beignets* (a kind of French doughnut that I ate six of), a couple of T-bones, coffee, juice, hot tea, and fresh hot chocolate. Mike was a big Cubs fan and he talked with this other guy, Paul, about their chances this year and the problem was their bullpen like it was every other year. Bennacio sat beside me, nibbled on some toast with strawberry jam, sipped coffee, and said nothing.

After breakfast, Mike led us up the stairs to the second floor and showed us the bathrooms where we could wash up. I stripped down and laid my clothes outside the door as Mike suggested, so they could be washed while Bennacio and I took our showers.

I stood for a long time under the hot spray. I think I may have had jet lag, because I kept dropping the soap, and everything seemed to be taking a very long time to accomplish: it seemed washing my hair took at least a couple of hours.

I stood in the shower until my fingertips pruned up; then I dried off and slipped into a white terry-cloth robe that I found hanging on a hook by the shower. The bathroom was very small and I kept knocking into the sink and hitting my elbows on the walls, but I felt better with a full stomach and a clean body. I found a toothbrush and some paste in the medicine cabinet and scrubbed my teeth. Brushing my teeth made me think of my mother, who was a real stickler for oral hygiene—I'd never had a cavity in my life.

I was late getting back downstairs. The meeting had already started without me. Mike, Jeff, and Paul were sitting on the sofa in the great room, with Bennacio sitting by himself in the rough-hewn rocking chair near the fire.

A lady sat next to Mike. She had large lips that looked very red and wet-looking in the firelight. Her platinum-blond hair was pulled into a tight bun on top of her head. She wore a pinstriped business suit and black high heels.

I leaned against the wooden beam in the entryway, feeling kind of silly in my bare feet, my hair still wet. Bennacio was fully dressed. Nobody acknowledged my presence. Mike was talking.

"So it's all set up," he was saying. "Last night I got final approval from headquarters. I can't tell you how much, that's classified, but I will say we think we've topped the highest bid by at least half a billion."

He stopped, almost as if he was waiting for an answer from Bennacio. He didn't get an answer, though. Bennacio said nothing. He was staring at the fire.

Mike pulled a piece of foil from his pocket, carefully wrapped his used gum in it, and slipped it back into his pocket. He popped another piece of gum into his mouth, wrapped up the foil, and just as carefully put the fresh foil into his pocket.

The lady with the shiny blond hair spoke up. She had a British accent. "Honestly, we think that was his plan from the beginning, to sell the Sword to us."

"Really?" Bennacio said. "You presume much."

"Who else could he turn to?" she asked. "We represent the richest countries in the world. And he can trust us. Not even the Dragon wants to see the whole world go up in flames."

"Right, Benny-boy, that's right!" Mike said. "I mean, how's he going to enjoy his money in a nuclear wasteland? He's known from the beginning he *has* to sell it to the good guys."

"I have told you," Bennacio said. "Mogart does not intend to give you the Sword. He will never part with it."

"How come?" Mike was smiling at Bennacio, a hard, unfriendly smile.

"Would you?"

"Hey, come on now, Benny. We're the good guys, remember? We're all on the same side here, right?"

"He will take your money and keep the Sword."

"World domination, huh? King Mogart. Well, we're just gonna have to take our chances on that one, Benny."

"You are a fool," Bennacio said, turning away from the fire and glaring at Mike. "He will betray you."

"That's precisely why we've invited you to the party." Mike turned to the British lady. "Right, Abby?"

Abby said, "We will not make the exchange until you've verified the Sword's authenticity."

"And then OIPEP returns the Sword of Righteousness to us, its friends," Bennacio said. Now he was the one smiling hard and unfriendly.

"I'm gonna be honest with you, Benny. That's not our call," Mike said. "Point of fact you guys didn't do such a hot job of protecting it in the first place."

"We have protected it for a thousand years," Bennacio shot back. "Only by a freakish accident was it lost."

Mike glanced over his shoulder at me, the freakish accident. Then he looked at Bennacio, smiled and shrugged, as if to say, *Look, buddy, you couldn't even protect it from this big loser*.

"Bennacio," Abby said in a kind voice. "We have nothing but admiration for what your Order has accomplished. But perhaps the time has come for the Sword to pass on to different protectors. Why else would Samson involve us?"

"Abby's got her hands around the issue's throat, Benny," Mike said. "There's nobody on the planet better equipped to keep it safe."

Bennacio wasn't buying it. "I will not do this without your assurance the Sword will be returned to me."

"Like I said, Benny, we can't promise that," Mike answered. "I've always been straight with you and I respect the heck out of you and your knightly buds. We wouldn't dream of busting your chops. But I will give you my personal guarantee The Company has no intention of using the Sword for any purpose. We want the same thing you want: to keep it out of the hands of all the baddies and loonies."

"I cannot betray my solemn oath," Bennacio said. "By my life or death I will hold and protect it. I can do no less. If Mogart indeed returns the Sword, you must kill me to keep it from me."

"Nobody wants to do that," Abby said. She didn't say they wouldn't kill Bennacio, though.

"Benny," Mike said. "We're a go whether you come along or not. We're just waiting for the Dragon to get back to us on the time and location for delivery of the Sword. We—I—want you along, of course, and once we get the Sword back, everything's negotiable. Let's take it one step at a time."

Bennacio sighed. Nobody said anything for a long time. Paul picked at a hangnail. Jeff smoothed creases I couldn't see on his pants. Mike smacked his gum. Abby was the only one looking at Bennacio.

Finally, he stirred in his chair and said, "I will come, on one condition."

"You name it."

"The vengeance is mine."

" 'Thus saith the Lord,' " Mike cracked, but nobody laughed.

34

I went back upstairs and found my clothes in the bedroom. Somebody had washed and laid them on the small bed by the window. I pulled back the curtains to look out, but there was nothing to look at: The window was boarded up. *Secure location.* As if I would know where I was in France. The only way I'd know is if I looked out and saw the Eiffel Tower in the backyard.

I dressed and sat on the bed. I didn't know what else to do. I didn't want to go back downstairs. Being around Mike and his gang of spies or whatever they were made me feel kind of twitchy.

There was a soft tap on the door and Bennacio came in. He closed the door and sat down beside me.

"Do you trust them?" I asked.

"Would you?"

I thought about it. "No choice?"

"We must use the tools given us, even those that are double-edged."

"How'd they find out about the Sword in the first place?"

"When the Sword was lost, Samson realized at once we would need their help. I counseled against it, but now I understand the bitter necessity of it, though it cost us our greatest loss since the founding of our Order."

"I thought I caused that."

He frowned at me. "I am not speaking of the Sword."

"They're not going to let you have it, are they?"

"I think not."

"How're you going to stop them?"

"I will do as I always have done: all that I must to protect it."

"Bennacio, you can't kill them."

He sighed. "Long ago, Alfred, I took a solemn oath as binding as gravity. I know of no other way."

"Well, I'm not sure exactly what you're trying to say, Bennacio. Maybe because I've never taken any kind of oath like that. I've never taken any kind of oath period."

He looked at me with those deep-set, intense eyes.

"Why not?"

"I guess I never had the chance."

"All of us have that chance. But we either choose not to or do not recognize it when it comes. On the plane, when I told you I believed all happens for a purpose, you thought of your uncle's death, and you wondered how something so seemingly useless could serve any purpose. In the past, Alfred, men cast about for reasons to believe. Now we find reasons *not* to."

"I'm not following you, Bennacio."

"The human race has grown arrogant, and in its arrogance assumes nothing is beyond the power of its reason. If we see no purpose, it follows there must be no purpose. It is the fallacy of our times."

"Bennacio," I said. "You can't just kill them. For every one of them you kill, they'll send a dozen to come after you. Sooner or later they'll find you, and I don't care how powerful the Sword is, they'll get it from you somehow. And then they'll kill you."

"Perhaps," he answered. "Yet mercy has cost us much. If I had killed you the night you took the Sword, your friends and mine would still be alive and the Sword would still be safe."

"Yeah, but I'd be dead."

He laughed, then patted me on the knee and stood up.

"I think I shall miss you, Alfred Kropp, when this is over."

He left me alone. I sat there for a few minutes, thinking. Mostly I was thinking the last knight was going to buy the farm. Either Mogart would kill him or the agents of OIPEP would.

I was convinced that Mike's plan was to use Bennacio to help get the Sword, and then kill him (and probably me). That's what Natalia meant when she told me I had sentenced Bennacio to death.

Thinking about Natalia made me feel especially rotten, though I'm not sure why. It's not easy being hated by anybody, but it's especially hard when the person who hates you also happens to be the prettiest girl you've ever seen.

35

Later that afternoon I was lying on my bed, thinking, when overhead I heard the slow *thumpa-thumpa* of a helicopter, growing louder as it approached. From downstairs there was clumping and bumping as the spies ran around in a panic, shouting at each other and looking for their guns.

I heard Mike shouting, "Breached! We've been breached!"

I jumped out of bed and ran into the hallway, where I literally bumped into Bennacio. He was wearing his brown robe and carrying his black sword.

"Mogart?" I asked.

He shook his head. "Something worse, I fear."

I tried to imagine something worse than Mogart. I followed Bennacio downstairs into the great room. Jeff and Paul corralled us and told us to stand back. Mike and Abby went to the front door and flung it open. Over their shoulders I could see a black attack helicopter landing on the sloping ground in the front yard. A big man wearing a black sweater jumped out. He reached into the helicopter and helped out a smaller person.

Mike's shoulders relaxed and he stuck the gun under his Windbreaker as the two people walked up the gravel path to the front door.

Abby glared at Bennacio. "Do you have an explanation for this?" she asked.

Mike stepped back, and then Cabiri came into the room, Natalia right behind him. She ignored Mike and Abby and rushed over to Bennacio. As she passed me, I could smell her hair—peaches.

"Hello!" Cabiri called to nobody in particular. "Hello, hello! And how is everyone? How are all my secret-agent friends?"

Mike slammed the door, threw the dead bolt, and whirled on Bennacio.

"You got an explanation for this?" he shouted.

"I've already asked him that, Michael," Abby said coldly.

"Please, do not hold Lord Bennacio responsible," Cabiri

said. "This is entirely my doing." He gave an apologetic smile. "*Scusi*."

"Save your '*scusis*,' pal," Mike shot back, as the *thumpa-thumpas* of the helicopter grew fainter. "How did you find us?"

"Oh," Cabiri said, "how does the fox find the chicken? How does the bird find the worm?" He smiled at Bennacio.

"*You* called them," Mike said, turning to Bennacio.

"How might I call them?" Bennacio asked. "I have no telephone."

"I am a Friend of the Sword," Cabiri said to Mike, his voice losing its jokey edge. "And Friends of the Sword have friends who have friends. Do you think your presence has gone unnoticed in Saint Étienne?"

Mike didn't seem to be listening. He brushed past Cabiri and bounded up the stairs, dialing his cell phone as he went. A door slammed above us and I could hear Mike's voice as he shouted to someone on the phone, but I couldn't make out the words. Abby sighed.

Cabiri said to Bennacio, "Forgive me, my lord. It was not my decision to come here." He was looking at Natalia.

Natalia was looking at Bennacio.

"I am coming with you," she said, her chin tilted up in defiance.

"You know you cannot," Bennacio answered, but not unkindly.

"And I," Cabiri said.

"No."

"Who then will stand by you when the test comes?" Natalia demanded. "Her?" And she jerked her head toward Abby.

"My name is Abigail," she said. "And you are?"

"Or *him*?" And now Natalia jerked her head toward me.

"Do not underestimate my friend Alfred Kropp," Bennacio said. "There is more to him than meets the eye."

"Then there is much indeed!" Cabiri said heartily, and he slapped me on the back. "For he is substantial!"

Mike came bounding down the stairs then, and jabbed his finger at Cabiri's nose.

"You are interfering with a matter of international security, mister!"

"Perhaps you should shoot me."

"Enough!" Bennacio said, and everybody shut up and stared at him. "They should not have come, but they have and so we must make the best of it. When Mogart calls, Cabiri will stay here with my daughter. I will return for them both once we have the Sword."

That ended the discussion. None of the OIPEP people seemed happy about it, but they couldn't come up with a good argument for sending Cabiri and Natalia away. There was some discussion of sleeping arrangements, since all the bedrooms were taken. Then Jeff volunteered to sleep on the sofa downstairs so Natalia could have his room. Cabiri decided he would bunk with me.

"For you and I are the only Friends here," he told me. "It

will be delightful, Alfred Kropp! Only I must warn you of my snoring and my flatulence."

Bunking with Cabiri didn't turn out to be delightful. He had been telling the truth about his snoring and farting.

Natalia and Bennacio holed up in his room for hours, and I could hear their voices through the walls as they argued. Sometimes I could hear her crying.

When she wasn't in the bedroom, she would be in the great room, sitting in the rocker by the fireplace, staring at the flames, her knees drawn up to her chest, her dark eyes reflecting the firelight. Sometimes she passed close to me coming down the hall or in the kitchen at dinner, and each time she passed I smelled peaches and thought of being a little kid, turning the handle of the ice cream churn while Mom dropped fresh peaches into its belly.

Natalia barely spoke to me, but sometimes I would catch her staring at me and she would look away quickly.

Then one night Cabiri's flatulence chased me from the room (his farts seemed to gather underneath the covers and attack any time I rolled over, fluffing the blankets). I padded downstairs, thinking maybe I'd wake up Jeff for a game of poker or pool. But Jeff wasn't on the sofa; Natalia was, curled up under a blanket, wide-awake, staring at the dying embers in the fireplace.

I stood for a second at the bottom of the stairs. I thought about going into the kitchen for a snack, but that was like covering up for disturbing her and didn't seem cool at all.

"Hi," I finally decided to say.

She didn't answer.

"I, um, I couldn't sleep. Cabiri won't stop farting."

She still didn't say anything.

"Look," I said, taking a step into the room. "About what happened in Halifax . . . it's okay."

She slid her dark eyes in my direction. I felt like a bug on a pin when she looked at me.

"What is okay?" she asked.

"You know, the fact that you kneed me in the groin."

"I should have stabbed you."

"Sure, I understand that." I eased myself into the rocker across from her.

She was looking at the fire again.

"Who are you?" she asked softly.

She whipped her head in my direction, her dark hair flying to her right shoulder.

"Who are you, that you have done this?"

"I was just a kid trying to help out his uncle."

"You are a thief."

"Yeah. As it turned out."

"My father should have killed you when you took the sword. *I* would have killed you."

"Don't you think life's funny that way?" I asked. She stared at me as if I were speaking a language she didn't understand. "I mean, I guess you've noticed, but there isn't a lot to do around here, and I'm not sure how long I've been here, but it seems like it's been a very long time, and all there is to do is eat and sleep and think. And I was thinking, look at how many things had to happen for me to end up here. You know, if only my dad hadn't run off on my mom. If only my mom hadn't died of cancer. If only Uncle Farrell hadn't volunteered to raise me. If only Mr. Samson had hired somebody else to be the night watchman at Samson Towers. Or if Uncle Farrell had just said no to Mogart like he should have. Or if I had said no to Uncle Farrell. I guess I could go on, but you probably get the point. Your father talks a lot about fate and doom, which is something I never really bought into, but now I'm thinking maybe something does guide us or use us for something bigger . . . What do you think?"

"What do I think?" she asked. "I think you are an idiot."

"You wouldn't be the first," I admitted.

"Your sympathy for my father disgusts me."

"Well," I said. "Maybe you shouldn't be so hard on me, Natalia. I know how it feels."

"You know how *what* feels?"

"Losing a parent."

She looked at me for a long time. It was so long, I started to feel very uncomfortable, more uncomfortable than usual.

"And at least there's a chance he won't die," I went on. "My mom didn't even have that."

36

Things changed between Natalia and me after that night. I'm not saying they got much better, but it was like we'd reached some kind of understanding. I still caught her staring at me sometimes, and once or twice I think Mike noticed too. Once at dinner, I looked up from my plate and saw her looking, and then I looked over at Mike and he was looking at her looking at me, and he was smiling.

One morning, after I finished my shower, I passed Bennacio's door and heard Natalia's voice, followed by the low hum of Bennacio's. It sounded like a heated debate was going on; I figured it was about Natalia going with him to the rendezvous with Mogart. I went to my room and closed the door. After a while I heard a door slam and the light tread of Natalia going down the hall.

I went to Bennacio's room and knocked softly on the door. There was no answer. I tried the knob. It was unlocked.

I stepped inside. The light was off, but there was a glow in the room from two candles sitting on the small table pushed against the far wall. Propped up between the candles was a small painting in a gilded frame of a man in a white robe, kind of floating against a black background, with great white fluffy wings outstretched on either side, holding a sword in his right hand.

Kneeling in front of this picture was Bennacio. He didn't lift his head or move when I came in. I felt ashamed, almost as if I had walked in on him naked. The main thing that struck me, though, was how terribly small he seemed, kneeling there in front of that picture, how terribly small and alone.

"Yes, Kropp?" he asked without turning or getting up.

"You should take her with you," I said.

He didn't move.

"Take her with you, Bennacio," I said.

"You do not know what you are asking," he said finally.

"Maybe I don't," I said. "There's a lot I don't get. Most stuff I probably never will, but this one thing I'm pretty sure of, Bennacio."

His shoulders dipped, his head fell to his chest, and when he stood up, for the first time he struck me as an old man, old enough to be a grandfather, even. He turned and looked hard at me.

"What are you so sure of, Kropp?"

"Look, Bennacio, when my mom got sick she would get on me all the time about coming to see her at the hospital. She was all worried about me missing school or sleep or meals, but she was dying. There was no hope for her. But I didn't care. I came every day anyway, for over a month, and I sat there for hours, even when she didn't know I was sitting there." All the memories came rushing back then, of Mom shrunken to the size of a pygmy in that hospital bed, bald from all the chemo, big black circles around her eyes. Her teeth seemed huge against her hollow cheeks and thinned lips. And the way she would whimper, *Please, please, Alfred, make it go away. Make the pain go away.*

"Maybe it was useless my being there. Maybe there was nothing I could do, but where else was I supposed to be? You say you don't have a choice, but you think she does. Well, maybe she doesn't have any more choice than you do. It's kind of hypocritical, if you ask me, saying you don't have a choice but she does."

I don't know if anything I was saying was making any sense. But he listened. He didn't say anything. He just stared at me, but he listened, I think.

"Okay," I said. "That's it. That's about all I had."

I walked out of the room, pulling the door closed behind me. Standing a couple of feet away was Natalia.

I wiped the tears from my cheeks and walked hurriedly past her, muttering as I passed, "There's no such thing as accidents." I don't know why I said that.

37

I went to my room and after a while—I don't know how long, maybe a couple of hours—there was a knock on the door and Bennacio came in, still wearing that brown robe. He was carrying a long box. He sat beside me, setting the box down on the bed behind us.

"Kropp," he said.

"Bennacio," I said.

"I cannot take her."

"Well," I said. "You should."

"One day, perhaps, you will have a child, and you will understand."

"Whatever," I said.

"Do not think too bitterly of me."

"Okay," I said, as if what I thought about Lord Bennacio, Last Knight of the Order of the Sacred Sword, really mattered. Bennacio was giving off some serious sadness sitting there beside me, as if an invisible cloak of sorrow was wrapped around his shoulders.

"That picture in your room," I said. "Is it Saint Michael?"

"The Archangel Michael, yes."

"You know, I was thinking about that. Mr. Samson talked about the master of the Sword and so did the Lady in my dream. Michael is the master of the Sword you're waiting for, isn't he?"

He slowly shook his head and smiled. I didn't know what he meant by that. Was I right or wrong?

"When I was a boy of thirteen," Bennacio said, "my father took me aside and told me that we were of the house of Bedivere. I had heard the story of the Sword, of course, but like you had always thought it merely a legend. My father took me to the head of the Order, Samson's father, who had just moved to America. I saw the Sword and I believed. Upon his deathbed, my father told me of Bedivere's failure."

Bennacio sighed. "Bedivere *was* to cast the Sword into the lake—those were the direct orders from Arthur—but he chose to keep it instead, and our Order was created. Of all the knights, he loved his king the most, and from this love rose the belief that one day another master would return for the Sword."

He sighed again, a longer, sadder sigh. "It is a particular burden, Alfred, to descend from the house of Bedivere. There have always been knights of our Order who saw what he did as a betrayal of his king's trust. Many believed the Sword should be cast back into the waters from which it rose, thus removing any possibility of the Sword being used for ill. By my honor, as the last knight and the last son of Bedivere, if ever I retrieve the Sword, that is what I shall do. I will atone for his sin, though his sin was of the most peculiar kind, born of love."

He picked up the box, laid it on his lap, and opened the lid. Inside, lying on the purple velvet lining, was a sword, thin and black-bladed. It looked like the same kind of sword he used the night I stole Excalibur. He held it up.

"This is the sword of my father. OIPEP recovered it when they stormed Mogart's keep. On the day my father died, I swore upon this sword the ancient oath of our Order."

He turned to me. "It may be my fate to fall to Mogart when the hour comes. If so, will you not make the same oath and take up this sword?"

"Gee, Bennacio," I said. I was shocked. "That's a big honor and I really appreciate your asking me, but I think you've got the wrong guy. Maybe you should ask Mike or Paul or one of those guys . . . Even that Abby woman would be a better choice. I think she might be the toughest one of the lot. Mike's kind of scared of her, you can tell."

"Those people, Kropp? They are arrogant and full of their own wisdom. They are fools."

"Well, some people might say I'm not the ripest apple on the tree, Bennacio. You gotta know your limitations, and what you're asking is way over my head. Basically, I'm a loser."

He stared at me with a stern expression. "What do you mean?" he asked.

"Well, I lost the Sword, for one. But besides that, there's nothing I'm good at. You know how most people have talents? Like some people are good at sports and others good at school—science and math and stuff like that? Well, I'm not very good at anything. I played football, but I wasn't very good at it, and my grades are pretty mediocre. You know, I'm just . . . average."

"Average," he said.

"Yeah. Just your average, um, Kropp. Though I've been screwing up more than usual lately. The idea of me taking up your sword and being some kind of hero—well, that's kind of ridiculous."

He put a hand on my shoulder. "But we fall only that we might rise, Alfred. All of us fall; all of us, as you say, screw up. Falling is not important. It is how we get up after the fall that's important."

He gave my shoulder a little pat. "And as for being a hero—who can say what valor dwells in the soul unless the test comes? A hero lives in every heart, Alfred, waiting for the dragon to come out."

38

Bennacio took my hand and placed it on the flat part of the blade.

"I'll just let you down," I said. I was about to cry. Maybe I should cry, I thought. That'll change his mind about a hero dwelling in my heart.

"Perhaps. Our will often falters. My mind tells me you are a weak young man, timid and unsure, but my heart tells me something altogether different. For all your faults, Alfred, you are without guile, without pretense. The Sword shall never be won or evil defeated through trickery and deceit, as those downstairs believe. Will you not speak the oath now, while there is still hope?"

I looked away. His expression was so desperate, I couldn't look at him. Things really couldn't get any worse, when a knight like Bennacio had to turn to Alfred Kropp to help him.

"Alfred," he said softly. "There is something else. Something you do not know that might help you make your decision."

I turned back. "What?"

"You asked if I had finished Windimar's training. It was indeed I who finished it, which is not uncommon, as I've said. Samson too completed a certain knight's training, when that knight pledged himself to the Order upon their first meeting in France. You can guess who that certain knight was."

He waited patiently for my Kropp mind to grasp what he was saying.

"Mogart?"

"Yes, Mogart was Samson's squire, and more. Samson named him his heir."

My Kropp mind couldn't get a grip on that one. "So why did Mogart turn on him?"

His dark eyes glittered beneath his shaggy eyebrows, the same way they had about a lifetime ago in the halls of Samson Towers.

"Have you not wondered, Alfred, more than once, why your name was the code to unlocking the secret chamber beneath Samson's desk? Have you not wondered why, at the most desperate hour, Samson ordered me to return to

America to find you? Have you never wondered why Samson hired Farrell Kropp, an underskilled mechanic, to be the night watchman at Samson Towers? Two years ago, Bernard Samson discovered he had another heir, a true heir, and he wanted to make sure his son was taken care of until he came of age and could be brought into his full inheritance as a Knight of the Order."

"Uncle Farrell was Bernard Samson's son? Wouldn't that make me his . . ." I tried to figure it out. "Grandnephew or something?"

"Alfred, Bernard Samson was *your* father."

I stared at him for a long time. "I don't understand, Bennacio."

"Sixteen years ago, the man you know as Bernard Samson fell in love with a woman he met on a business trip. A business trip to Salina, Ohio, Alfred. That woman's name was Annabelle Kropp."

I was slowly shaking my head. Even though it was larger than average, it wasn't big enough to hold what he was telling me.

"Samson did not wish to expel Mogart from the Order. In many ways, Mogart was the best of us: intrepid, clever; with sword and lance he had no equal. But Mogart wanted more than to be a mere knight like the rest of us. He desired Samson's place. But when *you* were born, he could not have it."

"Oh, great. This is just great, Bennacio. Now that's my fault too?"

"It is no one's fault, Alfred. It is merely a fact. You are

the last in the line of Lancelot, the greatest knight who ever lived."

I didn't know what to say. Of all the things that had happened to me since my mother died, this was probably the weirdest—and the worst.

"You're just making this up to get me to take this stupid vow or oath or whatever it is. I'm not his . . . He's not my father . . ."

I couldn't go on and Bennacio didn't make me. He sat very still while I cried.

"Why did he leave my mom?" I finally made myself ask.

"So as not to endanger her—or you."

"That didn't work out too well, did it?"

"Not all good intentions do."

"I still don't believe it."

"As with the angels, Alfred, that hardly matters."

I looked down and saw the sword across my lap.

"Why didn't you tell me, Bennacio? Why did you wait till now to tell me?"

"I was hoping I wouldn't have to."

Bennacio whispered, "Speak the words now, Alfred Kropp. Speak, son of my captain, heir to Lancelot. 'I, Alfred Kropp, swear in the name of the Archangel Michael, my guardian and protector, that I will sacrifice my life in defense of the Sword of Righteousness, and that by my life or my death, I shall defend it against the agents of darkness.'"

I repeated the words, and in the silence that followed,

waited for some heroic valor to swell my breast. I didn't feel anything except a little sick to my stomach.

Bennacio smiled, patted my shoulder again, and placed the sword back into its box.

Then from downstairs came the sound of Mike's cell phone ringing. I knew it was Mike's because the ringer played "Take Me Out to the Ballgame."

"Ah," he said. "At last. The call comes. Perhaps a good sign."

"Am I a knight now?"

"There are no knights left, save one, and his reckoning is soon upon him."

39

Mike knocked loudly on the door and stuck his head in. He was smacking gum and smiling.

"Great news, cowboys. We're a go. Let's load 'em up and move 'em out!"

He clapped his hands and clumped down the hall in those big hiking boots he wore.

"You want me to take up your sword," I told him. "But I don't even know how to use a sword."

"There is no time to teach you, Kropp. However, I suspect the day will not be lost or won through swordsmanship."

We went downstairs. Jeff had laid out sandwiches. He said Mike had given orders to eat before we left.

"Where are we going?" I asked Mike.

"That's classified."

Bennacio and I took our sandwiches into the great room and ate by the fire. Abby was standing off by herself, talking quietly on a cell phone and checking her watch. Cabiri was there, and Natalia, of course, but neither of them ate anything. Cabiri was very quiet too, not his usual jokey self, and Natalia looked like she was about to cry.

Everybody gathered by the front door.

"Okay, here's the game plan," Mike announced. "Jeff, Paul, Bennacio, and *moi* head for the rendezvous point. Everybody else hangs here until we get back." He was kind of smirking in Abby's direction.

"I am going with Bennacio," Cabiri said.

"No can do, pal," Mike said cheerfully. His mood was a lot better now that the game was finally on. "You don't have clearance."

"I do not need your clearance," Cabiri said. "I found you once . . ."

"You try to leave this château and I'll have you shot in the back of the head," Mike said with a smile. "I've already given the order."

Cabiri turned his head and made a spitting motion.

"Cabiri," Bennacio said. There was a faraway-ness in his voice and eyes, as if he were already at the rendezvous point, the Sword of Kings within his grasp. "Stay."

"Jeez, this is heartwarming," Mike said. "Parting, the

sweet sorrow thing and all that, but we're on a tight schedule here and we've got to get shaking."

He opened the door and waved at Bennacio. I stepped forward with him.

"You're staying here, Al," Mike said.

"Kropp is coming," Bennacio said. "He is my second."

"Your second *what*?" Mike asked.

"He will take up my sword should I fall."

"No offense, Benny," Mike said. "But if it were me, I'd take Cabiri here."

"But I have no clearance," Cabiri said sarcastically.

"Look, Ben," Mike said in a tone usually reserved for a little kid. "The kid can't come."

"Michael!" It was Abby. "We don't have time for this. Let him take the boy."

Mike's mouth moved a little, but no sound came out. His face grew red.

"Headquarters is going to hear about this in my report," he said.

"Headquarters is going to hear about many things," Abby shot back.

Then she nodded to Jeff, who stuffed my head into that black sack again.

As we were going through the door I heard Bennacio say, "No, I shall lead him." I felt a hand leave my elbow and another take its place.

Bennacio helped me into the backseat of the car and

closed the door. After a second it opened again. I heard Cabiri saying, "No, no, no, Natalia . . ."

And I smelled peaches.

"Good-bye, Kropp," her voice whispered. "Protect my father."

The hood lifted over my right cheek, and I felt something warm and moist press against my chin. From the front seat, Mike let out a whistle and a loud whoop.

" 'Love is in the air!' " he sang.

Then my door slammed closed and the gravel crunched beneath the tires as we started down the mountain.

I figured we had been driving for an hour at least before we finally stopped. I could hear the sound of a jet engine warming up. The hood was lifted and I was blinking in the blinding light, getting a sinking feeling when I saw the plane about a hundred feet away. Mike turned to me.

"It's not too late, Alfred. We can have another plane here in ten minutes."

I looked at Bennacio, who had come to stand beside me.

"That's okay," I said. "I'm coming."

We walked up the stairs and took our seats. I took the aisle because I didn't want to look out the window. Mike put on a big pair of headphones. He said something into the microphone and the plane began to taxi toward the runway.

"Well, here we go!" Mike said. His cheeks were flushed. "This reminds me of the time the US Defense Department called us in to help with their little containment problem in Area Fifty-one! Whew, what a mess! But 'nuff said—that's classified!" He was shouting now as the plane began to accelerate, pushing me back in my chair as I fumbled for the safety belt: I had forgotten to fasten it. "Or the time we were lost for six days in the Bermuda Triangle! Talk about some funky vibes! Saw things in that operation that would turn your hair white!" He laughed in Bennacio's face. "But yours already is, so what the hey!"

Bennacio didn't say anything, but he had a disgusted look on his face. I was pretty sure he was going to kill Mike before all this was over. I wondered if Mike knew that and had similar plans for Bennacio. I felt almost sorry for Mike; he didn't know who he was screwing around with.

Mike explained that we would proceed immediately to the rendezvous point, where we would exchange the cash ransom for the Sword.

He wouldn't tell us exactly where the rendezvous point was, but he did say we would be met by some agents of OIPEP, or "The Company." OIPEP agents never called OIPEP "OIPEP." Maybe it was *Officers Investigating Perpetrators of Evil Pranks.*

"Let us do the talking," Mike said. "All you got to do, Benny, is hang back and wait. I'll let you know when to step up and authenticate we've got the real McCoy."

"And then?" Bennacio asked quietly.

"And then he's all yours. Have fun with your vengeance."

"And the Sword?"

"Let's take it one step at a time, Benny. Let's get it back first, okay? Then you and my superiors can talk."

Bennacio nodded, but I could tell he wasn't happy about it. My stomach was knotting up. I reached for the airsick bag.

After we touched down, I waited for the hood, but Mike just stood at the plane door and smiled at me, smacking his gum, and jerked his head toward the door. The sun had set and a cold, dense fog had rolled in. I wondered what the date was; I had lost track.

Mike led us to a pair of Bentleys parked on the tarmac. Bennacio had to reposition his sword so he could sit. He leaned his head back and closed his eyes. After a minute his lips began to move as if he was saying a prayer. It probably *was* a prayer.

We turned off the main road onto a narrow lane that weaved through a forest. The headlights barely penetrated the fog, and I worried we'd run into a tree before we could even get there. Our driver was driving way too fast for the fog, but I had heard Europeans always drive too fast.

After another fifteen minutes or so the trees opened up and we were driving through a rolling countryside. In the distance, I could see floodlights shining on black shapes pointing like thick fingers at the night sky. I had seen this place before, and it wasn't until the car began to slow down that I realized that Mogart had chosen Stonehenge as the place where the fate of the world would be decided.

40

We parked about a hundred yards away from the lighted circle of stones. Huge spotlights had been set up just outside the circle, and the fog separated each beam as it shone into the center. The air was so cold, I could see my breath. Men in dark suits waited for us just outside the outer ring. One of them came over and said to Mike in an English accent, "No sign of our quarry yet, Mike. We've established the perimeter; he won't get within ten kilometers without us spotting him."

Mike nodded and clapped the Brit on the back, but Bennacio said calmly, "No, he is already here."

"I'm afraid that's quite imposs—" the British agent began,

then stopped, because just then a group of robed men stepped from behind one of the larger stones ringing the center. Six of them, in black robes, with a tall man in the middle, wearing a white robe with the hood thrown back.

Mogart.

We stepped into the circle on the opposite side. The guys from OIPEP stood in front of me and Bennacio, seven in all, not counting us two. An even match, except Mogart had the Sword that no army or combination of armies could resist. Mike took one step toward Mogart and raised his hand.

"You're very punctual, Monsieur Mogart! That sort of thing impresses the living daylights out of me!"

"And you are late, Mr. Arnold," Mogart answered. "I see you have brought some unexpected guests. How good it is to see you again, my brother knight."

He bowed at Bennacio, and then looked at me. "And you, Mr. Kropp! How extraordinary that you are here! Please accept my gratitude for delivering the Sword!"

"You can go to hell," I muttered under my breath. Bennacio touched me on the arm as if to say, *Be still*.

"Well," Mike said. "Now that we've dispensed with the pleasantries, do you think we could talk a little business?"

"You Americans," Mogart laughed. "Always so abrupt."

Mike motioned to Paul, who reached into his coat and pulled out a long white envelope. Mike tossed it toward Mogart. It landed about three feet away and one of Mogart's men snatched it off the ground and handed it to Mogart.

"That is the location and the account number," Mike

called over. "Deliver the item and we'll give you the access code."

Mogart peeked inside the envelope, a sly smile playing on the corners of his lips. He handed the envelope to the guy on his right and nodded to the one on his left. This guy walked into the circle holding something long and narrow wrapped in a golden cloth that shimmered in the glare of the floodlights. He laid it on the ground in the center of the ring and stepped back to rejoin Mogart.

"Okay, Benny," Mike breathed. "You're on."

Bennacio walked slowly past Mike. I started to follow him and he whispered to me, "No, Alfred. Only if I call."

He walked alone into the center of the ring of stones and knelt beside the bundle lying on the ground, the cloth glittering and sparkling as he unfolded it. He made some motion with his right hand. It was hard to see from where I was, but it looked something like the sign of the cross.

I don't know everything that happened next, because a lot happened all at once, though it seemed to go in slow motion, like a car wreck. All of a sudden black-robed figures were flying from everywhere, swarming toward Bennacio, swords raised high over their heads. Paul yelled something beside me; I turned, and there was a swirl of black robes and the flash of a long black blade before it sank into Paul's back. There was the pop of small-arms fire on the other side of me. A head flew past my nose. It was Jeff's.

A figure in a black robe twirled past me: One of the British agents had him in a headlock, but he shuffled backwards and slammed the agent into one of the stones, breaking his grip, before turning to sink his sword into him to the hilt.

That's when somebody forced me to the ground, hissing in my ear, "Get down!" A gun went off right next to my ear and my whole head hurt from the explosion. A body fell right on top of me. I rolled him off and saw the bullet hole through the center of his forehead.

I looked to my right and there was Mike, a gun in his hand, lying flat on his belly and staring into the middle of the circle. His left hand was on the small of my back, I guess to remind me to stay down.

I looked around and saw nobody left standing except Mogart and Bennacio. Around Bennacio lay four or five of the black-robed AODs, most of them without their heads, some with their legs still jerking. I could see a thin line of blood trickling down the side of Bennacio's face where one of the AODs must have smacked him as he knelt beside the Sword.

I looked for the Sword in Bennacio's hand, but it wasn't there. Mogart was holding the Sword.

Neither of them moved or said anything for a long time. They just looked at each other, standing about six feet apart, both taking in big gulps of air and breathing out in little jets of steam.

Finally, Bennacio said, "Surrender the Sword, Mogart." He sounded very calm. "Surrender it now and I will show mercy toward you."

"Oh yes, how I long for mercy from *you*," Mogart sneered. "Sir Bennacio! Gentle Bennacio! The kindest and bravest of knights! The last knight!" The mocking expression disappeared and a shadow fell over his face. "*I* am the last knight, Bennacio. I am the heir to Lancelot, the master of the Sword!"

I leaned over and whispered into Mike's ear. "Shoot him."

Mike shook his head. I could have grabbed the gun from him and fired, but I had never fired a gun in my life. I was afraid of guns, to tell you the truth. Mike was slowly chewing his gum, working it so hard, his jaw clicked as he gnawed.

Bennacio drew his black sword from the folds of his brown robe and held it by his side, casually, like a man carrying an umbrella.

"You always had poor taste in friends," Mogart said. "Cowards and fools. But what an admirable choice in your squire, Lord Bennacio! A fat, bumbling simpleton with hardly the intellectual wherewithal to tie his own shoes. You have outdone yourself, Bennacio."

"The Sword belongs to neither of us, Mogart." Bennacio used the same tone he had used with me sometimes, like a patient father talking to a thick-headed kid. "In your heart, unless it is totally corrupted, you know this. You may betray your sacred vow, but you cannot change the truth. You lay claim to something that is not meant for you. Abandon this madness that you might yet live."

"Wise words coming from the man whose sole purpose is to kill me."

"I wish harm to no man, Mogart. I shall ask you just once more. Relinquish the Sword that you might live. Answer now, yes or no."

Bennacio raised his sword, holding it with both hands, the hilt at chest level, the blade right in front of his face, about two inches from his sharp nose. Mogart smiled and raised Excalibur, holding it with both hands like Bennacio, so they mirrored each other, Bennacio with his brown robe and black sword, Mogart in his white robe and the much longer and wider Sword of Kings.

"Here is my answer," Mogart said softly, and launched himself at Bennacio.

41

Bennacio's blade was a black blur, its shiny surface sparking now and then in the glare of the floodlights. As he spun and turned and sidestepped around the circle, his brown robe fluttered and snapped. Bennacio was taller than Mogart, and he was faster. They held their swords with both hands as they fought, and each time Excalibur struck Bennacio's sword, I saw black flecks and sparks shooting off against the charcoal-colored backdrop of the great stones.

The blades whined and whistled as they cut through the cold air, and I don't know if it was the ringing in my ears from the gunshots, but there was a faint sound like a choir singing, and I remembered Bennacio telling me of the angels lamenting the last time he and Mogart met.

I remembered how it felt when I used the Sword, how it seemed a part of me or more like I was part of it. I remembered Bennacio telling me how it could not be defeated or destroyed, and then I realized what Bennacio had known all along: There was no winning against the Sword. Bennacio didn't have a prayer, and that made my chest hurt, because Bennacio didn't have a prayer—*and he prayed anyway*. He couldn't win, *but he fought anyway*.

Mogart was getting impatient. He must have thought Bennacio should be dead already. His blows came faster and Bennacio's parries a little slower, until Mogart swung the Sword high and brought it down in a sweeping arc straight at Bennacio's head. Bennacio raised his sword to block the downward blow and, when Excalibur struck, Bennacio's sword flew from his hands and skittered away into the shadows. The force of the blow knocked him to his knees.

Then he did a strange thing, a horrible thing, the strangest, most horrible thing I've ever seen anybody do: Bennacio raised his head and brought his arms straight out from his sides, very slowly, palms turned upward. He was offering himself!

Mogart hesitated, the tip of the Sword poised a few inches from Bennacio's heaving chest.

"No," I whispered.

Then Mogart slammed the Sword into the last knight's chest and Bennacio fell over without a sound, his eyes still open.

42

Somebody was screaming loud enough to drown out the high-pitched singing or ringing or whatever it was going on inside my head, and it took me a second to realize the screaming person was me.

The next thing I knew, I was running across the circle of stones, straight for Mogart, with Mike yelling after me, "Kropp! Kropp! Kropp!"

When I was about twenty feet away, Mogart pulled the Sword from Bennacio's chest, and the last knight fell to his side, eyes wide open staring right at me as I ran.

At ten feet, Mogart began to turn toward me.

At five, he was raising the tip of the Sword, its blade still glistening with Bennacio's blood.

At two, he actually started to smile.

I didn't let him finish that smile. I smashed my forearm into his face and he staggered backward. My forward momentum carried me right into him and we fell into the grass. I landed on top, knocking the wind out of him. He started to bring the Sword up, but I slapped my hand down hard on his wrist. When his hand struck the ground, I pulled the Sword out of his hand and stood up.

I backpedaled, gasping for air, my breath fogging and swirling. Mogart slowly sat up, gulping air.

A voice behind me said, "Alfred."

I turned, the Sword rising without me thinking about it. Mike was walking toward me, smiling widely, still holding the gun in his right hand, the left outstretched.

"Awesome, man! Simply awesome," Mike said. "You wanna come work for us?"

"It's the football," I gasped. "Finally paid off."

"Mr. Kropp," Mogart said. "I beg you to reconsider."

I took a couple of steps backward, so I could keep both of them in sight. Mogart was smiling now.

"It is not yours to take," Mogart said.

"It isn't yours either," I said. My voice sounded very small and quivery to me.

"Actually, it's mine," Mike said. "I mean, it's the property of my employer. Anyway, we bought it fair and square. Alfred, I'm gonna give Monsieur Mogart here the access code to the Swiss bank account so he can have his money and then you, me, and the Sword are outta here. How's that sound?"

"Not very good, Mike," I said, and then I ran.

43

Of course it was dark and foggy and I was in a strange country, but as I stumbled along I thought I'd try to make it to the forest we had driven through. The back of my neck tingled and my hair stood up, waiting for Mike's bullet. He wouldn't have hesitated to kill Mogart for the Sword and I didn't think he'd hesitate to kill me for it either.

I'm not a fast runner to begin with, and hefting the Sword didn't make me any faster. The long wet grass pulled at my feet and I might have just gone in circles in the dark, but the floodlights helped; I kept looking over my shoulder and they kept getting smaller as I ran. I listened for the sound of Mogart's army coming after me, but there was no sound at all except my huffing and puffing and the *swish-swish* of the grass rubbing against the soles of my shoes as I ran.

I stumbled onto the edge of the paved road. If this was the same road we drove in on, then following it would take me back into the woods. I still couldn't hear any sound of pursuit and I was too tired to run any more, so I started walking. Fog and sweat flattened my hair and I kept having to wipe the moisture off my face. My shirt clung to my chest and I shivered. I could feel a bad cold coming on. For some reason, the scar on my thumb was throbbing to beat the band. Maybe because the Sword was near it.

I was still walking with no woods in sight, just rolling hills that disappeared into the fog, when I heard the car coming up the road behind me.

I ran to the side of the road and threw myself onto the ground, making myself as flat as a fat, bumbling simpleton can get. But I didn't get flat enough, because the car stopped and a voice called out softly, "Alfred! Alfred Kropp, get over here!"

I lifted my head. Mike was sitting behind the wheel, smiling, smacking, waving his hand urgently at me.

"Come on! We don't have much time . . ."

He was probably right about that and I didn't have much of a choice. I scrambled up the embankment to the car and dived into the backseat. Mike hit the gas and the Bentley's back wheels spun out, screeching on the wet pavement like a wounded animal.

"Boy Howdy!" Mike yelled. "That was close, huh? Took

heavy casualties, but we kinda expected that goin' in, right? The main thing is we got the Sword. Got the Sword and saved the world, not bad for a night's work, huh?"

I leaned back, the Sword against my chest, still breathing heavily.

Mike said, "Pretty quick thinking back there, Al. You and Benny plan it that way, or was it all your idea?"

I didn't say anything. That didn't seem to matter to Mike. He kept talking.

"Darn it, dropped my cell back there in the fight. Well, everybody's on standby anyway. Me and Jeff have been together since Cairo—that wacky death-cult thing in the Valley of Kings. But, oh, jeez, enough about *that*, that's all classified. Anyway, I'm gonna miss that son of a gun and what a dingy-darn shame about Benny, huh? Heck of a guy. *Heck* of a guy. If I had my cell I'd call in a couple of Stealths and knock the living you-know-what out of that medieval madman, take out those thousand-year-old rocks with him. Small price to pay, don't ya think?"

"Did you kill him?" I asked.

He laughed. "What do you think, Al?"

"I don't think you did." I sat up and pressed the tip of the blade against Mike's neck.

He didn't react, except his hands tightened slightly on the wheel.

"Stop the car, Mike."

"Hey, Al. Ally boy. What the heck are you doing?"

"Stop the car, Mike."

He slowed down and pulled to the side of the road.

"Okay, now what? Talk to me, Al. What's this all about?"

I wasn't sure. I was making this up as I went along. "Give me your gun. No, Mike, with your left hand. Keep the right on the wheel. Slowly, Mike." I took the gun from over his left shoulder and slipped it under my belt.

"Okay," I said. "Now put your left hand back on the wheel."

"Al, I'm one of the good guys, remember?" His voice was calm enough, but he was working the gum hard. "Look, nobody's sorrier about Benny than me. That was a damn shame, but you were there, you saw—what did you want me to do about it?"

"You set him up."

"Ah, come on, Al!"

"You planned it from the beginning. Mogart didn't want just the money. He wanted Bennacio too."

Mike didn't have anything to say to that. He was watching me in the rearview mirror. I knew I was right when he didn't say anything.

"And you set up Mr. Samson and the rest of the knights in Spain. You tipped off Mogart they were coming."

He shook his head, smiling now. "Why would I do that, Alfred?"

"Because you both knew the same thing: As long as the knights lived, they were the only hope of ever keeping the

Sword safe. You both needed them out of the way. So you made them part of the deal."

"Man, that's a pretty interesting theory, Al."

"Mr. Samson trusted you to do the right thing," I said. "He didn't have to tell you about the Sword and you double-crossed him. Bennacio knew you were double-crossing us tonight, but he didn't see how he had a choice. He took a vow, see . . . he gave his word . . ."

"Look, Al, no offense, I know you mean well and everything, but you're in this thing way over your head. Put down the Sword, pal. We'll talk about this on the plane, okay? Don't you want to go home?"

"I don't have a home anymore."

"Really?" He whistled. "That's gotta be tough. I'm truly sorry to hear that, Al. Well, we could take you anywhere you want to go. Natalia is still at the château. You wanna see her? You got kind of a thing for her, don't you?"

I didn't say anything, but I could feel my face get hot. Mike Arnold noticed me blushing and smiled.

"Get out of the car," I said.

"Al . . ."

I pushed on his neck with the tip of the Sword.

"Okay, I'm getting out."

He opened his door and stepped onto the road. I got out and pointed the gun at his head.

"Get down on your stomach and fold your hands on the back of your head."

"You're making a huge mistake here, Al. A heck of a boner . . ."

"Lay down, Mike. I'll shoot if you don't."

"You think so? I'm sorry, Al, but I really don't think you can."

He took a step toward me and the gun went off. We both jumped. Neither of us was expecting that. I couldn't even remember pulling the trigger.

"All righty then," Mike said softly. He lay down.

"Hands on the back of your head," I told him.

He laced his fingers behind his head.

"Where do you think you're gonna go, Alfred? You can't get out of the country, and what are you goin' to do with the Sword? Take over the world? Donate it to the Smithsonian? You're not thinking this through, kid."

"Good-bye, Mike," I said, and I climbed into the car and drove off. I kept looking in the rearview mirror, but I never saw Mike get up.

44

The steering wheel was on the wrong side and I had trouble keeping the car on the road; the right wheels kept dropping off the road until I remembered I was supposed to be driving on the left side. That made it a little better, but it still felt funny. I knew I needed to ditch the car as soon as possible: A Bentley's a little too conspicuous for a getaway car.

I drove aimlessly through the English countryside, not even knowing what direction I was heading. I kept going until I came to a road that looked bigger and kept taking bigger roads until I came to a highway or whatever they're called in

England, and after a few miles passed a sign that read: "London 40 miles."

The traffic began to pick up as I got closer to the city. I drove with both hands on the wheel, my knuckles bone white, the Sword lying on the seat beside me. I couldn't stop yawning, and all I wanted to do was pull to the side of the road and go to sleep, but I kept driving.

The sun was rising by the time I reached the outskirts of London. I was definitely not driving into the heart of the city in a hot Bentley, so I pulled into the first hotel I saw in a place called Slough. I took off my jacket and wrapped the Sword in it, but that left the butt of the gun sticking up from my waistband in full view. I worried what to do about this and if the clerk would wonder why this fifteen-year-old kid was checking in without any bags or parents, and why I had a jacket in the shape of a large sword. But some things you can't do anything about, so I pushed the gun all the way down, into my underwear. The cold metal of the barrel pressed against my groin.

The hotel looked old, as if it had been something else before it was a hotel, maybe a nobleman's country estate. The lobby was very small, and just felt old compared to the American hotels I had been in. The clerk didn't say anything about my sword-shaped jacket. He put me in a room on the third floor, and told me I'd have to take the stairs because there was no lift. He asked how long I'd be staying. I told him I was taking a walking tour of England and I'd leave when I was tired of walking. He didn't ask anything else. He didn't smile once, and I thought maybe he had bad teeth. I had read some-where that's a problem in England.

In the stairwell, I took the gun out of my underwear and kind of tucked it under my arm. The hall was narrow and there were water stains on the baseboard. The paint job and carpet looked at least ten years old and smelled of mold. My room was at the end of the hall, next to the bathroom.

My bed was narrow, about six feet long, and shook a lit-tle when I sat on it. I was afraid it was going to break. I thought about calling the front desk and asking if they had rooms with bigger beds. I put the gun on the bedside table and laid the Sword down on the bed beside me. I took off my shoes, peeled off my wet socks, and lay down.

What was I going to do with the Sword now? Mike had a good point. They'd lock down the whole country and go door-to-door if they had to. They'd find the Bentley parked in the hotel parking lot, and I hadn't even used a fake name to check in.

I expected a knock on the door any second, but they probably wouldn't knock, just burst in with guns blazing, because after all, I had the Sword of Kings and might use it to take over the world.

I yawned. I needed sleep, but my instincts told me sleep should probably be the last thing on my to-do list. I pushed myself off the bed. On the wall next to the TV was a mirror. I looked at myself and decided I probably should take a shower, but that would mean leaving the room, and I didn't want to take the Sword with me into the shower or leave it in the room. I looked in the mirror and thought about Mogart calling me fat. I wasn't fat; I was just big. I had always been big and blocky, like one of those blocks at Stonehenge, wide and rectangular, the most boring shape next to a square there is.

I sat back on the bed and tried to figure out my next move. I couldn't stay here long—no more than a few hours. I should shower and brush my teeth and go, except I didn't have a toothbrush. I didn't have anything except the most powerful weapon on earth. I could declare myself the Emperor Kropp, King Alfred the First, Lord of the Earth, but right then all I wanted was a toothbrush.

If I made myself king, I could summon all the world's leaders to Slough and declare world peace. I could demand all the tanks and bombs and guns be melted down and turned into playground equipment. I could tell all the rich countries to feed the poor ones and outlaw war and tell them from now on every penny they used to spend on weapons they now had to spend on finding cures for diseases and making cars that burn clean fuel. I could demand the end to every evil under the sun. No more war or disease or famine. I could fulfill what Bennacio said was the reason the archangel gave the Sword to Arthur: I could unite mankind. I could finish what Arthur started. It might not bring Bennacio back, or Samson and the knights, or Uncle Farrell, or anyone who was lost because of me, but it might make up for what I had done. It might even make Natalia not hate me anymore.

Maybe my destiny was to be the sword-wielding savior

of the world, and wouldn't that just make Amy Pouchard regret not giving me her cell phone number! I had a vision of myself on a great throne, with a great big golden crown on my great big head.

The cold I had felt coming on was now fully on: My head hurt, my nose was running, and my forehead was hot. I lay on the bed and told myself in a minute I would get up and take a cool shower to bring my fever down and be ready to think more clearly. It's pretty sad when you reach the point of scheduling your clear thinking.

"That's it. You've figured it all out, Kropp," I told myself. I was pretty feverish by this point. "The Knights of the Sacred Order kept the Sword hidden for a thousand years, waiting for Alfred Kropp to come along and save the world. Right! It never occurred to any of them, from Bedivere on down, that maybe one of *them* could take up the Sword and bring peace to this rotten world. They were waiting for *you*, Mr. big-headed high school dropout, to take care of things."

I touched the cold metal of the blade—after a thousand years, how smooth and perfect it was! Just touching it made me happy and sad at the same time.

Eventually, I fell asleep, and I was back in the dream of the dark rider on the terrible battlefield, the Sword in the rider's hand. Just as he was about to slam the blade into the ground and blow away his enemies, he lifted his head and I could see his face. It was *my* face. Not Kropp the Benign . . . but Kropp the Conqueror, Kropp the Terrible.

When I opened my eyes again the room was dark and the

phone was ringing. I turned on the table lamp and wondered how long I had been asleep. I stared at the phone on the bedside table and wondered who was calling. Maybe the front desk, to tell me some guys in black robes were waiting for me down in the lobby.

I picked up the receiver. "Hello?"

"Bonjour, Mr. Kropp."

I picked up Mike's gun from the bedside table and held it in my lap.

"Mr. Mogart."

"Are you watching television?"

"Excuse me?"

"Is there a television in your room? If so, I suggest you turn it to channel one."

"Right now?"

"Immediately."

"I'm gonna have to put the phone down."

"That's quite all right."

I set the phone down and turned on the TV. The BBC news had just started. About five minutes into the show, they ran a story about the American attorney general's news conference that afternoon. He was announcing an update to the FBI's most wanted list. Before they flashed the photograph on the screen, I knew what I would see.

It was my picture.

The attorney general was saying I was an international fugitive with ties to terrorists and was responsible for the deaths of sixteen British and American personnel in an attempt to destroy one of England's most famous national treasures. Then he announced the Justice Department was offering a six-million-dollar reward for information leading to my capture and conviction.

The big-headed loser was finally tops in something: I was the most-wanted fugitive in the entire world, but all I could think of was how difficult it would be now to assemble my summit of world leaders and declare the founding of the Kingdom of Kropptopia.

I turned the set off and went back to the phone.

"I'm back," I said.

"Congratulations, Mr. Kropp. You are a celebrity. Perhaps you will even make the cover of *People* magazine."

"How—how did you find me, Mr. Mogart?"

I walked over to the window as I talked. I pulled back the curtain, expecting to see a SWAT team or their British counterparts storming the building. But all I could see was the empty parking lot and some woods. To my left, the dirty yellow lights of London glowed on the horizon.

"A fifteen-year-old boy—and not a particularly clever boy at that—alone in a strange country, afraid and without friends, driving a car equipped with a Global Positioning System—how difficult do you think that really is?"

"I guess not too difficult," I said.

I sat back down on the bed.

"I know what you want, Mr. Mogart. But, see, if I give it to you it's going to mean the end of the world. I'm only fifteen, like you said, and it's really important to me that the world sticks around for a while, at least until I'm forty. Maybe fifty, even."

"Ah, but you are missing the point, Alfred," Mogart said. It was the first time he had called me by my first name. "Whether you live to fifty is of little importance to me. I want only one thing, so you see we are both equally disadvantaged. You have something I want and I have something you want."

"What?" I asked, since I couldn't think of a single thing I had left that mattered. Everybody who mattered to me was dead. But that wasn't true and the funny thing was that, of the two of us, Mogart was the only one who knew it.

"Kropp."

It took a second for it to sink in that the voice on the other end wasn't Mogart's. It wasn't even a man's voice.

"Kropp," she whispered again.

"Natalia?"

I heard a little screech, then silence, and Mogart's voice came back.

"Understand, Mr. Kropp, that I care not for what I have, as you care not for what you have. I would sacrifice my life for what you possess, as you would sacrifice yours for what I possess. To my mind, there is only one way to satiate our particular desires. Are you following me, Mr. Kropp?"

"Wouldn't it have been easier just to come here and take it from me?" My voice was shaking badly.

"Why should I come there for it, Mr. Kropp, when you are bringing it to me?"

Just then I heard a sharp rap on the door. I jumped and gave a little yelp.

Mogart said, "Someone is at your door. Open it."

"I have a gun," I said. "I'll use it."

"Do so and she dies."

The rapping on the door continued.

"Who's at my door?" I asked.

"Answer it and find out. I'll wait."

I walked to the door and called out, "Who is it?"

"Your escort, Mr. Kropp," came a voice from the other side. I unlocked the door and shuffled backwards, lifting the gun, so when he walked into the room it was pointed right at his nose.

"Don't even think about going toward that bed," I told him.

He nodded. He was a big man, about my size. He wore a long gray cape over his shoulders, fastened by a dragon-shaped pin just below his Adam's apple. Under the cape, he was dressed in an expensive tailored suit. His long hair was greased and combed back from his face.

"Stand right there," I added, backing toward the bed, keeping the gun on him. He nodded again. "Don't make any sudden moves!" I said sharply to him. He nodded a third time. I picked up the receiver with my left hand and brought it to my ear.

"Mr. Kropp," Mogart said softly. "I believe I told you some time ago that the will of most men is weak. Thus nations crumble and decay, great enterprises are lost, needless suffering and humiliation ensue. I believe I also told you—in fact, demonstrated to you in the most graphic way—what would happen if your will opposed mine. You will accompany my associate to our little meeting or the girl will die."

My knees completely gave out then and I sat on the bed. The gun dropped to my side. I had made a vow and if I kept that vow, Natalia would die. I felt so miserable at that point, I almost picked up the Sword and handed it to the escort, who was still standing by the door, smiling at me.

Mogart's voice lost all its playfulness and it got hard. "Listen carefully, Kropp. You are not adept at what you're attempting to do. You are a boy playing a man's game. You might be enjoying this make-believe game of being a hero, but truly you are fortunate that I found you first."

"I don't know what you're talking about!" I screamed into the phone. "I never wanted to be a hero! I never wanted any of this!"

"They are coming, Mr. Kropp. Remember the report you just saw on television? The OIPEPs are coming for you and they *will* find you. And when they find you, they will take the Sword and I will kill the girl. You will have lost both. You have no choice now but to bring it to me."

"But if I bring it to you, you'll kill her anyway."

"You wound my feelings, Mr. Kropp."

"You'll kill her, because the last time I gave you the Sword you killed Uncle Farrell, and you didn't need to kill Uncle Farrell."

He sighed. "No. I should not have killed your uncle. I should have killed *you*."

"You're gonna do that too," I said into the phone.

"Then your answer is no?"

"You already know what my answer's going to be."

"Just so," Mogart said.

45

I hung up the phone. Mogart's associate, was still standing by the door, smiling at me.

"Come," he said. "The master is expecting us."

"I've got the Sword now," I said. "Doesn't that make me the master?"

"Do you claim it?" he asked mockingly.

I looked at it on the bed beside me. "No. But that's the point, I think. Nobody can. You could wait a thousand years, ten thousand even, but nobody can really claim it. I think that's where your boss has got it all wrong and why the knights kept it hidden all those years, maybe even why

Arthur had to die. It's not something you can own." He wasn't getting it. I asked, "Where are we going?"

"Did the master not tell you? To Dundagel, now called Tintagel."

"Oh. What's in Tintagel?"

"Camelot is in Tintagel, and the caves of Merlin."

"Sure," I said. "That would make sense."

Then I picked up the gun and shot him in the left kneecap.

He yelled and pitched forward onto the floor, wrapping his arms around his knee. I grabbed Excalibur from the bed beside me.

"In the name of Saint Michael!" I yelled, and brought the Sword, flat side down, toward his head. He didn't even see it coming. I hit him in the head with the broad part of the blade and he went still.

I knelt beside him and pressed my fingertips against his wrist. He wasn't dead. I remembered what Bennacio had told me after he dispatched those two thralls in the forest back in America: *You would not pity them if you knew them as I do.*

"Well, Bennacio," I murmured as I unhooked the dragon pin to remove the gray cloak. "I know what they did to my father. And I know what they did to you and to the rest of the knights, but at some point somebody's gotta say enough. At some point all the blood and guts have to dry up."

Underneath the cloak the escort had concealed one of those black-bladed swords. I searched his pockets and found a set of car keys.

I hooked the black sword around my waist and twisted the belt around so it hung on my right side. I slipped Excalibur into the other side of my belt, to hang on my left side. I threw the gray cape around my shoulders and hooked the dragon pin, then looked at myself in the mirror. Sir Alfred of the Castle Screws-up-a-lot.

I stepped over the escort, opened the door, looked both ways before going into the hall, and closed the door behind me.

I took the back stairs to the main floor, praying there was a back door to the place. The Sword pooched out of the cloak on the left side, and its shape was kind of obvious.

The stairs ended just to the right of a glass door that opened onto the parking lot. I slipped outside and walked around, looking for the escort's wheels. There was a black Lamborghini Murciélago parked in the handicapped space right by the door. I knew it was the right car before I even tried the key. These guys liked their cars.

I couldn't sit with both swords jutting out, so I pulled them from my belt and laid both in the small backseat, throwing the gray cloak over them. I cruised the lot once before leaving, to see if any spooks or other black robes were hanging around, but saw nothing suspicious.

I had no idea where Tintagel was, so I pulled into the first gas station I saw, though apparently it isn't called gas in England; it's called petrol. The clerk gave me a funny look when I walked through the door in my gray cloak with the dragon-shaped pin.

"And what are you supposed to be?" he asked.

"The heir to Lancelot, the greatest knight who ever lived."

One of his eyebrows went up and I said, "Yeah, it's a stretch. I've been having a heck of a time with it."

"If you're Lancelot, I'd hate to see Guinevere."

"I didn't say I *was* Lancelot. I'm *descended* from Lancelot."

"Oh, right. And I'm the Queen of bloody Sheba."

I told the clerk I needed a map of England and asked him where Tintagel was.

"Tintagel? That's in Cornwall."

"About how far is it?"

"Around two hundred miles."

He spread the map open on the counter and showed me where Tintagel was, on the southwest coast.

"Now here is Tintagel Head," he said, pointing out a spot on the map right by the Atlantic Ocean. "Lots of Yanks go there. Spectacular view, sits on a cliff with a three-hundred-foot drop to the sea."

"Is there a castle there?"

"Some ruins, yes. Not much to look at. King Arthur's castle is the legend, but you know that already, of course, being the descendent of Lancelot. Did you know he wasn't British? He was French."

"Was he? Well . . . *très magnifique*. Nothing but ruins there, you said?"

"Above, yes. Now, in the cliffs directly below is a cave they say was the sanctuary of Merlin, the king's wizard.

Some say when the tide is out and the wind begins to blow from the sea, you can hear the ghost of Merlin wailing for the kingdom that was lost—if you believe such things."

"Oh," I said. "You bet I do, mister."

"Of course, sir knight," he said. "You would."

46

So I drove to Tintagel at ninety miles per hour, expecting any minute to hit a roadblock or to see a helicopter gunship swoop out of the night sky and take out my tires. But nothing like that happened. I tried to think. I really needed a plan. In fact, this was probably my last chance to come up with one, but all I felt was naked, like I was caught up in a tornado, every scrap of clothing torn away, naked in the screeching wind with nothing to hold on to.

After an hour and a half I could smell the sea. I slowed down because the road signs were different and I couldn't read them very well going that fast. I bore off the main highway at the turnoff for Tintagel and followed the signs toward

Tintagel Head. I rolled down the window and could hear the ocean as well as smell it.

I came to a roadblock, just a couple of sawhorses painted red and placed in the middle of the lane. A sign beside them read: "Site Closed for Archeological Dig." I backed the Lamborghini up about fifty feet and floored the gas. One of the sawhorses sprung into the air and smashed into the windshield, making a series of intricately laced cracks, like a spiderweb.

I cut the headlights and crawled along the lane, expecting any second for men in black robes to jump out of the dark onto the hood of the car. The road ended about fifty yards from the cliff's edge. I turned off the engine and got out.

A cold, icy wind was blowing in from the sea. I stood for a second in the biting wind and my eyes were watering up pretty bad, the tears running straight back across my temples and into my hair. I should put the swords in my belt and march off to my doom like Bennacio—and the world's doom, since losing the Sword now left nobody to get it back, if you didn't count OIPEP. But I wasn't sure about which side OIPEP was on. Mike Arnold was kind of a jerk and I wasn't sure about Abigail either, except she seemed nice and didn't like Mike, which was a point in her favor.

But instead of grabbing the swords, I got back in the car again. I asked myself, "Okay, Kropp, which is it, Natalia or the Sword?" and that made me get out again and throw the car keys as far as I could into the darkness.

I put the swords back in my belt, the black one on the

right, Excalibur on the left. I threw the cloak over my shoulders. I patted my pockets, checking for the gun, and then remembered I had left it lying on the bed in the hotel room. Over my head, all right. Not very adept for sure.

I could see some squat, dark shapes silhouetted against the moonless sky, blocking out some of the stars. I hiked toward them, and I didn't see any sign of activity, just a bunch of whitish-looking blocks jutting out of the ground like gigantic discarded teeth. I couldn't quite imagine this as a gleaming white castle by the sea.

I noticed a path made of large white stones leading away from the ruins toward the edge of the cliff. I couldn't find any rope or handrails, nothing to hang on to as you descended. I skittered and slid on the wet stones as I crawled down sideways. Droplets of rain and sea spray clung to my cloak.

I stopped at the bottom of the path, wondering where Mogart's gang was. You'd think they'd be all over me by now.

About thirty yards away a light glowed from an opening in the cliff face. Merlin's cave.

I eased along the path, hugging the base of the cliff wall. The stones beneath my feet were smooth and wet, worn from centuries of the sea's coming and going. I let out my breath as I reached the edge of the opening. I could hear men talking quietly inside the cave, their voices echoing against the cave's walls. There was another sound too, a kind of high-pitched whistling that I guessed was the wind moving through cracks in the cliff. The cries of Merlin.

I didn't really have a plan. I'd never stormed a bad guy's

hideout before, and all I knew about it came from movies and books—and those weren't real. I stood to the right of the jagged cave opening, my back pressed against the cliff wall. Directly across from me was another, slightly shorter cliff that formed the other wall of the inlet, so I couldn't see the ocean. I could hear it, though, and taste the salt on my tongue. You'd think carrying the greatest weapon mankind had ever known would have given me some courage, but all I felt was insignificant.

I took a deep breath and said aloud, "I'm going to die."

Then I turned and stepped into the opening.

47

Two men sat by a small fire about twenty feet inside the cave. They stared at me for a second; then one of them stood up. He was wearing a black robe and held a thin black sword just like the one tucked into the right side of my belt.

"Where is the boy?" he snapped at me. "Where is the Sword?" He must have thought I was the escort.

"We're both right here," I said, and drew out Excalibur.

It took him a second to get it, and then he came at me with a loud cry.

He fell at my feet. I looked down at him, startled,

because he'd just dropped there; he hadn't even had a chance to raise his sword.

I stepped over him, fighting the feeling that I was going to throw up. I looked toward the second guy, who turned on his heel and made for the back of the cave, slipping on the wet rocks as he tried to run. He wasn't wearing a black robe, but a blue and gray Windbreaker, a pair of Dockers, New Balance running shoes, and a Chicago Cubs baseball cap.

I caught him at the back of the cave—it wasn't very deep, maybe fifty or sixty feet—spun him around, and held him against the wall with my left forearm while I pressed the tip of the Sword against his Adam's apple.

"Hey, Mike," I said.

"Hi, Al." He was smacking him gum and smiling, showing his large white teeth.

"Where's Mogart?"

"Dunno."

I pressed the tip of the Sword harder against his flesh. His eyes grew wide and he said, "Look, I swear, kid, you just killed the one guy who knows where he is. He was going to take us to him once you got here with the escort. I swear to God I don't know!"

"You gave him Natalia."

He didn't say anything. He was smiling, but his eyes were cold.

I said, "Tell me where she is."

"Even if I did know, what're you gonna do, Al? Give him the Sword? He'll kill her anyway. And if you try to take him,

298

he'll kill her before you can kill him. Don't you see you can't win? Time to cut your losses. You gotta step back and take a look at the big picture. We're talkin' the fate of the whole ding-dong world here, Al! You're going to sacrifice humanity for the sake of one person? I mean, let's be reasonable here!"

"Okay, Mike, I'll be reasonable. I'll make a deal with you. You bring me to Mogart and when it's over I'll give you the Sword."

He stared at me and slowed some on the gum.

I said, "That's why you're here, isn't it? Give me Mogart and it's yours."

Mike thought about it. "How do I know you won't double-cross me?"

"I guess you don't. But like Mr. Mogart told me, you don't have a choice."

I stepped back, but kept the Sword pointed toward his neck. "Give me your gun."

He reached into the pocket of his Windbreaker and held out the gun, his finger hooked around the trigger guard. I took it from him and slipped it into my pocket.

"Anything else?" he asked. He acted like he was trying hard not to laugh.

"No," I said. Then I thought of something. "Yes. What does OIPEP stand for?"

"'Only Idiots Pursue Extraordinary Persons.'" He laughed in spite of himself and smacked his gum. "Okay? Are we done now?"

"One more thing," I said. I held out my hand. "The gum."

He started to laugh again but saw I was dead serious. He took out the gum and dropped it into my hand. When he did that, about half his personality evaporated. I tossed it into the shadows.

He turned to his left and I followed him along the back wall of the cave. The walls were smooth and slightly concave. He stopped at a fissure in the wall near the south corner. It was barely the width of one person, running from the floor to the ceiling.

"You first," I said.

As we slipped into the opening, the sea sound became softer, and the drip of water and the wailing of Merlin a little louder. The floor here was rough, littered with stones and angled downward slightly. The path twisted right, then back left, then dropped steeply, and I had to press my free hand against the jagged wall to keep my balance. We eased our way down very slowly. Loose rocks and jutting outcrops as sharp as knives slowed our way down.

Gradually the walls drew back and the floor leveled and became smooth. A circle of light glowed in the distance. When we were about a hundred yards from the opening, Mike turned and whispered urgently, "Al, you gotta give my gun back."

"Why?"

"He's gonna think I've stiffed him. You've seen what he does to people who stiff him."

I thought about it. "Okay," I said. I took the gun from

my pocket and hit him in the head as hard as I could with the grip.

He fell straight down. I slipped the gun back into my pocket, stepped over him, and walked the final hundred yards to the portal, alone.

48

I stood at the entrance to a huge cavern whose walls and ceiling were lost in vast, arching shadows. The floor was as smooth and as dark as a frozen pond. My footfalls echoed against the unseen walls as I walked slowly across the floor. There was no other sound and nobody in sight. I walked holding the Sword in front of me, thinking maybe there was another passage somewhere and I'd knocked out Mike too soon. Then I heard Mogart's voice. It seemed to come from everywhere and nowhere.

"Mr. Kropp. You never cease to surprise me."

I stopped. I slowly pulled the gun out of my pocket and

held it loosely in my left hand, more to comfort myself than anything else.

"To have come this far, with so little experience and even less intelligence . . . I salute you, sir."

"Where's Natalia?" My voice sounded small and tinny, almost like a little kid's.

"Here."

His voice sounded right by my ear. I whirled around and saw them coming toward me, Natalia in front of him. He held the back of her neck with his left hand. In his right he held a tapered dagger.

They stopped about twenty feet away and Mogart smiled.

"I'm glad to see you have taken care of Mr. Arnold," he said, nodding toward the gun. "I never cared for that man."

Natalia's eyes were dry, but very red; she must have been crying. Her dark hair was tangled around her face and there was a large bruise near the hairline.

"I'm sorry," I told her. "Are you okay?"

She nodded, cutting her eyes at Mogart. I said, "I brought the Sword, Mr. Mogart. Let her go."

"First the gun, yes? It's hardly necessary, Mr. Kropp, and you might make a terrible mistake. You might strike the wrong person."

I thought about it. If I refused, he might stab Natalia before I had a chance to get off a shot, a shot that would probably miss. But I'd still have the Sword and he knew if he killed her there'd be no reason for me to let him live. But that didn't really matter to me, since Natalia would be dead.

I threw the gun and it slid across the smooth floor into the shadows.

"Very good," Mogart said. "Now, the Sword, please."

"Let her go first."

He laughed. "My, how bold we've become! But boldness, Mr. Kropp, can never be a substitute for intelligence."

The dagger pressed into Natalia's side. Her eyes went wide and she cried out, "Kropp!"

Mogart said, "Decide now, Alfred Kropp. Throw down the Sword or watch her die."

Natalia was just one person and, like Mike said, what was one person when the whole world was at stake? If I refused to give him the Sword he'd kill Natalia; if I gave him the Sword he would probably kill her anyway and my sacred vow—and the only vow I ever made—would be broken.

I knew whatever decision I made would probably turn out to be wrong, as wrong as every decision I had made since this whole thing started. I kept screwing up and then just kept coming back for more. Maybe to fix it I needed to decide what the best thing to do was, and then do the opposite.

Looking at Mogart, I realized the plain truth was that he wasn't my greatest enemy. My greatest enemy was the fifteen-year-old homeless loser holding the Sword of Kings.

"Choose, Mr. Kropp," Mogart said softly.

I chose.

I tossed the Sword toward him. It clattered to the ground about halfway between us. I expected him to throw Natalia to the floor and dive on the Sword, but he didn't move. He wasn't even looking at the Sword; he was looking at me and I got that sinking feeling I had in Uncle Farrell's apartment, right before Mogart rammed the Sword into his body.

"Don't, Mr. Mogart," I pleaded. "You don't need to do that now. Don't hurt her, please."

"Oh, Mr. Kropp," Mogart answered. "After all that has happened, have you learned so little?"

And with that he plunged the dagger into Natalia's side.

49

She fell without a sound. I froze for a second, watching her fall, before lunging for the Sword, but I was too late. Mogart dived on it first, rolling out of the way as I launched myself at him.

I scrambled to my feet and pulled the black sword from my belt, meaning to switch it to my right hand, but Mogart was on me too fast, the Sword of Kings whistling toward my head.

I lifted my blade just in time and then cried out when Excalibur smashed against it with a ringing crash. The force of it almost snapped my wrist. I stepped back, flailing my sword in the air as Mogart, almost leisurely, took swings at me. He smiled, enjoying himself, and he was saying things like, "Good, Mr. Kropp! Excellent! Fine parry, sir! On the balls of your feet, step lightly and keep your sword up!"

He kept advancing and I kept backing up. He came from the right, then the left, then the right again, very fast, and finally the force of a blow slung my arm away so hard, I heard the joint in my shoulder pop.

His free hand caught the wrist of my blade hand, and his grip was cold and hard. I felt the tip of Excalibur pressing under my chin. Mogart brought his face very close to mine and he whispered, "There is one thing that has always troubled me about you, Alfred Kropp: Why do you persist? I kill your uncle, and you join Bennacio. I kill Bennacio, and you strike out on your own. I kill Natalia, and still you fight. So tell me, boy, tell me why you persist."

"I . . . I made a vow . . ." I stammered.

He cocked his head to one side, and his eyes twinkled as he started to smile.

"A vow! Alfred Kropp has made a vow!" He laughed harshly. "To Lord Bennacio, no doubt."

"No," I answered. "To heaven."

And I brought my knee up into his crotch as hard as I could. I ripped my blade arm free and stepped back as he went down to the stone floor. This was it! Go, Kropp, while he's down—take him out with your sword! But something stopped me. Instead of killing him, I just stood there, gulping air, waiting for him to stand up.

"It isn't yours, Mr. Mogart," I said. "Don't you see? It isn't anybody's."

Mogart stood up, his face distorted by pain and something else, not anger exactly, but something like anger and sadness mixed together, like a pouty little boy who's just learned he can't have his favorite candy.

"Who are you?" he gasped. "Who are you, Alfred Kropp? How is it that I find you at every turn, like a fat stone in my path, blocking my way?" With each question, he took a step toward me. And with each step he took forward, I took one backward.

"Why did Bennacio come to you after Samson's fall?" Step. "And bring you here?" Step. "Why did he demand the vow of you?" Step. *"Who are you, Alfred Kropp?"*

"I'm Bernard Samson's son and the heir to Lancelot."

He stopped. He looked as if I had slapped him. Then all the pain and sadness drained out of his face and left nothing but anger.

He launched himself at me with a terrible roar. I raised my black sword just in time to block the downward arc of Excalibur, and the impact made my ears ring with pain. Mogart's eyes glittered with rage as he swung at me, so fast, Excalibur was just a silvery blur.

As Mogart swung furiously at me, I backed up until I ran out of room and smacked into the wall behind me. Now I was left with two choices: Stand up and fight, or give up and die.

I was moving on just instinct, holding the sword in both

hands as Mogart's shoulders dipped and hunched and swiveled, and the sound of our swords meeting was an awful screech of metal striking metal. I could feel the jagged teeth of the wall behind me cutting through the gray cloak, taking nibbles from my back.

I screamed Bennacio's name as loud as I could. This only made Mogart angrier, and he slammed his left hand against my right shoulder. The force of the blow jarred the sword from my hand, and the blade clattered to the floor.

Mogart pressed his forearm against my neck, and as I struggled to breathe against the pressure, I knew the fight was over.

"The heir to Samson!" he hissed into my face. I felt the tip of Excalibur pressing into my stomach, penetrating the cloak and tearing slowly into the shirt under it. "The heir to Lancelot! The reason for my exile! How things have come full circle, Alfred Kropp!"

"Please," I whispered. "Please, Mr. Mogart . . ." I wasn't sure exactly what I was begging him to do. Or not do.

"Did noble Bennacio tell you how your father met his fate? Did anyone tell you, Alfred Kropp, how Daddy died?"

I felt the steel tip pierce my skin, and the sickening warmth of my own blood trickle down my stomach.

"Please," I whispered. "Please."

"I tortured him. I cut him a thousand times, until upon his knees he begged me to finish it, to end his miserable life. Just as you are begging now."

His arm moved forward. The blade sank deeper into my

body, maybe four or five inches, and I could taste blood in my mouth.

"And when he had no more breath for begging, I lopped off his miserable head."

His right arm jerked forward, harder this time, and now my mouth was full of my own blood.

His face was fading and his voice was growing fainter.

"And then I took Bernard Samson's head and mounted it on a steel pike. I placed his head at the entrance to my keep, where the carrion fed upon it, where the crows feasted on his eyes and tongue. And so you see we have indeed come full circle, Mr. Kropp. The time has come for our parting. The time has come for you to leave me and join your father."

And with that he slammed the Sword all the way into my body, up to the hilt, and I heard the cloak rip as the tip passed out through my back and bit into the stone wall behind me as easily as if the rock were sand.

Mogart let go and backed away. His smile came back.

"Now," he said. "*Die,* Alfred Kropp."

I'll never be sure, but I think when he said that, I did.

50

I saw some things after I died.

First, I was floating near the cave's roof, looking down at myself impaled against the wall. Mogart had both hands wrapped around the hilt of the Sword, pulling with all his strength, his face contorted with the effort. His roars of rage and frustration echoed against the walls of the cavern.

He pulled and pulled, but he couldn't pull the Sword from the stone.

He staggered backwards, then turned and found the two-foot dagger he had dropped when he dived for the Sword. I guess he was going to cut my body away from the Sword because you can't get much leverage against a human body—it's too soft—and then that faded.

There was silence, and then the sound the wind makes whispering through leaves.

Suddenly, I was sitting beside Mom's bed in the hospital and she was saying, *Take it away. Please take the pain away.*

I couldn't take that, so I turned away and Uncle Farrell was on the sofa and the Sword was in his gut, and I watched as he pulled it out and held it toward me. *Take it, Al. Take it away.*

I turned away from Uncle Farrell, and Bernard Samson, my father, was beside me, saying, *They are part of an ancient and secret Order, bound by a sacred vow to keep safe the Sword until its Master comes to claim it.*

I turned again, and saw Bennacio. I heard us speak, but it was more like I was remembering hearing us speak.

Who is the master if Arthur's dead?

The master is the one who claims it.

And who would that be?

The master of the Sword.

Then Bennacio turned away and I was sad to see him turn away, because I think I missed him most of all.

Then I saw the Lady in White sitting beneath the yew tree, and I felt no wind, but her dark hair was flowing behind her and the folds of her white robe were rippling like waves.

She didn't look at me as I stopped under the tree beside her. Her cheeks were wet.

"Am I dead?" I asked.

Do you wish to be?

"I think so. I'm awfully tired." More than anything, I wanted to lie down with my head in her lap and feel her stroke my brow.

A tear rolled down her cheek and I said, "Please don't. It's not like I didn't try. From the beginning I did what any-body asked. Uncle Farrell asked me to help him get the Sword, and I did. Bennacio asked me to help him get it back, and I did. Mogart asked me to bring it to him, and I did. But every time I did what they asked, somebody got killed. Uncle Farrell, Bennacio, and now Natalia. So, you see, Lady, there's nobody left now. Nobody left for me to help and nobody left to die because I tried. There's no reason for me to go back."

I turned away because I couldn't bear to see her cry. She was still there, only I couldn't see her, but I could see the memory of her and the memory of the yew and the long grasses and the glittering shards like teeth in the slag heap below. And, over my head, the butterflies.

The hour has come. Do you remember, now, Alfred Kropp, what has been forgotten?

Then there was nothing. Even the blackness wasn't black, because my memory of *black* was gone. No light, no sound, no sensation or memory—there wasn't even any *me* anymore. Alfred Kropp was gone.

And when the last of me was gone, I remembered what I had forgotten.

I reached into the yew tree and pulled a silver pin from the body of a butterfly. Freed, it burst into flight, black and red and gold against the bright blue sky, soaring higher and higher, until it was gone.

Darkness came back, but this time only because my eyes were closed.

So I opened them.

I was back in Merlin's cave, with the silver Sword of Kings jutting from my stomach.

And I knew, I finally knew, who the master of the Sword was.

51

Mogart came toward me, the black dagger in his hand, but he stopped when he heard the sound of my voice.

"The master . . ." I gasped. "The master of the Sword is . . . the one . . ." I coughed and blood filled my mouth and ran down my chin. "The one . . . *who claims it*."

I brought my hands up and wrapped my fingers around the hilt. Behind me, metal screeched against the rock as I pulled the Sword from my body. Mogart was opening his mouth to either scream or say something, I'll never know, because I was free of the Sword now—or it was free of me—and, free, I swung the Sword around in one gigantic arc, my own blood flying from the blade, and I cut off his god-damned head.

I dropped to the cold stone floor. I realized I might die again, but I had already died once and I wasn't worried about it anymore, at least not once I finished what I had started.

I started to crawl toward Natalia, but my arms gave out and I flopped onto my belly on the cold stone. I let go of the Sword; I needed both my hands to push myself along the floor.

There was a soft white glow surrounding her and through my tears, in the trick of the light, I thought I saw a shadow hovering over her and the shape of wings.

My head felt hollow and black stars began to bloom before my eyes. I would never make it to her in time, but I told myself I could go one more inch. One more inch, Kropp, I told myself. One more inch. And after that inch, another inch.

My teeth chattered and I was very cold, colder than I ever remember being. The soft light around her burned my eyes to look at, so I closed my eyes and felt something warm around me, as if someone had wrapped me in a blanket.

There was a rushing sound and I thought of a great river running to the sea. Hundreds of years, thousands, whole centuries passed, and I still didn't know how close I was or if I was even close at all.

Then I breathed in the scent of peaches.

I opened my eyes and saw the face of the most beautiful girl I had ever seen.

I whispered in her ear, "By the power of the Sword, Natalia . . . in the name of the Archangel Michael . . ."

Dipping my fingers into the wound in my stomach, I brought the blood to her side where Mogart had stabbed her.

I bathed her wound in my blood, whispering in her ear, "See, I remembered. I remembered what I had forgotten. I was going to stay dead, mostly because I was just so darned tired, but then I remembered what I'd forgotten, which is *the power to heal as well as to rend* . . . so get up, Natalia, get up, because I am the master now and you have to do what I say."

I smoothed her hair and stroked her forehead with my other hand. "Live," I said. "Live."

And after what seemed a very long time, her eyes opened, she took a deep breath, and I knew I had saved her.

52

I guess after all that, I would have bled to death beside her, but Mike came to and found us inside the cave. Soon we were loaded onto stretchers and men carried us up the path to the top of the cliff, where a helicopter was waiting. We were flown to a hospital in London.

After a couple of weeks I was able to sit up and eat some solid food, though hospital food in the best of circumstances isn't that good, and this was England, after all, so the food was really lousy.

They did two operations on me to remove part of my lower intestines and fix up my left lung, which Mogart had torn with his final thrust. After another couple of weeks I could walk around, and sometimes Natalia would walk with me in the hallway. We didn't talk much on these walks, though she did thank me for saving her life. Once I asked her if she believed in angels.

"As a little girl I thought I had a guardian angel."

"That doesn't count," I told her. "Little kids believe in Santa Claus too. Your father said the angels live whether we believe in them or not."

She looked away then. I could have kicked myself for mentioning her father. For once she was actually talking to me as if I were a halfway normal person.

"I guess it would be tough for you to forgive me," I said. "I can't seem to, no matter how hard I try."

"You should have left me to die," she said. "It would be better. Why didn't you leave me to die?" She began to cry.

I had apologized, but that only made it worse for her. I was beginning to think that was my special gift: taking something bad and making it worse. I tried to hold her hand while she cried, but she turned away from me. I could save her life but not her broken heart.

After Natalia left, I felt really bad, the worst I'd felt since this whole thing with the Sword started. You would think the prospect of saving six billion lives might make me feel better, but it didn't. I could save the world, but it wouldn't bring Uncle Farrell back. It wouldn't bring my father back.

Or Bennacio. I kept seeing him fall, the way he raised his arms and just let Mogart run him through. Why hadn't Bennacio fought? He could have lunged forward and tackled

Mogart by the knees. Why had he just given up like that? How was that keeping his precious vow? I was pretty sore at him for that. If he hadn't quit, I wouldn't have ended up with the Sword, he would be alive, and Natalia's heart would not be broken.

A shadow fell into the room but I hardly noticed it. I just wanted it all to go away. The hospital, London, my memories, me.

The shadow came closer and I heard her ask softly, "Alfred, why are you crying?"

I said, "It works on everybody but me, Natalia. I can heal everybody but myself."

She sat in the wooden chair beside the bed. She had changed into a long red cloak over a gray dress with one of those soft, high collars, and her earrings were fat diamonds about the size of green olives. Her reddish gold hair was loose and flowed over her shoulders. She looked like some medieval princess, beautiful and terrifying at the same time. Seeing her dressed like that, I realized Natalia was leaving.

"You are forgetting something," she said.

"I can't forget anything," I said. "That's the problem."

"You are forgetting you saved the world."

I didn't say anything. I wondered why she had come back, but at the same time I knew why, though I couldn't put it into words.

Then she did. "I'm leaving, Alfred."

"When?"

"Tonight."

"Don't."

"I must." She drew a deep breath. She was sitting very straight in the chair.

"But before I go," she went on, "I wanted to pay homage to the master."

She looked down at my snotty face.

"I'm not the master of anything," I said.

"Alfred," she answered softly. "Like my father, I have waited a very long time for your coming. My father would tell me stories of our ancestor Bedivere, how he betrayed the king by refusing his command to return the Sword to the waters from which it rose. I would spend hours imagining what the master would be like. Tall, handsome, brave, honest, chaste, modest, the knight of all knights—in short, everything that I believed my father to be." She looked sideways at me, clearly not the guy she had pictured as the master of the Sword. "In fact, when I was still very young I told him that *he* might be the master, that perhaps it was his destiny to claim the Sword as his own, a fitting end to Bedivere's shame."

"What did he say?"

"He told me of the prophecy Merlin made before he departed the world of men, that the master would not come until the last male heir to the house of Bedivere had perished. My father believed that prophecy, Alfred. He believed it because he believed in the justice of it. It was the price we would pay for Bedivere's failure, our atonement for his sin."

I thought of Bennacio kneeling before Mogart, and I understood then why he had spread his arms in that way, as if saying, *Here I am. Here I am.*

"Oh, jeez," I said. "Like I didn't feel bad enough, Natalia. What am I supposed to do, huh? What do you want me to do? I was just, you know, helping out my uncle. I didn't know my father and I sure didn't know I had stolen the Sword of Kings for a black knight or an agent of darkness or whatever he was. I mean, what rational person believes in all this stuff, Merlin and King Arthur and magic swords and angels and prophecies—who believes in that kind of stuff these days? I don't know what you want from me, Natalia. Can you tell me what I'm supposed to do? Somebody better tell me and they better do it quick, because I'm just about at the end of my rope here."

She came to the bed, and her hair fell over my face. She whispered, "He is at peace, Alfred. His dream is fulfilled, and he is at peace. Now you be at peace."

Then she kissed me on the forehead, and her hair was like the walls of a cathedral around me, a sanctuary, and she murmured into my ear, "Be at peace, Master Alfred."

53

One afternoon, about a week before I was to be discharged, the door opened and a dark-suited man came into the room. Tall and stoop-shouldered, with a hound-dog face and very long earlobes, he reminded me of a sad-eyed Basset. He closed the door behind him as I pushed myself up in the bed, thinking, What now?

He didn't say a word; he barely looked at me. He crossed the room and peeked through the curtains, then strode to the bathroom and looked in there. Then he opened the door and spoke softly to someone in the hallway. He stepped back and a woman came in next, dressed in a tailored pinstriped business suit with shiny black heels that made a clicking sound on the linoleum as she walked. Her bright blond hair was pulled into a tight bun on her head. She carried a bundle wrapped in white satin.

"Abigail?" I said.

"Alfred." She smiled, and I was impressed by the excellent condition of her teeth. "How good of you to remember."

She handed the bundle over to the hound-dog man and sat down beside my bed.

"How are you feeling?" she asked.

"Pretty lousy," I said. "Physically I'm doing okay; it's the other departments that are bothering me."

"You have been through a great deal," she said.

There was an uncomfortable silence. I blurted out, "I don't have it."

"Don't have what, dear?"

"You know what. I don't have it. And I don't know where it is, though I have a guess."

"And where would that be?"

I bit my lip. Her smile didn't leave her face and her blue eyes were glittering brightly.

"You don't trust me," she said calmly. "I don't blame you, Alfred. We've done little to earn your trust. At any rate, you don't need to tell me. I believe I already know. The gift has been returned to its giver." I didn't say anything and she lowered her voice. "The master claims the Sword and, in claiming it, understands that it can never be claimed."

She was just beaming by this point. "We tore that cave apart, Alfred, and dragged the inlet. The Sword is gone, which is both a great loss and a great boon. Its time on earth has passed, and now there is one less piece of wonder in our world. Perhaps it is the price we must pay for our . . . growing up."

I stared at her. "Who *are* you, anyway?"

"I thought you knew, dear."

"All I know is you guys double-crossed Mr. Samson and his knights, and you double-crossed Bennacio and you double-crossed his daughter and nearly got her killed, and *did* get me killed and—"

"OIPEP didn't double-cross them, Alfred, Mike Arnold did." She made a little sour face, as if just saying the name bothered her. "You of all people can understand the effect the Sword can have on the minds of . . . weaker men. Mike was seduced by it from the beginning. Without our knowledge he contacted the Dragon and gave away Samson's plans to storm his castle in Spain, and he did agree to sacrifice Bennacio in order to gain the Sword. He also told Mogart where he might find Natalia—all without our knowledge. He was what you might call a 'rogue agent,' and he has been terminated."

"You killed Mike Arnold?"

She smiled. "He is no longer with The Company."

"The Company," I said. "What is The Company? What is OIPEP and why does it care so much about the Sword?"

"It cares because its purpose is to care."

I stared at her for a second, and then I said, because I had learned some things along the way, "That was my fault. I asked two questions, which allowed you to choose which one to answer."

She laughed one of those gentle trills you associate with very cultivated people or people from England.

"Our organization dedicates itself to the research and preservation of the world's great mysteries," she said.

"Really? And all this time I thought you were some kind of supersecret spy outfit dedicated to killing people you don't like."

"We are not spies, Alfred. Not in the sense you mean. We are clandestine in that few know of our existence; and we do have certain . . . technologies that have yet to be officially acknowledged, but we are more likely to wear pocket protectors and carry laptops than body armor and guns. OIPEP has more scientists, historians, and theoreticians than field operatives like Mike Arnold. The head of my department is a doctor of thaumatology. And I hold a doctorate in eschatology."

"What's that?" I asked. She was being very Bennacian: The more she explained, the more confused I got.

"Eschatology is the study of final things. Death. The afterlife. The end of the world."

"Oh. Gotcha."

"And thaumatology is the study of miracles. So you see, it was only natural that Samson should involve us once the Sword was lost."

She motioned to the large man with the dog face and the big flappy hands, and he brought her the long object wrapped in satin. She laid it on my lap.

"What's this?" I asked. But I figured it out before she could answer. I pulled on a corner of the cloth and the black blade tumbled out.

"Bennacio's sword," she said. "We recovered it at Stonehenge and thought you might like to have it."

I stared at the sword. "Thank you," I whispered.

Abigail said, "There is one other thing before I go, Alfred. I must say The Company is quite impressed."

"Impressed by what?" I asked.

"With you," she said. "It is nothing less than extraordinary."

"What is?"

"That you not only survived your ordeal, but accomplished what we, with all the resources at our disposal, could not."

"Well," I said. "The whole thing was basically my fault, so I kind of thought it was the right thing to do."

"Don't be so hard on yourself. You're very young. You have no idea how rare that is."

"Youth?"

"Doing the right thing. Not only doing the right thing, but understanding what the right thing is."

"Oh," I said. "You bet." Though I wasn't completely sure what she was getting at or why we were having a philosophical conversation.

"We will be keeping an eye on you, Alfred Kropp," she said.

"You will?" That didn't sound good.

"We are very interested in your . . . development."

A shiver went down my spine. "Look, Abby . . . Abigail . . . ma'am . . . I don't have any intention of getting involved in anything like the Sword again, so if you're worried—"

She raised her hand to shut me up. "We're not worried at all. In fact, I wanted to give you this, in the event you decide you want to know more about The Company. We are always looking for fresh talent—for the extraordinary, if you will."

She dropped a business card in my lap, shot up from the chair, nodded to hound-dog man by the door, and left me alone. I picked up the card and read it:

OFFICE OF INTERDIMENSIONAL PARADOXES
&
EXTRAORDINARY PHENOMENA
(OIPEP)

Abigail Smith, MD, PhD, JD, MBA
Special Agent-in-Charge
Field Operations Division

Washington • London • Paris • Tokyo
Brussels • Rome • Moscow • Sydney

54

My foster parents, the Tuttles, arrived in London the next day to take me back to America. I had no idea they were coming. They just showed up in the doorway and Horace Tuttle shouted, "Alfred Kropp, you big-headed pain in the rump! What in heaven's name are you doing in London, England?"

"If you ever run away like that again, we'll have to let you go, Alfred," Betty Tuttle told me tearfully.

"Might do that anyway," Horace puffed. "You have a lot of explaining to do, young man!"

"Actually," I told them, "I saved the world from total annihilation."

"Of course you did!" Horace shouted. "And I'm Tarzan, Lord of the Apes!"

"Now, Horace," Betty said. "You know what the social worker told us: Alfred is a *troubled youth*."

"We all have troubles," Horace grumbled.

"I'm sure Alfred has every intention of getting back into school and living up to his potential as a solid citizen and contributing member of his community," Betty said. She patted my arm. "Don't you, dear?"

"That's right," I said. "You bet."

"Well, I didn't fly all the way across the Atlantic to this God-forsaken foreign English country to chitchat," Horace said. "Where're your things, Alfred? We're leaving."

"I don't have anything," I said. "Except this."

I showed them Bennacio's black sword. Horace tried to grab the sword and I told him not to touch it; the blade was very sharp. I also didn't want him touching it because the thought of Horace Tuttle touching the blade of the Last Knight of the Order of the Sacred Sword made my stomach heave.

"We'll never get this through Customs," he said.

"Then I'm not going," I told them. "I won't leave without it."

And I didn't either. I stuck the sword in Horace's bag and, when the screeners went nuts over it, I showed the supervisor Abigail Smith's card. A call was made and in five minutes we were cleared through Customs.

55

So that's how I ended up back in Knox-ville, Tennessee, after saving the world and everybody in it, including the Tuttles.

After a week, I was back in school, but my picture had been flashed around the globe after the Stonehenge incident and now I was something of a celebrity. I don't know what calls were made or who said what to whom, but I was back in school like nothing had happened. There was a rumor that I was an international terrorist because that's what they called me on television, but I guess some people just can't grasp nuances.

Amy Pouchard pulled me aside after math class on my first day back. She was working a piece of gum really hard, which reminded me of Mike Arnold, and suddenly I didn't like Amy Pouchard as much as I thought I did.

"You disappeared, blew up something, and now you're back," she said.

"I didn't blow up anything," I told her. "I did kill somebody, though."

Her eyes got wide. "Get out!"

"But he kind of had it coming."

"Was he a terrorist or something?"

"No, but you might call him an agent of darkness."

"Whoa. That's too cool!" She touched my forearm with her hand. Her hand was very cold, and I wondered if she had a circulation problem. "You shot him?"

"I beheaded him."

Her mouth opened a little and I could see the knobby bright green of her gum between her tongue and her teeth.

"Kropp! You! Kropp!"

It was Barry Lancaster, pushing people out of the way in the crowded hall to get to me.

"Are you still his girlfriend?" I asked Amy Pouchard.

"Sort of. Not really. I mean, he's never beheaded anybody or anything like that. Do you want my cell phone number?"

Barry had reached me by that point. He shoved me hard in the right shoulder and said, "What are you doing here, Kropp? Aren't you supposed to be in jail or something?"

"Actually," I said, "I'm supposed to be in social studies."

"But instead you're talking to my girlfriend. Pretty stupid, Kropp."

"She's not your girlfriend, Barry."

"Like you would know."

He shoved me again.

"Don't shove me, Barry."

"Yeah? Who's gonna stop me, Kropp?"

He shoved me again.

"Barry," Amy Pouchard said. "Cut it out."

A crowd had gathered by that point. The bell rang but nobody paid attention.

"Maybe this is the point I should tell you that the last guy who shoved me around like this got his head chopped off," I told Barry.

"You're so full of it," he snarled, and then he launched himself at me.

He really didn't have a chance. I sidestepped to the right and landed a haymaker to the side of his blond head as he flew past. Barry went down and he stayed down, and I guess if I had been Barry, I might have kicked him in the ribs. But I wasn't Barry Lancaster. I was Alfred Kropp, not exactly a knight bound by the code of chivalry, but I was the descendant of the greatest knight who had ever lived. Plus I guess dying gives you some perspective on what's worth fighting about.

I held out my hand.

"This is nuts, Barry," I said. "We're both gonna get expelled."

"That was just a lucky punch," he gasped, and he slapped my hand away.

"The odds are against that," I answered. "I've never had too much luck."

I pulled him to his feet and he spat, "You're a freak."

But he didn't shove me again or try to punch me, and after that nobody teased me about my size or the remark about my IQ. People left me alone. Even my teachers kept their distance and went out of their way to give me a break. Of course, it got all around school that I had admitted to killing someone, and the rumor about me being a terrorist persisted.

I spent most afternoons in the Old City, walking aimlessly or sitting in the Ye Olde Coffee Shop, where I had met Bennacio. I always took the last stool at the end of the counter and sipped lattes, staring at the people walking past the big window. Sometimes I took out the card Abigail Smith had given me in London and stared at it. Most of the time, though, I just stared out the window. And I always dreaded going home to the Tuttles.

Sitting in the coffee shop made me feel close to Bennacio, the nearest thing to a father I ever had, and sometimes I would hear his voice in my head: *Do not concern yourself so much with guilt and grief, Alfred. No battle was ever won, no great deed ever accomplished by wallowing in guilt and grief.*

I began to understand I had claimed more than the Sword of Kings in Merlin's cave. I had claimed something even more powerful and scary.

I had claimed who I was.

One afternoon, after I finished my coffee, I looked at my watch and realized it was almost six o'clock. Dinner would be over by the time I got to the Tuttles', and Betty would fuss at me and wonder where I wandered off to every afternoon instead of coming home and studying like a good boy. Horace would stomp and shout, and the thin walls of the little house would shake. I would eat the leftovers and retreat to the little room I shared with Lester and Dexter. The next morning I would go to school and that would be my life, the life of Alfred Kropp, Heir to Lancelot, Son of the Sacred Order, Master of the Sword of Kings, and Adventurer Extraordinaire.

I left the coffee house and turned on Central to Jackson, but instead of walking toward the bus stop I went straight to the pay phone half a block down and dialed the 800 number scrawled on the back of the card.

"This is Alfred Kropp, Abby . . . Abigail . . . Ms. Smith, *Doctor* Smith, ma'am," I said. "I was wondering about what you said. About, um, needing fresh talent . . ."

ACKNOWLEDGMENTS

From the beginning, my wife has been there, through the long dry season of the repetitious rejection letters, the unreturned phone calls, the cold silence that dragged on for months—hiding rejected manuscripts under the bed and rescuing them from the trash, encouraging, pleading, cajoling, helping me fight the inner demons and, when my strength gave out, fighting them herself, in battles that should never be fought alone.

My failings belong to no one but me. All success, however, I owe to her. She was there before the agents and book deals and television appearances, behind the door long before Hollywood—or anyone—came knocking. God willing, she will be behind that same door, by my side, long after the world has passed me by.

Though no poor words of mine can begin to express it, thank you, my love.

**READ ON FOR A SNEAK PEEK AT ALFRED'S NEXT
EXTRAORDINARY ADVENTURE**

11

Every summer when I was a little kid, my mother threw me into our old Corolla and drove us down to Destin, a beach town in the Florida Panhandle. I loved those trips. We stopped at roadside restaurants to eat, greasy spoons with the vertical coolers that held the pies and cakes, and little one-story motels two blocks from the beach, like the Seabreeze Motor Court or the Conchshell Conclave.

The Seabreeze was my favorite, mostly because the beds had this vibrator built in: you dropped a quarter into the timer and the bed would vibrate for five minutes. Two quarters got you twelve minutes. As soon as we hit the door, I flopped on one of those beds, feeding it quarters. Mom wouldn't let me use the vibrating function at night, though. She thought the vibration while I slept would give me vertigo or bad dreams, or maybe both.

I woke with the name *Destin* on my lips. I could hear the low, deep-throated hum of engines, one of those sounds that seem to come from everywhere and nowhere.

I started to notice other things too, things that came in flashes as I slowly woke up.

Crisp white sheets. The smell of lavender. Gray walls lined with rivets; even the floor was riveted. A round door with a ship's wheel for a handle. A porthole on the wall opposite the bed, nothing beyond the glass but darkness.

"Destin," I whispered again in the semidarkness of the little cabin.

Mom in her jean shorts and halter top, sunglasses covering almost her entire face, tiny beads of sweat on her forehead, a paperback novel resting on her stomach, calling to me, *Don't go out too far, Alfred! Don't go out too far!* Because I can't swim. She knew I wouldn't go far: there were scary things in the ocean, jellyfish and the sharp spines of dead horseshoe crabs and busted aluminum beer cans and sharks, of course. Swimming in the ocean is a little crazy when you think about it. The ocean is nature untamed, just like the woods, and who in their right mind would strip to their shorts and go running through the woods?

I remember wearing old bathing trunks with the starfish on the butt, faded from a bright yellow to a kind of dingy white, and a wide white stripe of sunscreen on my nose. I waded knee-deep in the languid surf of the gulf, kicking up little underwater puffs of sand, never worrying where she was, because I was sure she would always watch over me.

The wheel spun counterclockwise and the round door swung open. A big man dressed in black, with enormous ears and a face that reminded me of a bloodhound, stepped inside and looked down at me beneath the lavender-smelling sheets.

"Hi," I said. "I'm Alfred Kropp."

"I know who you are," he said.

"I know who you are too," I said. "Well, not your name, but I remember you. You came to my hospital room in London. Where's Abigail . . . I mean, Dr. Smith?"

As if on cue, Abigail Smith, Special Agent-in-Charge, Field Operations Division, of the Office of Interdimensional Paradoxes & Extraordinary Phenomena, stepped into the cabin and swung the door shut behind her.

"Hello, Alfred," she said.

She looked just like I remembered, her bright blond hair in a tight bun. She wore a black turtleneck and pants, and her lips were as red as I remembered, but this time her three-inch heels were replaced with black lace-up boots.

"Where am I?" I asked.

"Aboard the jetfoil *Pandora,* somewhere off the coast of Oman," she answered.

"Oh." I had no idea where Oman was. "Why?"

"There has been a . . . development that has necessitated your extraction from the civilian interface," the dog-face man intoned.

"Huh?"

"What Operative Nine means is you were kidnapped for your own good, Alfred."

"Operative Nine?"

"Yes," she said, nodding toward Mr. Dog-Face. "Op Nine for short."

"What's his real name?"

"Whatever it needs to be," Op Nine said.

Abby said, "Only the director knows his real name."

"How come?"

"The nature of his work."

"And that is?"

"Classified," he said.

"That's pretty clunky, though, Operative Nine," I said. "Why don't you just use a code name like 'Bob'?"

"'Bob' would be more an alias than a code name, don't you think?" Abigail was smiling.

"What's going on?" I asked, struggling to sit up, but my head was throbbing and the room was spinning, and I decided sitting up wasn't such a good idea at that moment.

"We don't know the answer to that question," Abby said. "It seems an odd turn of events, given what we know about Mike Arnold's plans."

"Maybe that's something you could share with me," I said. "Mike's plans."

"After he was terminated, Michael Arnold stole two very valuable items from the OIPEP vaults. We are on our way to intercept him before he can put them to use."

"What did he take?" I asked, and waited for the usual answer: *That's classified.*

Op Nine glanced at Abby, who gave him a sharp nod. He looked at me. His eyes were very dark, almost black.

"The Seals of Solomon," he said in that deep, undertaker-like voice. If he was waiting for some sign of recognition from me, he was going to be waiting for a long time. I just stared back.

"You have heard of King Solomon," he said.

"From the Bible, right?"

"Yes. In the days of his reign, Solomon possessed two items of great power, immeasurable gifts from heaven. The Great Seal and the Lesser Seal, also called the Holy Vessel. These two charges he jealously guarded until his death three thousand years ago. The Great Seal was lost in antiquity, but the Lesser Seal was recovered from its hiding place in Babylon by an archeological expedition in 1924—"

Abby cut off the lecture. "The Greater Seal, or Seal of Solomon, is a ring, Alfred. The Company recovered it in the 1950s from a now-defunct apocalyptic death cult in the Sudan—"

"Wait a minute," I said. "Did you say the Seal of Solomon is a *ring*? Like a wear-on-your-finger-type ring?"

"Precisely.

"Have you paged Elijah Wood? I think I saw this movie."

She smiled. "The ring to which you refer is a product of art, a fiction. The Great Seal of Solomon is an artifact of history. It belongs to our world, not an imaginary one. Most significantly, Solomon's ring is not the creation of evil. Of course, in the wrong hands it could be used to that purpose, and that is precisely why we recovered it and kept it safe for the past fifty-five years—"

"Until Mike stole it."

"We have since launched a complete overhaul of our security protocols."

"Boy, that's a comfort. So Mike stole these two things from you guys . . . and then comes to Knoxville to kill me. Why?"

They looked at each other.

"We don't know," Abigail said. "We were hoping you might."

"Me? OIPEP's looking to me for answers? We're in bigger trouble than I thought. What about Ashley?"

Op Nine frowned. "What about her?"

"Why was she spying on me?"

Again they looked at each other.

"The Company often assigns operatives to keep tabs on Special Subjects."

"'Special Subjects'? I'm a Special Subject?"

"How could the last son of Lancelot *not* be a Special Subject?"Abby asked tenderly. "Mike's entrance into your particular interface took all of us by surprise. Fortunately, Ashley was watching your house when Mike made his move."

"So you knock me out and bring me to this boat off the coast of Oman—where is that, Africa or something?—to do . . . what?"

"Intercept Michael Arnold before he can use the

ring to open the Lesser Seal."

"Lesser Seal . . ."

"The Holy Vessel," Op Nine said.

"Why don't you want the Holy Vessel opened?"

For the third time they exchanged a glance. I was like the little kid in the room while the parents danced around the facts-of-life lecture.

"The ring, the Great Seal," Op Nine said slowly, "is the key. Without it, the wearer cannot control the . . . agents confined within the Vessel. Indeed, without the ring, the Lesser Seal cannot even be broken. One without the other is useless. With both . . ." He took a deep breath. "Catastrophe."

The door swung open and a guy in a black jumpsuit like Ashley's stepped in, carrying a tray with orange juice and two slices of toast.

"Ah," Op Nine said. "The food is here." He seemed relieved.

"Not much of it, though," I said, trying again to sit up. Op Nine bent to help me. The room whirled around my head. I wondered why I felt so light-headed and weak. What was in that shot Ashley gave me on the chopper—and why had she given me a shot in the first place?

I drank the tall glass of orange juice down in three gulps. The toast was cut into quarters and that's how I ate it, stuffing a whole quarter in my mouth and barely chewing before I swallowed.

"Okay," I said. "Let me see if I have all this. After you guys fired Mike for trying to take Excalibur, he breaks into your vaults and steals the two Seals of

Solomon. I'm still not clear on what they are or what they do, but anyway, after that you assigned Agent Ashley to keep tabs on me because now I'm a person of special interest or something. Mike shows up, kidnaps me, takes me up into the mountains to kill me— only Mike knows why —and Ashley rescues me in the nick of time. Now we're on a boat on our way to . . . where?"

"The nexus," Op Nine said.

"The what?"

"The center. The place of opening."

"Right. Gotcha. And the plan is to stop Mike before he can pull off this opening."

"Correct."

"Or else . . . ?"

"Catastrophe."

A bell went off, a blaring sound that seemed to come from everywhere and nowhere. Op Nine checked his watch.

"It's time for the briefing," he said to Abigail.

She nodded, then turned to me and gave my shoulder a little pat.

"We have to go, Alfred."

"When are you taking me home?"

They both looked away.

"You're not taking me home, are you?" I asked.

"You'll be safe here, Alfred," Abby said.

"I'd rather go home and take my chances."

Abby was looking at Op Nine. She pursed her fat red lips and for some reason I thought of goldfish, those big koi you see sometimes in little ponds outside

Japanese restaurants.

He said, "Perhaps we will discuss it, once the Seals have been recovered."

They left, slamming that big round metal door closed behind them. The wheel turned and I heard a clanking sound, like a dead bolt sliding home. It hit me then that I had traded one kidnapper for another. OIPEP might not want to kill me like Mike did, but I was at their mercy just the same.

ALFRED MEETS ARTHUR:
THE REAL LEGEND OF KING ARTHUR AND THE KNIGHTS OF THE ROUND TABLE

King Arthur: Man or Myth?

"You're talking about King Arthur, right?"

"Yes, King Arthur."

"That's just a legend, a story, Mr. Samson."

"I don't have the time to convince you of anything, Alfred. You held it tonight. In your inexperienced hands, the Sword bested three of the finest swordsmen in the world." (pg. 77)

Despite watching the movie *Excalibur* about fifty times, Alfred Kropp doesn't 100-percent buy into the whole King Arthur thing until he's cruising down the highway in a silver Mercedes with Bennacio, the last descendent of the Knights of the Round Table. Alfred isn't alone. For centuries, people have questioned whether King Arthur was, in fact, a real person.

The first significant reference of King Arthur and his exploits appeared in a twelfth-century text called *The History of the Kings of Britain*. But what isn't agreed upon is whether the author, Geoffrey of Monmouth, made up Arthur or not.

Three hundred years after the book's publication—long after Geoffrey had taken the secret with him to the grave—historical debate ignited, and the flames have been burning ever since. During the Renaissance, Tudor monarchs vigorously defended Arthur's authenticity—and even justified their rights to the throne by claiming to be his descendents. Apparently, the Tudor mentality prevailed. Today it is generally assumed that there was an actual person at the heart of the legends, and, after reading *The Extraordinary Adventures of Alfred Kropp,* you might, too!

Two Awkward Youths,
Both Destined for Greatness

Arthur was this kind of goofy kid, actually, a squire to his brother Kay, toting around his sword and taking care of Kay's horse and his armor, kind of his lackey, not even a knight. Nobody believed this kid could actually pull the Sword from the Stone until Arthur did it and told them, "If you would be knights and follow a king, then follow me!" (pg. 88)

So let's assume Arthur was a real guy. Like Alfred Kropp, Arthur didn't discover who his real father was until *after* his father's death. Legend claims that Arthur was the illegitimate son of Uther Pendragon, king of Britain during the late fifth century. Since Arthur was born out of wedlock, King Uther could not raise him as a prince in the castle. Instead, the king's magician, Merlin, stole away with the newborn heir under the cover of night to the countryside estate of Sir Ector, an English nobleman. Until Arthur was a teenager, he had no knowledge of his royal lineage.

When Arthur was fifteen, King Uther died. No one but Merlin knew the king had a son, and there was much debate over who should inherit the throne. One day a mysterious stone with a huge sword stuck in its middle appeared in the churchyard of St. Paul's Cathedral in London. It was said that whoever pulled the sword from the stone was the rightful king of Britain. Men from far and wide tried in vain, but not even the strongest knight could make the sword budge. You can imagine the amazement when the least likely candidate succeeded: a scrawny teenage boy from the countryside, named Arthur.

So you see, sometimes heroes appear in strange packages. Remind you of anyone?

The Master of the Sword Is the One Who Claims It

"The sword is in this world, Alfred, but it is not of this world. Forged before the foundations of the earth, not by mortal hands, it is the True Sword, Alfred, the Sword of Kings. In another time it was known as Caliburn. You may know it by its other name, the sword Excalibur." (pg. 77)

Many people in England didn't think a fifteen-year-old kid like Arthur should (or could) be king. Luckily, Merlin was on Arthur's side. He led Arthur to a magical lake where an enchantress living beneath the surface of the water gave Arthur a gift of great power: the sword Excalibur.

Excalibur was kept in a magic scabbard that protected the wearer from hurting himself. Whoever used Excalibur in a fight always defeated his opponent. This is why our hero, Alfred Kropp, was able to use Excalibur as if he'd been sword-fighting his whole life, and why the descendents of King Arthur's knights were willing to give up their lives to protect the artifact.

With such a powerful weapon at his side, Arthur was able to secure his kingdom and set up his royal palace at Camelot. Arthur also married a princess named Guinevere. As a wedding gift, Guinevere's father presented Arthur with a large round table. Only the twelve bravest knights in the country were allowed to sit at this table. Because it was round, the positions of all the seats, including Arthur's, were equal, and he gained the reputation of being a fair and noble king.

"Samson too completed a certain knight's training, when that knight pledged himself to the Order upon their first meeting in France. You can guess who that certain knight was."

He waited patiently for my Kropp mind to grasp what he was saying.

"Mogart?"

"Yes, Mogart was Samson's squire, and more. Samson named him his heir."

My Kropp mind couldn't get a grip on that one. "So why did Mogart turn on him?" (pg. 244)

Sir Lancelot was the bravest of Arthur's knights, and it wasn't long before he and Queen Guinevere fell in love and began an affair that would end in disaster. Trouble arose when Mordred, King Arthur's evil nephew, discovered the infidelity. Mordred saw the affair between the king's best knight and the king's wife as the perfect opportunity to create discord in Arthur's Camelot. When Mordred happily revealed the news to Arthur, Lancelot and Guinevere fled to France and Arthur followed them across the English Channel.

King Arthur left Mordred in charge while he was away. As Arthur had no children, Mordred would inherit the kingdom when Arthur died; but he did not want to wait. Instead, Mordred told everyone King Arthur had been killed while fighting in France and made himself king of Britain. But Arthur would not take defeat lying down. He raised an army and returned to Britain to squelch the insurrection. The mighty armies of Arthur and Mordred fought at the climactic Battle of Camlann.

The Final Act?

Bennacio whispered, "Speak the words now, Alfred Kropp. Speak, son of my captain, heir to Lancelot. 'I, Alfred Kropp, swear in the name of the Archangel Michael, my guardian and protector, that I will sacrifice my life in defense of the Sword of Righteousness, and that by my life or my death, I shall defend it against the agents of darkness.'" (pg. 246)

The battle was so brutal, only a few people were still alive by its end, including King Arthur and Mordred. Grueling man-to-man combat ensued. Arthur killed Mordred, but Arthur was very badly injured himself. Knowing he was going to die, Arthur gave Excalibur to Sir Bedivere and asked him to return it to the magical lake. Bedivere pretended to do what he was told, but he hid Excalibur under a bush instead. Arthur knew he had disobeyed and told him to go and do the job properly. The traditional legend says that Bedivere then threw the sword into the lake and saw the hand of the Lady of the Lake come out of the water to catch it. But as you'll learn in *The Extraordinary Adventures of Alfred Kropp*, the story doesn't end there . . .

Bennacio sighed. "Bedivere was to cast the Sword into the lake—those were the direct orders from Arthur—but he chose to keep it instead, and our Order was created. Of all the knights, he loved his king the most, and from this love rose the belief that one day another master would return for the Sword." (pg. 240)

To learn more about the legend of King Arthur, visit these cool sites:

www.legendofkingarthur.com

www.arthurian-legend.com

www.britannia.com/history/h12.html

www.kingarthursknights.com

A Note on the Author

It was, perhaps, inevitable that Rick Yancey would chronicle Alfred's quest. Writing and Arthurian legend have been his passion and fascination since he was a teenager. Rick wrote his first book when he was fourteen—roughly Alfred's age. Around the same time, he saw the movie *Excalibur* and has been captivated by the story (and swordplay) ever since.

"I've wanted to write a great adventure story that combined my love for swords with the Arthur stories," he said. "It's also an incredibly romantic legend, set in a time that I think we all idealize and in some way long for."

As a boy, reading was Rick's favorite subject in school—math his least favorite. The books he enjoyed most were *Charlie and the Chocolate Factory*—he loved the humor; *The Hobbit*—for its whimsy and adventure; *The Borrowers*; and *A Wrinkle in Time*.

Rick lives in Florida with his wife, three sons, and their two dogs, Maddie and Casey. Maddie is a little dog and Casey is a big dog. But Maddie is definitely in charge! He wrote most of his novel while sitting in his car during his sons' soccer and karate practices.

Visit the author at
www.rickyancey.com

CHECK OUT THESE OTHER HIGH-FLYING ADVENTURES FROM BLOOMSBURY!